# Haydn

Karl Geiringer was born in Vienna and studied at the University of Berlin and the University of Vienna, where he obtained a Ph.D. Between 1930 and 1938 he was curator of the Archives of the Society of Friends of Music in Vienna. He came to the United States in 1940 and was naturalized five years later. He has taught at the Royal College of Music in London, at Hamilton College in Clinton, New York, and at Boston University. At present he is professor emeritus of music at the University of California, Santa Barbara. Dr. Geiringer is the author of *Musical Instruments: Their History in Western Culture* (third edition: *Instruments in the History of Western Music*), *Brahms: His Life and Work*, *The Bach Family: Seven Generations of Creative Genius*, and *J. S. Bach: The Culmination of an Era*. He has edited the anthology *Music of the Bach Family* and works by Chr. W. Gluck and J. Haydn in the Collected Editions. Dr. Geiringer has received fellowships from the Bollingen Foundation and the Guggenheim Foundation and grants from the American Philosophical Society. He was president of the American Musicological Society in 1955 and 1956 and was elected a fellow of the American Academy of Arts and Sciences in 1959. He is an honorary member of the American Musicological Society, of the Austrian Musicological Society, and of the American chapter of the New Bach Society. His books have been published in ten different languages.

Irene Geiringer is a niece of the psychoanalyst Dr. Wilhelm Stekel. She received a Ph.D. from the University of Vienna, where she studied philosophy and German literature, and has taught German on the university level. Mrs. Geiringer assists her husband in his research and has collaborated on all of his books, concentrating in particular on the biographical sections.

# HAYDN
# A CREATIVE LIFE
# IN MUSIC

*by*

KARL GEIRINGER

*in collaboration with*

IRENE GEIRINGER

UNIVERSITY OF CALIFORNIA PRESS

BERKELEY   LOS ANGELES   LONDON

**University of California Press**
**Berkeley and Los Angeles**

*Haydn: A Creative Life in Music* was originally published by W. W. Norton & Company in 1946.
Second revised edition 1961 by Doubleday and Company, Inc.
Reprinted with revisions 1968 by the University of California Press
Third revised and enlarged edition 1982 by the University of California Press, Berkeley and Los Angeles
Copyright © 1963, 1982 by Karl Geiringer
Copyright 1946 by W. W. Norton & Company, Inc., New York, New York.

**Library of Congress Cataloging in Publication Data**
Geiringer, Karl, 1899–
Haydn: a creative life in music.
Includes index.
Bibliography: p.
1. Haydn, Joseph, 1732–1809.  2. Composers—Austria—Biography
ML410.H4G4   1982    780'.92'4 [B]      82-2821
ISBN 0-520-04316-2 (cloth)              AACR2
ISBN 0-520-04317-0 (pbk.)

M 9 8 7 6 5 4 3 2 1

# Contents

# PART TWO    *Works*

*HCaW*  H. C. Robbins Landon. *Haydn: Chronicle and Works.*
Bloomington: Indiana University Press, 1976–1980.
5 vols.

Hob.  Anthony van Hoboken. *Joseph Haydn: Thematisch-*
*bibliographisches Werkverzeichnis.* Mainz: Schott,
1957–1978. 3 vols. (The generally used listing of
Haydn's works in which the different categories of
composition are designated by Roman numerals and
individual pieces by Arabic numerals.)

*H-St*  *Haydn-Studien.* Edited by Joseph Haydn Institute,
Cologne. Munich: Henle, 1965–  .

*HYb*  *Haydn Yearbook.* Edited by H. C. Robbins Landon and
colleagues, Vienna: Universal Edition, 1962–  .

*JHW*  *Joseph Haydn Werke.* The collected edition of Haydn's
compositions, edited by the Joseph Haydn Institute,
Cologne. Munich: Henle, 1958–  .

# Preface

This book represents the results of half a century of Haydn research and in the course of time has undergone various changes. As curator of the Society of Friends of Music in Vienna, which owns the extensive Haydn collections assembled by C. F. Pohl and E. Mandyczewski, I was invited to contribute a book on the composer. It was published in 1932 to commemorate the bicentenary of Haydn's birth. My Haydn research continued in the following years, and in 1946, after I had moved to the United States, a more extensive work appeared in English. In due course, translations of this book into German, Swedish, Hungarian, and Japanese followed. When in 1968 the University of California Press decided to incorporate the book into its catalogue, a revision appeared to be necessary again, as great advances in many areas of Haydn research had occurred since the end of the Second World War. Moreover, I had been able to study the vast Esterházy collection of documents and scores in Budapest taken over by the National Széchényi Library.

In the following decade, Haydn studies advanced with breathtaking speed. Our knowledge of Haydn's life work broadened considerably and at the same time gained depth. A thematic catalogue of the composer's works was available for the first time, and a substantial part of the composer's vast creative output was accessible in critically revised editions, presented by the Haydn Institute in Cologne or the indefatigable H. C. R. Landon.

In order to deal adequately with the large amount of new material, it was necessary to readjust and rewrite substantial parts of the present book. The discussion of a few compositions whose authenticity could no longer be upheld was removed, and the space thus won was used to include important new discoveries. However, the basic character of the study and the arrangement of the material remained unaltered. From the picture I had tried to provide of Haydn's personality and creative activity, a few details had to be eliminated, while others were added and reinforced. It is my hope that, as a result, the character of the man and artist may appear with greater clarity and strength. Footnotes were added not only to indicate the sources of information, but also to direct the reader to the best editions available of Haydn's various compositions. The substantial Bibliography is intended as a help in further studies.

It would seem redundant to repeat here the sincere thanks expressed in former editions to the numerous librarians in more than half a dozen different countries who supported the author's Haydn studies. However, mention should be made of Dr. István Kecskeméti, since 1966 head of the music division of the National Széchényi Library, Budapest, who continued the tradition of friendly assistance established by his predecessors. On the home front, Mr. Martin Silver, head of the music library at the University of California, Santa Barbara, proved unfailingly cooperative. My young friend Dr. Michael Meckna provided valuable assistance in various practical matters. Special thanks for advice and help are due the staff of the University of California Press, in particular Ms. Doris Kretschmer and Ms. Mary Lamprech.

My wife, Dr. Irene Geiringer, who for many years has participated in all my research, was also my collaborator in the present venture, dealing in particular with the biographical section.

Santa Barbara, California                             Karl Geiringer
May 1982

# PART ONE

## *Life*

# The Haydns and the Kollers

The question of Joseph Haydn's origin has been much disputed. No less than four different theories have been put forward; all are interesting and merit examination, although they fail to furnish a complete solution to the problem. The families of Haydn's parents had their homes in eastern Lower Austria, north of the large Neusiedler Lake, a district of many different races. Since 1533, besides the predominant German element, a large number of Croats have settled in this district, and from the adjacent Hungarian border there has come, through the centuries, a steady stream of Hungarian immigrants. The Slav ethnologist, Dr. Franz Kuhač,[1] has contended that Haydn's family was by race Croatian, that the names of Haydn and Koller (the family name of the composer's mother) were both Croatian, and that many of Haydn's melodies bear a close resemblance to Croatian folk songs. Undue publicity was given to this theory by Sir Henry Hadow, who declared in both the *Oxford History of Music* and Grove's *Dictionary of Music and Musicians*[2] that Haydn was a typical Croatian composer. On the other hand, the Hungarian historian Elemér Schwartz has attempted to prove

---

[1] This champion of the importance of Croatian art had, incidentally, the purely German name of Koch, which he changed later to the Slav form of Kuhač.

[2] Hadow's statements are to be found in the "Haydn" articles of the second and third editions of Grove's *Dictionary of Music and Musicians*. See also Henry Hadow, *A Croatian Composer* (London, 1897).

Haydn's Hungarian descent.[3] He bases his theory on the fact that the village of Tadten (Hungarian: Tétény), where Haydn's great-grandfather lived before he moved to Hainburg, was predominantly Hungarian in the seventeenth century. However, in 1659 the Bishop of Raab wrote about Tadten: "All the members of the parish are Hungarian Lutherans, with the exception of a few German houses."[4] There has even been an attempt by the Slav philologist Dedaelus to claim a gypsy origin for Haydn. This induced Ernst Fritz Schmid to undertake elaborate genealogical research, tracing the family names in German districts back to the Middle Ages and producing most valuable data about Haydn's ancestors.[5] According to his final conclusions, there can be no doubt that the Haydn and Koller families were of German origin.

But blood and race alone do not determine one's nationality. By race Haydn was a German, by nationality an Austrian. He lived in a melting pot of races, in a country in which cultural elements from both central and eastern Europe were fused together. It was quite natural that he should be familiar with the way of life of the Croats and the Hungarians. He heard their music from his childhood on and attended their festivities; he admired their artistic craftsmanship and the color of their holiday garb. With the instinct of genius he absorbed all these impressions and brought them to life in his music. The inner enrichment that he owed to his acquaintance with the different cultures of Austria and Hungary was more than a minor factor in making him the great artist he was.

Great composers often have someone of artistic or intellectual leanings among their ancestors. Joseph Haydn, one of the most independent spirits of musical history, was exceptional also in this respect. Going back to his great-grandfathers on both sides, we fail to find among them a single musician or even a man who pursued any kind of intellectual occupation. They all toiled with their hands as vinegrowers, farmers, wheelwrights, or millers. They were hard-working, honest men whose infinite diligence, patience, and pertinacity succeeded in raising them from extreme poverty to well-ordered circumstances and esteemed positions in the community. This they achieved under the most difficult conditions, for war raged almost continuously in that part of central Europe during the seventeenth and eighteenth centuries. The little section of eastern Austria where the Haydn family lived lies close to the Hungarian

[3] In the daily publication *Magyarság* (Budapest, April 20, 1932).
[4] *"Parociani omnes sunt Lutherani Hungari praeter aliquot domos Germanos."*
[5] Ernst Fritz Schmid, *Joseph Haydn . . .* (Kassel, 1934).

border. It was feebly fortified and thus fell easily to any nation that chose to make war on Austria. Haydn's great-grandfather, the wagonmaker Caspar Haydn, and his wife lost their lives when the town of Hainburg was captured by the Turks in 1683. Of the house and possessions acquired with heartbreaking toil only ruins were left to their one surviving son, Thomas. But less than seven years later Thomas had already built himself a new house and had been nominated a "citizen" of Hainburg. This meant definite progress, for his father had started his career at Hainburg as a modest *Burgknecht*, a day laborer with a permanent domicile.

On the other side, Haydn's maternal grandfather, the farmer Lorenz Koller (b. 1675), after witnessing as a boy of eight the ravages wrought by the Turkish invasion, lost all his possessions in 1704 when the *Kuruczes*, the peasant army of the anti-Habsburg Hungarian party, plundered the border village of Rohrau. One year later he rebuilt his house, only to see it go up in flames a second time when the Hungarians returned in 1706. But Lorenz Koller was not a man to give up. Again and again he started from the beginning, and so good was his progress that in 1713 he was offered the office of *Marktrichter* (a magistrate supervising peace and propriety in the village), a position in which his son-in-law, Joseph Haydn's father, was to succeed him.

As to Haydn's parents, the information supplied by documents is supplemented by stories based on the master's own accounts. Haydn's mother, Anna Maria Koller, was baptized on November 10, 1707, to the sound of cannon firing against the *Kuruczes* who were attempting another assault on the village of Rohrau. Her father died when she was eleven years old. She became a cook for the lords of Rohrau, the Counts of Harrach, and in their castle she saw something of the way of life of the Austrian nobility. The kitchen staff comprised nine persons, for whom a yearly salary of a thousand florins was budgeted. Menus preserved in the archives of the castle show that the Harrachs demanded high culinary skill from their cooks. Maria had to handle such delicacies as tortoises and crayfish and had an abundance of material at her disposal. We are told, for example, that something like eight thousand eggs, two hundred capons, and three hundred chickens were delivered annually to the castle by the inhabitants of Rohrau as part of their duties to their patron. It must have been quite a change for Maria Koller when, in 1728 at the age of twenty-one, she left the castle to marry the wagonmaker Mathias Haydn. Although she brought her husband a dowry of one hundred and twenty florins and an "honest outfit" (according to the marriage contract), every penny had to be accounted for in the little house, especially when there was a large family to rear. Maria bore her husband twelve children, but six of them died in infancy. Her famous son often testified to Maria's excellent housewifely qualities. She was scrupulously clean and neat, an indefatigable worker; and these were the qualities that she stressed in bringing up her children. She was deeply religious, this being a characteristic trait of the family. We know that her father bequeathed eighty-eight florins to the church, a considerable sum for the modest people of Rohrau. It was Maria Haydn's great dream to see Joseph's talents devoted to the Catholic Church, and great must have been her disappointment at his preference for the irresponsible life of a musician to that of the sacred profession of a priest. Haydn often lamented that his dear mother did not live to see him succeed. Before he got his first post Maria Haydn, worn out by a life of ceaseless toil, had died in 1754, at the age of forty-seven.

Haydn's father, Mathias Haydn, was born on January 31, 1699, in the town of Hainburg, a son of the wheelwright Thomas Haydn. Only two years after the infant's birth, Thomas died, leaving a widow of thirty with six sons, the eldest being barely twelve. In those troubled times, with war and plague threatening the population, Katharina Haydn naturally sought male support, and four months after her husband's death she married Mathias Seefranz, also a wheelwright. She bore him four children, among them Juliane Rosina, whom we shall meet again as the wife of the schoolmaster Franck. Seefranz, who later became a member of the Hainburg council, was a rather difficult and quarrelsome person, and life with him may not have been easy for his young stepsons, who were all learning the family trade under his instructions. In 1717 Mathias Haydn finished his apprenticeship and set out on the traditional travels of the journeyman, which brought him as far as Frankfort on the Main. When he came home, he brought with him a harp, which someone had taught him to play. Although he could not read a note, it was his great delight to accompany himself on the harp when he sang his favorite folk tunes in a pleasant tenor voice. In 1727 Mathias decided to settle down in the nearby town of Rohrau, remaining at the same time a member of the Hainburg guild of wheelwrights. Why his choice fell on this rather uninviting little market town is not known, but it is not unlikely that the person of his future bride attracted him to it. In 1728 Mathias Haydn and Maria Koller were married, and for twenty-six years they lived happily together. But Haydn's father was certainly no sentimentalist. When his good wife died, the man of fifty-five did not hesitate to marry his servant girl of nineteen.

Mathias lived in Rohrau in a cottage built by himself, and from the outset was fairly prosperous. It has been the custom of Haydn's biographers to stress the extreme poverty of his father, and judging from the appearance of the house in which the Haydns lived throughout their lives, this attitude seems to be justified. The little low-roofed, thatch-covered cottage is bound to fill us with pity, and we all feel like Beethoven, who on his deathbed, when shown a picture of the Haydn house, exclaimed, "Strange that so great a man should have been born in so poor a home!" For all that, Mathias Haydn was by no means a poor man, and he could probably have built himself a much better house if he had felt his cottage to be inadequate. Several of the bills that he made out have been preserved, and it is known that he was given plenty of work and was not paid badly by the Counts of Harrach for making wheels, repairing wagons, and painting houses. From the taxes he paid we see that he ultimately had his own wine cellar, his own farmland, and some cattle. The high esteem in which he was held is proved by his nomination to succeed his father-in-law in the office of *Marktrichter*, a position that he filled from 1741 until 1761, one year before his death. The list of his duties is imposing, but only a few can be mentioned here. He was responsible for the good conduct of the population and had to keep a sharp lookout for adultery or excessive gambling. He had to see that people went to church and did not break the Sunday rest. It was his job to allot among the inhabitants of Rohrau the labor required by the patron, Count Harrach, and he was responsible for keeping the local roads in good repair. On Sundays at six in the morning he had to report on all such matters to the count's steward.[6] Every two years an open-air meeting of the whole community took place at which the *Marktrichter* rendered a detailed account of the work done during the past period. To be at the same time a wagonmaker, farmer, vinegrower, wine producer, and important official and to carry out all these duties well was no small matter. Mathias Haydn must have been as efficient as he was diligent.

No personal documents of Haydn's parents or any of his forebears have been preserved. No portraits, letters, or diaries have

[6]These early hours were kept during the period from April to September. In the other months, the *Marktrichter* did not have to report until 8 AM once every fortnight.

come down to us. Nevertheless we know that it was not a mean heritage that they passed on to their great offspring. A deep religious sense, a stubborn tenacity of purpose, and a passionate desire to rise in the world are qualities that we find in his ancestors. Combined with them were a great pride in good craftsmanship, a warm love of the soil, and a healthy streak of sensuality. Indeed, it might be said that this heritage gave Joseph Haydn the very qualities necessary for the life he was to lead.

# CHAPTER ONE

# Rohrau and Hainburg

## 1 7 3 2 – 1 7 4 0

Rohrau, Haydn's hometown, is by no means an attractive place. The surrounding country is flat and marshy (as may be inferred from the name, which means reedy meadow), and the houses in the little township are mainly low, thatched cottages built of clay. Life is not easy there, for the Leitha River, which at Rohrau forms the border between Austria and Hungary, has an unpleasant tendency to flood the countryside; and in the hot dry summers, fires frequently play havoc with the thatched houses. The Haydn house, for instance, was burned in 1813, 1833, and 1899, but it was always carefully restored to its original form. Today it serves as a museum.

Franz Joseph[1] Haydn, the second child of Mathias and Maria, was born on March 31, 1732, and baptized on April 1.[2] His earliest childhood would have been spent like that of any Austrian peasant boy but for one important difference. His musical talent began to show itself at a very early age, and many anecdotes reflect this. In the evenings, when work was done, his father and mother used to sit by the fireplace and sing their favorite folk tunes to the accom-

---

[1] The Haydns, like many other families, used to call their children by their second names.
[2] There is some difference of opinion about the date of Haydn's birth, as both March 31 and April 1 were mentioned by members of the family. Haydn himself always maintained that it was March 31, and the diary of the Esterházy official, J. C. Rosenbaum (edited by E. Radant, *HYb*, V [1968]) states that the birth took place at 4 PM.

paniment of the harp proudly handled by Mathias. Little Sepperl, as the boy was called in the Austrian fashion, joined in with perfect intonation and a beautiful voice, attracting the attention of all the neighbors. Before long the boy's ambition went further. He wanted to play an instrument as his father did, and having seen the school-master perform on a violin, he took two sticks and pretended that they were a violin and a bow. Thus he accompanied the songs, keeping time with amazing accuracy. People began to comment on Sepperl's unusual behavior, and in the hearts of his parents there stirred a hope that one day their son might rise to a position far above theirs. Perhaps he would work with his brains instead of his hands; perhaps he would become a schoolmaster or even, as his mother fervently hoped and prayed, a priest. The auspices seemed good, for Sepperl showed a deep religious faith that was never to desert him.

Both parents must have felt dimly that the poor little village could not offer sufficient opportunities for the education of their eldest son. Then one day a cousin, Johann Mathias Franck, the hus-band of Mathias Haydn's stepsister, Juliane Rosina Seefranz, came from Hainburg to pay the Haydns a visit. He was the school princi-pal as well as the choir director of the Church of SS. Philip and James in Mathias's native town. In the eyes of the wheelwright and the former cook, he was a person of indisputable authority. Franck soon noticed Sepperl's musical talent and suggested taking the boy to Hainburg, where he could get a proper education, mainly in music. This offer was not wholly prompted by unselfish motives, however, for any payment Franck might receive for Sepperl's board and tuition would be a most welcome addition to his meager bud-get.[3] As Maria Haydn wanted Sepperl to be trained for the priest-hood, Franck argued that, if the boy should decide later to take holy orders, his musical education would be most helpful. Still it was a hard decision for the mother to make. The boy was not yet six years old, and she knew that if he left home her chances of seeing him would be few, for traveling was practically impossible for a woman as busy as she. But finally the parents decided to accept Franck's offer, feeling that they were unable to give the boy a fitting education in Rohrau. It was certainly the best thing they could have done for Joseph. His intellect was craving nourishment that his na-tive village could not provide. To satisfy it seemed imperative,

---

[3] Just what sum was paid by Haydn's parents is not known: Schmid mentions that as late as 1760 Mathias owed Franck thirty florins.

much more imperative than that he should be given loving care and understanding. So Sepperl at the age of five-and-a-half[4] was sent away, never to return to Rohrau except for rare, short visits. All close contact with his father and mother ceased, and gradually the thoughts of the narrow life he had shared with them at home became tender memories, mellowed by distance and nostalgia. When Haydn, as an old man, told his biographers about his youth, he described his mother—who had surrendered her child while he was still an infant—as "having always given the most tender care to his welfare." And when in 1795 the then world-famous composer visited Rohrau to see the monument erected in his honor by Count Harrach, he knelt down and kissed the threshold of the humble cottage he had shared with his parents for less than six years.

Rohrau once left behind, Sepperl breathed a very different air and saw a new and different landscape. Gone was the dreary monotony of the marshes, and the boy's eyes could hardly take in all the new sights that he saw on his way. There were many relics of times past to admire, for in this part of Austria the Romans had built important cities. In the middle of the plain stands a gigantic triumphal arch, now called the "Heathen Gate," and not far from it are the remains of the city of Carnuntum, which witnessed the coronation of Septimius Severus as Roman Emperor. Even if Sepperl did not understand the historical meaning of such monuments, he could not help being thrilled by the lovely surroundings of the city he was approaching.

At Hainburg the mountains slope down steeply to the imposing Danube and, covered with rocks or dense woods among which appear the ruins of the castle that gave the city its name, they make a picturesque background for the little town. Even today the visitor to Hainburg feels that he is back in the Middle Ages. The enormous, ancient gates through which the city is entered still stand, and next to one of them, the Vienna Gate, lived Haydn's grandmother. Imposing walls and towers testify to the part that Hainburg once played as a fortress against foes from the East, and within the gates are beautiful baroque façades and the interesting Church of SS. Philip and James. Truly Sepperl had entered a new world.

Here his artistic and intellectual curiosity found full satisfaction. It was fortunate for him that by old Hainburg custom Franck's

---

[4]Haydn's exact age when he left Rohrau is a matter of conjecture. It seems likely that the departure occurred sometime between his fifth and sixth birthdays.

duties were much more numerous than those that a schoolteacher of the present time would be willing to undertake. With the aid of two assistants paid by him, he had to instruct some eighty children in reading, writing, arithmetic, singing, and prayers; he was in charge of church music, playing the organ himself and directing the singers and instrumentalists, who by south German tradition took part in every service. In addition, Franck had to keep the church register, look after the church clock, and ring the bells both for the services and for special occasions such as thunderstorms or fires. To many of these activities little Sepperl was introduced without delay. The daily schedule of the six-year-old boy became very crowded indeed. School began at seven in the morning and lasted for three hours, after which all the children went to Mass, some participating as altar boys. At eleven they went home for their noonday meal, and from twelve to three there was school again. For the rest of the day, there was the study of homework and, what was most important of all, very extensive musical instruction. We do not know exactly which instruments Haydn studied with Franck, but he himself wrote in his autobiographical sketch:[5] "Our Almighty Father had endowed me with so much facility in music that even in my sixth year I stood up like a man and sang Masses in the church choir and I could play a little on the clavier and violin." Furthermore, Georg August Griesinger,[6] in the biography based on direct infor-

[5] *Das gelehrte Oesterreich. Ein Versuch* (Vienna, 1778), I, p. 309 (Cf. p. 67).

[6] Georg August Griesinger, a Saxon diplomat who lived in Vienna during the last decade of Haydn's life, served as representative for the Leipzig publishers Breitkopf and Härtel (with whom Haydn had various dealings) and frequently visited the old composer to discuss matters relating to the publication of his works. On such occasions he induced Haydn to tell him a great deal about his life, and noted all the information thus received. In Leipzig in 1810 Griesinger published his important *Biographische Notizen über Joseph Haydn*. In the same year in Vienna appeared the *Biographische Nachrichten über Joseph Haydn* by the painter A. C. Dies, who had called on the famous composer to obtain biographical information. These two volumes, based on first-hand information, form the most significant foundation for our knowledge of Haydn's early years. A third biographical study, entitled *Le Haydine*, appeared in Milan in 1812. The author was Giuseppe Carpani, an Italian poet who spent several years in Vienna. As Carpani translated the text of *The Creation* into Italian, and wrote a sonnet on Haydn for the memorable performance of *The Creation* in 1808, it seems quite likely that he met the composer in person and obtained valuable information for his biography. Thus his work may also be considered important source material (cf. also p. 16).

Our Chapters 1–3 are largely based on information provided by the biographies of Griesinger (pp. 8–14), Dies (pp. 16–44), and Carpani (pp. 14–30), which often resemble each other in content. It seemed redundant to furnish individual references for each little episode or remark extracted from these chronicles for our narration.

mation from Haydn, states that he studied the "kettledrum as well as other instruments." How he learned to play the drum at the age of six was told by another contemporary biographer, the painter Albert Christoph Dies, and is quoted here as evidence of the child's peculiar gift for self-instruction:

It was in the Week of the Cross [May 11–18], when many processions take place, that Franck was in great distress because of the death of his drummer. He thought of Joseph; the boy should learn to play the instrument at once. He showed Joseph how to make the strokes and left him alone. Joseph took a little basket, such as peasants use for baking bread, covered it with a cloth, placed his contrivance on an upholstered chair, and drummed with such enthusiasm that he did not notice the flour pouring out of the basket and ruining the chair. He was scolded, but his teacher was easily appeased when he saw to his amazement that Joseph had already become a perfect drummer.[7]

So the boy proudly marched in the procession. The instrument was strapped upon a hunchback to make it possible for the little fellow to play it. What a comical sight this pair must have been— the hunchback in front with the kettledrum on his back, little Haydn following, beating his drum and probably not always aiming quite straight. When Haydn showed an English orchestral musician how to play the timpani fifty years later, he may have remembered with amusement his own first efforts with these instruments. Though Haydn probably did not learn properly to play the other instruments mentioned by Griesinger, he certainly had ample opportunity to become acquainted with them. The standards of the music directed by Franck were not too low. The inventory of church instruments included, for example, as many as eight trumpets and eight violins. Although on ordinary Sundays the music was confined to a four-part chorus, two violins, and organ (the ensemble still used in Haydn's first Mass), on great feast days and the first Sunday of the month a violoncello, double bass, trumpets, horns, and timpani were added. Franck had a rather extensive collection of manuscript music, which he even lent to the churches of

[7]If this had really happened, it would show Haydn as an extremely precocious child. Learning to play the timpani in a very short time using a basket covered with a limp cloth in lieu of the resilient surface of a real drum would require genius.

larger cities. In all likelihood he made his gifted little pupil copy music for him; in this way Haydn may have become familiar at an early age with the sacred music of the period.

Apart from the ordinary routine, in itself interesting enough for the lad, there were special occasions when even a small town like Hainburg displayed the baroque splendor so dear to the Austrian heart. In 1738 the Roman Catholic Church arranged a *jubileum universale*. For two weeks, to the accompaniment of an abundance of music that must have kept young Sepperl tremendously busy, prayers were said for a victory over the Turks. Another great event was the solemn entry of the imperial Commissary Cetto a Cronstorff into Hainburg on May 2, 1739. He came to witness the election of the city councilors, and little Hainburg wanted to pay every possible honor to the guest from Vienna. He was received at the Vienna Gate by the city judges and councilors and conducted in state to the church. Before the portal stood trumpeters and drummers in their red cloaks and the civil guard resplendent in their uniforms. To the sound of fanfares the commissary entered the church, where Franck directed a motet *Veni Sancte Spiritus* before the Mass and a *Te Deum* after it. On the following day the elections took place, followed by another solemn church service. To the sound of impressive fanfares the names of the new councilors were announced from the high altar, among them, to Joseph's pride, that of Mathias Seefranz, the second husband of his grandmother and Franck's father-in-law. Two months later Hainburg celebrated with all the splendor it could afford the peace concluded between Austria and France. Besides such outstanding events, there were the many great feast days of the Catholic Church, and the processions then held followed age-old tradition, the Almighty being entreated to protect the people and their holdings from thunderstorms, hail, frost, and other disasters. In these processions little Sepperl took an active part, and they must have made a deep impression on his fertile brain. Particularly attractive was Corpus Christi day, the feast day of the guilds, among them that of the wheelwrights. Masters were admitted and journeymen discharged, all with the solemn ritual that Haydn's grandfather, father, and uncles had witnessed in this very place. To Sepperl's joy, in 1738, his own father attended a meeting in order to bind new apprentices. Such occasional contacts with his parents meant much to the little boy who, in spite of a life filled with new discoveries, must often have felt homesick.

It is necessary now to reveal another side to the Hainburg picture, one that was much less pleasant. The Francks were very poor.

On his modest salary, consisting mainly of allowances in kind, the school rector had to support a steadily growing family. Juliane Franck seems to have lacked the housewifely qualities of Haydn's mother. Her home was never kept in good order, and she was already so busy with her two infant daughters, who were joined by a son in November 1739, that she saw in her nephew of six not a child needing love and care, but a useful helper with the housework. Sepperl may not have resented doing the tasks she set him, but he did suffer from the neglect of his person. He, who had been trained by his mother in unimpeachable cleanliness and order, lost his neat appearance. The few clothes he possessed were not washed and mended very often. Dies relates that when talking of Hainburg, as an old man Haydn said: "I could not help perceiving, much to my distress, that I was gradually getting very dirty, and though I thought rather highly of my little person, I was not always able to avoid stains on my clothes, of which I was dreadfully ashamed—in fact, I was a regular little ragamuffin." At that time Haydn also began to wear a wig "for the sake of cleanliness." His meals were insufficient, and he admitted in later years that he got from his strict teacher "more floggings than food." Regarding the floggings, we should not blame Franck too much; they were the customary method of education. For instance, Schmid tells us of an "Instruction for the Schoolmaster" in which the Hainburg Council admonished the rector to refrain from pulling out the hair of his pupils, but to keep them strictly in order with the cane.

Still, if we balance the two sides of Haydn's life at Hainburg, the final result was certainly favorable. Haydn got what he most needed, extensive musical instruction. Furthermore, he was endowed by nature with a rare combination of gifts, wiry resilience, and a contented disposition. Hardships never made him bitter and never broke him. In spite of being hungry and dirty, in spite of the rough treatment occasionally meted out to him, Sepperl was happy. Throughout his life, whenever Franck's name was mentioned, Haydn had words of praise for his first teacher. "I shall be grateful to that man as long as I live for keeping me so hard at work," he said to Griesinger. In his house Haydn piously kept a portrait of Franck which he left in his last will, together with one hundred florins, to his teacher's daughter, Anna R. Schimpel.[8]

Little Sepperl progressed fast, and after a time Hainburg had given him all it had to offer. To stay longer within its medieval

[8] See Johann R. von Lucam, "Haydn und die beiden Originalportraits seiner Eltern," *Wiener Allgemeine Zeitung* (1852).

walls would have meant a retarding of his artistic and intellectual growth. Fortunately some natural law appears to direct the artistic destiny of a genius and lead him to the path best suited for his art, even though it may not contribute to his personal happiness.

Karl Georg Reutter the younger, court composer and newly appointed chapel master at the famous Cathedral of St. Stephen in Vienna, went on a tour in search of good choristers, in the course of which he visited Hainburg and stayed at the house of the parish priest, Anton Johann Palmb. On hearing of Reutter's quest, Palmb recommended young Haydn, whose "weak but sweet voice" he had noticed. The rest of the story is best told in the words of Giuseppe Carpani:[9]

> Reutter gave him a tune to sing at sight. The precision, the purity of tone, the spirit with which the boy executed it surprised him; but he was more especially charmed with the beauty of the young voice. He remarked that the lad did not shake (trill) and smilingly asked him the reason. The boy replied promptly: "How can you expect me to shake when my cousin does not know how to himself?" "Come here," said Reutter, "I will teach you." He took him between his knees, showed him how he should produce the notes in rapid succession, control his breath, and agitate the palate. The boy immediately made a good shake. Reutter, enchanted with the success of his pupil, took a plate of fine cherries and emptied them into the boy's pockets. [According to Dies, he also gave Sepperl a piece of money.] His delight may be readily conceived. Haydn often mentioned this anecdote to me, and added, laughing, that whenever he happened to shake he still thought he saw those beautiful cherries.

Reutter offered to take Sepperl to Vienna as a chorister at St. Stephen's and to give him a thorough musical education if his parents would consent to it. A meeting was quickly arranged, and Sepperl's father and mother were overjoyed with Reutter's promise that he would look after their boy. It was agreed that Sepperl should go to the imperial capital when he reached his eighth year. Reutter urged him to practice singing scales and solfeggios in the meantime so as to develop his voice. As Franck was unable to teach Sepperl

[9] Giuseppe Carpani, *Le Haydine* (Milan, 1812).

anything of the kind, the boy himself found a practical method and with characteristic diligence and ambition worked so hard that he made good progress.

The last few months before his departure were filled with joyous anticipation. Haydn was all impatience; he could hardly wait to see with his own eyes the wonders of the Austrian capital and to begin the musical training that Vienna's great cathedral had to offer.

# CHAPTER TWO

# At St. Stephen's

## 1740–1749

There is one building in Vienna that never fails to fill even the least sensitive inhabitant of the Austrian capital with awe and amazement: the Cathedral of St. Stephen. This Gothic church is so full of power, so imbued with the mystery of life in all its aspects, whether lofty or humorous, that it would be impossible ever to know it completely or to plumb its profundities. The outside of the cathedral displays a bewildering variety of high slender buttresses, gargoyles in the form of dragons, and countless statues of the great of the Church and of the House of Austria. The big south tower of St. Stephen's is the distinctive feature of Vienna. From its top, more than four hundred feet above the ground, one can look east far into the Hungarian plain, north toward the Danube and the fertile fields of Moravia, west and south toward the green Vienna woods and the foothills of the Alps. Although the outside of the church is entirely medieval, there are many baroque decorations and altars inside. In the typical Austrian manner, purity of style is completely lacking, but the daring mixture of old and new is in good taste and works of the fourteenth to eighteenth centuries succeed in being beautifully harmonious. In this imposing cathedral the imagination is never at rest. Every step brings new surprises and wonders, and the whole building is filled with a sense of great mystery, always eluding one, always leading one further. This Gothic architecture seems to lift one from earth into higher and more spiritual spheres, filling the soul of even the most matter-of-fact person with awe. How great must have been the effect of St. Stephen's upon the highly imaginative child whose constant resort it was for nine years.

While the surroundings in which Haydn dwelt in Vienna were all that he could have expected, and even more, closer acquaintance with the man in whose hands his fate lay proved sadly disappointing. Georg Reutter[1] lived with the six choir boys, a subcantor, and two preceptors, various vocalists, an organist, and string players in the *Cantorei* house next to the cathedral. He was entirely responsible for the pupils' education and musical training, as well as for their board, for which he received a yearly sum of twelve hundred florins from the city of Vienna. Unfortunately the man who had so generously filled Sepperl's pockets with cherries at Hainburg had turned into a stern principal who provided the boys with even less and poorer food than Sepperl had received from his impecunious relatives in Hainburg. Dies relates: "Joseph's stomach had to get accustomed to continuous fasting. He tried to make up for it with the musical academies [concerts that the choir gave in the houses of the Viennese nobility], where refreshments were offered to the choristers. As soon as Joseph made this discovery, so important for his stomach, he was seized with an incredible love for academies. He endeavored to sing as beautifully as possible so as to be known and invited as a skilled performer, and thus to find occasions to appease his ravenous hunger." But the insufficient food was not the worst, for "it seemed as if they wanted to starve the mind as well as the body." To Reutter the boys were merely choristers. He saw that they became expert singers and sight readers; he also made them learn to play the clavier, the violin, and the organ, but he was not interested in their general education, and they received no instruction in musical theory. Sepperl lacked any encouragement or help in his groping attempts at composition. Once Reutter found him writing a *Salve Regina* in twelve parts, for at that time the boy thought that to write good music he had only to fill a page with plenty of notes. The kapellmeister merely laughed mockingly and exclaimed: "Oh, you silly child, aren't two parts enough for you?" But he made no attempt to show Sepperl how to work out these two parts, contenting himself with advising the boy to arrange the

[1] There were two Viennese composers of this name. Georg Reutter, the father (1656–1738), was choir director of St. Stephen's and court organist. His son, J. A. Karl Georg (1708–1772), was Haydn's teacher. It is not always easy to distinguish between the compositions of the father and those of the son. See Norbert Hofer, "Die beiden Reutter als Kirchenkomponisten," a thesis manuscript (Vienna, 1915).

motets he sang in church. The diligent, ambitious lad must certainly have followed his teacher's advice, but it is doubtful that Reutter ever deigned to correct his efforts. Haydn said later that he had no more than two lessons from the kapellmeister during the many years he stayed with Reutter, who could have taught him so much.

The younger Reutter was, in fact, a very fertile and experienced composer. His music was distinguished by brilliance, harmonic richness, and excellent instrumentation. Burney, it is true, characterized his work by the terse comment, "great noise and little meaning," but even if this opinion (which was by no means shared by the Viennese public) were correct, Reutter's good workmanship could have been of immense help to young Haydn. The fact that the kapellmeister did not choose to give such assistance was not because of any animosity toward Haydn; he was simply too busy. Ambition and continual lack of money turned him into that unpleasant type of man who accumulates appointments as a confirmed pluralist. In 1731 he became court composer, seven years later conductor at St. Stephen's, and thus head of the choir school. These two positions should have been sufficient, but Reutter, who was knighted in 1740 by the Emperor Charles VI, succeeded in also being appointed second conductor of the court chapel in 1747. His position was further improved in 1756 when the Empress Maria Theresa appointed him first court conductor. Thus Reutter, besides diverse musical duties at court, was in charge of music in both the great cathedral and the venerable court chapel, a state of affairs that had never before occurred in Vienna. Still another position at St. Stephen's fell to him. The cathedral employed a special group of vocalists and instrumentalists for services in a small chapel adorned with a miraculous painting of the Virgin, which was believed to shed real tears. In 1740 Reutter became provisional leader of this ensemble, but subsequently had to cede the appointment to a certain Ferdinand Schmidt. On the latter's death in 1756, Reutter became Schmidt's successor. It is hard to imagine how he could have carried out all these duties. As he was more interested in his duties at court, music at St. Stephen's had to be neglected. Carl Ferdinand Pohl[2] quotes a reprimand of the city council that "the church music was becoming worse and worse, thus leading to inattention and even disgust instead of gracious Christian edification." Reutter's income from various sources must have been considerable, and to it was added the unusually high salary of thirty-five hundred florins

[2]Carl Ferdinand Pohl, *Joseph Haydn* (Leipzig, 1878–1882), I, p. 41.

paid to his wife, the excellent court singer Therese Holzhauser. Even so, he kept the boy choristers, for whose support he was paid, on the shortest possible rations.

Lack of a thorough musical education, however, did not mean lack of work for the boys, and therein lay Haydn's salvation. The choristers' duties were very heavy; they had to take part every day in two full choral services (High Mass and Vespers), besides innumerable extra appearances on feast days, especially during Holy Week, and at festivities, private academies, funerals, processions, and even in Latin shows given by the Jesuits.[3] Reutter's double duties brought, as a great advantage, repeated invitations to court, where the singers of St. Stephen's and the court chapel joined forces. The practical musical knowledge that the impressionable boy derived from these various performances was enormous. He became thoroughly acquainted with the sacred music of such contemporary composers as Caldara, Fux, Reutter, Wagenseil, Tuma, Ziani, Palotta, and Bonno, and he also heard many secular works. According to Johann Friedrich Rochlitz, Haydn once said: "Proper teachers I have never had. I always started right away with the practical side, first in singing and in playing instruments, later in composition. I listened more than I studied, but I heard the finest music in all forms that was to be heard in my time, and of this there was much in Vienna. Oh, so much! I listened attentively and tried to turn to good account what most impressed me. Thus little by little my knowledge and my ability were developed."[4]

In addition to these rich musical impressions, baroque Vienna offered many thrilling sights. Young Haydn would certainly not have shared the opinion of Lady Mary Wortley Montagu, who in 1716 wrote from Vienna: "The processions I see very often are a pageantry, as offensive, and apparently contradictory to all common sense, as the pagodas of China."[5] He was too much of an Austrian and a Catholic to be anything but elated by the lavish display of color and sound on festive occasions. One unforgettable experience was the jubilee of Vienna's cardinal archbishop Sigismund Count Kóllonicz in 1749 to celebrate the fiftieth year of his

---

[3]The *Wiener Diarium* mentions a performance in the Jesuits' Theater on December 16, 1743, when a Latin drama on the Emperor Constantine with music by Reutter was performed by a cast of two hundred, including the pupils of the Jesuit College, St. Stephen's, and other institutions. The show was attended by the Empress Maria Theresa and the highest nobility and clergy.
[4]Johann Friedrich Rochlitz, *Für Freunde der Tonkunst* (Leipzig, 1832), IV, p. 274.
[5]See the letters of Lady Mary Wortley Montagu in Everyman's Library (1906).

priesthood, when an enormous procession of clergy and dignitaries marched solemnly into the cathedral, which was lighted by myriads of candles. Archbishops, bishops, and prelates assisted at High Mass, all dressed in the most ornate robes and carrying gorgeous wreaths on their arms. Cardinal Kollonicz's wreath was of pure gold, a present from the Empress Maria Theresa, and the chalice he used was adorned by a magnificent wreath wrought in silver, a gift from the Queen of Portugal. Members of the imperial family were carried to the building in golden sedan chairs and accompanied by the Knights of the Golden Fleece, the ambassadors, and the high nobility, all resplendent in robes of gold and silver encrusted with precious stones.[6] Surely such magnificence must have made any pageant that Sepperl had seen in Hainburg seem mean by comparison.

The boys from St. Stephen's also frequently took part in outdoor performances. Thus, in honor of St. John, music was performed on brilliantly illuminated boats lying in the Danube Canal opposite the saint's statue, while on St. Nepomuk's Day an evening performance of a Reutter oratorio was given on the beautifully decorated Vienna "High Bridge" in the presence of a distinguished audience.

Young Haydn must have greatly enjoyed such outings, for in spite of the beauty of St. Stephen's, its atmosphere could at times be oppressive. Sepperl had the natural craving of any healthy boy for exercise and fun, and even the very rigid discipline of the *Cantorei* did not prevent him from breaking loose occasionally. Once the choir was ordered to sing before the Empress Maria Theresa at her newly erected castle of Schönbrunn. The scaffolding had not yet been removed, and what was more natural than for the boys to climb on it with shouts of delight and laughter? Angrily the Empress appeared at a window and commanded the noisy group to get down immediately, threatening a good thrashing to anyone seen there again. The next day Joseph could not resist the temptation. Alone he climbed to the top and was duly observed by the Empress, who instantly ordered the kapellmeister to give this "fairhaired blockhead" the threatened punishment.

Not often, however, did Joseph displease Her Majesty. Usually she was well satisfied with his execution of important solos, which she was qualified to judge, being herself, like most of the Habsburgs, a well-trained musician. (It was reported that her beautiful

[6] See *Wiener Diarium* (1749).

singing made the famous male contralto Senesino burst into tears.)
Altogether, young Haydn, during his first years at St. Stephen's,
was very successful, though he never created a sensation. However,
from 1745 on, things seemed to grow steadily worse. Slowly the
voice of the boy approaching puberty began to deteriorate. This
became all the more noticeable as a newcomer had joined St. Stephen's choir school, a fine soprano with the remarkable compass of
three octaves. This voice belonged to Joseph's brother, Michael,[7]
who had joined the *Cantorei* in 1745 at the age of eight. At first
Joseph may have been delighted to have a member of his family
with him, and felt very proud when he was ordered to instruct his
younger brother in various subjects. Michael showed outstanding
gifts and seemed even more brilliant than Joseph. He learned rapidly,
and before long he played the organ so well that for the payment of
a few pennies he acted as deputy for the cathedral's organist. He
also showed initiative by organizing among his schoolmates a club
for the detection of plagiarism in their own compositions. We do
not know what Joseph's feelings were, for he was not the man to
dilate on such personal matters to his biographers. It seems highly
unlikely, however, that his "pleasure" in Michael's presence, mentioned by the contemporary writers, could have persisted when his
young brother snatched all the laurels from him. Joseph was given
no more solos after the Empress had complained about his "crowing like a cock"; instead they were entrusted to Michael. In point of
fact, Michael earned from the imperial couple applause such as had
never been given to Joseph. It was customary for the Empress to
celebrate annually the festival of St. Leopold, the patron saint of
Lower Austria, in the magnificent nearby monastery of Kloster-
neuburg. In 1748, when the imperial chapel, enlarged by St. Stephen's choir, had the task of executing the music for this festive
occasion, Michael sang a *Salve Regina* so admirably that the Emperor and Empress received the boy in a special audience, compli-
mented him, and gave him twenty-four golden ducats. Asked by
Reutter what he would do with such a fortune, Michael answered:
"Half of it I'll send my father, who has just lost a cow. The other
half please keep for me until my voice breaks too." Reutter agreed,
but apparently he never bothered to give the money back.

   According to Haydn's pupil, Ignaz Pleyel, Reutter, noticing
Joseph's distress about his breaking voice, hinted that there was a

[7]Johann Michael Haydn, a gifted composer in his own right, was born on September
14, 1737, at Rohrau. Cf. Hans Jancik, *Michael Haydn* (Vienna, 1952).

means of preserving the fine quality of his singing. Quite a few castrati still had good positions in the imperial chapel, and Joseph could imitate their example if he would submit to castration. Fortunately, Mathias Haydn, hearing about this plan, rushed to Vienna to put a stop to any such project.

More and more Joseph Haydn became useless to St. Stephen's as a singer. Had Reutter bestowed any thought on the welfare of the boy who for nine years had given him valuable service, he might of course have employed him as a violinist until his voice had regained its strength. But Reutter was no sentimentalist and did not have a good memory of promises given long before to anxious parents. At last the blow fell. A pretext was provided by none other than the victim himself. Joseph, always keen on playing practical jokes, could not resist testing a new pair of scissors by cutting off the pigtail of a fellow chorister. When Reutter heard about it, he exclaimed: "You will be caned on the hand." Joseph, seventeen years old, thought such punishment unbearable and rashly cried: "I would rather leave the *Cantorei* than be caned." This was the opportunity for which Reutter had been waiting. "Of course you will be expelled," he answered, "after you have been caned." And so it happened. On a cold November day in 1749, Haydn, with three ragged shirts and a worn coat as his sole possessions, without money, without any recommendation, was turned out into the street to fight for his existence.

# CHAPTER THREE

# "*Making Something Out of Nothing*"

## 1750 – 1761

The writers of the eighteenth century are full of praise for Vienna as a musical center. Dr. Burney, after visiting it in 1772, wrote: "Vienna is so rich in composers, and incloses within its walls such a number of musicians of superior merit, that it is but just to allow it to be, among German cities, the imperial seat of music, as well as of power." And the Prussian court conductor, J. F. Reichardt, declared: "The court made music with passion and the Austrian nobility was perhaps the most musical that ever existed." The Empress Maria Theresa, following a firmly established tradition in the Habsburg family, was enormously interested in music and the stage. Although not a composer herself, as many of her ancestors had been,[1] and in her struggle for the very existence of her empire unable to spend money for music as lavishly as her predecessors had, she saw to it that artists of the very first rank were invited to Vienna and engaged for academies and festive occasions at court. The high nobility of the country followed the example of the imperial dynasty. They vied with each other in establishing their own

---

[1] Ferdinand III, Leopold I, Joseph I, and Karl VI all composed sacred music, while Maria Theresa once jokingly called herself the oldest virtuosa in Europe because her father had made her sing on the stage when she was but five years old. See Charles Burney, *The Present State of Music in Germany,* . . . (London, 1773–1775), I, p. 206ff.

excellent orchestras. The academies, such as those which Prince Joseph Friedrich von Hildburghausen arranged with his own band in the exquisite palace built by the great architect Johann Fischer von Erlach, were of the very highest standard.

From 1750 onward the middle class also began to become more interested in music. Public concerts were inaugurated, following the model of the Paris Concerts Spirituels, and before long they enjoyed great popularity. The love of the Viennese for spectacles found satisfaction in its two theaters, the Theater nächst der Burg, in which mainly opera was played, and the Theater nächst dem Kärntnerthor, which concentrated on German and French plays. Under the Habsburgs, Vienna became a center of the reigning Italian opera of Naples. On the other hand, the city was also the first to witness, in 1762, the birth of Gluck's musical drama. Great attention was also given to the art of the ballet, which was to achieve in this century a summit of perfection under the great ballet master Noverre. Such native composers as Fux, Wagenseil, Dittersdorf, Reutter, and Starzer added a specifically Austrian touch to the colorful picture of Vienna's music culture during the reign of Maria Theresa.

Bearing all this in mind, one might be inclined to regard as fortunate any young and gifted musician ambitious to make his way in Vienna of 1749. Surely, one would think, some one of the aristocratic music lovers who spent such enormous sums on the cultivation of this passion must have discovered young Haydn's talent and given him the opportunity to develop it. In reality nothing of the kind happened. Haydn, as he bitterly complained in his autobiographical sketch, "had to eke out a wretched existence for eight whole years" before his luck began to change. The reasons for this predicament are clear enough. When he left St. Stephen's, he did not play any instrument more than moderately well (even on the violin, his favorite, he was, as he said, not "a conjuror"), his voice for the time being was nonexistent, and his compositions were groping attempts lacking any theoretical foundation. He was miserably dressed, unattractive in appearance, and on account of his secluded life in the *Cantorei*, unused to the great world and therefore shy and uncouth. What could such a destitute young musician do? Help from his family was neither given nor expected.[2] His parents might have considered assisting him if Joseph had followed his

---

[2] Just at the most critical time, Haydn's parents had to use all their resources to provide a dowry for their eldest daughter, Franziska, who married the baker J. Vieltzwiser on February 8, 1750.

mother's ardent desire and taken holy orders. The young man, however, for all his innate faith and the strong ties that bound him to the Catholic Church, never seriously considered this possibility. With the tenacity that had made his grandfather Lorenz Koller rebuild his house again and again after each devastation, young Haydn clung to his intention. He wanted to be a musician—not merely a mediocre performer, but a real composer. Therefore the position of a musical valet, which was very common in the eighteenth century, when a footman had to be able to play in his master's band,[3] had no appeal for and was not sought by him. It would take up too much of his time and not bring about the artistic development he craved. On the other hand, Haydn fully realized how sadly unprepared he was for the career he had chosen. He needed a good teacher of theory, or at least sufficient time for self-instruction. There seemed only one way open to him: to support himself by odd musical jobs and to spend all the time and energy he had left on the improvement of his musical knowledge. It was a long and tortuous way, a way filled with privations, but it led him to his ultimate goal.

When the young musician left St. Stephen's in November 1749, he did not even know where to spend the night. At this critical point he was first helped, characteristically enough, by one who himself was not much better off. As he wandered desperately through the chilly streets, Haydn chanced upon a man he knew slightly, Johann Michael Spangler, a singer in the Church of St. Michael and a private teacher. When Spangler heard of Joseph's misfortune he invited him to share the poor garret where he lived with his wife and a baby boy nine months old. The homeless lad accepted this generous offer with relief. A roof was found, and now he had only to earn his food (for here the impecunious singer was unable to help). Slowly Joseph began to make connections. He played at dances, he arranged compositions for various instruments, he took pupils for miserably small fees. Most of all, he went *gassatim*, which means that he took part in serenades. Like Italy, old Austria had a great fondness for open-air music at night, and many musicians were needed to fill the continuous demand. An eighteenth-century Viennese almanac[4] gives a lively description of this custom:

[3] A typical advertisement in the *Wiener Zeitung* (1789) states: "Wanted by nobleman a servant who plays the violin well and is able to accompany [on his instrument] difficult piano sonatas."
[4] *Wiener Theater-Almanach* (1794), p. 173.

On fine summer nights you may come upon serenades
in the streets at all hours. They are not, as in Italy, a mere
matter of a singer and a guitar. Here serenades are not
meant for declarations of love, for which the Viennese have
better opportunities. Such night music may be given to a
trio or a quartet of wind instruments, and works of some
extent may be played. The evening before the name day of
some fair lady will produce a lot of this kind of entertainment; and however late a serenade is given, all windows
are soon filled and in a few minutes the musicians are surrounded by an applauding crowd.

Haydn made the best use of this fashion. He earned a little
money this way and drew from the rich well of Viennese folk music, which has been a source of inspiration to Mozart, Beethoven,
Schubert, Brahms, and many others.

In this way he somehow got through the first difficult months,
but he was aware that this state of affairs could not and must not
last. In the Spanglers' crowded garret it was impossible for him to
undertake the serious studying upon which he was determined.
Moreover, Frau Spangler was expecting another baby, and after its
arrival there simply would be no room for him.[5] In the spring of
1750, as a temporary escape from his problems, he joined a party of
pilgrims to the miraculous shrine of the Virgin at Mariazell, a beautifully situated village in Styria that was, and still is, frequented by
crowds of worshipers. By this time, apparently, he was in full command of his voice, for he introduced himself to the choirmaster,
Father Florian Wrastil, as a former chorister of St. Stephen's and
asked to be admitted to the choir. His shabby appearance did not
inspire confidence, and apparently Father Wrastil had had unfortunate experiences with other traveling musicians; so he rudely sent
him away. Thereupon Haydn stole into the church choir, snatched a
vocal part out of a singer's hand, and sang the solo with such perfection that "all the choir held their breath to listen." The choirmas-
ter repented; young Haydn was invited to stay with him for a
week. During this time he was able to enjoy the exquisite, and for
him unfamiliar, sensation of getting all the food he wanted. He
returned to Vienna well rested, full of confidence in his ultimate

[5] The child was Maria Magdalena, born September 4, 1750. In 1768 Haydn engaged
her as a singer for Prince Esterházy. She performed the soprano solo in the first
performance of his *Il ritorno di Tobia* in 1775. Her husband was Haydn's good friend,
the tenor Karl Friberth.

success, and even with a little cash collected from the musicians of Mariazell. Before long this confidence bore fruit. A tradesman and *Marktrichter* in Vienna (a sort of colleague of Mathias Haydn) by the name of Anton Buchholz decided to help the young musician to pursue his studies and lent him unconditionally one hundred and fifty florins, a sum which must at that time have seemed enormous to Haydn. In 1801 the composer wrote in his will: "To Fräulein Anna Buchholz, one hundred florins, inasmuch as in my youth her grandfather lent me one hundred and fifty florins when I greatly needed them, which, however, I repaid fifty years ago." If the date mentioned is correct, Haydn must have repaid the loan as early as 1751, a year after he had received it. It seems more likely, however, that Haydn merely wanted to imply that it had not taken him long to square his debt. It is true that two legacies came his way in these critical years: seventy-seven florins due to him, as to the other five Haydn children, on the death of his mother in 1754, and sixty-one florins on the death of his maternal grandmother in 1756. However, these sums were paid to him only much later.

Now Haydn was in a position to leave the good Spanglers and settle down in a room of his own. He chose, of course, the cheapest place available. It was a garret, partitioned off from a larger room, in the old Michaelerhaus near Vienna's ancient Romanesque Church of St. Michael. His neighbors in the attic were a cook, a journeyman printer, a footman, and a house-stoker who tended the fires in the house of some wealthy man. To all outward appearances the new lodgings were anything but pleasant. Indeed, Haydn's early biographers did their utmost to stress the hardships he endured there. Karl Bertuch wrote: "He lived on the sixth story, and his room in the garret had neither stove nor window; in winter his breath froze on his coverlet, and the water that he fetched himself from the spring in the morning for washing was frequently changed into lumps of ice before his arrival in these elevated regions."[6] Such drawbacks were, however, of no great consequence to a youth like Haydn. Here he was, as he said, "too happy to envy the lot of kings," for he had at last the privacy he craved for his studies and he was the proud owner of an "old, worm-eaten clavier." Haydn now set about to fill the big gaps in his theoretical knowledge. He devoured Johann Joseph Fux's famous *Gradus ad Parnassum*,[7] Johann

---

[6] See Karl Bertuch, *Journal des Luxus und der Moden* (Weimar, 1805).
[7] Haydn's own copy, held in the Esterházy Library, was destroyed by fire in the Second World War. However, Pohl had the forethought to enter all comments by Haydn into another volume of the *Gradus*, which is retained by the Gesellschaft der

Matteson's *Der vollkommene Kapellmeister*, and David Kellner's *Unterricht im Generalbass*. The copies he used and their numerous annotations reveal the thoroughness with which young Haydn threw himself into the study of these subjects.

Perhaps even more important than these manuals was his discovery of the first six keyboard sonatas by Carl Philipp Emanuel Bach, which opened a new world to him. "I did not leave the clavier," he said to Dies, "until I had mastered them all," and to Rochlitz he remarked: "Innumerable times I played them for my own delight, especially when I felt oppressed and discouraged by worries and always I left the instrument gay and in high spirits."[8]

One of the reasons for Haydn's reactions was the strong emotional appeal emanating from the works of the "Hamburg Bach." Up to then he had been familiar with the gay and superficial idiom of the musical rococo; here he found compositions that deeply stirred and excited him. "Who knows me well," he was later to remark, "must have found out that I owe a great deal to Emanuel Bach, that I have understood and diligently studied him." As a matter of fact, no other composer except Mozart influenced him as much as the north German master.

But while the works of Carl Philipp Emanuel Bach opened new vistas to the young musician, it was only natural for him to maintain connection with Austrian folk music, and in 1752 this resulted in his first dramatic attempt. The story is best told in the words of Bombet—Stendhal[9]—based on the report of Giuseppe Carpani:

> Haydn composed for his amusement, a serenata for three instruments, which he performed with two of his friends in different parts of Vienna. The Kärntnerthortheater was at that time directed by Kurz-Bernardon, a celebrated harlequin who amused the public with his puns and drew crowds to the theater by his originality. He had,

Musikfreunde in Vienna. Interestingly enough, Haydn's entries are all in Latin, as is Fux's own text. Cf. A. Mann in *Studies in Eighteenth-Century Music* (London, 1970), p. 324.

[8]Johann Friedrich Rochlitz, *Für Freunde der Tonkunst* (Leipzig, 1832), IV, p. 274. Rochlitz was in personal contact with Haydn.

[9]In 1814 Marie-Henri Beyle (writing mostly under the pseudonyms of L.-A.-C. Bombet or Stendhal) published his *Lettres écrites de Vienne, en Autriche, sur le célèbre compositeur, Joseph Haydn*. This was actually a translation, with very slight adaptations, of Carpani's *Le Haydine* (Milan, 1812). It was translated into English in 1817, and an American edition appeared in 1839.

moreover, a handsome wife; and this was an additional reason for our nocturnal adventurers to perform their serenade under the harlequin's window. Bernardon was so
struck with the originality of the music that he came down
into the street to ask who had composed it. "I did," replied
Haydn boldly. "Come upstairs." Haydn followed the co-
median, was introduced to the handsome wife, and rede-
scended with the libretto of an opera, entitled *The Limping
Devil* [*Der krumme Teufel*]. The music, composed in a few
days, had a brilliant success. But a nobleman, who probably was not handsome, suspected that he was being ridiculed under the name of the "Limping Devil" and caused
the piece to be prohibited. Haydn often said that he had
had more trouble in devising a mode of representing the
motion of the waves in a tempest shown in this opera than
he afterward had in writing fugues with a double subject.
Bernardon, who had spirit and taste, was difficult to please
and there was also another obstacle. Neither of the two
authors had ever seen either sea or tempest. How can a
man describe what he knows nothing about? Bernardon,
all agitation, paced up and down, while the composer was
seated at the harpsichord. "Imagine," said he, "a mountain
rising and then a valley sinking, and then another mountain and another valley; the mountains and the valleys follow rapidly one after the other." This fine description was
of no avail and in vain did the actor add thunder and lightning. At last, young Haydn, out of all patience, extended
his hands to the two ends of the harpsichord, and bringing
them in a glissando rapidly together, he exclaimed: "The
devil take the tempest!" "That's it, that's it," cried the harlequin, springing upon his neck and almost stifling him.
Many years later when Haydn crossed the Straits of Dover
in bad weather, he laughed during the whole of the passage, remembering the storm in *The Limping Devil*.

Haydn's music to the little opera is unfortunately lost. We
know that the work was performed on May 29, 1753, and apparently had substantial box office receipts.[10]
While most of the lessons Haydn gave were—as he remarked

[10] Cf. Franz Hadamowsky, "Das Spieljahr 1753/54 des Theaters nächst dem Kärntnerthor und des Theaters nächst der K. K. Burg," in *Jahrbuch der Gesellschaft für
Wiener Theaterforschung* XI (1959), pp. 3–22.

in his autobiographical sketch—just "a miserable mode of earning daily bread," one played an important part in his career. As luck would have it, there lived on the third floor of the old Michaeler-haus the great Italian writer, Pietro Metastasio, poet laureate of the Habsburgs since 1730 and author of numerous operatic librettos that were set to music by a greater number of operatic composers than those of any other librettist. According to Dr. Burney, who was Metastasio's first biographer, the Italian poet's writings "con-tributed more to the refinement of vocal melody, and consequently of music in general, than the joint efforts of all the great composers in Europe." The great man shared his apartment with the family of a Spanish friend, Niccolò de Martinez, and was highly interested in the education of his two daughters. In particular the elder one, Marianne (born on May 4, 1744), was the apple of his eye, and he bestowed the greatest care on the development of her outstanding musical talent. Somehow Metastasio must have noticed Haydn. Perhaps in quiet nights the sounds of the clavier on which the young man was improvising penetrated from the miserable garret down to Metastasio's elegant apartment. He decided to engage the unknown youth as piano teacher for Marianne, then ten years old. For three years Haydn worked daily with the girl, receiving free board in exchange for his labors, and there is no doubt that he learned a great deal himself while studying with so unusual a pupil, whose subse-quent achievements as pianist, singer, and composer earned her election to the famous Philharmonic Academy of Bologna and were praised by all Viennese musicians. (Even Mozart played piano duets with her.)[11] Besides, Haydn was naturally brought into con-tact with the gentle Metastasio, whose "simplicity and decorum" (Burney) may have exercised a good influence on the young teacher's demeanor. The lessons with Marianne had, moreover, another re-sult of still greater importance. She received singing instruction from the famous Italian composer and singing teacher Niccolò Por-pora, who lived in Vienna from 1753 to 1757. Haydn acted as ac-companist in these lessons, and thus had the good fortune to meet the "patriarch of melody." Porpora was then seventy years old, and had probably forgotten his own early struggles, about which the following amusing story is told.[12]

[11] As a mature composer Haydn still maintained contact with Marianne Martinez. They both appear in an album belonging to Mozart's pupil Babette Ployer. Haydn wrote into it the canon he had composed for Oxford University; Marianne contrib-uted an Italian canzonetta. Cf. Roland Tenschert, *Frauen um Haydn* (Vienna, 1946).
[12] F. S. Kandler, *Cenni storïco critici di Hasse* (Venice, 1820).

In the time of Charles VI [father of Maria Theresa], the celebrated Porpora lived at Vienna, poor and unemployed. His music did not please the imperial connoisseur, being too full of trills and mordents. Hasse wrote an oratorio for the emperor, who asked him for a second. He entreated His Majesty to permit Porpora to execute it. The emperor at first refused saying that he did not like that capering style; but, touched by Hasse's generosity, he at length complied with his request. Porpora, having received a hint from his friend, did not introduce a single trill into the whole oratorio. The emperor, surprised, continually repeated during the rehearsal: "It is quite a different man; here are no trills!" But when they came to the fugue, which concluded the sacred composition, he observed that the theme began with four trilled notes. Now you know that in fugues the subject passes from one part to another, but does not change. When the emperor, who was said never to laugh, heard in the full height of the fugue this deluge of trills, which seemed like the music of some enraged paralytic, he could no longer maintain his gravity, and laughed, perhaps for the first time in his life. It was the beginning of Porpora's fortune.

Those days were passed, and now Porpora was "sour beyond all that can be imagined" (Carpani). This did not deter Haydn. Here was an excellent teacher within his grasp, and he did not mean to let the opportunity slip away. He asked for permission to become Porpora's accompanist in order to study his method, and in exchange he offered menial service. Porpora accepted and took Haydn to the fashionable baths of Mannersdorf, where they were both to stay in the house of the Venetian ambassador, Pietro Correr, whose mistress was Porpora's devoted pupil. In this favorite summer resort Haydn seems to have met various prominent composers like Gluck, Wagenseil, and Bonno and attended the famous academies of the Prince of Hildburghausen. He was, however, much more interested in the "old bear," whom he served diligently, "cleaning his shoes, beating his coat, and arranging his antique periwig." The treatment he received was not very good, for the choleric Italian was quite fluent with his tongue and active with his hand, but Haydn did not really resent being called a "blockhead" or a "beast" and receiving sundry cuffs as long as Porpora was willing to correct his valet's compositions. When he left the maestro, after three months, he had improved enormously in singing and in Italian, which he could write in later years nearly as well as German, and had learned, as he said, "the genuine fundamentals of composition."

While Joseph was thus acting as a valet to Porpora, his brother Michael was treading the path toward a successful career. Just as he had outshone Joseph at St. Stephen's, so now he seemed to show more ability than his elder brother. After leaving the Vienna cathedral and eking out his existence by odd jobs as his brother was doing, he was engaged, at the age of twenty, as conductor to the Bishop of Grosswardein in Hungary. Joseph must have felt deeply impressed and somewhat shaken when he heard this news, for he remembered only too well in what utter poverty he had lived when he was twenty. Even now, five years later, he had nothing to show his father that could match Michael's success. Considerations of this kind, however, only strengthened his determination to persevere; and though he could not display visible proofs of success, he felt that he was steadily climbing upward, that he was, in his own words, "making something out of nothing."[13] Slowly he began to gain admission to the only circle in eighteenth-century Vienna that could assure a composer's fortune, that of the nobility. The charming Countess Thun,[14] after coming across one of Haydn's sonatas, wanted to meet the composer. When Joseph first stood before her, she was somewhat shocked by his appearance. Could this undersized, dark-complexioned youth with a face pitted by smallpox, a large aquiline nose, and legs too short for his body, really be the creator of such lovely and graceful tunes? But a closer inspection revealed a noble forehead and dark gray eyes sparkling with humor and kindness which somehow made the Countess forget the young man's general ugliness, awkward manners, and very shabby clothes. When she had made sure that she was not being tricked by an impostor, the Countess began to study the clavier and singing with Haydn. This meant a decisive step forward, as the Thun family, thanks to its social position and good relationship to important musical friends, could do a great deal for a young unknown composer. Perhaps the Countess' recommendation helped him to establish an even more important contact. He was invited by the ardent music lover Karl Joseph von Fürnberg to his country home, Weinzierl, to take part in chamber music performances. Haydn spent a delight-

[13] According to Dies, Haydn said once: "Young people can learn from my example that something can come out of nothing. What I am is all the result of the direst need."

[14] Cf. the report in Nicholas E. Framery, *Notice de Joseph Haydn* (Paris, 1810).

ful time in the hospitable little castle, charmingly situated in a hilly country and offering a splendid view of mountains six thousand feet high. There three other musicians joined him: his host's steward, the local priest, and the violoncellist Albrechtsberger (not J. G. Albrechtsberger, the famous teacher of Beethoven, but possibly a brother of his). For this group Haydn composed his first string quartets, which were received with such praise that he was encouraged to continue in this line. Music was also made in the village of Purkersdorf, at the home of Fürnberg's eldest son, Joseph, likewise a passionate music lover.[15]

Haydn's situation certainly was improving since he had gained access to such music lovers as the Countess Thun and the Fürnberg family. It is significant that around 1755 he was taking part in chamber music at the castle of his native town's patron, Count Harrach.[16] This is attested to by the report of a certain Major Weirach, who stayed as prisoner of war in the Harrach castle after the battle at Kolin. He remembered that Haydn's compositions were received with great acclaim, to which the young and shy composer reacted with the utmost modesty.

In Vienna the number of Haydn's pupils grew, he raised his fees, and other engagements filled his time. He worked from sixteen to eighteen hours a day. At daybreak he took the part of first violin at the church of the Brothers of the Order of Mercy;[17] thence he repaired to the chapel of Count Haugwitz, where he played the organ; at a later hour he sang the tenor part at St. Stephen's; and last, having been on foot the whole day, he passed a part of the night at the harpsichord. And so it went on from day to day.

At last he was able to harvest the fruits of such concentration. Around 1758, Fürnberg recommended him to the Bohemian Count Karl Joseph Franz von Morzin and Haydn was engaged as music director and *Kammercompositeur*. Not only socially, but also financially this was a great step forward. Now he was paid two hundred florins a year, besides receiving free board and lodging. Both the

---

[15] Landon (*HCaW*, I, p. 239ff.) conjectures that Joseph von Fürnberg bought a large number of Haydn's early works from Count Morzin when the latter disbanded his Kapelle (see p. 40). On Fürnberg's death it was, according to Landon's theory, purchased by another music-loving aristocrat, the Hungarian Count Festetics, who took the collection to Keszthely, his castle in Hungary. There it was discovered at the end of the Second World War, taken to Budapest to be catalogued, and then returned to Keszthely. Landon's theory seems quite intriguing, though unproved. At any rate, the collection discovered in Keszthely is of the greatest value, as it throws light on Haydn's early production.

[16] Cf. Leopold Nowak, *Joseph Haydn*, 2d ed. (Zürich, 1959), p. 82.

[17] According to Griesinger, he received for this work a yearly salary of sixty florins.

Count and his wife, the beautiful Countess Wilhelmine, were great lovers of music. They had their own orchestra of about sixteen musicians which played in the winter in Vienna and in the summer at Lukavec, their country house in Bohemia. The new responsibilities paved the way for Haydn's great artistic development. It was at the Morzins' that his first symphony was composed, and in all likelihood several others followed and were performed by the Count's own orchestra under Haydn's direction. According to Landon,[18] who bases his analysis on the Fürnberg-Morzin collection to be found in the castle of Keszthely (see n. 15), Haydn displayed intense creative activity while serving the Morzin family. For his patron's wind band he contributed a number of divertimenti. These works helped him to acquire a true mastery of the employment of wind instruments, especially the horns.

Very little is known about Haydn's life with Count Morzin, but one little episode mentioned by Griesinger is not without significance. The Countess was a good singer and it was Haydn's duty to accompany her on the clavier. Once, while she was leaning over him to look more closely into the music, her neckerchief became unfolded, whereupon Haydn stopped playing, as if struck by lightning. Reprimanded by the fair Countess, he exclaimed naïvely, "But, Your Highness, who would not lose his head over this?" There can be no doubt that the composer's interest in the fair sex began to develop much more strongly once he had outgrown his artistic apprenticeship and gained a modest foothold on the social ladder. He felt that the time had come to consider marriage seriously. The events leading to this fateful step are unfortunately rather obscure and contemporary statements contradict each other. The only fact established beyond doubt is that Haydn did not marry the girl of his choice. Among his pupils in Vienna were the daughters of a wigmaker, Johann Peter Keller. Haydn fell in love with the younger one, Theresa. However, her deeply religious parents insisted that Theresa devote herself to the Catholic Church and paid for her entrance into the nunnery of the Poor Clares[19] at the Convent of St. Nicholas. For the ceremony of her profession as Sister Josepha, Haydn offered an Organ Concerto in C major. This work as well as the *Salve Regina* of 1756, possibly also written for her, are the earliest compositions extant that bear a date in his hand. Maybe these youthful works held a special significance for Haydn because

[18] Cf. *HCaW*, I, pp. 260–296.
[19] Cf. Ernst Fritz Schmid, "Josef Haydns Jugendliebe," in *Festschrift Wilhelm Fischer* (Innsbruck, 1956).

of their personal implications and were therefore carefully preserved by him.

Haydn did not stop visiting the Keller family, and when he entered the service of Count Morzin and his financial position was much improved, the wigmaker naturally tried to secure the promising young artist for another member of the family. There was the elder daughter, Maria Anna Aloysia Apollonia, thirty-one years old and so much less attractive than Theresa, that there seemed little prospect of her entering the state of holy matrimony. We do not know what pressure the Kellers brought to bear on Haydn, but unfortunately they succeeded, and the composer took a wife who was probably the most unsuitable life partner that he could have chosen. His blindness and passivity are hard to understand, for it is known that he was a keen judge of human nature, and many recorded facts prove his skill and shrewdness in dealing with other people. It seems most likely he was prompted by reasons similar to those that Mozart expressed in a letter to his father before he married. Mozart had suffered a fate not very different from Haydn's. After falling passionately in love with the singer, Aloysia Weber, and being jilted by this "false coquette," Mozart felt induced to marry her sister Constanze. Here is the explanation he gave to his father:

> The voice of nature speaks as loud in me as in others, louder perhaps, than in many a big strong lout of a fellow. I cannot possibly live as do most young men in these days. In the first place, I have too much religion; in the second place, I have too great a love for my neighbor, and am too honorably minded to seduce an innocent maiden; while in the third place, I have too much care for my health. . . . I can think of nothing more necessary to my disposition than a wife, inclined as I am to quiet domesticity more than to revelry. A bachelor, in my opinion, is only half alive.[20]

Haydn, too, felt that he needed marriage, and the partner herself did not seem of such great importance to him now that the one who really mattered was inaccessible. So, though Maria Anna Aloysia Apollonia was three years his senior, not good-looking, not pleasant, and not interested in music, he married her on November 26, 1760.

[20] Letter from W. A. Mozart to his father dated December 15, 1781.

The marriage contract has been preserved in the *Archiv für Niederösterreich.*[21] According to the custom then prevailing among middle-class people, either partner had to deposit a certain amount of money. The bride offered three hundred and fifty florins in goods and five hundred florins in cash; the bridegroom one thousand florins. How Haydn could have afforded so sizable a sum at this stage is not clear. Maybe he displayed even in the early years considerable business acumen in selling his compositions, such as the first quartets, which seem to have been very popular from the start. On the other hand, shrewdness was not displayed in his selection of Maria Anna Keller. Haydn expected marriage to provide him with a comfortable, peaceful home and with children, for whom he felt a great fondness. Neither of these hopes was fulfilled. Maria Anna was quarrelsome, jealous, bigoted, not even a good housekeeper, and Haydn reproached her particularly for being a spendthrift. As to progeny, Haydn once remarked: "My wife was unable to bear children, and for this reason I was less indifferent toward the attractions of other women." What irritated him most, however, was his wife's utter lack of appreciation of his work. "She doesn't care a straw whether her husband is an artist or a cobbler," he exclaimed indignantly. Members of Haydn's orchestra even said that Frau Haydn, out of pure mischief, liked to use the master's manuscript scores as linings for her pastry or for curl papers. Haydn must have felt a diabolical pleasure when he came across the following poem by Lessing, for which he composed a canon:

> If in the whole wide world
> But one mean wife there is,
> How sad that each of us
> Should think this one is his!

It would not be entirely fair to put all the blame for the couple's domestic misery on Frau Haydn, whose position, indeed, was not an easy one. That she was unable to grasp the importance of her husband's creative work was, after all, not her fault. She was not made that way, and if Haydn had tried to know her better before their marriage, he would have found that music meant nothing to her. In her own peculiar way, Maria Anna may have been fond of her husband. It is known, for instance, that she cared so much for a

[21] Cf. Robert Franz Müller, "Heiratsbrief . . . der Gattin Joseph Haydns," *Die Musik* (Nov. 1929), pp. 93–99.

certain portrait of Haydn by Ludwig Guttenbrunn that she brought it with her when taking the cure at Baden and did not want to part with it even when it was required for copying. Haydn, it must be admitted, interpreted her behavior in a less flattering way, declaring that the reason his wife liked the picture so much was because Guttenbrunn had once been her lover. Be that as it may, unless she was quite indifferent toward her husband, Frau Haydn must have suffered agonies of jealousy throughout her married life. She may not have forgotten that Haydn had cared deeply for her younger and prettier sister. That she was right in this respect is proved by the fact that as late as 1801 he remembered his first love in his will.[22] Quite apart from that, the sight of her husband, whose inflammable nature she knew, working constantly with the attractive singers of his ensemble was not easy for this plain woman to bear. The difference between their ages further aggravated the situation. Haydn, who had developed with extreme slowness, was unusually young for his age, while Frau Haydn, according to the views of the time, felt and behaved like an elderly matron while still in her middle thirties. The way each of them spent money proved to be another source of irritation. Frau Haydn may have been as much annoyed at her husband's supporting scores of his poor relatives as he was at his wife's liberality toward the clergy. There is no doubt that in this unhappy union both partners suffered deeply. Yet Haydn behaved with great loyalty toward other members of the Keller family. A touching instance was brought to light by A. van Hoboken.[23] A brother of Maria Anna had, because of his odd behaviour—he owned up to ten dogs which he fed sumptuously—been taken to the insane asylum. In 1797 Haydn sent a petition to the Ministry of Justice to get his brother-in-law released, claiming the man was not insane, only feeble-minded. He succeeded and Joseph Keller was reunited with his wife. However, a year later Keller was again taken to the asylum. This time Haydn took the matter into his own hands. He removed Keller from the asylum, and returned the unhappy man to his home where Keller remained until his death in 1801. Haydn also lent him the sum of one thousand florins, which was repaid from the estate on the brother-in-law's death.

[22] He describes her as "ex-nun." In the course of Emperor Joseph II's reform activities, the St. Nicholas convent had been dissolved and Josepha forced to return to secular life. As we learn from the last will of Haydn's wife, who also left her sister a legacy, the latter had become engaged in social work for the poor.
[23] Cf. Anthony van Hoboken, "Joseph Haydns Schwager," in *Festschrift Josef Stummvoll* (Vienna, 1970).

Soon after the marriage, at the very time when Haydn must have become aware of his fatal error, all his energies were required to cope with a new situation. Count Morzin found himself in financial difficulties, and decided to give up his expensive orchestra. Haydn was left without a position, though not for long. Prince Paul Anton Esterházy, hearing of Morzin's troubles, may have remembered Haydn's performances with the Morzin band, and realized that now he could secure this musician for his court at Eisenstadt. As he already had a conductor, old and ailing Gregorius Joseph Werner, Prince Esterházy offered the young composer the post of vice-conductor. Haydn accepted with enthusiasm.

# CHAPTER FOUR

# The Honorable Officer of a Princely Court

## 1 7 6 1 – 1 7 6 6

The years of ceaseless toil, of poverty and intense self-education now seemed to have been worthwhile, as they had led to a truly important appointment for Haydn. The Esterházys stood at the very top of the powerful Hungarian nobility. They were the oldest and wealthiest magnates of the country and had the longest record of zeal in the promotion of music and the fine arts. The first member of the family of barons to be raised to the rank of Prince of the Holy Roman Empire had been Paul (1635–1713), a staunch supporter of the House of Habsburg, who was instrumental in promulgating the law that made the Austrian monarch hereditary King of Hungary. Paul was a great Maecenas. He acquired a fine picture gallery for his castle of Forchtenstein and established his own band of musicians in his residence at Eisenstadt. He was also a composer, and in 1711 published a series of church hymns with orchestral accompaniment written for all the holidays of the ecclesiastical year. The grand scale on which he liked to organize his enterprises is clearly illustrated by the account of a pilgrimage that he had his subjects make to the shrine at Mariazell in 1692. It consisted of no less than 11,200 persons, who walked for six days, among them members of the high nobility, clergy in ornate robes, girls with golden crowns on their heads, musicians, and banner bearers. The Prince visited this shrine fifty-eight times, though certainly not always with so large a retinue. Under his reign, the old castle in

41

Eisenstadt was rebuilt. In this magnificent baroque edifice, with proud towers at the four corners, there were no less than two hundred rooms for guests and a beautiful reception hall adorned with frescoes. The building also contained a chapel, a library, and a picture collection (which was acquired in 1860 by the Hungarian State and served as the basis for the Budapest Museum of Fine Arts). Great care was given to the planning of the immense park surrounding the castle, and it abounded in artificial waterfalls, ponds, grottoes, and beautiful trees.[1] Young Count Karl von Zinzendorf, who had become a friend of the family on his arrival from Dresden, remarked in his diary:[2] "There is no park as beautiful in Vienna."

Prince Paul's successors continued the tradition established by this Maecenas, at the same time consolidating their enormous wealth. (At the beginning of this century the Esterházy estate comprised twenty-nine lordships, with twenty-one castles, sixty market towns, and four hundred fourteen villages in Hungary alone, besides several lordships in Lower Austria and a county in Bavaria.) Prince Paul Anton (1710–1762) began his reign in 1734. He had a genuine love of music and played the violin, flute, and lute himself. During his travels through Italy and Germany, he collected a great number of manuscript scores, and he had a detailed catalogue of them made in 1759 by the violinist Champée. Military duties at first made it impossible for the Prince to plan for the improvement of the Esterházy orchestra, functioning, since 1728, under the leadership of Gregorius J. Werner (b. between 1695 and 1701). For some years Paul Anton was ambassador at the Court of Naples, besides taking a very active part in the wars that Austria fought during the reign of Maria Theresa. As a reward, he was given the rank of field marshal. When at last, at the end of the 1750s, the Prince was able to settle down at Eisenstadt, he showed that he had a perfect understanding of what was needed to raise the standard of music-making at his court. New musicians were engaged, among them the excellent tenor Karl Friberth, who was destined to become one of Haydn's great friends, and, one year later, the soprano singer Anna Maria Scheffstoss. The Prince's most important act, however, which has awarded him a permanent place in the history of music, was his engagement of Joseph Haydn. As Landon has pointed

[1] The park, built on the slopes of the Leitha hills, was changed several times according to the fashion of the period. In 1754 it was arranged in the style of the gardens at Versailles, while in the nineties of that century it was reorganized in the English fashion.
[2] Cf. *HCaW*, I, p. 358.

out,[3] Haydn worked for the Esterházys some time before he was formally appointed. He thus started his musical activities for the princely house in Vienna, where the Esterházys resided every year for several months. Haydn's contract was concluded on May 1, 1761, less than a year before Prince Paul Anton's death, at the age of fifty-one, on March 18, 1762. The interesting document, which has been preserved in the Esterházy archives, is quoted here in full:[4]

This day (according to the date hereto appended) Joseph Heyden, native of Rohrau in Austria, is accepted and appointed a Vice-Kapellmeister in the service of His Serene Princely Highness, Herr Paul Anton, Prince of the Holy Roman Empire, of Esterházy and Galantha, etc., subject to conditions here following:

1. Whereas the Kapellmeister at Eisenstadt, namely Gregorius Werner, having devoted many years of true and faithful service to the princely house, is now, on account of his great age and infirmities, unfit to perform the duties incumbent on him, it is hereby declared that the said Gregorius Werner, in consideration of his long service, shall retain the post of Ober-Kapellmeister, and the said Joseph Heyden as Vice-Kapellmeister at Eysenstatt shall, so far as regards the music of the choir, be subordinate to the Kapellmeister and receive his instructions. But in everything else relating to musical performances, and in all that concerns the orchestra, the Vice-Kapellmeister shall have the sole direction.

2. The said Joseph Heyden shall be considered and treated as a house officer. Therefore His Serene Highness is graciously pleased to place confidence in his conducting himself as becomes an honorable officer of a princely court. He must be temperate, not showing himself overbearing toward his musicians, but mild and lenient, straightforward and composed. It is especially to be observed that when the orchestra shall be summoned to perform before company, the Vice-Kapellmeister and all the musicians shall appear in uniform, and the said Joseph Heyden shall take care that he and all his subordinates follow the instructions given, and appear in white stockings,

[3] Cf. *HCaW*, I, p. 346.
[4] Cf. Carl Ferdinand Pohl, *Joseph Haydn* (Leipzig, 1878–1882), I, p. 391ff.

white linen, powdered, and either with pigtail or hairbag, all, however, of identical appearance.

3. Whereas the other musicians are referred for directions to the said Vice-Kapellmeister, he shall therefore take the more care to conduct himself in an exemplary manner, so that the subordinates may follow the example of his good qualities; consequently the said Joseph Heyden shall abstain from undue familiarity, from eating and drinking and other intercourse with them, so as to maintain the respect due to him and preserve it; for these subordinates should remember their respectful duties and consider how displeasing the consequences of any discord or dispute would be to His Serene Highness.

4. The said Vice-Kapellmeister shall be under obligation to compose such music as His Serene Highness may command, and neither to communicate such compositions to any other person, nor to allow them to be copied, but he shall retain them for the exclusive use of His Highness, and not compose for any other person without the knowledge and gracious permission of His Highness.

5. The said Joseph Heyden shall appear daily (whether here in Vienna or on the estates) in the antechamber before and after midday, and inquire whether His Highness is pleased to order a performance of the orchestra. On receipt of his orders he shall communicate them to the other musicians, and take care to be punctual at the appointed time, and to ensure punctuality in his subordinates, making a note of those who arrive late or absent themselves altogether.

6. Should, contrary to expectation, any quarrel or cause of complaint arise, the Vice-Kapellmeister shall endeavor to arrange it in order that His Serene Highness may not be incommoded with trifling disputes; but should any more serious difficulty occur, which the said Joseph Heyden is unable to set right, His Serene Highness must then be respectfully called upon to decide the matter.

7. The said Vice-Kapellmeister shall take careful charge of all music and musical instruments, and be responsible for any injury that may occur to them from carelessness or neglect.

8. The said Joseph Heyden shall be obliged to instruct the female vocalists, in order that they may not forget in

the country what they have been taught with much trouble and expense in Vienna, and, as the said Vice-Kapellmeister is proficient on various instruments, he shall take care himself to practice on all those with which he is acquainted.

9. A copy of this Convention and Rules for Behaviour shall be given to the said Vice-Kapellmeister and his subordinates, in order that he may be able to hold them to their obligations therein laid down.

10. It is considered unnecessary to detail the services required of the said Joseph Heyden, more particularly since His Serene Highness is pleased to hope that he will of his own free will strictly observe not only these regulations, but any others that may from time to time be made by the high *Herrschaft*, and that he will place the orchestra on such a footing, and in such good order, that he may bring honor upon himself and deserve the further favor of the Prince his master, who thus confides in his zeal and discretion.

11. A yearly salary of four hundred florins to be received in quarterly payments is hereby bestowed by His Serene Highness upon the said Vice-Kapellmeister.

12. When on the estates, the said Joseph Heyden shall board at the officers' table, or receive a half-gulden per day in lieu thereof.

13. Finally, this agreement shall hold good for at least three years from May 1, 1761, with the further condition that if at the conclusion of this term the said Joseph Heyden shall desire to leave the service, he shall give His Highness six months' previous notice of his intention.

14. His Serene Highness undertakes to keep Joseph Heyden in his service during this time, and should he be completely satisfied with him, he may look forward to being appointed Ober-Kapellmeister. This, however, must not be understood to deprive His Serene Highness of the right to dismiss the said Joseph Heyden at all times, also during the period in question, should He see fit to do so.

Duplicate copies of this document shall be executed and exchanged.

Given at Vienna this first day of May, 1761.

*Ad mandatum Celsissimi Principis,*

JOHANN STIFFTELL, *Secretary*

The number and variety of duties expected from Haydn are staggering, and they had to be carried out to the satisfaction of a new patron, Prince Nicolaus, who succeeded his brother, Prince Paul Anton, as the ruling head of the family. Fortunately for Haydn, this new sovereign was an ardent music lover and a fairly good performer. Yet he was evidently convinced that the varied activities demanded of the new vice-kapellmeister could reasonably be expected to be discharged satisfactorily. Three different spheres of activity were entrusted to him. He was conductor, which meant daily practice with the orchestra and very frequent performances; he had to compose a great part of the enormous amount of music performed; finally, he was an important officer of administration, uniting in his person the positions of music librarian, supervisor of instruments, and chief of the musical personnel. All this Haydn did, and he performed his duties extremely well. That he succeeded as a composer far beyond Prince Esterházy's fondest hopes need not be emphasized here. As a conductor, playing the violin or the harpsichord, he was outstanding too. There is a humorous report that his face while conducting was so expressive that society snobs who wanted to demonstrate their understanding of music just dexterously placed themselves in a situation where they could see Haydn and regulate by his smile the ecstatic applause by which they testified to their neighbors the extent of their own rapture. Despite the important duties entrusted to him and despite unceasing creative work, he also found time to carry out tasks of a more practical nature, which he executed with the conscientiousness typical of a descendant of diligent farmers and wheelwrights. He supervised the work of the copyists, occasionally even taking a hand himself, and, according to Griesinger, he liked to tune his own clavier. He also saw to it that old instruments were repaired at the lowest possible cost. As chief of personnel, Haydn revealed his innate tact and good nature and even this part of his duties was performed with a skill not granted to other great composers. (One remembers Handel's fights with the members of his opera company and Bach's difficulties in Leipzig.) Haydn's task was by no means easy and often he had to mediate quarrels among the musicians. We know, for instance, of a settlement between the oboist Zacharias Pohl and the cellist Xavier Marteau concluded in Haydn's presence and doubtless thanks to his intervention. During a brawl in the castle tavern, Marteau had knocked out the oboist's right eye with his ring and now had to undertake to pay Pohl a compensation of forty-nine florins and forty-three kreutzer in monthly installments. The act of

December 21, 1771, explicitly remarks that the cellist did not inflict damage on the oboist intentionally, a remark that reflects the conductor's conciliatory attitude. On the other hand, Haydn had to establish some kind of *modus vivendi* with the higher-ranking court officers, in particular with the administrator, Güterregent Ludwig Peter von Rahier, a former military man who held full judicial powers over the musicians, whom he could incarcerate or subject to fines for some failing in their duties. Von Rahier regularly sent reports to the Prince on his dealings with the musicians, and as a rule his verdict prevailed with Prince Nicolaus. However, Haydn learned eventually to reach some sort of compromise with the haughty administrator and often managed to achieve in one way or another the desired end. Haydn even went so far as to endeavor to dissuade the Prince from carrying out an order of dismissal. A letter like the following[5] partially changed the patron's mind, especially in view of its final remark:

> Your Noble Serenity graciously let me know recently that the present rent-collector Frantz Nigst was found to be expendable as violinist and that the same was true of Joseph Diezl, tenorist, wherefore I was ordered to have the former return his two uniforms. Regarding Nigst, may I submissively state and confess that in the operas produced up to now he was the only one to take proper care of the second violin part; therefore, should he be dismissed, I would live in fear of possible errors occurring unless Your Serene Highness was willing to engage another second violinist or have one come from Vienna for our opera performances, as my second violin would be merely handled by the horn-players Frantz and May, which is not enough. It is true, of course, that if the whole band goes to the Eszterháza castle next year, Nigst could not constantly be with them because of his duties at the rent office in Eisenstadt, but I would humbly suggest to have him called to Eszterháza, should a visit by the Imperial Court or other august personages occur. I therefore submissively petition Your Serene Highness also henceforth to grant to Nigst the yearly fifty florins as well as the winter and summer clothes (in which he has al-

[5]Cf. Arisztid Valkó, *Zenetudományi Tanulmányok* VI (1957)—henceforth quoted as Valkó I; and VII (1960)—henceforth quoted as Valkó II. Here Valkó I, p. 47.

ready served). . . . On the other hand, if the whole band
leaves for Eszterháza, Joseph Diezl is especially needed in
the choir loft [of Eisenstadt] so that the regular church
service can be held by him, his preceptor, and the choir-
boys. I hear from various sides that he cannot possibly
subsist on his salary as schoolteacher, and I therefore most
humbly petition Your Serene Highness graciously to allow him enough for his livelihood.

In the next days I will obediently submit to Your
Serene Highness a few new [Baryton-] Trios. I most
humbly commend myself to Your Highness' favor and
grace and remain,

Your Serenity's most obedient servant

JOSEPHUS HAYDN

Eisenstadt, 22 December 1768

This letter was sent to the princely secretary, Scheffstoss, for approval, and Haydn added the following characteristic remark:

Should anything in the above seem inadvisable to
you, kindly let me know by return. I flatter myself that
through this petition and your confirmation regarding
these men's characters His Highness will be favorably impressed. Should this not be the case, I cannot be blamed
for loving my neighbor.

Haydn succeeded as far as the tenorist Diezl was concerned. Nigst,
however, was dismissed.

Instances proving Haydn's concern for the welfare of his musicians are found again and again in the Esterházy archives. Once[6] he
reminded the princely secretary that the cellist Marteau had not
been supplied with the firewood, candles, and lodging money that
the Prince had promised; this oversight was quickly remedied.

All this makes it understandable that his musicians loved their
"Papa," as they came to call him. The nickname must not, however, lead to the conception that Haydn was in any way easygoing.
While he did his utmost to intercede with the Prince on behalf of
personal misdemeanors, he was certainly adamant as far as the musical activities were concerned. The instructions he wrote down for

[6]Letter to Secretary Scheffstoss dated January 9, 1772, in Valkó I, p. 51.

the execution of his *Applausus* at the Monastery of Zwettl (see p. 245), where he could not attend rehearsals, show very vividly to what extent he insisted on the clearness and accuracy of every detail, and how well he knew what mistakes the musicians were likely to make.

Yet it cannot be denied that Haydn, despite his diplomatic skill, met with difficulties time and time again. As he remarked in 1791, when this type of life lay far behind him: "I had a gracious Prince, but sometimes I was forced to be dependent on base souls."[7] An episode of this kind which took place in 1765 is revealed by documents in the Esterházy archives. The flautist Franz Sigel had, with a gunshot, started a small fire, whereupon he was dismissed by von Rahier. The whole band was greatly upset, and a dispute arose between the administrator and Haydn, who felt the punishment meted out to the flautist to be too severe. Thereupon the administrator complained to the Prince, and Haydn, receiving a reprimand from his patron, wrote a lengthy letter of explanation, which, despite the routine flowery phrases inserted, manages to take an energetic stand for the writer's rights.[8] It reads:

> The letter Your Serene Highness sent me on the 8th was received with the most submissive respect, and I learned from it that Your Illustrious Serenity was displeased by my protesting to Herr von Rahier, with all due respect, against the arrest of the flautist Frantz Sigl. . . . However, nothing could be achieved with the administrator and I even had to see the door slammed in my face and hear him threatening us all with detention. Likewise Friberth, who did not lift his hat to Herr von Rahier (certainly owing to an oversight), is anxiously hiding from the administrator and now out of fear of detention does not dare go home. The administrator asserts that Friberth acted rudely toward him and must accept his punishment. But I testify together with all the other musicians that when the administrator threatened everybody with detention—and this without any justification—Friberth merely remarked that he had no other master but His Serene Highness, Prince Esterházy. I myself said to the administrator that if he should feel that he had suf-

[7] Letter to Marianne von Genzinger dated September 17, 1791.
[8] Valkó I, p. 49.

fered a personal insult, he ought to take the matter up with His Serenity, but he answered that the administrator was his own judge and would inflict the penalty himself. Everybody is very disturbed about this, and to respectable people such treatment seems very hard to take. We hope that Your Serene and Gracious Highness will not entertain intentions of this kind and will graciously prevent a procedure whereby anyone can be his own judge without distinguishing between guilty and innocent ones.

As Your Serene Highness is doubtless aware, the commands of the aforementioned administrator have always been properly carried out by me, and whenever I receive through him orders from Your Gracious and Serene Highness I will be intent on executing them. Therefore, if the administrator has complained about me on this account, that was due only to his angry pen. Moreover, Your Serene and Noble Highness will be graciously aware that *I cannot serve two masters* and cannot accept and submit to the administrator's commands, for Your Serenity Yourself once said to me: henceforth he ought to come to me first, for I am his master.

This gives me confidence that Your Serene Highness will not consider ungraciously my most submissive report, but will regard me and the whole band with gracious eyes and afford us fatherly protection, as everyone else is treating us with ill will. In the hope of further marks of favor from Your Serene and Noble Highness, I remain for life, with the most submissive respect,

> Your Serene and Gracious Highness'
> very obedient and humble
>
> Josephus Haydn

Eisenstadt, 9 September 1765

Anyway, from a letter written by von Rahier on September 13, 1765, we learn that the dispute was settled with the conductor and Friberth, and that the administrator asked his patron not to take any further steps. Apparently Haydn was too shrewd to continue a quarrel with the powerful officer. Though Haydn did not prevent Sigel's dismissal in 1765, he apparently succeeded in winning the musician again for his band. Sigel was reinstated on February 1, 1767, and retained his position until April 1771.[9]

The documents reprinted here, especially the contract, deserve our interest for various reasons. Modern readers may be shocked to see a genius treated not much better than a servant. Imagine a composer in the throes of inspiration having to wait twice a day, at certain hours, in the Prince's antechamber, to receive his patron's orders; or having to compose whatever the Prince wishes; and who, even in his appearance, had to conform absolutely to the instructions of His Serene Highness. It would, however, be wrong to view such regulations from the vantage point of the twentieth century. Haydn himself, at least at that time, considered them matters of course. Composing to order was the usual practice of every musician of his time; it was only with Beethoven that the attitude of musicians began to change. To await the commands of so exalted a personage as Prince Esterházy, who used to say, and prove by action, that what the emperor did he too could do, was not humiliating for a man who had only recently risen from the depths of poverty. Concerning Haydn's clothes, Griesinger remarked: "Mathias Haydn lived to experience the joy of seeing his son in the princely blue uniform braided with gold."[10] Haydn himself probably felt much the same way, all the more as the uniforms, which were issued twice a year, for winter or summer, saved him from paying considerable amounts for festive clothing. As we learn from a most interesting report on conditions at the Esterházy court by János Harich,[11] Haydn's uniforms were made from much better cloth than those of his musicians. There was also the possibility of using the same uniform for more than the prescribed time, provided it was kept in perfect condition. In this case the Prince paid Haydn a redemption of some three hundred forty florins.

A clause in the contract that could create difficulties was the stipulation that all the compositions of Haydn were to belong to Prince Esterházy, and that he was not to compose for anyone else. Haydn, however, soon succeeded in modifying this condition. Apparently, a kind of gentlemen's agreement was reached between the kapellmeister and his princely patron; for shortly after his appoint-

---

[9] Cf. Ulrich Tank, "Die Dokumente der Esterházy-Archive," *H-St*, IV/3-4 (May 1980), p. 222.

[10] Mathias Haydn died on September 12, 1763.

[11] Cf. János Harich, "Das fürstlich Esterházy'sche Fideikommiss," *HYb*, IV (1968), p. 5ff.

ment, the composer's works began to be distributed outside the court of Eisenstadt and later he derived a substantial and steadily growing income from the sale of his compositions to publishers. Incidentally, this clause was modified in a new contract concluded in 1779. Another stipulation (to be found in all the Esterházy contracts with musicians) seems unfair indeed to us. While Haydn, if desiring to leave the Esterházy court, was to give notice six months in advance, the Prince reserved for himself the right to dismiss Haydn at any time, should he see fit to do so. This deprived Haydn of any true security, for the Prince might die and his successor desire to appoint another kapellmeister. Here we see one of the reasons for Haydn's never-ceasing concern for increasing his earnings, which induced him at times to sell his music under conditions hardly to be termed ethical.

When Haydn settled down in Eisenstadt, the Esterházy orchestra was still rather small, but in that year various musicians joined it. The most important member was the outstanding violinist Luigi Tomasini (born in 1741), whom Prince Paul Anton brought from Italy to Eisenstadt as a valet in 1757. The youth's unusual musical talent induced the Prince to send Tomasini to Venice in 1759 to pursue musical studies. As he arrived in the summer when musical activities had come to a virtual standstill, the visit proved unproductive and Tomasini was called back. However, through self-instruction he succeeded in developing into a truly first-class violinist whom Haydn greatly appreciated. The Prince also favored the violinist, who had to accompany him on several of his travels. The new vice-kapellmeister may have been responsible for the engagement of the eminent violoncellist Joseph Weigl. These two artists, hardly more than twenty years old, together with the new conductor, brought a breath of fresh air into Eisenstadt's musical life, and it was not easy for the head conductor, Gregorius Werner, to adapt himself to the altered conditions. Old Werner was a most conservative musician who excelled in sacred compositions in the polyphonic style.[12] A composer so deeply rooted in the past considered everything new to be a symptom of decline. For Haydn's music Werner had nothing but derision, and he called the newcomer a "mere fop" or "a scribbler of songs." Still, he could not help notic-

[12]The old composer had long since lost the sense of humor shown in such burlesque compositions of his younger years as *The Old Clothes Market of Vienna*, *The Election of a Village Justice*, and *A New and Very Curious Musical Instrumental Calendar*, all published in 1748.

ing the great esteem enjoyed by the vice-kapellmeister, whose salary, as early as November 1761, was raised to six hundred florins (an increase of fifty percent), considerably exceeding his own four hundred twenty-eight. Naturally enough, the old man grew more and more embittered.

The Esterházy archives preserve a letter of Werner's from October 1765,[13] voicing serious complaints about his young colleague. He claimed that Haydn did not maintain discipline among the musicians. He let them get away with everything, including prolonged absences which prevented the church choir from achieving a good performance. The instruments were in bad repair, and the music material seriously depleted. Haydn had been requested to make a catalog of the music available but had not kept his promise so far.

The Prince sent the letter to von Rahier, asking him to deal with it, and the administrator thereupon issued the notorious *Regulatio Chori Kissmartoniensis* (Kismarton being the Hungarian name for Eisenstadt) in which Haydn was rebuked for the "indolence and lack of discipline among the musicians," and at the same time ordered "to apply himself to composition more diligently than heretofore."[14] However, it did not take Haydn very long to change his patron's attitude, for as early as January 4, 1766, the Prince asked his administrator to pay the composer twelve ducats as a sign of approval of three new pieces just submitted.

In his last years Werner displayed astounding productivity. Between 1761 and 1766, the year of his death, he wrote no less than sixteen Masses, five *Salve Regina*'s, and eight other sacred works. Haydn, on his side, treated the learned conductor with the great respect that he really felt for him. Many years after Werner's death when the "scribbler of songs" stood at the summit of his fame, he arranged six of Werner's fugues for string quartet and had them published by Artaria "out of sincere esteem for this celebrated master." Nevertheless, in spite of his esteem, the young vice-kapellmeister managed to take complete charge of the whole musical organization and to increase its size whenever there was a chance to do so. In this he was helped by the new ruler, who evidently surpassed his predecessor in his passion for music and in his Medi-

[13] Valkó II, p. 84.
[14] Landon (*HCaW*, I, p. 420ff.) established the date of the document as November 3, 1765. He conjectures that this reprimand was responsible for Haydn's decision to start on his draft catalogue (cf. p. 196), a document of the greatest significance for posterity.

cean dream of creating a center of culture at his court. Prince Nicolaus was called the Magnificent because of his love of splendor and
display; his coat covered with diamonds was a sensation in many
capitals of Europe. The man who wore it was certainly worth
knowing. Goethe, who saw the Prince in 1764 when Nicolaus attended the coronation of Joseph II in Frankfurt, professed a "particular sympathy for him" and described him as "not tall, but well
built, vivacious and distinguished, and at the same time without
haughtiness and coldness."[15] Prince Nicolaus often showed himself
to be generous and kindhearted and by and large displayed a degree
of social-mindedness uncommon at that time. He paid pensions to
aged employees, and bestowed small sums on their widows. He
supported a modest hospital in Eisenstadt and another in Eszterháza, which were available to the court employees. The medicines
dispensed by the monastery of the Brothers of the Order of Mercy
were, in most cases, paid for by the Prince. Any employee was
entitled to consult one of the three physicians attached to the court,
and, if the doctor so advised, an ailing servant was sent at the sovereign's expense to a spa to receive treatment. (A favorite was the
village of Baden near Vienna with its hot sulphur springs.) On the
other hand, the Prince insisted on strict discipline that was painstakingly maintained through the supervision of the princely administrator, von Rahier. A musician who absented himself without
princely consent could expect deduction of a fine from his salary, or
even detention in jail. In the treatment of the Prince's employees,
pedantry and autocratic treatment went hand in hand with great
generosity. Golden ducats were showered on the performers after a
successful opera performance. (Haydn himself received within ten
years no less than two hundred ducats, viz. 1126 florins from his
patron.) However, Prince Nicolaus, though truly generous by nature, could be forgetful in money matters, which may not be too
hard to understand in a man of such vast means. It slipped his mind
that his late brother and predecessor had bequeathed in his last will
a gift of one year's salary to each member of his musical band. A
question had arisen regarding the deduction of income tax, and the
Prince evidently forgot about the matter. It took eleven years until,
on a written petition by Haydn, payment reached the legatees. During that time Haydn had to obtain loans to buy a house, the re-
payment of which caused him quite a few problems.[16] The four

[15] Cf. Johann Wolfgang von Goethe, *Dichtung und Wahrheit*, bk. V, pt. I.
[16] Cf. Harich, "Das fürstlich Esterházy'sche Fideikommiss," *HYb*, IV (1968), p. 1ff.

hundred florins he received after this long wait would have been welcome indeed. Yet the relationship between Haydn and his patron was certainly a good one, and it improved through the thirty years of cooperation. The Prince did love and understand music, and he was able to appreciate Haydn's greatness. Moreover, Haydn was a true diplomat. Evidently he was able to choose the right tone in his conversations with the Prince. That the sovereign was aware of Haydn's diplomatic gifts is shown by the fact that the Prince, planning a severe action against a musician, asked von Rahier not to tell the kapellmeister of such intention, a ruse that proved, however, unsuccessful.

The archives preserve a letter that the administrator wrote to the Prince on January 24, 1769,[17] reporting that the tenor Karl Friberth was about to marry the newly engaged singer Magdalena Spangler and that as His Highness had forbidden them to marry, they were to leave the princely service. The administrator had therefore ordered Haydn to have the couple return all clothes supplied for their service at court. Evidently the Prince assumed the right to grant or refuse his employees permission to be married and expected such decree to be final. In this case the matter, fortunately, seems to have been settled amicably, for the two singers, although married, remained at the Esterházy court until 1776, when they moved to Vienna, where Friberth obtained a position as music director of a church. We may assume that Haydn helped to placate the Prince; naturally he was eager to do so, as Magdalena Spangler was the daughter of the man who had granted him asylum at the critical moment when he had been expelled from St. Stephen's (see p. 27).

On May 17, 1762, Prince Nicolaus made his solemn entry as new ruler into Eisenstadt with the splendor that was to characterize the numerous festivities of the years to come. Even more splendid was the pompous celebration of the marriage of Prince Nicolaus's son to Countess Erdödy in 1763, when Eisenstadt, as the *Wiener Diarium* stated,[18] saw "greater festivities and more exalted personages than ever before." Haydn wrote for the wedding his pastorale *Acide* and appeared at the performance in the new Esterházy uniform of crimson and gold. During the next year the Prince had to attend the coronation of the Austrian Archduke Joseph as Holy Roman King at Frankfurt. Nicolaus—the Magnificent in the true sense of the word—outshone every other ambassador by arranging

---

[17] Valkó II, p. 191.
[18] *Wiener Diarium*, no. 9 (January 20, 1763).

a "fairylike" (Goethe) illumination of a main street in celebration of the great event. The Prince's return to Eisenstadt was celebrated by the performance of a new Haydn cantata *Da qual gioja improvviso* (Hob. XXIVa:3). Music, however, may have played a secondary role at that time with Prince Nicolaus, as he had embarked on a major architectural project which required a great deal of planning.

# CHAPTER FIVE

## At Eszterháza

### 1 7 6 6 – 1 7 7 9

The castle of Eszterháza, which Prince Nicolaus built, was a typical product of the eighteenth century. It reflected the attitude toward life adopted by the high aristocracy when neither trouble nor money was spared to satisfy a whim. Prince Nicolaus the Magnificent, having heard various reports about the Palace of Versailles, decided to rival the King of France in Hungary. In choosing a site for his palace, he felt no reluctance about selecting a truly unsuitable location that somehow appealed to him. The Esterházy family owned a little hunting lodge at Süttör near a large lake known as the Neusiedler See. The lake had overflowed the surrounding country, producing a huge swamp covering no less than sixteen square miles. It was a desolate place, filled with mud as far as the eye could see. Every sort of insect abounded there, and fever was a permanent guest. There Nicolaus had lived after leaving the Austrian army as a lieutenant field marshal. When he succeeded his elder brother as ruler of the Esterházy estate, he decided to erect his Versailles in this very place. Recollections of his former, much more modest, way of life at Süttör may have influenced him; perhaps he also enjoyed the thought that he, the Magnificent, would triumph over nature at its worst. So the swamps were cleared, canals were dug, a magnificent dam was built, and after tremendous difficulties and the expenditure of something like thirteen million florins (more

than six million dollars), the castle of Eszterháza came into existence. Music was performed there starting in 1766, but it still took
years to accomplish all the Prince's ambitious plans. In 1784 it was
completed. A large, richly illustrated book was devoted solely to
the description of its wonders.[1] A few selections from it may help to
give an idea of the place where Haydn was to spend so much of his
time during the following twenty-five years.

> The castle is in Italian style. . . . surrounded by a
> beautifully proportioned stone gallery. Most valuable are
> two rooms used by the Prince. One of them contains ten
> Japanese panels in black lacquer adorned with golden flow-
> ers and landscapes, each of which cost more than a thou-
> sand florins. The chairs and divans are covered with golden
> fabric. There are also some extremely valuable cabinets
> and a bronze clock that plays the flute. In the second room,
> richly adorned with golden ornaments, is another gilded
> clock with a canary on top that moves and whistles pleas-
> ant tunes when the clock strikes, as well as an armchair that
> plays a flute solo when you sit on it. The chandeliers are
> made from artistically wrought rock crystal. In the library
> there are seventy-five hundred books, all exquisite edi-
> tions, to which novelties are being added daily. It also con-
> tains numerous manuscripts and many excellent old and
> new engravings by the best masters. The picture gallery is
> liberally supplied with first-class original paintings by fa-
> mous Italian and Dutch masters which fill the eye of the
> connoisseur with delight and admiration.
>
> In an alley of wild chestnut trees stands the magnifi-
> cent opera house. The boxes at the sides open into charm-
> ing rooms furnished most luxuriously with fireplaces, di-
> vans, mirrors, and clocks. The theater easily holds four
> hundred people. Every day, at 6 PM, there is a performance
> of an Italian *opera seria* or *buffa* or of German comedy, al-
> ways attended by the Prince. Words cannot describe how
> both eye and ear are delighted here. When the music be-
> gins, its touching delicacy, the strength and force of the
> instruments penetrate the soul, for the great composer,
> Herr Haydn himself is conducting. But the audience is also

---

[1] *Beschreibung des hochfürstlichen Schlosses Esterháss im Königreich Ungarn* (Pressburg,
1784). Its author was probably Prince Nicolaus himself.

overwhelmed by the admirable lighting and the deceptively perfect stage settings. At first we see the clouds on which the gods are seated sink slowly to earth. Then the gods rise upward and instantly vanish, and then again everything is transformed into a delightful garden, an enchanted wood, or, it may be, a glorious hall.

Opposite the opera house is the marionette theater, built like a grotto. All the walls, niches, and apertures are covered with variegated stones, shells, and snails[2] that afford a very curious and striking sight when they are illuminated. The theater is rather large and the decorations are extremely artistic. The puppets are beautifully formed, and magnificently dressed; they play not only farces and comedies, but also *opera seria*. The performances in both theaters are open to everyone.

Behind the castle is the park. Everyone entering it stands still in amazement and admiration at the majestic sight, for it fills the soul with rapture. The park was built after the Prince's own designs, and is without doubt the most gorgeous example of its kind in the whole kingdom. Art and nature are here combined in an extremely noble and magnificent way. In every corner there is something to attract the eye—statues, temples, grottoes, waterworks; everywhere are the glory of majesty, gentle smiles of nature, joy, and delight!

At the gates stands the princely guard consisting of one hundred and fifty grenadiers, very handsome and finely trained men, mostly six feet tall. Their uniform is a dark blue coat with red flaps and lapels, white tie, white vest and trousers, and black bearskin cap with yellow visor.

Only a few of the splendors are described here. There were also marvelous hothouses and orangeries and immense game preserves in the park, while the castle boasted one hundred twenty-six richly gilded and paneled guest rooms and two exquisite halls for entertainments—the parade hall, decorated entirely in white, and the *sala terrena*, tiled with white marble and overflowing with art treasures. This latter hall was used for music on festive occasions. Truly Nicolaus the Magnificent had achieved something worthy of his reputation. It must have given him real satisfaction when he read in

[2]The rocaille style applied here was made fashionable by Louis XV.

the *Letters of a Traveling Frenchman on Germany* by Risbeck:[3] "In France, there is perhaps no place, except Versailles, that equals this castle in splendor."

Eszterháza proved to be for the Prince much more than a passing whim. The more he improved it, the more attached he became to this, his own, creation. Planned first as a summer resort, Eszterháza became the Prince's residence for the greater part of the year. Eisenstadt, though much more healthful and richer in natural beauties, was completely eclipsed by the new castle. The Prince returned to the old residence for a short sojourn during the winter and spent the rest of the winter in Vienna, but as soon as spring approached he moved back to his beloved new castle. The unpleasantly damp climate, not greatly changed even by the canals he built, did not appear to affect Prince Nicolaus nor did he suffer from the "vexatious, penetrating north wind" that caused Haydn much discomfort. As long as he could be at Eszterháza, busily engaged in some new scheme and enjoying the excellent music and theater performances provided there, he was the best of patrons and the most charming host to the exalted visitors he liked to entertain.

A great staff had to be engaged to fulfill the Prince's dream of a cultural center. There were the painters, Johann Basilius Grundmann with various assistants; Ludwig Guttenbrunn, who stayed only for a short time, as he was sent for further training to Italy and never returned to Eszterháza; and (from 1771) Pietro Travaglia,[4] who painted the portraits of the family, adorned the castle with frescoes, and designed the stage scenery.[5] A librarian, a director of the picture gallery, landscape gardeners for the constantly growing park, and a great number of employees connected with the two theatres were also part of the staff. The marionette theatre was entrusted to the pantomime master Bienfait, to P. G. Bader, and (up to 1778) to J. K. von Pauersbach, who supplied the librettos. The dialogue for the puppets was recited by actors from one of the well-known troupes whom the Prince used to hire for several months at a time. After Werner's death, Haydn had become kapellmeister in 1766,

[3] Cf. Risbeck, Johann Kaspar, baron von, *Briefe eines reisenden Franzosen über Deutschland*, 2d ed. (1784), I, p. 354.
[4] Travaglia also painted parts of the decorations for the performance of Mozart's *La clemenza di Tito* at Prague.
[5] As Landon (*HCaW*, II, p. 30) rightly observes, it is significant that the Prince, in spite of the grandiose plans for his castle, did not appoint truly famous Austrian painters like Maulpertsch or Troger for the adornment of Eszterháza. He rather economized in this respect, while spending a fortune on opera and theatre performances offered in his palace.

and eventually he engaged excellent singers, mostly from Italy or, at least, trained by Italian masters. Among the male singers Friberth, Dichtler, Specht, Braghetti, Moratti, Lambertini, Jermoli, Griessler, Bianchi, Totti, Ungricht; among the women Weigl, Dichtler, Spangler, Cellini, Prandtner, Jermoli, Boschwa, Puttler, Ripamonti, Zannini, Valdesturla, and the Bologna sisters deserve mention because they appeared in Haydn's operas. The orchestra was made up of from sixteen to twenty-two players whose artistic qualities more than compensated for the smallness of their number. Haydn saw to it that only highly promising musicians were engaged, and it can be imagined how they developed under the continual training of so outstanding a conductor. In the first chair throughout Haydn's stay at Eszterháza sat Luigi Tomasini, a great favorite of the Prince, and also of the kapellmeister, who used to remark that no one (himself included) could play his string quartets like his "brother Luigi." Of the violoncellists, Haydn's friend Joseph Weigl[6] stayed from 1761 to 1769, when he joined the Vienna court orchestra; his successors, Franz Xavier Marteau and Anton Kraft, maintained the same high standard. The Prince could always afford to choose the best, as the salaries he paid were even higher than those offered by the imperial court at Vienna.

That the musical world was aware of the artistic standard maintained at Eszterháza is shown by a remark of the *Gotha Theater-Calendar* for 1778: "The orchestra consists of thirty (*sic!*) players, mostly virtuosos, and therefore ranks among the most excellent ensemble groups."

This costly staff of musicians and artists was kept constantly busy by the Prince. Apart from two concert academies a week (and it should not be forgotten that concert programs in the eighteenth century were much longer than they are today), there was chamber music in His Serene Highness' private apartments, with Nicolaus often taking part himself. The Prince was a passionate lover of the baryton (see p. 229), a now obsolete instrument related to the viola da gamba. The baryton is extremely hard to play; this may be why the ambitious Prince preferred it to the violin or violoncello. He became quite an adept player and Haydn could hardly keep pace with his patron's demands for new baryton compositions. To give the Prince a pleasant surprise, Haydn began secretly to practice playing the baryton, and when he had acquired some skill, offered

[6] Haydn was godfather to Weigl's son, Joseph, who became famous as the composer of German Singspiele, including *Die Schweizer-familie*. See also p. 136.

to show his art to the Prince. To his disappointment, his attempt
was received with icy indifference, and he realized that his patron
wanted him only to compose for the baryton, not play it. Likewise,
when the cellist Kraft played baryton duets with the Prince, all the
solos had to be planned so that there were no great technical difficulties, for they were to be executed by the Prince and not by Kraft.
As Nicolaus remarked: "It is no credit to you to play better than I
do; it is your duty." At times changes had to be made in Haydn's
compositions so as to make them acceptable to the august baryton
player. This is illustrated by the following, very typical letter[7] addressed to the Prince, which also throws light on the conductor's
manifold concerns:

> [undated, but marked "Received 5 December 1766"]
>
> The most welcome arrival of my patron's name day
> (which may Divine Grace let Your Serene Highness spend
> in perfect well-being and happiness) causes me not only
> to offer to Your Serenity in dutiful submission six new
> divertimenti, but also to kiss the hem of your robe for
> graciously presenting us with our new winter clothes,
> which a few days ago were handed to us. May I add that
> despite Your Highness' most regrettable absence, we shall
> venture to wear them for the first time at the celebra-
> tion of High Mass on Your Highness' name day. Order
> was given to me to have bound the twelve divertimenti I
> composed. But as Your Highness sent me a few of them
> to be changed and I had not noted these alterations in my
> score, I venture to ask to let me have the first twelve
> pieces for three days and later also the others, so that,
> with all alterations entered, they may be carefully copied
> and bound. May I also submissively inquire in what man-
> ner Your Serene Highness wishes them to be bound?
> Incidentally, the two oboists report to me (a statement
> I have to corroborate) that their instruments are deterio-
> rating because of old age and do not stay on pitch any
> longer. I therefore submissively mention that there is a
> Master Rockobauer in Vienna who, in my opinion, is best
> qualified in this field. Although this master is constantly
> engaged in such tasks, he would at present manage to
> produce a pair of fine and durable oboes with an extra

[7] Valkó I, p. 53.

piece of reed pipe (allowing all the necessary notes to be sounded), for which work the best price would be eight ducats. May I expect Your Serene Highness' gracious consent to acquire the two urgently needed oboes at the above-mentioned price.[8]

Hoping for Your Noble Highness'
favor and grace I remain,
your most obedient

HAYDN

Frequently the ordinary routine was interrupted by the visit of some distinguished guest and preparations for such an occasion had to be made a long time ahead. These visits usually lasted for three days filled to the brim with concerts, theater and marionette performances, masked balls, and hunting. An outstanding event was the visit of the Empress Maria Theresa herself in 1773. The *Wiener Diarium* and a special booklet[9] afford detailed accounts of the festivities, a résumé of which is given here as an example of the entertainments provided amid the marshes and swamps of Hungary:

On her arrival the Empress and her retinue were escorted in fifteen of the Prince's magnificent carriages through the park, the wonders of which Maria Theresa could not sufficiently admire, though she was used to a beautiful park in the French style at her own residence of Schönbrunn. In the evening Haydn's burletta *L'infedeltà delusa* was performed, which so impressed the imperial guest that she was overheard to say: "If I want to enjoy a good opera, I go to Eszterháza" (a remark that before long was repeated all over Vienna). The performance was followed by a masked ball in the luxurious hall of the castle. Then the Empress was taken to the Chinese pavilion whose mirror-covered walls reflected countless lampions and chandeliers flooding the room with light. On a platform sat the princely orchestra in gala attire, playing under Haydn's direction various of his works.

The Empress then retired to her magnificent suite, while her retinue continued to enjoy the masked ball until dawn. The next day a great banquet took place in the *sala terrena*, during which the virtuosos of the orchestra demonstrated their skill. In the afternoon

[8] Apparently Haydn's advice was not heeded. The Esterházy archives merely mention payments to Rockobauer for the purchase of woodwind mouthpieces and repair of an English horn.

[9] *Relation des fêtes données à Sa Majesté l'Impératrice . . . le 1ᵉʳ et 2ᵉ 7ᵇʳᵉ 1773.* (Vienna: Ghelen, n.d.).

the Empress attended a performance of Haydn's opera *Philemon and Baucis* in the marionette theater,[10] and she was so fascinated by it that four years later she had the complete outfit sent to Vienna for some special festivities. After the "souper" the august guests watched huge fireworks planned by the pyrotechnist Rabel, their variety and brilliance surpassing all expectations. Afterward, the Prince took the monarch to an immense open space, which was hung with multicolored lights forming artistic designs. Suddenly, about a thousand peasants appeared in their beautiful Hungarian or Croatian costumes and performed national dances to the entrancing tunes of their own folk music. The next morning the Empress left after distributing costly presents. Haydn received a valuable gold snuffbox filled with ducats. He was proud to have impressed Her Majesty not merely as a musician, for during her stay he succeeded in killing with one shot three grouse that were graciously accepted for the Empress' table. During the festivities, emphasis was laid on Chinese artifacts, which at that time enjoyed a great vogue. At the masked ball, Chinese decorations prevailed and even the princely musicians appeared in gorgeous Chinese robes. Among the countless treasures amassed at Eszterháza, the newly erected Chinese pavilion particularly impressed the Empress. The Prince, however, waved aside her praise with the airy remark that this was merely a "bagatelle," a designation henceforth applied to the exquisite building.[11]

Entertainment of this kind took place once a year or even more frequently, and most of Haydn's operas were written for such occasions. For visitors who would enjoy a more robust form of entertainment than appealed to the Empress, the Prince took care not to neglect the comic element in arranging his plans. In 1775, for example, when an Austrian Archduke and Archduchess visited Eszterháza, a whole country fair was set up in the park with quack doctors, mountebanks, cheap-jacks, and stalls and booths. There the guests had all the fun they desired, and the merry mood was heightened by an entrancing parody of Gluck's *Alceste* by Carlos

[10]The topic of the opera was well chosen. It dealt with conjugal love, and thus was apt to deeply stir the Empress, who had lost her beloved husband in 1765, and who since that time always appeared in mourning weeds. She must also have liked the ending: out of the clouds rose a dazzling vision of the Habsburg coat of arms held by Justice, Wisdom, Clemency, and Valor. It was crowned by Fame, before which knelt figures in Hungarian attire symbolizing Obedience, Diligence, and Fidelity, praising the monarch in song.

[11]Cf. Mátyás Horányi, *Das Esterházysche Feenreich* (Budapest, 1959), p. 46.

d'Ordonez in the marionette theater. No less than fourteen hundred guests attended the masked ball arranged in honor of the exalted visitors. Again peasants were invited to dance and sing, each village appearing with its own flag and band, and as the Prince liberally provided food and drinks for the villagers, a hilarious mood prevailed.

Time never hung heavy on the hands of Prince Esterházy's retainers. But in spite of the interesting work under the leadership of their beloved "Papa," in spite of the good salaries they received, the musicians were often much discouraged when their stay at Eszterháza dragged on and on far into the autumn. The Prince, who never hesitated to adorn the park with a new and expensive monument, and who spent about six thousand florins on the production of the marionette opera *Dido*, saw no necessity for providing living quarters ample enough to house his musicians and their families. All the instrumentalists and singers, all the actors, painters, copyists, and some of the servants, had to live in a single moderate-sized building. In 1772 the Prince therefore gave strict orders that no musician was to bring his wife or children to Eszterháza. Only Haydn, Friberth, Dichtler, and Tomasini were exempted from this rule. Three rooms were reserved for the kapellmeister, whereas two musicians generally had to share a single chamber. By paying the married members an extra fifty florins for the expenses incurred in keeping the double households, the Prince felt that he had settled the matter generously enough, and it did not trouble him that these husbands had to live for the greater part of the year away from their families. The musicians felt differently. According to Griesinger: "The affectionate husbands appealed to Haydn to help them. Haydn decided to write a symphony [Hob. I:45, known as the "Farewell" Symphony] in which one instrument after the other ceases to play. The work was executed as soon as an occasion presented itself, and each player was instructed to put out his candle when his part was ended, seize his music, and leave with his instrument tucked under his arm. The Prince instantly understood the meaning of this pantomime and the next day he gave the order to leave Eszterháza."

The biographer fails to tell us what happened in the following years. Surely Haydn was not always able to invent something new to humor the Prince. The musicians actually had to give in or accept a position elsewhere, which many did. The kapellmeister himself was tied to Eszterháza just as closely as his subordinates. He once complained in a letter to a friend[12] about how difficult it was for him to obtain even a short leave: "It is scarcely credible, and yet the refusal is always couched in such polite terms as to render it utterly impossible for me to urge my request." Haydn had to resort to diplomacy to achieve results. His tactics are illuminated by the following letter[13] to the princely secretary Anton Scheffstoss. Here the petition for leave is clothed in a report of the praise given to Haydn by a famous master, and thus was calculated to be pleasing to the vanity of his august patron, who certainly was also inclined to believe that the singers in his service were far superior to those employed in Vienna:

Eisenstadt, 20 March 1768

Doubtless you are aware that last year I set to music with all the power at my disposal the highly respected hymn called Stabat Mater, and I sent my music to the great and world-famous Hasse out of the desire that if I had failed adequately to express the most valuable words, this might be remedied by the Master, so successful in all his compositions. Contrary to my merits, this outstanding artist honored me with inexpressible praise and desired nothing more but to hear my work performed by a proper ensemble of musicians. But as there is a great lack of singers of both sexes in Vienna, I venture to present through you my humble petitions to His Serene Highness to allow me, Weigl, and his wife, as well as Friberth, to leave next Thursday for Vienna in order to promote the honor of our most gracious prince through performances by his servants on Friday afternoon at the Brothers of Mercy. Saturday night we would be back in Eisenstadt. Should His Highness thus command, I would send up someone else instead of Friberth. Dearest Monsieur Scheffstoss, do please expedite my petition. I remain with profound respect,

Your most devoted servant

HAYDN

---

[12] Letter to Marianne von Genzinger dated May 30, 1790. The English version of this and various other Haydn letters quoted herein is partly based on the translation by Lady G. M. Wallace (London, 1867).
[13] Valkó I, p. 56.

P. S. My compliments to all the gentlemen. The promised divertimenti will certainly be handed this week to His Highness.

Mrs. Weigl, who from 1760 to 1769 sang important soprano parts in Haydn's operas as well as in the church service, was the secretary's daughter, and we may therefore assume that he helped to obtain the requested leave. Such an event was a rarity, however, and most of Haydn's trips were made officially in the retinue of the Prince. Thus, on March 22, 1770, the Esterházy ensemble successfully performed Haydn's opera *Lo speziale* in the house of a Viennese nobleman, Freiherr von Sumerau, and followed it a few days later by a concert. In 1775 Haydn conducted in the capital the first performance of his oratorio *Il ritorno di Tobia* for the Tonkünstlersocietät, a charitable institution for assisting destitute musicians' widows and children. The performance was up to the Esterházy standard, as Haydn brought with him three singers as well as Tomasini and Marteau. This was the first occasion on which Haydn sought the approval of a large audience in a capital city. Its success was notable. The public was enchanted, and after the deduction of expenses, almost two thousand florins remained for charitable purposes. Some of the critics were very enthusiastic. The *K.k.priv.Realzeitung der Wissenschaften* declared: "Nature and art were so delicately interwoven in this work that the audience had to love the one and admire the other. The choruses especially displayed a fire to be found previously only in Handel's compositions." [14]

The great success of *Il ritorno di Tobia* may have been responsible for the request sent to Haydn in 1776 to write an autobiographical sketch for Lucca's publication *Das gelehrte Oesterreich*, a sort of Austrian *Who's Who*. The invitation apparently was handed to a certain Mr. Zoller, probably an employee at the Esterházy court. He transmitted it to Mademoiselle Leonore, an important official and subsequently the wife of the Esterházy estate director, Lechner. Haydn addressed his reply to her. It reads: [15]

Estoras, 6th July, 1776.

Mademoiselle,

You must not take it amiss that I send you a kind of medley in complying with your wish. To describe such

---

[14] *K.K. priv. Realzeitung der Wissenschaften* (Apr. 6, 1775), p. 218.
[15] We reproduce this important document in the translation by H. C. Robbins

things requires time, and this I do not possess. I thought it best, therefore, not to write myself to M. Zoller, which I hope you will excuse.

I only offer you a rough sketch, for neither pride nor the love of fame, but solely the great kindness, and marked satisfaction, that so learned a national society has displayed towards my works, have induced me to comply with their request.

I was born on the last day of March in 1733 [*sic*], in the market town of Rohrau, near Prugg, on the river Leitha, in Lower Austria. The calling of my late father was that of a wheelwright (in the service of Count Harrach). He was a great lover of music by nature, and played the harp without knowing a note of music. While as a boy of five, I sang all his short simple pieces very fairly; this induced my father to send me to the rector of the school at Hainburg, a relative of ours, in order to learn the first elements of music and other juvenile acquirements. Our Almighty Father (to whom above all I owe the most profound gratitude) had endowed me with so much facility in music that even in my sixth year I was bold enough to sing some masses in the choir, and also played a little on the piano and the violin. In my seventh year the late Kapellmeister von Reutter, when passing through Hainburg, heard by chance my weak but pleasing voice. He forthwith took charge of me, and placed me in the Kapell-Haus [in Vienna], where, in addition to my other studies, I learned singing, the piano, and the violin, from very good masters. I sang soprano both at St. Stephen's and at Court with great applause, till my sixteenth year, when I finally lost my voice, and was forced for eight whole years to gain a scanty livelihood by giving lessons; many a genius is ruined by this miserable mode of earning daily bread, as it leaves no time for study. This I, alas, know too well myself from experience, and I could never have accomplished even what I did, if in my zeal for composition I had not pursued my studies through the night. I wrote diligently, though not quite correctly, till at length I had the good fortune to learn the

Landon. Cf. *The Collected Correspondence and London Notebooks of Joseph Haydn* (London, 1959), pp. 18–20.

genuine rudiments of composition from the celebrated
Maestro Porpora (who was at that time in Vienna).

At length, by the recommendation of the late Herr
von Fürnberg (from whom I received unusual kindness), I
was appointed *Directeur* of Herr Count von Morzin's, and
subsequently as Kapellmeister to his Highness Prince Esterházy, in whose service I wish to live and die.

Among my works, the following have been most approved of—the operas *Le pescatrici*, *L'incontro improvviso*,
and *L'infedeltà delusa*, performed in the presence of Her
Imperial and Royal Majesty; the oratorio *Il ritorno di
Tobia*, given in Vienna; also a *Stabat Mater*, for which I
received, through a kind friend, a testimonial from our
great composer Hasse, containing many undeserved eulogiums. This letter I will treasure like gold as long as I
live, not owing to its content, but for the sake of so admirable a man.

I have had the good fortune to please almost all na-
tions (except, indeed, the Berliners) in chamber music, as
testified by the public papers, and by letters addressed to
myself; I only marvel that those judicious Berlin gentlemen preserve no *medium* in their criticism of my works,
as in one weekly paper they laud me to the skies, and in
another bury me sixty fathoms deep in the earth, and
without any valid reason; but I know why it is: because
they are unable to perform these pieces of mine, and are
too conceited to give themselves the trouble to understand them properly, and from other causes which, God
willing, I will bring forward at the right time. Kapellmeister von Dittersdorf, in Silesia, recently wrote, en-
treating me to defend myself against their cruel attacks,
but I replied that one swallow does not make a summer;
that perhaps one of these days some impartial authority
would stop their tongues, which happened to them once
before when they had accused me of monotony. In spite
of this, they eagerly strive to get all my works, which I
was told only last winter by the Imperial Ambassador at
Berlin, Baron van Swieten; but enough of this.

Dear Mademoiselle Leonore, you will be so good as
to give this sketch, with my kind regards, to M. Zoller,
for his consideration; my highest ambition is to be regarded by the world as the honest man I really am.

I offer up to Almighty God all eulogiums, for to Him alone do I owe them. My sole wish is neither to offend against my neighbor nor my gracious Prince, but above all our merciful God.

I remain, Mademoiselle, with high esteem, your sincere friend and obedient servant,

JOSEPHUS HAYDN

Though many of the biographical facts have been mentioned earlier in our book, this significant document is reproduced as a whole. It clearly pinpoints Haydn's position among contemporary composers. In spite of his steadily growing fame, praise of his music was by no means unanimous, and this was not only true of north Germany (which he singles out in his letter), but of Vienna itself. A strong movement against him was led by people who either envied him his excellent position or did not understand his style. Dr. Burney's quotation from a letter that a friend from Hamburg wrote him about Haydn in 1772 reveals exactly the attitude of many Viennese musicians. "His mixture of serious and comic is disliked, particularly as there is more of the latter than the former in his work and, as for rules, he knows but little of them." That was the way Maria Theresa's subsequent successor, Joseph II, felt. For him, Haydn's music was just "tricks and nonsense," and this dictum did not make the kapellmeister from Esterházy popular at the Viennese court.

Even when dealing with the Tonkünstlersocietät, which was greatly indebted to him for his *Il ritorno di Tobia*, Haydn had good reason for anger. To obtain a kind of insurance for himself and his wife, Haydn applied to the society for admission in 1778, depositing the amount of three hundred sixty-eight florins requested from him as a nonresident. The society, however, was not satisfied and asked him to sign an agreement pledging himself to supply compositions of importance whenever required. Haydn, highly indignant, declined this offer as being incompatible with his duties toward Prince Esterházy, remarking with a fire rarely to be found in his letters: "The fine arts and the beautiful science of composition cannot bear any fetters; soul and spirit must be free," whereupon the Societät calmly refused to enroll him among their members.[16]

---

[16] Mozart's petition for admission in 1785 was equally unsuccessful. Although he had played repeatedly for the society, they insisted on his presenting his certificate of baptism before they would make him a member. Mozart apparently neglected get-

The incident in Vienna made Haydn appreciate more and more the advantages of his life at Eszterháza. As he once remarked to Griesinger (24): "My prince was always satisfied with my works. Not only did I have the encouragement of constant approval, but as conductor of an orchestra I could make experiments, observe what produced an effect and what weakened it, and was thus in a position to improve, to alter, make additions or omissions, and be as bold as I pleased. I was cut off from the world; there was no one to confuse or torment me, and I was forced to become original."

It is true that from the middle of the seventies his duties steadily increased. As Dénes Bartha and László Somfai pointed out in a valuable study,[17] 1776 marked a decisive change in Eszterháza's cultural life that greatly affected Haydn's responsibilities. The Prince, who up to then had used his fine theater mainly for dramatic performances by traveling theatrical troupes, decided to allot opera a prominent place. In earlier years opera had been presented only for special festive events, the composition of the work always being entrusted to Haydn. Now Eszterháza was to have a repertoire of Italian operas by renowned contemporary composers. Several reasons may have induced the Prince thus to change his policy. The fact that Italian opera was being stressed at the imperial court in Vienna after a pause of several years certainly constituted an important factor. Moreover Nicolaus the Magnificent apparently was now less interested in performing on the baryton and preferred to spend his leisure hours attending good operatic performances. With his customary largess, he purchased a sizable number of Italian opera scores and had new singers engaged in 1776. Haydn, though relieved from the continual necessity of supplying new baryton compositions for his patron, had his hands full conducting operas twice a week in the period from February to November or December, novelties appearing between four and eight times per season. Besides coaching the singers and the orchestra and supervising the copying of the material, in most cases Haydn felt obliged to make considerable changes in the works so as to adapt them to the specific conditions of the Esterházy court. The orchestra pit was small and held only about twenty musicians; as a rule clarinets, trumpets, and timpani were not available, and Haydn had to arrange the scores accordingly. On the other hand, he liked to enrich the or-

---

ting this document from Salzburg, and thus his petition was left pending. Cf. Otto Erich Deutsch, *Mozart, die Dokumente seines Lebens* (Kassel, 1961), p. 209.

[17] Dénes Bartha and László Somfai, *Haydn als Opernkapellmeister* (Budapest, 1960).

chestration of an opera by giving to the second violin and the viola more important parts and adding wind instruments such as oboes and horns where the original used only strings. At Eszterháza no chorus was available, and if choral numbers could not be entrusted to a group of soloists, they had to be omitted. Apart from cuts necessitated by the limitations of his ensemble, Haydn did not hesitate to shorten considerably most of the operas performed, and even had no compunction about changing the form of a number if he felt it to be overlong. Similar motives may have been responsible for his alterations of tempo. Haydn made it a habit to accelerate slow numbers, changing, for instance, larghetto to andante con moto, and once even andante maestoso to allegro vivace.[18] Also, intricate coloraturas were occasionally omitted.

Whether the many cuts and the accelerations of tempo were entirely owing to the taste of the conductor or were owing rather to that of his patron cannot be ascertained today. However, one would think it likely that Haydn himself reacted with impatience to the hollowness and long-windedness so often present in Italian *opera seria*. On the other hand a few works like Paisiello's *Il barbiere di Siviglia*, Martin's *L'arbore di Diana*, and Sarti's *Didone abbandonata* seem to have been accepted by him without cuts.

The majority of the works performed required, however, a great deal of work before they were ready for production. Thus a tremendous new responsibility was entrusted to Haydn. Prince Esterházy, conscious of the increased demands made on his music director, expressed his appreciation by concluding in 1779 a new contract with Haydn under greatly improved terms.[19] The fourteen stipulations of the original document (cf. p. 43) were now reduced to six. The original salary of four hundred florins was increased to seven hundred eighty-two florins and thirty kreutzer, and delivery of certain quantities of wine, firewood, grain, meat (including a whole pig), salt, lard, candles, vegetables, and forage for two horses was guaranteed. The clause regarding the Prince's right to dismiss the kapellmeister whenever he wished was omitted, and a mutual right to give three months' notice established. Most significant was the omission of the old clause according to which all compositions by Haydn were to belong solely to the Prince who was the only one entitled to commission music from him. Although

[18] An aria in Salieri's *La fiera di Venezia*. Cf. Bartha and Somfai, *Haydn als Opernkapellmeister*, p. 55.

[19] Cf. Dénes Bartha, ed., *Joseph Haydn, Gesammelte Briefe und Aufzeichnungen* (Kassel, 1965), p. 83f.

Haydn had managed not to be fettered by the old restriction, he could not but be pleased that the new contract accorded him a more dignified position.

No one was more aware of Joseph Haydn's good fortune at the Esterházy court than his brother Michael. The positions of the two brothers had now changed. Michael had been appointed music director and concertmaster to the Archbishop of Salzburg (the patron of Leopold Mozart and his son Wolfgang) in 1763, a position he retained until 1800. The Archbishop was not so devoted to music or in any way so generous as Prince Esterházy. Michael's annual salary was only three hundred florins, and though it was doubled when he had reached the summit of his career, these six hundred florins were no more than Joseph had received after a single year of service with the Esterházys. As a composer also, Michael was more and more eclipsed by Joseph. He felt, however, that he had just as great a talent as his elder brother and is reported to have often exclaimed: "Give me an encouraging hand, like that lent to my brother, and I will not fall behind him."

Although this was far from the truth—Michael's talent could never have competed with Joseph's genius—it cannot be denied that Haydn's life in the service of Prince Nicolaus gave him just the opportunities he needed for his artistic growth. The very monotony of the daily routine, the lack of diversions of any kind, which probably would have been unbearable to an artist like Mozart, helped him to find himself. At Eszterháza he was by no means deprived of intellectual and artistic stimulation; the performances of the traveling dramatic troupes offered, for instance, works by Goethe, Lessing, and Shakespeare, the last still a rarity in this part of the world. The "originality" attained at Eszterháza therefore did not mean that Haydn was unaware of the great spiritual and artistic movements of the time. Indeed, this period offered very interesting proof of Haydn's sensitiveness to contemporary trends.

The eighteenth century was the age of rationalism. Religion, culture, and art—everything was governed by the intellect. But before long a reaction set in. In all countries Jean-Jacques Rousseau, with his motto of "return to nature," called forth a storm of opposition to things purely intellectual. The result was a new attitude toward the arts, the first traces of which can be found in England. Edward Young showed in 1759, in his *Conjectures on Original Composition*, that the man of genius creates not by means of his intellect, but with the aid of divine inspiration. A scintilla of this inspiration can be seen in the folk song. When, in 1765, Bishop Thomas Percy published his collection of old English and Scotch ballads under the title *The Reliques of Ancient English Poetry*, everyone began to be deeply interested in folk songs. Laurence Sterne wrote his humorous works, one of which, *A Sentimental Journey through France and Italy* (1768), revealed the poesy of the human heart and made the word "sentimental" the great fashion of the time. This movement, which in Germany was called *Sturm und Drang* (Storm and Stress), was not limited to literature. We find it in the music of that time, in compositions by Dittersdorf and Mozart, and especially in Haydn's works. A trend toward deepening and intensifying the emotional content had been noticeable in his output even earlier. Encouraged by the prevailing tendency to express darker moods, Haydn followed this line to such an extent that the French musicologist Théodore de Wyzewa [20] felt justified to speak of a "romantic crisis" in his music, reaching its climax in the works of 1771 and 1772. The passion and melancholy breaking forth in many compositions of this period were apparently not owing to external occurrences or to a specific unhappy experience. If anything in Haydn's personal life was responsible for these unrestrained outbursts, it was not the excess, but rather the starvation of his emotional life. Here lay the danger in his existence at Eszterháza. His wife meant nothing to him; friends like Tomasini, Weigl, and Friberth, while very pleasant comrades, were receivers rather than givers in their relation to him. So all the emotional forces of which he was capable inundated his music, sometimes almost marring its artistic quality. What Haydn needed for full mastery in his art was the inner enrichment supplied by vital human contacts.

[20] Théodore de Wyzewa, "A propos du centenaire de la mort de Joseph Haydn," *Revue des deux mondes*, LXXIX/15 (June 15, 1909).

# CHAPTER SIX

# $\mathcal{L}ove$ $and$
# $\mathcal{F}riendship$

## 1 7 8 0 – 1 7 9 0

In 1779, Prince Esterházy engaged an Italian violinist, Antonio Polzelli, and his wife, Luigia, a mezzo-soprano. Neither proved very
satisfactory. The violinist suffered from poor health and often could
not fulfill his duties; his wife, with the help of much coaching from
kapellmeister Haydn, was able to master only roles of secondary
importance. Although their salaries were the lowest paid to any
member of the musical personnel—they received jointly four hundred sixty-five florins a year—the Prince felt that their performances did not justify even this expenditure. Their contract was
due to expire at the end of 1780, but even before that date they were
told that their services would no longer be required. In spite of this,
the Polzellis stayed on, receiving their former salaries, even though
the consumptive Antonio in time disappeared from the orchestra
and was not even mentioned in the list of its members. For once the
Prince did not insist on his wishes being carried out, for it became
clear to him that if he wanted a contented kapellmeister, he must
put up with the presence of Luigia Polzelli.

The singer was twenty-nine, eighteen years younger than
Haydn. She seems to have been a typical Italian brunette, with dark
vivacious eyes, an oval face, an olive complexion, and a graceful
figure. Her marriage with the aged and infirm Antonio was most
unhappy. Haydn understood her plight only too well. The helpless-
ness of the young singer roused all his protective instincts, and be-

fore long his sympathy grew into a deep passion. He seemed to feel that the miseries that for years he had suffered in his union with Maria Anna absolved him from any obligation to his marriage vows.

We know practically nothing about Luigia. No portrait of her is in existence, and we have to imagine what picture we can make of her from the dry description in a passport issued many years later. Her character remains equally obscure; in fact, the only thing we know is that, in later years, after her husband's death, the widow continually asked for and received Haydn's financial assistance. This shows her, of course, in not a very pleasant light, but it does not prove—as many biographers seem to assume—that Luigia had submitted to Haydn's love ten years before for mercenary motives. It is known that women were often attracted to Haydn. The composer himself admitted it, sarcastically adding that his good looks could not have been responsible for it. There is no reason why Luigia should not have succumbed to the strong personality and abounding vitality of her musical mentor or why she should not have genuinely loved him.

Today we cannot ascertain whether Luigia was worthy of the love of a man like Joseph Haydn. Probably she was not, just as Constanze Weber was not worthy of that of Wolfgang Amadeus Mozart. Nevertheless, at the time when Haydn was deeply in love, Luigia gave him what he needed, and by awakening his emotional life played an important part in his development. It seems doubtful that Haydn ever could have achieved the artistic maturity that his works of the 1780s reveal so splendidly if his passion for the Italian singer had not opened to him new vistas of life.

We do not have any letters from the time when their love was at its peak, but other documents throw light on Haydn's feelings for the young singer. Luigia had but a small mezzo-soprano, a type of voice for which the current Italian operas offered little scope. Haydn went out of his way to help her overcome these inadequacies. He transposed arias for her to adapt them to her range; he also subtly enriched their orchestral garb so as to make the music sung by her more attractive. In the scores preserved in the Esterházy archives one can follow his preoccupation with Luigia's problems. Typical is his action in the case of Gazzaniga's opera *La vendemmia*.[1] Here Luigia had to sing a cavatina with a comparatively high tessitura. Haydn had the piece transposed a third down so as to make it more easily

[1] Cf. Dénes Bartha and László Somfai, *Haydn als Opernkapellmeister* (Budapest, 1960), p. 51, 221.

accessible to her range. Apparently he also noticed during rehearsals that Luigia found it difficult to hit the aria's first note correctly, since the voice part started without any instrumental introduction. To help her, he inserted three forte chords played by the orchestra at the beginning of the cavatina, a device he did not use when the same tune was later sung by two more experienced singers. He even tried to sketch for her an effective coloratura passage to be sung in Salieri's opera *La scuola de' gelosi*.[2] As Luigia's voice was inferior to those of the other opera singers employed, Haydn found it impossible to entrust a leading part to her. Except for the somewhat more important role of Silvia in his own opera *L'isola disabitata*, she played mostly minor parts such as chambermaids. In order to improve this situation, Haydn wrote special arias for her, tailored to her vocal capacities and revealing her talent at its best. These were inserted into the respective operas in which she held small parts, and the exquisite pieces thus assured her success. The first of these "insertion arias" was provided for Anfossi's opera *La Metilde ritrovata*, in which Luigia represented the chambermaid Nannina. The Esterházy archives preserve five such "insertion arias" definitely composed for her, and five others rearranged for her, but we have reason to assume that in reality many more pieces were especially composed for Luigia.

That the providing of such arias was a work of love is proved by the quality of these delightful pieces and still more by the fact that Haydn, burdened with countless responsibilities, still managed to find time for such labors. It is true that he occasionally contributed an "insertion aria" for another singer in order to improve an opera. Yet no other of his singers was as frequently favored as Luigia.

Operatic life at Eszterháza was certainly gaining in intensity and every year witnessed a number of first performances. Even after a fire had destroyed the theater in 1779, opera performances were not cut down, but merely transferred to the marionette theater. Particularly impressive was the repertoire in 1786. One hundred twenty-five opera performances took place then, seventeen different works being presented alternately, among them eight novelties. Almost every year changes occurred in the vocal personnel and Haydn had to engage and subsequently train new singers. Some of them brought operatic scores with them from Italy, and

---

[2]Cf. László Somfai, *Joseph Haydn: Sein Leben in zeitgenössischen Bildern* (Budapest, 1966), p. 83.

thus the Esterházy repertoire reflects the prevailing taste among the supporters of Italian opera. At Eszterháza twelve works by Cimarosa, ten each by Anfossi and Paisiello, five by Dittersdorf, four by Guglielmi, and three each by Traetta, Salieri, and Zingarelli, were performed in the period from 1776 to 1790. Naturally enough under these circumstances Haydn had no opportunity to compose many operas himself, and we find his creative work in this field more and more curtailed by his duties as opera conductor. In this period he wrote but three operas. *La fedeltà premiata* originated in 1779 to celebrate the opening of the new theatre at Eszterháza. There followed *Orlando paladino*, intended for the visit of Grand Duke Paul of Russia and his wife, the Grand Duchess Maria Fedorovna (a visit that was canceled, whereupon Haydn's opera was presented on his patron's name day, December 6, 1781). In 1784 he composed *Armida*, his last opera written for Prince Esterházy. It is noteworthy that these two very last operas enjoyed the greatest success at court, a success exceeding that of his previous dramatic works. *Orlando* was played thirty times through the seasons from 1782 to 1784. *Armida* received twenty-one performances in 1784, seventeen in 1785, seven in 1786, and remained in the repertoire in succeeding years.

Studying the casts of the various operatic performances, one notices that Luigia Polzelli was quite active during the eighties but did not appear on the stage in 1783. This was because of her pregnancy. A son, Aloysius Antonio Nicolaus, was born to her on April 22, 1783. Rumor persisted that he was Haydn's son. Probably this will never be clearly proved, but the imputation cannot be definitely rejected. In the Polzelli family his paternity was taken for granted, and Antonio's daughter did not hesitate to describe herself as Haydn's granddaughter when making an appeal for help in the *Musikalisches Wochenblatt* of December 31, 1875. Haydn himself never made a statement about this matter. He took a loving interest in Antonio as well as in Luigia's elder son, Pietro, born in 1777 in Bologna, but did not differentiate between the two. If anything, he rather preferred the elder. He taught them both music, watching with pleasure the unfolding of their talents, gave them much financial assistance, and helped them to obtain their first appointments.[3]

[3] Pietro Polzelli, known as Pietrucchio, after working as second violinist in a Vienna orchestra, died at the age of nineteen from tuberculosis. Antonio Polzelli entered the Esterházy orchestra in 1803 and became its vice-concertmaster and music director in 1803. Later he turned to agriculture, working as an estate agent for various Hungarian magnates. In 1826 he was knighted in Rome. Through speculations and law-

After their mother ceased to mean much to Haydn, the two Polzelli boys were still sure of the composer's unfailing sympathy. He certainly had the feelings of a father for both, and he made this so clear that even Frau Haydn, in spite of her hatred for Luigia, was resigned to this state of affairs and received Pietro Polzelli for a prolonged stay in her home "very kindly."[4]

Absorbed though Haydn was in his personal affairs through his love for Luigia, these years brought him another experience of equal or perhaps even greater importance. He met Wolfgang Amadeus Mozart, who had moved from Salzburg to Vienna in 1781. Naturally they had known of each other before this; now, however, a very close personal friendship was established between them that grew stronger from year to year.

It is difficult to conceive of two personalities fundamentally more different than these two great men. Mozart developed with amazing rapidity. Haydn's progress was incredibly slow. Indeed, at the age of thirty-six (Mozart died at this age) Haydn had written none of the compositions that are most admired in our time. In person, Mozart was the typical artist, his moods undergoing rapid changes from buoyant gaiety to deep melancholy, from fits of temper to an almost feminine gentleness. Haydn was of a rather even temperament, mostly calm and cheerful, and had a great sense of humor. Mozart was a born dramatic composer and a brilliant virtuoso on both the piano and violin; thus he gained tremendous success as a performer. Haydn's gifts as a composer for the stage were limited; he preferred to conduct his own works inconspicuously from the harpsichord and was free from any ambition to gain laurels as a soloist. There was little sense of order and regularity in Mozart's life, and he had no understanding of the value of money. Haydn's existence throughout the greater part of his life had something of an automatic precision; neatness and regularity were indispensable to him; in financial matters he was a match for his publishers and he left considerable property at his death, while Mozart died a pauper.

Perhaps the very differences between these two men of genius drew them to each other. Had they constantly lived together they might have got on each other's nerves, but as they did not visit each other very frequently, every meeting became an event. Haydn may

---

suits he lost his fortune and returned to music, dying a music teacher in Budapest in 1855. Various compositions show him as a talented disciple of Haydn's.
[4] Postscript by Haydn to one of Pietro's letters to his mother dated October 22, 1792.

have been fascinated by Mozart's quicksilver personality, while Mozart derived a sense of security from the friendship of a man as steadfast and warm as Haydn.

But for both of them, their artistic relations far transcended in importance their personal contacts. At the time of their first meeting, Mozart was twenty-five, Haydn forty-nine, but the older composer who had developed so slowly and the younger master who had grown so rapidly had much to impart to each other. Whenever Haydn went to Vienna he had the joy of attending chamber music performances at Mozart's home. In 1785, Leopold Mozart visited his son, and Wolfgang's new string quartets were played for Haydn by the composer, his father, and the two barons Tinti. Then Haydn took Leopold Mozart aside and said to him: "I tell you before God as an honest man that your son is the greatest composer known to me either in person or by reputation. He has taste and, what is more, the most profound knowledge of composition."[5] Mozart would not accept this praise for himself, but insisted that it was solely from Haydn that he had learned how to write string quartets. To acknowledge this to the musical world, he published in 1785 six quartets dedicated to his "beloved friend Haydn," expressing his deep gratitude in touching words. But he went much further than that, for he allowed no one to say anything against Haydn in his presence. Typical indeed was his reply to Leopold Koželuch, teacher of the pianoforte at the Vienna court. This composer, on hearing a daring passage in one of Haydn's quartets, remarked somewhat contemptuously: "I would never have written that." Whereupon Mozart replied: "Nor would I! And do you know why? Because neither your nor I would have had so excellent an idea." And on another occasion he exclaimed to Koželuch: "Sir, even if they melted us both together, there would still not be stuff enough to make a Haydn." This attitude was reciprocated by Haydn. After the Vienna premiere of *Don Giovanni*, sundry passages were criticized in his presence and he exclaimed: "I cannot settle this dispute but this I know: Mozart is the greatest composer that the world possesses now." And when someone expressed surprise at a daring disregard of the rules of harmony in Mozart's Quartet in C major, he replied sharply: "If Mozart wrote it so he must have had a good reason for it." Other examples could be mentioned to illuminate the deep respect each composer felt for the other. Not only reports and anecdotes, but their works themselves testify to this. When the older

[5] Letter from Leopold Mozart to his daughter, Nannerl, dated February 14, 1785.

master created his "Sun" quartets in 1772, the younger felt inspired to work in the same field, the result being compositions that in some respects follow Haydn's model. Then a considerable pause occurred in Haydn's quartet composition, and the same was true of Mozart's. But when Haydn had presented his "Russian" quartets, "written in a new and special way," Mozart composed the six exquisite quartets that he dedicated to Haydn.

Mozart's influence on Haydn is mainly noticeable in the late works, and we shall have to mention the name of the Salzburg master frequently when discussing Haydn's output in the 1790s. Before that, the young friend's operas had helped the older composer to clarify the limitations of his own talent. A few passages from letters may illustrate this. In his dealings with the Artaria publishing house, Haydn often boasted of his operas. On May 27, 1781, he remarked, for instance, about his *La fedeltà premiata*: "I do assure you that no such work has hitherto been heard in Paris or perhaps in Vienna either." On March 1, 1784, he wrote: "Yesterday my *Armida* was played for the second time with general applause. They say it is my best work up to now." But when he became acquainted with Mozart's *Le nozze di Figaro*, *Così fan tutte*, and *Don Giovanni*, his own achievements in this field appeared to him in a new light. In December 1787 a great admirer from Prague, by the name of Franz Roth, asked him to write an opera for Prague (as Mozart had done) and Haydn answered:

> You wish me to write an *opera buffa* for you. Most willingly if you are desirous of having a vocal composition of mine for yourself alone; but if it is with the idea of producing it on the stage at Prague I cannot comply with your wish, all my operas being too closely connected with our personal circle [Prince Esterházy's, in Hungary], so that they could never produce the proper effect, which I have calculated in accordance with the locality. It would be very different if I had the invaluable privilege of composing a new opera for your theater. But even then I should be taking a big risk, for scarcely any man could stand comparison with the great Mozart.
>
> Oh, if only I could explain to every musical friend, and to the leading men in particular, the inimitable art of Mozart, its depth, the greatness of its emotion, and its unique musical conception, as I myself feel and understand it, nations would then vie with each other to possess

so great a jewel within their frontiers. Prague ought to strive not merely to retain this precious man, but also to remunerate him; for without this support the history of any great genius is sad indeed, and gives very little encouragement to others to adopt a musical career, and for lack of this support many promising talents are lost to the world. It enrages me to think that the unparalleled Mozart has not yet been engaged by some imperial or royal court. Do forgive this outburst—but I love that man too much.[6]

Such an "outburst" was indeed a rarity for Haydn. It proves how much Mozart's welfare meant to him, that he was willing to disparage his own achievements if by so doing he could put the genius of his colleague in the right light.

That Mozart could exert so strong an impact on the older master testifies to Haydn's broadmindedness and flexibility. Even as a man of fifty he was by no means set in his ways. Fundamentally there was an amazingly small difference between the youth who twenty-five years previously had devoured manuals on music while nearly starving in his Vienna garret and the master who by now had achieved world fame.

World fame it was indeed that came to Haydn while he worked in the solitude of Eszterháza. His name traveled far beyond the borders of his country, and in the whole of Europe there was hardly a music lover who did not know of, and admire, the works of Joseph Haydn.

The first indications of the composer's widespread reputation came from Spain. As early as 1779 the poet Yriarte wrote glowing praise of his music in the poem *La música*. Two years afterwards, the Prince of Asturias, later King Carlos IV of Spain, sent Haydn a golden snuffbox set with diamonds. This was a reward for the gift of Haydn's score of the opera *L'isola disabitata* that the Prince had received. What pleased the composer perhaps even more than the costly present was the manner in which it was presented. The secretary of the Spanish Legation went to Eszterháza for the sole purpose of handing over the royal gift and expressing his monarch's great esteem for Haydn's music—a ceremony that must have afforded keen satisfaction to both the composer and his ambitious patron. What the Spanish court thought of Haydn is also reflected

[6]The letter was first published by Franz Xavier Niemetschek in his *Leben des K. K. Kapellmeisters Gottlieb Mozart* (Prague, 1798), p. 51.

in the attitude of two members of the highest ranking aristocracy, the Duke of Alba and the Duchess of Benavente and Osuña. Both entered into a formal agreement with Haydn to receive from him yearly a certain number of symphonies, quartets, and other chamber music scores. The contract was concluded with a Spanish resident in Vienna, C. H. de Lelis,[7] and Haydn seems to have delivered from 1783 to at least 1789 a considerable amount of music against sizable payments. More important than these commissions was another one, also from Spain, about which Haydn reported in his preface to the score of the work published by Breitkopf and Härtel in 1801:

> About fifteen years ago I was requested by a canon of Cádiz to compose instrumental music on *The Seven Last Words of Our Saviour on the Cross*. It was customary at the cathedral of Cádiz[8] to produce an oratorio every year during Lent, the effect of the performance being not a little enhanced by the following circumstances. The walls, windows, and pillars of the church were hung with black cloth, and only one large lamp hanging from the center of the roof broke the solemn obscurity. At midday the doors were closed and the ceremony began. After a short service the bishop ascended the pulpit, pronounced the first of the seven words (or sentences) and delivered a discourse thereon. This ended, he left the pulpit and prostrated himself before the altar. The pause was filled by music. The bishop then in like manner pronounced the second word, then the third, and so on, the orchestra following on the conclusion of each discourse. My composition was subject to these conditions, and it was no easy matter to compose seven adagios to last ten minutes each, and succeed one another without fatiguing the listeners.

However, Haydn overcame these difficulties and he was justified in writing to the English publisher William Forster:[9] "Each word is

---

[7] Cf. Georg Feder, "Manuscript Sources of Haydn's Works and Their Distribution," *HYb*, IV (1968), p. 134.

[8] A. van Hoboken (Hob., I, p. 845) remarks that the exercises took place in a church situated in the grotto Santa Cueva, which the priest Marqués de Valde-Inigo had decorated. It was the marqués who conceived the idea of commissioning a composition for the Passion from Haydn, asking Father Don Francisco Micón, known to Haydn, to serve as intermediary.

[9] Letter of April 8, 1787.

expressed by purely instrumental means in such a way as to make the most profound impression on even an inexperienced listener's soul." The work won instant success and before long was played and printed in other countries. Thus, as early as 1793 the first performance took place in the United States.[10] The Spanish canon, incidentally, presented the honorarium in an original way. Haydn received a little box from Cádiz. Upon opening it, he saw to his surprise a chocolate cake. Angrily he cut into it and found it filled with gold pieces.

France shared its neighbor's admiration for Haydn's music. On March 27, 1781 the composer could report to his Vienna publisher, Artaria: "Monsieur Le Gros, director of the Concerts Spirituels, wrote me a great many nice things about my *Stabat Mater* which had been given there [at Paris] four times with great applause; so this gentleman asked permission to have it engraved. They made me an offer to engrave all my future works, on very advantageous terms, and are much surprised that my compositions for the voice are so singularly pleasing." In 1784 another society, the Concerts de la Loge Olympique invited Haydn to write six symphonies specially for them, an invitation to which we owe the famous Paris symphonies (Nos. 82–87). The triumphant success of these works induced one of the society's directors, the Comte d'Ogny, to commission three more symphonies from Haydn (Nos. 90–92). The composer received twenty-five *louis d'or* for each of the Paris symphonies, which, according to the Comte's report, appeared "colossal" to him. Haydn's prestige in France is also reflected in a remark made to Adalbert Gyrowetz when this composer discovered that one of his own works was circulating in Paris under Haydn's name. "One answered Gyrowetz," the composer reports in his autobiography, "that he should consider it a great honor to have his symphonies taken for works by Haydn" (cf. n. 19). As a matter of fact, enterprising French publishers like Nadermann and Sieber published a sizable amount of alleged "Haydn works" that were not contributed by the composer, a method by no means unusual in that era.

The year 1781, which brought Haydn the letter from Monsieur Le Gros and the present from the Prince of Asturias, also saw the beginning of the master's direct connection with England. The eminent violinmaker William Forster applied to the British ambassador

[10] See M. D. Herter Norton, "Haydn in America," *Musical Quarterly*, XVIII/2 (Apr. 1932).

in Vienna for help in securing Haydn's works for his newly established publishing house. The ambassador, General Jermingham, was successful, and within six years Forster published no less than one hundred twenty-nine works by Haydn, among them eighty-two symphonies, for which he paid considerable sums. Forster's example was followed by the firm of Longman and Broderip. When the Professional Concerts was founded in 1783, Lord Abingdon tried to induce Haydn to take over its direction. The newspapers were full of doubts and hopes that the great man would come to London, but Haydn declined, since giving up the service of his Prince appeared to be out of the question, and he knew that a leave of absence would certainly not be granted to him by his patron. So the directors of the Professional Concerts had to be satisfied with a less famous musician, who opened the series with a Haydn symphony. That rumors persisted regarding Haydn's visit to England is revealed in a note from the north German town of Königsberg appearing in April 1783 on page 92 of Cramer's *Magazin für Musik*. It also testified to the fame Haydn had by now acquired in Germany: "Mr. Joseph Haydn, who in his exquisite sonatas has given to many a clavierist an antispasmodic against grief and misfortune, certainly would not take it amiss that the large number of yearning violinists dares hereby most submissively to ask him to bear them in mind and to regale them with some violin sonatas. As to the labor expended by the great artist, is it not payment enough when any violinist offers to the good man his sincere gratitude? According to newspaper reports, Haydn has undertaken a trip to England. Crowned with laurels and, if his merits are sufficiently rewarded, paid in good guineas, he will return to his affectionate and admiring fatherland. Should this note then come into his hands, he might fulfill the wishes of the German violinists, who hold him in so great respect."

Haydn, though unable to accept the invitation to London, did not find it easy to give up any plan of this kind, and as the years went by, it became more and more alluring. On April 8, 1787, he wrote to Forster[11] in London that he hoped to see him personally at the end of the year, and on July 19, 1787, he outlined to the London impresario John Gallini terms under which he would come to London.[12] We cannot ascertain whether this was meant seriously. In all

[11] Cf. H. C. Robbins Landon, *The Collected Correspondence and London Notebooks of Joseph Haydn* (London, 1959), p. 59.
[12] Ibid., p. 66.

likelihood Haydn derived some satisfaction from toying with such plans while being tied firmly to his duties at Eszterháza. Meanwhile he kept in touch with his English admirers.

A particularly enterprising publisher, John Bland, took the trouble to travel from London to Eszterháza to obtain new works and to persuade Haydn to visit England. The master presented Bland with two autographs. One was the cantata *Arianna a Naxos*, the other the String Quartet Op. 55, No. 2. About the latter work Bland used to tell an amusing story, which brought it its peculiar nickname of the "Razor" quartet. He said that he visited Haydn just when the master, while shaving with a very blunt razor, exclaimed in despair, "I would give my best quartet for a good razor." Bland rushed to his inn and brought back his own excellent set of razors. Haydn was delighted and scrupulously kept his promise, for the "Razor" quartet was certainly among the best he had written.[13]

Nor was England the only foreign country that invited the master. Haydn was also a great favorite in Italy. The Philharmonic Academy of Modena elected him a member in 1780, thus putting to shame the Viennese Tonkünstlersocietät. In 1786, King Ferdinand IV of Naples, a passionate lover of music, commissioned several concertos for his favorite instrument, the lira organizzata (see p. 292). The works that Haydn wrote satisfied the king so completely that he urgently invited the composer to visit his court. Haydn felt much inclined to do so, and in the aforementioned letter to Forster he remarked: "Since I have not heard from Mr. Cramer [London impresario] up to now, I shall accept an engagement to go to Naples this winter."

All in all, royalty was gracious to the son of the wheelwright. Friedrich Wilhelm II of Prussia, an excellent violoncello player,[14] after receiving from Haydn the Paris symphonies, sent him a magnificent diamond ring worth three hundred ducats. Haydn was delighted with the gift and thanked the monarch by dedicating the string quartets Op. 50 to him. He made a habit of wearing the ring when he composed an important work. Carpani even declares that when the master forgot to put on the ring, no ideas came to him.

Another royal admirer of Haydn was the Russian Grand Duch-

---

[13] Though this sounds not improbable, the story may have originated in Bland's imagination. Van Hoboken remarks quite rightly (Hob., I, p. 414) that the quartet was not published by Bland, and the autograph is lost.

[14] Mozart wrote his last three quartets for the King; Beethoven dedicated the two violoncello sonatas, Op. 5, to him.

ess and subsequent Empress Maria Fedorovna, who took lessons from him while visiting Vienna in 1782, and as late as 1805 sent him a valuable ring in thanks for his new songs for three and four voices. Such proofs of success naturally gave Haydn a great deal of gratification. But his fame did not in the least turn his head. He remained the same kind, simple man whose "eyes beamed with benevolence" (Dies), and he never forgot his humble origin. "I have had intercourse with emperors, kings, and many a great personage," he remarked once to Griesinger, "and have been told by them quite a few flattering things. For all that, I do not care to be on intimate terms with such persons and prefer to keep to people of my own station."

The aim of keeping his distance from the highborn is illustrated in a letter of July 28, 1787, to G. A. Kreusser, conductor to the Elector of Mainz.[15] Here the composer employed a servility of expression that we find not at all in keeping with the fame he enjoyed at that time:

> I take the liberty of asking you kindly to hand with my deepest submission the present two symphonies to His Serenity, your most gracious Prince, and as His Illustrious Highness desired to know the cost of all the music sent so far, I venture most obediently to mention the expense of fifty florins for the copying and one hundred talers for my undeserving self. Should this request in any way whatever seem offensive to your most gracious Prince, I won't demand a penny. I consider myself fortunate indeed merely to be favored by His Serene Highness' condescension in listening to my humble efforts.

We may assume that the elector found Haydn's demands reasonable, he being aware of the value the "humble efforts" of the renowned master represented.

Naturally enough, Vienna could not but be influenced by the attitude of the whole musical world. The publishing firm of Artaria and Company entered into a close business connection with Haydn and did much to promote the master's fame in his own country. In 1781, when Artaria published a collection of pictures of the greatest

[15] Letter of June 23, 1781. See Landon, *Collected Correspondence*, p. 67.

men of the time, they included the portrait of Haydn by Johann Ernst Mansfeld.[16] The composer was, as he wrote to them, "exceedingly pleased," and the Prince "was even more delighted."[17] Although certain court circles in Vienna still maintained their old attitude, the number of Haydn's friends in Vienna steadily increased. They belonged mostly to the lower aristocracy or to the wealthy middle classes whose role in Austria's musical life was acquiring more and more importance.

Among them were the sisters, Caterina and Marianne von Auenbrugger, to whom Haydn dedicated six piano sonatas, and about whom he wrote to Artaria:[18] "The approval of the Misses von Auenbrugger is most important to me, as their style of playing and their genuine insight into music equal those of the greatest masters. Both deserve to become known in all Europe through public newspapers."

An important friend was the high official Franz Bernhard von Kees, who, according to the report of the Czech composer Adalbert Gyrowetz,[19] "was recognized as the first friend of music . . . in Vienna." In his home, orchestral concerts of amateurs regularly took place under the host's direction. The catalogue of Haydn symphonies compiled for von Kees was used in 1805 as a valuable source by Haydn and his helper Johann Elssler for his own list (see p. 197). Both Mozart and Haydn considered it an honor to have their new works performed in the von Kees house, and we understand their attitude when we read in a letter from Mozart to his father[20] that his symphony had been executed by forty violins, ten violas, eight violoncellos, and all the wind instruments doubled. Another friend was Hofrat Greiner, who chose the texts for Haydn's songs (though often not pieces of great artistic value). As we learn from the memoirs of Greiner's daughter, his house was also frequented by Mozart, Salieri, Paisiello, and Cimarosa. Moreover Haydn liked to visit the Anglo-Italian composer, Stephen Storace, at that time living in Vienna, and his sister, the highly successful singer Nancy, who interpreted the role of Susanna at the first performance of *Le*

---

[16] It was reproduced in 1784 in the *European Magazine*, London, with a biography of the "Celebrated composer."
[17] Letter of June 23, 1781. Cf. Franz Artaria and Hugo Botstiber, *Joseph Haydn und das Verlagshaus Artaria* (Vienna, 1909).
[18] Letter of February 25, 1780.
[19] Cf. Gyrowetz's memoirs in *Lebensläufe deutscher Musiker*, ed. A. Einstein (Leipzig, 1915).
[20] Letter from W. A. Mozart to his father dated April 11, 1781.

*nozze di Figaro.* The Irish singer Michael Kelly tells us in his *Reminiscences* of a chamber music party in Storace's home, when the quartets were played by no lesser masters than Haydn, Dittersdorf, Mozart, and Vanhall, while Paisiello and the Italian poet, Abbate Casti, were among the listeners. As Kelly remarks: "A greater treat, or a more remarkable one, cannot be imagined. . . . After the musical feast was over, we sat down to an excellent supper and became joyous and lively in the extreme."[21]

There was also the music-loving merchant, Johann Michael Puchberg, who besides being an unfailing friend to Mozart (which of course spoke in his favor from Haydn's point of view), helped Haydn with financial matters. Puchberg and Haydn were the only people whom Mozart invited to the first rehearsals of *Così fan tutte.*

It was probably on the recommendation of Mozart and Puchberg, both ardent Freemasons, that in 1785 Haydn joined the highly reputed Masonic lodge, *Zur wahren Eintracht.* This he apparently did for the pleasure of associating with men of high culture; moreover, becoming a member of a Masonic lodge was the general trend among his friends. On January 24, 1785, he was voted in "by unanimous and delighted consent," and he was initiated on February 11. However, he never attended another meeting, and in 1787 his name was removed from the membership list. Whether his neglect of the lodge was due merely to lukewarm interest in the freemasonic movement cannot be ascertained. Landon[22] seems to believe in Haydn's genuine interest in the movement. He points to the Masonic songs Haydn composed for the lodge *Zur wahren Eintracht,* songs found among his effects after his death and removed by the censor, since after 1795 the Order of the Freemasons was prohibited in Austria. It is also noteworthy that Haydn maintained contacts with the French *Loge Olympique* that commissioned his Paris symphonies. Thus Haydn's attitude remains unclear. However, it should not be forgotten that he was a loyal son of the Catholic Church, deeply rooted in its ritual, and may have felt somewhat out of tune with the Freemasons, a group proscribed by the Church.

Despite his numerous Viennese friends there was, with the possible exception of Mozart's home, no place in the city that proved so attractive to Haydn as the house of Peter L. von Genzinger, a very successful doctor who had been Prince Esterházy's physician for many years. Both the doctor and his charming wife,

[21] Cf. Stewart Marsh Ellis, *The Life of Michael Kelly* (London: Gollancz, 1930), p. 119f.
[22] *HCaW*, II, p. 508ff.

Marianne, an excellent singer and pianist, were real friends of music. On Sundays the musical elite of Vienna used to assemble at the Genzingers' home for performances of the first quality. Haydn attended these gatherings whenever he was in Vienna, and they meant a great deal to him. There he found an atmosphere that seemed like the fulfillment of his old dreams: a comfortable, pleasant home; a woman of high culture who took the keenest interest in every one of his new compositions and who at the same time was so thoughtful a hostess that she prepared his favorite dishes; musically gifted children whom he could guide. The Genzinger home offered him all that he had missed throughout his married life. He basked in this congenial atmosphere, only to feel all the more strongly the misery of his lonely existence when he returned to Eszterháza.

Fortunately for us, letters were exchanged between Haydn and Marianne von Genzinger after she had sent him in January 1789 a pianoforte arrangement of an andante from one of his symphonies which she had made herself, and which, according to Haydn, was an excellent piece of work. Among the personal documents that have come down to us from Haydn, there is probably nothing more important than his letters to Marianne.[23] The master ordinarily found it difficult to get away from the florid and stilted style of his time. When he wrote to Marianne, however, the words seemed to come from his heart, and they convey to the reader the impression that he is actually hearing Haydn talk to his dear friend. Most revealing is the long letter that he wrote to his "much esteemed and kindest Frau von Genzinger" on February 9, 1790, after a visit to Vienna:

> Well here I sit in my wilderness; forsaken, like some
> poor orphan, almost without human society, melancholy,
> dwelling on the memory of past glorious days. Yes, past,
> alas! And who can tell when those happy hours may re-
> turn—those charming meetings where the whole circle
> has but one heart and one soul—all those delightful musi-
> cal evenings that can only be remembered and not de-
> scribed? Where are all those inspired moments? All gone
> —and gone forever. You must not be surprised, dear lady,
> that I have delayed writing to express my gratitude. I

---

[23] They are preserved in the National Library, Vienna, and were first published in T. von Karajan, *Joseph Haydn in London* (Vienna, 1861).

found everything at home in confusion; for three days I
did not know whether I was kapellmeister or kapell-
servant. Nothing could console me; my apartment was all
in confusion; my pianoforte, which I formerly loved so
dearly, was perverse and disobedient, and irritated rather
than soothed me. I slept little, and even my dreams per-
secuted me, for when I fell asleep and was under the pleasant illusion that I was listening to *Le nozze di Figaro*, the
blustering north wind woke me and almost blew off my
nightcap. I lost twenty pounds in weight in three days,
for the effects of the good fare at Vienna had disappeared
on the journey back. Alas! alas! thought I to myself,
when forced to eat at the tavern a slice of a fifty-year-old
cow instead of your admirable beef, an old mutton with
turnips instead of a ragout with little forcemeat balls, a
tough grill instead of a Bohemian pheasant, Hungarian
salad instead of good juicy oranges, and dry apple fritters
instead of pastry. Alas and alas, thought I to myself,
would that I now had many a tidbit that I despised in Vienna! Here in Eszterháza no one asks me, "Would you
like chocolate with or without milk? Will you take coffee
with or without cream? What can I offer you, my good
Haydn? Will you have vanilla ice or strawberry?" If only I
had a piece of good Parmesan cheese, particularly in Lent,
to enable me to swallow more easily the black puddings!
Today I gave our porter a commission to get me a couple
of pounds.

Forgive me, dear lady, for taking up your time in
this, my very first letter, by so wretched a scrawl and
such stupid nonsense; you must forgive a man spoiled by
the Viennese. Now, however, I begin to accustom myself
by degrees to country life, and yesterday I rehearsed for
the first time, and somewhat in the Haydn style, too.

No doubt you have been more industrious than myself. The pleasing adagio from the quartet has probably
now received its true expression from your fair fingers.
I trust that my good Miss Peperl [Marianne's daughter]
may be reminded of her master by often singing the cantata *Arianna a Naxos*, and that she will pay particular attention to distinct articulation and correct vocal production, for it would be a sin if so fine a voice were to remain
shut up in her chest. I beg, therefore, for a frequent smile,

or else I shall be much vexed. I also advise master François [the eldest son] to cultivate his musical talents. Even
if he sings in his dressing gown, it will do well enough,
and I will often write something new to encourage him. I
again kiss your hands in gratitude for all the kindness you
have shown me, and am unchangeably while life lasts,

Yours, etc.

HAYDN

Soon after this letter was written an event occurred that was bound
to increase Haydn's depression. Princess Maria Elisabeth, the wife
of his patron, died on February 25, 1790. Haydn described the
gloomy atmosphere at Eszterháza in the following letter, which
also shows that he kept his friend informed of what was happening
to him:

March 14, 1790

Most valued, esteemed, and kindest Frau von Genzinger,

I ask your forgiveness a million times for having so
long delayed my answer to your two charming letters.
This has been caused not by negligence (a sin from which
may Heaven preserve me so long as I live), but by the
pressure of business that devolved upon me on behalf of
my gracious Prince in his present melancholy condition.
The death of his wife has overwhelmed the Prince with
such grief that we have been obliged to use every means
in our power to rouse him from his profound sorrow. I
therefore arranged for the first three days a selection of
chamber music, but no singing. The poor Prince, however, the first evening, on hearing my favorite adagio in
D, was affected by such deep melancholy that it was difficult to dispel it by other pieces. On the fourth day we had
an opera, on the fifth a comedy, and afterward our daily
theater as usual. I also commanded them to study Gassmann's old opera *L'amor artigiano*, as our master had recently expressed a wish to hear it. I composed three new
arias for it which I will shortly send you, not on account
of their beauty, but to demonstrate my industry. You shall
receive the new symphony I promised in April, so that it
may be performed at the Keeses' music party.

You must now permit me to kiss your hands grate-
fully for the rusks you sent me, which came exactly at
the right moment, when I had just finished the last of the
others. That my favorite *Arianna* has been successful at
Schottenhof[24] is delightful news to me, but I recommend
Miss Peperl to pronounce her words clearly, especially in
the phrase *che tanto amai.* . . .

As I feel sure, dear lady, that you take an interest in
everything that concerns me (far greater than I deserve),
I must let you know that last week I received a present of
a handsome gold snuffbox, of the weight of thirty-four
ducats,[25] from Prince Öttingen-Wallerstein, accompanied
by an invitation to pay him a visit this year, the prince
defraying my expenses. His Highness is desirous of making my personal acquaintance (a pleasing fillip to my depressed spirits). Whether I shall be able to make up my
mind to the journey is another question.

I beg you to excuse this hasty scrawl.

I am always, etc.

HAYDN

P.S. My dutiful compliments to Your Grace's husband,
your relatives, and the von Hacker family.—I have just
lost my faithful and honest coachman; he died on the
twenty-fifth of last month.

The question has often been asked whether Haydn was in love
with Marianne von Genzinger. It is not easy to answer. Marianne
certainly showed no more than friendliness in her letters. They
leave indeed the impression in one's mind that she was always on
guard to convey by her words nothing but great esteem. We do not
know what lay behind it. Haydn exhibited less reserve. That he
maintained such friendly relations with her but not with Dr. Genzinger is hinted by his mentioning merely in a postscript his "dutiful compliments to Your Grace's husband"; clearly his letters are
meant only for her. Once he went so far as to exclaim:[26] "I have so
much to say and confess to you, from which no one but yourself
can absolve me." And in the same letter he employs a revealing

---

[24] The Genzingers' residence.
[25] Haydn does not mention that the snuffbox also contained fifty ducats.
[26] Letter of June 20, 1790.

method of punctuation by adding after the customary respects to the doctor: "I kiss Your Grace a thousand times—on the hands."

It would not be surprising if Haydn had been in love with this charming admirer of his art who, at the time when these letters were exchanged, was only in her middle thirties. When writing a sonata specially for her, he called her attention in particular to the adagio and added, "It has a deep significance that I will analyze for you when opportunity offers." On another occasion, when a letter that he had written to her went astray and they suspected that it had been stolen by some curious person, Haydn reassured his friend in the following words: [27]

> You need be under no uneasiness, dear lady, as re-
> gards either the past or the future, for my friendship and
> esteem for you (warm as they are) can never become rep-
> rehensible because I have always in mind my respect for
> your elevated virtues, which not only I, but all who know
> you, must revere. Do not let this deter you from consol-
> ing me sometimes by your charming letters, as they are
> so needed to cheer me in this wilderness and soothe my
> deeply wounded heart. Oh, that I could be with you, dear
> lady, even for a quarter of an hour, to pour forth all my
> sorrows, and to receive comfort from you!

This letter gives a clear picture of what Marianne meant to him. Here was a woman to whom he could "pour forth his sorrows," who understood and comforted him.

But why should Haydn have needed comfort at that time? Why was "his heart deeply wounded"? To all outward appearances he was leading a highly satisfactory existence. His fame by far exceeded anything he might have hoped for in his proudest dreams; indeed probably no living composer had a more widespread reputation. He had an excellent and well-paid position. His health was good, his productivity in fullest bloom. The unhappiness of his married life was a burden he had become used to carrying, and all the more so since he and his wife now mostly lived apart. Still, many remarks in his letters point to an increasing moodiness and dissatisfaction, which are always ascribed to the same reason. In his autobiographical sketch of 1778, he had proudly said of his position: "Kapellmeister to His Highness Prince Esterházy, in whose

[27] Letter of May 30, 1790.

service I hope to live and die." Now he wrote: [28] "I am doomed to stay at home. What I lose hereby, Your Grace can certainly realize. It is indeed sad always to be a slave. Yet Providence decrees it so. I am a poor creature." Other similar outbursts could be mentioned, showing that Haydn had ceased to be happy at Eszterháza. He complains of "the many annoyances from the Court," [29] annoyances he had undergone often enough in the past and been able to overcome through skillful diplomacy. Right now he was apparently unwilling to make such efforts. It was natural for him to long for Vienna, where he could enjoy the inspiring company of Mozart and the wonderful sympathy of Marianne von Genzinger. Moreover, the various invitations to foreign countries that reached him were a great temptation and made him increasingly restless. But these were only symptoms of a more deeply rooted trouble. Haydn had outgrown Eszterháza. The problems that had confronted him in his position there had ceased to interest him. Even his attachment to his patron had somewhat diminished. Like a person of half his age, Haydn, now a man of nearly sixty, craved for change, new tasks, new experiences. With the sure instinct of genius, he felt that the immense creative forces still slumbering in him could be released only by a clean break with the way of life that for nearly thirty years had been dear to him.

[28] Letter of June 27, 1790.
[29] Letter of May 30, 1790.

# CHAPTER SEVEN

# Sweet Liberty

## 1790 – 1792

When Haydn was writing his melancholy letters during the early months of 1790, he could not have guessed how soon the dreary monotony of Eszterháza would become only a memory. In the autumn of that year things began to happen with a speed that he had never experienced before. Prince Nicolaus, the patron whom Haydn had faithfully served for twenty-eight years, died on September 28, 1790, thus removing the fundamental reason for his staying at Eszterháza. Fortunately for Haydn and for the history of music, Prince Anton, who succeeded Prince Nicolaus, did not share his father's interests. He immediately dismissed all the musicians with the exception of Haydn, Tomasini, and a few instrumentalists who were to carry on the church services. Haydn's old patron and friend had bequeathed to him a yearly pension of a thousand florins, to which Prince Anton added four hundred florins, thus keeping the master nominally in his service, but at the same time leaving him perfectly free to do whatever he wished. Haydn jumped at this opportunity and without making any further plans, rushed off to Vienna. Indeed, he was so anxious to get away from Eszterháza that he left behind most of his belongings. Hardly had he moved into an apartment in the house of his friend, Nepomuk Hamberger, when various offers were made to him. Prince Anton Grassalkovics, a son-in-law of Haydn's deceased patron and also a great lover of music, wanted him to come to his court at Pressburg. Such an offer naturally did not tempt Haydn, as it would have meant exactly the same kind of life he had been leading at Eszterháza. King Ferdinand IV of Naples, who had come to Vienna for the triple marriage of two of his daughters and a son to members of the Habsburg family, repeated his former invitation with great urgency. While Haydn was still weighing the pros and cons of this proposition, he was swept off his feet by the bearer of a third proposal. One day a stranger appeared in his room and introduced himself with the blunt words: "I am Salomon of London and have come to fetch you. Tomorrow we will arrange an accord." In fact a detailed agreement was instantly worked out by Salomon that stipulated considerably better terms than Haydn himself had outlined in 1787 in his letter to the impresario Gallini. He was to receive three hundred pounds for a new opera to be written for the King's theater, the same sum for six new symphonies, two hundred pounds for the copyright of them, another two hundred for twenty new smaller compositions to be performed by him at twenty concerts, and a guarantee of two hundred pounds for a benefit concert. As advance on these twelve hundred pounds, five thousand florins were to be deposited with the Viennese bankers, Fries and Company.

Italy or England, which was it to be? Haydn was confronted by a crucial problem. For many years he had cherished the dream of traveling to the classical land of opera. Again and again he had suggested such a trip to his patron, always to be put off with some excuse or other. Now, however, when the decision rested entirely with himself, Italy seemed much less glamorous. His interest in composing operas had waned considerably—partly because of the supremacy of Mozart's masterpieces—and he felt keenly that instrumental music was his particular language. In this field, England with its large, excellently trained orchestras was definitely the leader. Moreover, there was the question of personal freedom, which had become extremely vital for Haydn. At the court of a king, he would again have to wait in antechambers, conform to strict etiquette, and in short be treated once more as an upper servant. So Haydn chose England in spite of all the problems connected with such a venture. In a way, to go to England required more courage than a journey to Italy; it was, to a far greater extent, a step into the unknown. Haydn spoke and wrote Italian fluently and was used to working with Italian singers. But he did not know a word of English and had no chance of becoming even slightly conversant with it before reaching that country. The journey itself was more complicated, too, for it entailed the dreaded crossing of the Channel, which, even a hundred years later, deterred a less intrepid nature, that of Johannes Brahms, from accepting an honorary degree at Cambridge. In Haydn's time, crossing the Channel was certainly no minor venture, even for people brought up near the sea. There was the tragicomic experience of Dr. Burney, for instance. After leaving Calais on a stormy December day he had been "so nearly annihilated by his sufferings," that on arriving at Dover he had not enough energy left to move. Some time later, when he came out of his torpor, he found himself, to his unspeakable horror, on the way back to France. Haydn may have heard stories of this kind. Even if he had not, his Viennese friends did not restrain themselves from pointing out all the dangers awaiting a man fifty-eight years old starting for the first time on a great journey. But all their Cassandra-like cries were in vain, for the very novelty of the prospective experiences attracted Haydn. He was brimful of energy, in excellent health, and felt himself able to cope with any difficulty. So, when Mozart exclaimed, "Oh, Papa, you have had no education for the wide world, and you speak so few languages," Haydn answered serenely, "But my language is understood all over the world."

In his attitude Haydn was greatly sustained by Salomon, who became Haydn's shadow in his anxiety not to lose this invaluable prize. They got on very well together, in Vienna as well as in London, so that at a much later date Haydn spoke of Salomon as his "dearest friend." It therefore seems appropriate to say a few words about the artist who played an important part in the history of music by taking Haydn to England.

Johann Peter Salomon was born in 1745 at Bonn, the birthplace of Beethoven, and it is worthy of record that for some time the Salomons shared a house with the Beethoven family. In 1816, Beethoven wrote to Ferdinand Ries: "Salomon's death grieves me deeply, for he was a noble-minded man whom I remember well ever since I was a child." Salomon was an eminent violinist who filled various positions in Germany and, in 1781, went to England, where he soon won success and a great reputation. A correspondent for the *Berliner Musikzeitung*,[1] after praising Viotti as the greatest living violinist in Europe, declared that Salomon almost equaled him as a virtuoso, though not as a composer. In 1786, Salomon began to give subscription concerts, successfully competing with the older series of the Professional Concerts. He had been an ardent admirer of Haydn for a long time, and it was for these concerts that

[1] *Berliner Musikzeitung* (June 29, 1793).

he wanted to engage the master. It chanced that he was at Cologne, on his way to Italy, when he heard of Prince Nicolaus Esterházy's death. Taking the next coach, he rushed to Vienna and carried Haydn off in triumph. This was generally considered to be Salomon's greatest achievement. It is noteworthy that on his tomb in the cloisters of Westminster Abbey the tablet with his dates contains the remark: "He brought Haydn to England in 1791 and 1794."[2]

Despite Haydn's eagerness for the great adventure, it was by no means easy for him to tear himself away from Vienna, to which he was bound by so many ties. There was Marianne von Genzinger, whom he had so greatly pined for at Eszterháza. How delightful it was now to go regularly to her lovely home, to have long and friendly chats, and to make music together! Haydn's sad feelings on leaving this cherished companion could not be better expressed than in the "Farewell Song" for a lady friend. Words like "now when we have just begun to know each other well we have to part" and "think of me when sea and land are between us," with their tenderness and gentle melancholy, might well have been uttered by the composer himself. The song is not by Haydn, but by Adalbert Gyrowetz.[3] However, it is not unlikely that Haydn got hold of it, somewhat revised it, and in this improved form handed it to his friend, or sang it to her when taking his leave.

It was probably easier to leave Luigia Polzelli, for whom his passion had somewhat subsided. Luigia, of course, had also lost her position at Eszterháza and moved to Vienna. Her husband, who had been failing rapidly, died in a hospital a few months after Haydn's departure. She depended mainly on Haydn's financial support and would have liked very much to go to England with him. But this was out of the question for so mediocre a singer, and Haydn much preferred to get engagements for her in Italy.

Finally there was the parting from his beloved Mozart. They spent the last day together, both deeply moved. When they said good-bye, Mozart exclaimed with tears: "I am afraid, Papa, this will be our last farewell." Neither of the friends could guess the terrible truth in these prophetic words.

On December 15, 1790, Haydn and Salomon set forth on their journey, which was made as rapidly as possible because the manager was eager to start the preparations for his subscription series.

---

[2] Cf. *HCaW*, IV, p. 27.
[3] Cf. Alexander Weinmann, "Joseph Haydn's 'Abschiedslied,'" *HYb* II, (1964), p. 88. Up to now the piece has appeared in all editions of Haydn's songs.

Only two stops of any length were made, one at Munich, the other at Bonn, where, according to Griesinger, Haydn was received very cordially and introduced to the court orchestra, of which young Beethoven was a member. On New Year's Eve the travelers arrived at Calais, and Haydn, in a short note to Marianne, described himself as "very well, although somewhat thinner, owing to fatigue, irregular sleep, and eating and drinking so many different things." Appropriately enough, it was on New Year's Day that Haydn started his life in England. The journey itself seems to have been but moderately unpleasant and, unless Haydn was boasting to his friend, this elderly man, who had never seen the sea before, had stood on firmer sea legs than most of his fellow passengers. Anyway this is how he described the great event to Marianne:[4]

> I must now tell you that on New Year's Day, after attending early Mass, I went on board at 7:30 AM, and at five in the afternoon arrived safe and well at Dover, for which Heaven be praised! During the first four hours there was scarcely any wind and the vessel made so little way that in that time we went only one English mile. Fortunately toward eleven-thirty such a favorable breeze began to blow that by four o'clock we had come twenty-two miles. I remained on deck during the whole passage, in order to gaze my fill at that huge monster, the ocean. So long as there was a calm I had no fears, but when at length a violent wind began to blow, rising every minute, and I saw the boisterous waves rushing on, I was seized with slight alarm, and a little indisposition likewise. But I overcame it all and arrived safely in harbor without being actually sick. Most of the passengers were ill and looked like ghosts. I did not feel the fatigue of the journey until I arrived in London, but it took two days before I could recover from it. But now I am quite fresh and well, and occupied in looking at this mighty and vast town of London, its various beauties and marvels causing me the most profound astonishment.

Haydn's "astonishment" can well be imagined. What his young friend, Adalbert Gyrowetz, expressed in his autobiography (written in the third person) may also reflect the older master's attitude:

[4]Letter of January 8, 1791.

"The first moment Gyrowetz stood on English soil, he felt as if he were seeing a new world. Everything was different: a different air, a different architecture, different regulations, different customs, the highest degree of cleanliness in everything, and quite different people." And Gyrowetz had traveled a great deal through Italy and France, whereas Haydn had never before been beyond a small section of his own country, a territory corresponding in area approximately to that of the state of Connecticut.

It was not only the strangeness of English life that made Haydn's head whirl; it was also the size of London and its enormous traffic. The figures relating to London's population interested him tremendously. We find twice in his diary[5] a remark that in thirty-one years thirty-eight thousand houses had been built in London, that in 1791, twenty-two thousand persons died in this city, that it consumed annually eight hundred thousand cartloads of coal and kept four thousand carts for cleaning the streets. London fascinated and at the same time frightened him. "The noise in the streets and the cries of the common people selling their wares" seemed "unbearable" to him. As to the traffic, we can well imagine what Haydn felt if we refer to a letter that Horace Walpole wrote in 1791 to Miss Berry:

> Though London increases every day, the town cannot hold all its inhabitants, so prodigiously is the population augmented. I have twice been going to stop my coach in Piccadilly, thinking there was a mob, but it was only nymphs and swains sauntering. The other morning I was stopped five times before I reached Northumberland House, for the tides of coaches, chariots, and phaetons are endless. Indeed, the town is so extended that the breed of chairs is almost lost, for Hercules and Atlas could not carry anybody from one end of this enormous capital to the other.

[5] There exist three diaries (or notebooks) from the English visits. Two, preserved by the National Library, Vienna, refer to his first stay; one, in the Mozarteum, Salzburg, refers to the second. An additional notebook from the second visit must have existed, since Griesinger and Dies quoted excerpts from it, but it cannot be traced today. Large sections of the first two notebooks were translated in H. E. Krehbiel, *Music and Manners* (New York, 1898). The third diary has been reprinted by Johann Evangelist Engl, *Joseph Haydns handschriftliches Tagebuch aus der Zeit seines zweiten Aufenthaltes in London, 1794 und 1795* (Leipzig, 1909). Landon in *The Collected Correspondence and London Notebooks of Joseph Haydn* (London, 1959), p. 251ff., translates and reprints all three notebooks and reconstructs the missing fourth from the excerpts reproduced by Griesinger and Dies.

Added to these difficulties was the strange tongue. Perhaps Haydn was right in assuming that he, with his music, could make himself understood everywhere, but it was another matter for him to understand others. This elderly man with the soul of a youth was filled with insatiable curiosity regarding all aspects of English life, and he did not like at all being left out of anything. John Taylor in his *Records of My Life* describes a dinner party at the house of the singer Madame Mara that was attended by the satirist Dr. John Wolcot (Peter Pindar), and the violoncellist, John Crosdill,[6] and continues:

> Before the wine was removed, Mr. Salomon arrived and brought Haydn with him. They were both old friends of Madame Mara. Haydn did not know a word of English. As soon as we knew who he was, Crosdill proposed that we should celebrate the arrival of Haydn with "three times three." This proposal was warmly adopted and commenced, all parties except Haydn standing up. He heard his name mentioned, but not understanding this species of congratulation, stared at us in surprise. He was so confused by this unexpected and novel greeting that he put his hands before his face and was quite disconcerted for some minutes.

Incidents like that must have happened often enough. Haydn, of course, did his best to study English and in the early mornings he used to walk in the woods alone with his English grammar,[7] but for him to follow and take part in the conversations of his new English friends was a continuous strain.

The numerous old acquaintances that Haydn renewed in London were a great help. The British capital attracted artists and virtuosos from all corners of the earth. When Haydn visited there, it was one of the most important centers of music (although the British composers of the time could not compare with those of Vienna). The most eminent musicians flocked to England, received great honors and excellent salaries, and helped to build up a musical life which, in volume at least, was quite dazzling. Many of these artists had been in Vienna, and with them Haydn naturally established contact.

[6] Crosdill was the violoncello teacher of the Prince of Wales.
[7] Letter to Marianne dated September 17, 1791.

Mention has already been made of Adalbert Gyrowetz, whom Haydn had met years before at the private concerts of their common friend, Hofrat von Kees.[8] Gyrowetz had arrived in London two years before Haydn; he was a great success and moved freely in society. According to his autobiography, he helped Haydn by introducing him to the right people.

There was also Gertrude Elisabeth Mara, a singer of German origin who had captivated London by the "irresistible fire, dignity, and tenderness of her vocal appeal" (Gardiner) at the Handel Festival of 1784. Madame Mara had been in Vienna in 1780, after escaping from Prussia, where King Friedrich II had held her almost as a captive because of his enthusiasm for her art. Haydn admired her and was glad to have Salomon engage her for appearances at his own concerts.

The distinguished Croatian violinist, Giovanni Mane Giornovichi, who according to Dittersdorf, played "with art and heart," was also known to our master from his participation in the von Kees concerts.

One of the most successful pianists in London was Muzio Clementi. Haydn had probably met him in 1782, when Clementi had gone to Vienna for his contest with Mozart on the pianoforte. Clementi apparently was fond of Haydn, for he presented him with a goblet made of coconut shell adorned with rich silver ornaments.

Haydn also had friendly relations with the Czech pianist Jan Ladislav Dussek, who lent him his own excellent piano when the master moved to a more rural apartment in Lisson Grove. In a charming letter to Dussek's father,[9] Haydn described the son as "one of the most upright, moral, and, in music, most eminent of men."

Stephen and Nancy Storace were delighted to meet Haydn again. He had visited them and played chamber music at their home in Vienna. The master's diary, in mentioning a dinner with them on June 3, 1792, adds the obscure remark "sapienti pauca," which may have meant that the food offered was not too plentiful. Among the Storaces' circle of friends was Michael Kelly, the Irish tenor, returned to London from Vienna, where he had sung Don Basilio and

---

[8] Gyrowetz in his autobiography of 1848 (new edition by Alfred Einstein [Leipzig, 1915]) describes his first meeting with various masters at the von Kees house as follows: "Haydn smiled a bit roguishly, Dittersdorf was serious, Albrechtsberger quite indifferent, Giornovichi somewhat somber though noblehearted, and Mozart the kindest of all."

[9] Letter of February 26, 1792.

Don Curzio at the premiere of *Le nozze di Figaro*. He probably was not a great creative musician—this is implied at least by Sheridan's remark that "Kelly composed his wines and imported his music"—but he was a pleasant companion, and Haydn could chat with him about their various mutual friends in Vienna.

Another man who, though not personally known to Haydn, had been corresponding with him for some time, was the great musicologist, Dr. Charles Burney. He welcomed the master with an enthusiastic poem, and one of Haydn's first visits was to Chelsea College, where the English scholar held the post of organist.

Such was the circle of fellow musicians who gathered around Haydn, a circle that was to be greatly widened during the following eighteen months. And there was always Salomon, who helped Haydn get a footing in the strange and fascinating new world into which he had been plunged. To find one's way through the intricacies of London's musical life, with all its different currents and undercurrents, was indeed not easy and Haydn needed Salomon's guidance. A preview that appeared in the *Morning Chronicle* on December 30, 1790, may help us to get some idea of the number of musical events in the British capital:

> The musical arrangements now being made promise a most harmonious winter. Besides two rival opera houses a Concert [meaning a whole series] is planned under the auspices of Haydn, whose name is a tower of strength, and to whom the amateurs of instrumental music look as the god of the science. Of this concert Salomon is to be the leader and Madame Mara the principal singer.
>
> The Professional Concerts under the able conducting of Cramer, are to be reinforced by Mrs. Billington, assisted occasionally by Mr. and Mrs. Harrison.
>
> The Ancient Concerts under the patronage of Their Majesties will continue soon after the Queen's birthday, with Cramer as their leader and Storace as the principal singer. The Ladies' Subscription Concerts are to be continued as usual on Sunday evenings by permission (we hope) of His Grace the Archbishop of Canterbury.
>
> There will be oratorios twice a week at the theaters of Drury Lane and Covent Garden during Lent.
>
> These, with the Academy of Ancient Music will constitute the principal public musical entertainments of this winter.

Five different subscription series of orchestral concerts—an amazing quantity of music to be offered to a city of less than a million inhabitants. And all this was eagerly absorbed. Most of the concerts were crowded; thus, on the very day when Haydn's sensational first concert took place, oratorio performances in the two theatres also had very full houses. Present-day historians might find the artistic standard of the London audiences of 1791 not high enough—Marion Scott, for instance, in her delightful study "Haydn in England"[10] warns us against mistaking quantity for quality. Anyway, it cannot be denied that the Londoners of Haydn's time loved music very much and that it was natural for them to hear a good deal of it and, if we may believe Gyrowetz,[11] also to perform it. To be sure, the element of competition played some little part in rousing the public's interest in the various concerts. There was, for instance, a fierce rivalry between the English and the Italian opera (Covent Garden versus the Pantheon), between the Professional Concerts and the Salomon series, rivalries in which the press took a very active part. But this was a common occurrence in the eighteenth century, and London certainly took such matters no more passionately than Paris did. Leaving aside those snobs who went to the concerts only for the sake of fashion or faction, enough sincere music lovers remained to give Haydn the satisfaction of being truly valued and understood.

Returning to that memorable New Year's Day of 1791, when Haydn set foot on English soil, we find the master spending his first night at 45 High Holborn, the home of John Bland, who had visited Haydn at Eszterháza. Haydn's host received him with open arms and good pea soup (which meant much to our master, for in a letter to Marianne he pined for her delicious soups). Mrs. Bland may have somewhat disconcerted this lover of female beauty at first sight for she was "short and fat, pitted with smallpox and on the whole the most inharmonious-looking person that can be imagined."[12] Later, however, Haydn may have learned to share the general verdict that "when she sang, she threw a charm and magic on all she did that was perfectly entrancing."

The next day Haydn moved to a "neat, comfortable, though very expensive" lodging provided by Salomon in the house where

---

[10] Marion M. Scott, "Haydn in England," *Musical Quarterly*, XVIII/2 (Apr. 1932).

[11] He writes in his autobiography: "The girls are mostly musical and either well versed in the pianoforte or in singing, and know how to spend their evenings very pleasantly in this way. The men, however, are slightly or not at all musical, but they love to listen to music."

[12] Henry Phillips, *Musical and Personal Recollections* (London, 1864).

he himself lived (18 Great Pulteney Street, Golden Square). The Italian landlord was an excellent cook, and Haydn would have liked to enjoy the meals he offered in the sole company of Salomon, so as gradually to get his bearings. This was not to be, however, for Salomon had paved the way for Haydn extremely well. The newspapers made much of his arrival, and when Haydn wrote to Marianne on January 8, he confessed that he had "already dined out six times" in this first week and that he could be invited every day if he chose.

With a certain naïve pride Haydn describes his social life in a letter to Prince Esterházy,[13] significant in that its tone definitely deviates from that of former letters to the princely patron. Here Haydn is incomparably less submissive, and one has the impression that in 1791 it would not have occurred to him to employ such an expression as "kissing the hem of the princely coat," which was used by him in 1766. Thus, just eight days after his arrival in England the process of detaching himself from the way of life known to him for thirty years had begun. He wrote:

> I report respectfully that despite very poor weather and many bad roads throughout the journey I arrived safe and sound in London on January 2. My arrival caused a great sensation and forced me to move on the very same evening to larger quarters. I am so burdened with visitors that I will hardly be able to reciprocate within six weeks. Both ambassadors called, that is, Prince Castelcicala of Naples and Baron von Stadion. I also had the privilege of having dinner with them at six in the evening.
>
> The new opera libretto I have to compose is entitled *Orfeo*, in five acts, and I will receive it one of these days. It is said to be quite different from that used by Gluck. The prima donna is Madame Lops of Munich, a pupil of the great Mingotti, seconda donna is Madame Capelletti, primo homo the famous Davide. The opera is only for three persons, Madame Lops, Davide, and a castrato who is said to be not very outstanding. Moreover, it is to contain many choruses and ballets and great changes of scenery.
>
> In a fortnight the first opera, *Pirro*, by Paisiello will

---

[13] Valkó I, p. 55. The letter is dated January 8, 1791.

be presented. The concerts will start only next month, on February 11, about which I will later dutifully report to Your Highness, and meanwhile I remain, Your Serenity's

Respectful and most obedient

Haydn

I venture respectfully to kiss the hands of the most beautiful Princess, Your Highness' charming wife, as well as of Princess Marie and Her Highness' husband.

My address for the time being is: No. 18 Great Pulteney Street, Golden Square, London.

Besides making social contacts Haydn was eager to get a true impression of English musical life. He attended various concerts, at which great honors were bestowed on the illustrious guest, and the impressions he received from the size and high quality of the English orchestras were responsible for various alterations he made in the works he had brought with him.

Eighteen days after his arrival he made his real debut in society. He was invited to the court ball given in honor of the Queen's birthday, and to the amazement of the guests was greeted very respectfully by the Prince of Wales, though he had not yet been presented at court. Haydn was very favorably impressed by this "most handsome man on God's earth," as he once described him to Marianne.[14] Indeed, the appearance of the future George IV must have been dazzling even to one used to Prince Esterházy's splendor, for on this occasion he wore diamonds worth some eighty thousand pounds. The next day Haydn's interest in the Prince was heightened further, for when he was invited to take part in one of the famous musical evenings at Carlton House, the residence of the Prince, he found that his host possessed "an extraordinary love of music, and a great deal of feeling."[15] The chamber music, played by Haydn, Salomon, and Giornovichi, and sung by the Italian tenor Davide, took place in the small music room, the "jewel" of Carlton House. Again Haydn's impressions may best be expressed in the words of

[14]Letter dated December 20, 1791.
[15]The following story mentioned by Carl Ferdinand Pohl in *Mozart und Haydn in London* (Vienna, 1867) proves the Prince's musical aptitude. When he was three years old, he heard the violinist F.-H. Barthélemon and was so impressed by the "harmonics" the artist produced that he exclaimed: "There must be a flute hidden in the violin," and eagerly tried to find its hiding place.

Horace Walpole: "In all the fairy tales you never were in so pretty a scene. Madam, I forgot to tell you, how admirably all the carving, stucco, and ornaments are executed, but whence the money is to come, I conceive not—all the tin mines in Cornwall would not pay a quarter."

The Prince's gigantic debts were known even to Haydn. He mentioned the fact to Marianne, adding anxiously: "*Nota bene*, this is *entre nous*." He need not have worried on this account, as the Prince's financial problems were a common topic of conversation. But although His Royal Highness was generally considered to be "above a low attention to pecuniary matters,"[16] Haydn was one of the very few musicians rewarded adequately for his work. Following the advice of English friends, he sent on his return to Vienna to the commissioners of Parliament a bill for one hundred guineas as the honorarium for twenty-six appearances at Carlton House and obtained prompt payment.

Haydn, by the way, seems also to have enjoyed the fare offered by his royal host. Anyway, he took pains to note in his diary the recipe of the Prince of Wales's punch as follows: "one bottle champagne, one bottle burgundy, one bottle rum, ten lemons, two oranges, a pound-and-a-half of sugar."

While the master was starting on an extremely successful social career under the auspices of the Prince of Wales, he was at first prevented from appearing in public in his real capacity. Salomon, though most eager to open his concert series at the earliest possible moment, found himself unable to carry out his intention. For the first concert he had engaged the singer, Giacomo Davide, the "first tenor of his time," as Lord Mount-Edgcumbe described him. Signor Davide, however, was under contract to make his first public appearance in the Italian opera at the King's Theater and as (for reasons to be mentioned later) that performance could not take place, Salomon was twice forced to postpone his concert. This was most fortunate for the rival enterprise, the Professional Concerts, which started on February 7. Considerately a symphony and a quartet by Haydn were performed and the composer received a free ticket of admission to all the concerts. Haydn went and declared that he had never heard a symphony of his played so well. In spite of this exchange of courtesies, Salomon's rivals were not above circulating rumors injurious to the visiting composer. Remarks could

---

[16]Letter of Lady Montagu, the "Queen of the Bluestockings," dated June 4, 1795.

be overheard or read in certain newspapers that Haydn, although undoubtedly a great composer, was after all an old man whose powers were exhausted and who was bound to disappoint the high expectations of British friends of music. Haydn could not help being aware of such undercurrents. He tried not to let them discourage him, and with characteristic persistence, used the extra time to rehearse most carefully, playing important passages to the orchestra on the violin and gradually imbuing them with a perfect understanding of his ideas and wishes.

When the great day finally came, he swept the London audience completely off its feet. The concert took place on March 11, 1791, at the famous Hanover Square rooms, the scene of so many great events in music. Opened in 1775 by Johann Christian Bach, they were destined, after Haydn's triumphs, to witness the spectacular appearances of Liszt, Rubinstein, Mendelssohn, Joachim, and many others, until they were closed in 1874. Haydn's audience was a very brilliant one: the ladies all in hoops, the gentlemen in full dress with swords, the solo performers preceded by the sword-bearer who girded them in front of the audience with a special weapon. The artists Salomon had engaged were of the first class and earned much applause. The climax was reached with Haydn's new symphony (No. 92).[17] At the special request of the composer, it was played as the first number of the second part, Haydn hoping that by that time the many latecomers would be in their seats. The orchestra was much stronger than the Esterházy ensemble. It contained some forty players, including sixteen violins, four violas, three violoncellos, and four double basses. Salomon was the leader, playing on a Stradivarius instrument that had previously belonged to Corelli, and Haydn conducted from the pianoforte. Dr. Burney attended the concert and described the reaction of the public in the strongest words he could think of, speaking of Haydn's "electrifying" the audience so as to "excite . . . a pleasure superior to any that had ever been caused by instrumental music in England." The slow movement of the symphony had to be encored, and this made Haydn so proud that he asked Griesinger to record this "unusual occurrence." To Luigia Polzelli he reported[18] the fact adding that, he was told, such a thing had never before happened in London.

---

[17] We follow herein Landon's (*HCaW*, III, p. 53ff) lengthy discussion concerning the symphony performed at Haydn's first concert. Number 93, which was generally assumed to be the choice for the first concert, had its premiere in 1792.
[18] Letter of March 14, 1791.

"Imagine," he wrote, "what it means to hear this from an English-man's lips!" March 11 definitely assured Haydn's success in English musical life, and it is significant that the *Morning Chronicle* ended its report with the words: "We cannot suppress our very anxious hope that the first musical genius of his age may be induced by our liberal welcome to take up his residence in England."

The succeeding concerts of the series, taking place from March to June, were a continuous triumph; the peak was reached with Haydn's benefit concert on May 16, when he earned three hundred fifty pounds, almost double what had been guaranteed to him.

The brilliant success won in the Salomon concerts had far-reaching consequences. It increased Haydn's confidence in himself enormously. He had, of course, before his journey to London, re-ceived numerous proofs of his outstanding reputation in various countries. Still, it is one thing to read an enthusiastic letter and another to experience directly the response of a huge and brilliant audience. This was a novel sensation for the master, used to per-forming his works mostly to a very small and intimate circle of musical connoisseurs. The frenzied applause he was given by the exacting audience of the world's largest capital did not go to his head; it was only a challenge for him to offer London the very best he could give. Haydn's creative powers were taxed to the utmost, and the result took the form of the twelve London symphonies (six of them written for his first stay in London, six for his second) in which Haydn's music for orchestra attained its very climax. For these masterworks the musical world has to thank London; it is indeed doubtful that Haydn's genius would ever have unfolded so brilliantly without the stimulus of his English adventures.

On the other hand, Haydn's presence in London gave British music an inspiration and impetus of the greatest value which ulti-mately reached far beyond the frontiers of Great Britain. Musicians who had the privilege of playing under him or, at least, of becom-ing acquainted with the master's interpretation of his own works, traveled from London to the New World, taking with them an in-sight into how Haydn's works should be performed. There is a direct line from Haydn to such pioneers of American musical life as Graupner, Menel, Hewitt, and Bergmann.

Haydn's triumph was crowned, so to speak, at the instigation of the faithful Dr. Burney, when he was invited in July 1791 to the Oxford Commemoration in order to receive the honorary degree of Doctor of Music. Unlike Brahms, who received a similar invitation from Cambridge, Haydn went and was immensely feted. Three concerts took place on this occasion with brilliant soloists, among them "little Clement," for whom Beethoven was to write his violin concerto. As a thesis Haydn was obliged to offer a new symphony. The work in G major (No. 92), composed in 1788 for the Comte d'Ogny, was chosen, and thenceforth was named the Oxford Symphony. Later Haydn sent the university as his "exercise" a three-part canon cancrizans, *Thy Voice, O Harmony*. Haydn felt strange in his doctor's gown of cherry-and-cream-colored silk, which he had to wear for three days. But he was not above a bit of naïve pride. "I only wish my Viennese friends could have seen me," he wrote to Marianne. In his diary he commented on the event in these words only: "I had to pay one-and-a-half guineas for the bell peals at Oxforth [*sic*] when I received the doctor's degree, and half a guinea for renting the gown. The journey cost six guineas." This matter-of-fact statement is not surprising, as Haydn never expressed any personal feelings in his notebook, but confined himself to jotting down mere facts. A letter to Marianne on the event mentioned by Haydn apparently did not reach her. To his biographer, Dies, however, Haydn stressed the importance of the degree, to which he owed, as he declared, "much, I might say everything, in England; for thanks to it I met the first men and was admitted to the most important houses." Although this seems to be somewhat exaggerated, it is certain that the man, who still remembered so well how he had striven desperately as a penniless youth to instruct himself in all that Reutter had failed to teach him, felt satisfaction in signing his letters wih the words "Doctor zu Oxford." After being acclaimed as a fellow scholar by one of the oldest universities of the world, Haydn easily could disregard those critics in the German-speaking countries who had found his music too light and not learned enough.

Strangely there is no comment in Haydn's notebook on the exquisite buildings of Oxford. Perhaps he was too much occupied with rehearsals and social functions to take in all the beauty around him. That he observed such things when traveling in a more leisurely way is shown by his account of Cambridge, which he visited in November of the same year:

> Each university has at the back of it a very roomy and beautiful garden, besides stone bridges, in order to afford passage over the stream that winds past. The King's Chapel

is famous for its carvings. It is all stone and so delicate that nothing more beautiful could have been made of wood. It has already endured four hundred years, yet everybody judges its age at about ten years because of the firmness and peculiar whiteness of the stone . . .

At this time, when Haydn was reaping the greatest triumphs as a symphonic composer, his efforts in the domain of opera were doomed to failure. In accord with his contract with Sir John Gallini, he worked during the first part of his stay in London on the opera *L'anima del filosofo*, based on a book by Badini. He had completed the work (having written one hundred and ten pages, hardly less than the scores of all the first six London symphonies) when it turned out that Gallini was unable to perform the opera for reasons beyond his control. The old Italian opera at the Pantheon was supported by the monarch, and the management exerted all its influence to prevent a second Italian opera from being established in the King's Theater. Although the Prince of Wales espoused Gallini's cause, the Pantheon's adherents pointed out that two Italian opera houses were not needed. Haydn's opera was to be performed in May, but after long controversies Gallini was refused a license for opera altogether in this "edifice, grand and capacious beyond all parallel" (*London Chronicle*). When Haydn was conducting the first rehearsal, officials appeared and forced him to stop after forty measures had been played. Gallini had to be content with arranging entertainments of music and dancing, using the soloists he had engaged. Frequently Haydn's music, such as the chorus "The Storm" (on words by Peter Pindar, pseudonym for John Wolcot), was included. There was now no opportunity for a performance of *L'anima del filosofo*; nevertheless Gallini paid the agreed-upon sum for the composition. The composer naturally regretted having spent so much time on this work, but it seems that he was not especially interested in it, for he never had it performed elsewhere. As for Gallini, who had paid three hundred pounds without being able to produce the opera, no pity need be wasted on him, for in spite of various accidents during his career as a manager he left the tidy sum of £150,000 when death took him in 1805.

Although Haydn's creative output in the field of opera came to an abrupt end in England, it was there that he received the incentive to enter a new field. Here again we have to thank London for a most decisive influence on Haydn's work.

In 1784 a Handel Commemoration on a gigantic scale took place in Westminister Abbey, celebrating the centenary of that master's birth. Its success was so great that similar performances were arranged in the three succeeding years. Then an interval of four years followed, after which a Handel Festival of the same kind took place in May 1791, with Haydn among the enraptured audience. William Gardiner gives a lively description of the scene:

On entering the Abbey I was filled with surprise at the magnitude of the orchestra; it rose nearly to the top of the west window and above the arches of the main aisle. On each side there was a tier of projecting galleries and I was placed in one of these. Above us were the trumpeters and appended to their instruments were richly embossed banners worked in silver and gold. We had flags of the same description which gave the whole a gorgeous and magnificent appearance. The arrangement of the performers was admirable, particularly that of the sopranos. The young ladies were placed upon a framework in the center of the band in the form of a pyramid, as you see flowerpots set up for a show. This greatly improved the musical effect. The band was a thousand strong, ably conducted by Joah Bates upon the organ. The orchestra was so steep that it was dangerous to come down and some accidents occurred, one being of a ludicrous nature. A person falling upon a double bass, as it lay on its side, immediately disappeared; nothing was seen of him but his legs protruding out of the instrument. For some time no one could assist him for laughing. Haydn was present at this performance and with the aid of a telescope, which had been placed on a stand near the kettledrums, I saw the composer near the king's box. The performance attracted persons from all parts of Europe and the demand for tickets was so great that in some instances a single one was sold for twenty pounds.

The female fashions of the day were found highly inconvenient, particularly the headdresses, and it was ordered that no caps should be admitted of a larger size than the pattern exhibited at the Lord Chamberlain's office. As everyone wore powder, notwithstanding a vast influx of hairdressers from the country, such was the demand for these artists, that many ladies submitted to have their hair dressed the previous evening and sat up all night to be ready for the early admission in the morning.

We do not know how familiar Haydn was with Handel's oratorios before he went to England, but certainly he had never heard anything like the performance in Westminster Abbey. Although Hadow contends that the number of 1068 performers frequently mentioned is exaggerated, it must have been gigantic. Listening to the immortal masterworks performed by the enormous musical body in one of the loveliest churches of the world, feeling the veneration with which Handel's music was received "in a silence almost devotional" (Mount-Edgcumbe) by an audience taught by their king to see in this music the most sublime achievement, Haydn was so deeply moved that at the "Hallelujah" chorus, when all the audience, including the royal family, rose to their feet, he burst into tears, exclaiming: "He is the master of us all." He was tremendously impressed at finding Handel's oratorios still so alive in the hearts of the English people, and he may have conceived at that time the plan of trying his hand at this form.

On another occasion in the following year, Haydn was deeply stirred by great choral masses. This time he wrote in his diary: "No music has ever moved me so much in my life as this devout and innocent one," which is the only emotional utterance in the entire notebook. Haydn referred here to the annual meeting of the charity children at St. Paul's Cathedral, when he heard four thousand children sing a hymn by the organist of the cathedral, John Jones. (Haydn's profound emotion was shared, many years later, by Hector Berlioz and his companion, the tenor Louis-Gilbert Duprez, who "wept and raved.")

Truly, England had revealed to Haydn what human voices in great numbers can accomplish. The consequences of such experiences were to manifest themselves later when he again had firm ground under his feet. At the moment he was unable to start on any new experiment in composition, for he was too much absorbed by the various aspects of the fascinating new country, which he was determined to explore as fully as he possibly could. Through the summer and autumn, when concert activities had ceased, he traveled and visited and had a wonderful time. This does not mean that he stopped working, for he had to prepare for the next season, but that he was free to go wherever he pleased without asking anybody's permission and to indulge in any passing whim. In a way it was the first vacation for this man of fifty-nine. The following outburst in a letter[19] to Marianne is characteristic: "Oh, my dear gracious lady, how sweet is some degree of liberty! I had a kind prince, but was obliged at times to be dependent on base souls. I often sighed for release and now I have it in some measure. I am quite sensible of this benefit, though my mind is burdened with more work. The consciousness of being no longer a bond servant sweetens all my toil."

Some of the visits Haydn paid at this time are mentioned in his diary. For instance we find the following entry: "In the month of August I journeyed at noon in an East India merchantman with six cannon. I was gloriously entertained. In this month, too, I went with Mr. Fraser on the Thames from Westminster Bridge to Richmond, where we had dinner on an island. We were twenty-four persons and a wind band." (How Haydn, with his deep love of nature, must have enjoyed the picnic in such a beautiful spot!)

For five weeks he was "very well entertained" in the house of the rich banker, Mr. Brassey, teaching his daughter at the same time. His hosts, with typical English tact, left him alone as much as he chose, and Haydn describes his life to Marianne in these words: "I have been residing in the country, with a banker, whose heart and family resemble the Genzingers' [what higher compliment could he pay to the Brasseys?], and where I live as if I were in a monastery." After the noise of London, which caused him much suffering, the quiet and peace of the English countryside must have done him a great deal of good. Unfortunately a letter from his patron caused him some worry. Prince Esterházy complained of his long absence, and exacted, as Haydn described it, "his speedy return in the most absolute terms" because he wanted him to compose an opera for a fete planned in honor of the Emperor. Haydn could not comply with the request because he had already concluded a contract with Salomon for the coming season. He had to inform the Prince accordingly, which was not easy for a man used to obeying every demand coming from an Esterházy, and he expected his dismissal and the cancellation of his pension. None of this happened, however, as even an unmusical Esterházy like Prince Anton was too conscious of the renown that his connection with the world-famous composer gave him to desire to sever it.

In September, Haydn again took up his residence in London, but since concert life was almost stagnant during the months before the New Year, he frequently interrupted his work to make visits

[19]Letter of September 17, 1791.

and trips to the country or to attend important official functions. His diary devotes a long description to the dinner of the new lord mayor on November 5, which he attended, sitting at the second table with Mr. Silvester, the "greatest lawyer and first alderman of London." Haydn was naturally interested in the music played on this occasion, and his comments are not very flattering, though quite amusing. Mentioning the small hall where he first watched the dancing, he wrote:

> Nothing but minuets are danced in this room; but I could not stay longer than a quarter of an hour. First, because of the heat caused by so many people being crowded into so small a room; secondly, because of the wretched dance band, two violins and one violoncello composing the whole orchestra. The minuets were more Polish than German or Italian. Then I went into another room that looked more like a subterranean cave. There the dance was English and the music was a little better because there was a drum that drowned the blunders of the fiddlers. I went on to the great hall where we had dined; here the music was more tolerable. The dance was English but only on the elevated platform where the Lord Mayor and the first four members had dined. The other tables were all occupied again by men who, as usual, drank right lustily all night long. The most curious thing of all, however, was the fact that a part of the company danced on without hearing a note of the music, for first at one table, then at another, some were howling songs and some drinking toasts amid the maddest shrieks of Hurrah! Hurrah! and the waving of glasses.

Very different is the description of the three days during which Haydn stayed at Oatlands, the castle where the Duke of York was spending his honeymoon. The bride of seventeen was a daughter of the music-loving King Friedrich Wilhelm II of Prussia (whose beautiful ring Haydn valued so much). It gave her the greatest pleasure to meet the composer whose music she knew quite well, and Haydn was received in the most gracious way by the young couple as well as by the Prince of Wales, who was responsible for the invitation. He wrote about it to Marianne:[20]

[20]Letter of December 20, 1791.

The duchess is the most charming lady in the world, possesses much intelligence, plays the piano, and sings very pleasingly. She remained beside me from ten o'clock at night, when the music began, until two hours after midnight. No compositions were played but Haydn's. I directed the symphonies at the piano. The sweet little lady sat close beside me at my left hand and hummed all the pieces from memory, having heard them often in Berlin. The Prince of Wales sat on my right and accompanied me very tolerably on the violoncello. They made me sing, too. The Prince of Wales is having me painted just now[21] and the portrait is to be hung in his private sitting room.

The same month Haydn visited Sir Patrick Blake at Langham, but in spite of having traveled a hundred miles, he left after three days to attend the performance of Shield's comic opera *The Woodman* at Covent Garden. The magnet that drew him was the celebrated singer Mrs. Billington, whom Kelly described as "an angel of beauty and the St. Cecilia of song." These words faithfully reflect the verdict of the majority of Londoners, at least of the male sex. In point of fact, Sir Joshua Reynolds painted Elizabeth Billington as the saintly musician. Haydn, according to the report of Carpani, visited the artist while he was working on the picture and pointed out that a strange mistake had been made: "You have painted her listening to the angels, but you should have represented the angels listening to her." Although the story in this form is inaccurate, as the portrait was painted in 1790 before Haydn arrived in England, it is not unlikely that he made the remark when seeing the completed picture. Nice compliments like that were what endeared Haydn to the ladies. When a scandalous book, the so-called *Memoirs of Mrs. Billington*, appeared, his diary commented indignantly on the "shameless exposure" and continued: "It is said that her character is far from faultless, but that she is a great genius, and all the women hate her because she is so beautiful."

Haydn's caustic report on the performance of *The Woodman* by William Shield is rather interesting:

She [Mrs. Billington] sang rather timidly this evening but very well. The first tenor has a good voice and a fairly good style but he uses the falsetto to excess. He sang a trill

[21] Haydn's portrait by John Hoppner is now in the collection of Buckingham Palace.

on high C and ran up to G. The second tenor tried to imitate him but could not master the change from the natural
voice to the falsetto; besides he is most unmusical. He
creates a new tempo, now three-quarter then two-quarter,
and makes cuts wherever he pleases. But the orchestra is
used to him. The common herd in the galleries, as is the
case in all theaters, is very impertinent, and the performers
are obliged to give encores according to its noisy wishes.
The parterre and all the boxes frequently have to applaud a
great deal to secure a repetition, but they succeeded this
evening with the duet[22] in the third act, which is very
beautiful. The dispute lasted nearly a quarter of an hour
before the parterre and boxes triumphed and the duet was
repeated. The two performers stood in a fright on the
stage, now retiring, now again coming to the front. The
orchestra is sluggish.

Haydn's admiration for Reynold's St. Cecilia by no means
made him less sensitive to other beautiful women. Among the
music that the master took back from England was a song, which
he commented upon: "This song is by Mrs. Hodges, the loveliest
woman I ever saw in my life, and a great pianoforte player." Again,
when Haydn visited his great admirer Mr. Shaw in December 1791,
he found his hostess to be "the most beautiful woman he ever saw."
How pleased he must have been when he noticed that this attractive
lady had prepared a special homage for him. She, her daughters,
and all the ladies present "wore on their headdresses a pearl-colored
band embroidered in gold with the name of Haydn, while Mr.
Shaw wore the name worked on the ends of his collar in the finest
steel beads" (Diary). One can well imagine how Haydn basked in
this atmosphere of beauty and admiration and how he repaid it in
his particular way. Perhaps he sat down at the pianoforte and sang
merry songs to them, with the humor that English people could
appreciate so well.[23]

There were certainly quite a few such innocent friendships with
beautiful women, but they did not prevent the inflammable master
from enjoying a more significant romance as well. This time the

---

[22] The duet is not by Shield, but a piece taken from the Serenata *Solomon* by W.
Boyce. Cf. H. C. Robbins Landon, *Collected Correspondence and London Notebooks of
Haydn* (London, 1959), p. 274.
[23] According to Gyrowetz, it was this singing that made Haydn so popular with his
English hosts.

story can be followed only in the letters of the lady. Haydn copied them faithfully into his notebook, but what happened to the originals is not known. It may be that the lady wanted them returned to her when Haydn left England. None of the master's answers has been traced, nor is there any further mention of the affair in his diary, except for a note of the lady's address. Many years later, Haydn showed the letters to Dies and remarked: "They are letters from an English widow in London who loved me. Though sixty years old, she was still lovely and amiable and in all likelihood I should have married her if I had been single." There must be an error in this statement, committed by either Dies or Haydn, whose memory at that time was not as good as it had been. Haydn indeed was sixty when he became attached to the widow, but his partner was certainly considerably younger. She was a Mrs. Schröter, the widow of Johann Samuel Schröter, who had been music master to the Queen and the first exponent of skilled pianoforte playing in England. Dr. Burney, mentioning the musician Schröter in Rees's *Cyclopedia*, described his wife as "a young lady of considerable fortune." As Schröter was about thirty-six when he died in 1788, his wife would have been approximately eighteen years his senior to conform to Dies's description and certainly not "a young lady" when she married him, after eloping with him to Scotland.[24] It seems more likely that the amiable English widow was about the same age as Marianne von Genzinger. The two ladies had in common a great love of music, and whereas Marianne arranged Haydn's works for the piano, Mrs. Schröter did copying for the composer. Here the similarity ends, however, for the English widow did not show any of Marianne's reserve. There is preserved, for instance, the following love letter, copied in the original spelling from Haydn's diary:

My D[eare]st

Inclosed I send you the verses you was so kind as to lend me, and am very much obliged to you for permitting me to take a copy of them. Pray informe me how you do, and let me know my D[ear] L[ove] when you will dine with me. I shall be happy to see you to dinner either to morrow or Tuesday whichever is most convenient to you. I am truly anxious and impatient to see you

[24] Cf. *The New Grove Dictionary of Music and Musicians* (London: Macmillan, 1980), XVI, p. 747.

and I wish to have as much of your company as possible:
indeed my D[eare]st H[aydn] I feel for you the fondest
and tenderest affection the human heart is capable of, and
I ever am with the firmest attachment my D[eare]st Love
    Most Sincerely, Faithfully and most affectionately

                                                    Yours

Sunday Evening June 10    792

After the last Salomon concert, Mrs. Schröter wrote:

My D[ear]:

    I can not close my Eyes to sleep till I have returned
you ten thousand thanks for the inexpressible delight I
have received from your ever Enchanting compositions
and your incomparably charming performance of them.
Be assured my D[ear] H[aydn]: That among all your numerous admirers no one has listened with more profound
attention, and no one can have such high veneration for
your most brilliant talents as I have. Indeed my D[ear]
L[ove] no tongue can express the gratitude I feel for the
infinite pleasure your Music has given me, accept then
my repeeted thanks for it, and let me also assure you,
with heartfelt affection, that I shall ever consider the happiness of your acquaintance as one of the chief Blessings
of my life, and it is the Sincere wish of my heart to preserve to cultivate and to merit it more and more. I hope
to hear you are quite well. Shall be happy to see you to
dinner and if you can come at three o'clock it would give
me great pleasure, as I should be particularly glad to see
you my D[ear] before the rest of our friends come. God
bless you my D[ear]: I ever am with the firmest and most
perfect attachment

                                                    Yours

Wednesday night June 6th    92

Mrs. Schröter liked to mother Haydn a little. She was always
inquiring about his sleep and his health, and on April 19, 1792, she
wrote: "I am told you was five hours at your Study's yesterday;
indeed my D[ear] L[ove] I am afraid it will hurt you. . . . I almost

tremble for your health, let me prevail on you my much-loved H[aydn] not to keep to your Study's so long at one time. My d[ear] love if you cou'd know how very precious your welfare is to me I flatter myself you wou'd endeavor to preserve it, for my Sake as well as your own."

This sounds as if the lady were pretty sure of Haydn's affection, and indeed there is no reason to assume that he did not respond to the lovely widow's feelings. According to the letters, Haydn must have been a fairly frequent visitor at No. 6 James Street, Buckingham Gate, and the music lessons that first took him there probably soon were considered unimportant.

During the time that Haydn was living through this delightful romance, he regularly exchanged letters with his old love, Luigia Polzelli. It cannot be denied that they are ardent in tone. Once he remarked: "I esteem and love you as I did on the very first day. I am very sorry for you and it pains me terribly that I cannot do more for you. But be patient, perhaps the day will arrive when I can show you how much I love you."[25] And another time he exclaimed: "Oh, my dearest, you will always live in my heart. Never, never, shall I forget you, my beloved."[26] Luigia was at that time in Italy and very eager to go to London, where her sister was living. This of course was the last thing that Haydn wanted, for both personal and professional reasons. It seems likely that in order to dissuade her and at the same time extinguish her innate (and probably well-founded) jealousy, Haydn expressed more passion than he really felt. He sent her money in answer to her requests and gladly declared himself willing to have her elder son, Pietro, join him in London.

Evidently the emotional situation was none too easy for Haydn, and it was further aggravated by sundry venomous letters from his wife, for apparently she also had got wind of Haydn's recent successes with the fair sex. In a letter to Luigia, Haydn reacted with these strong words: "My wife, that infernal beast, wrote me so many things that I was forced to answer that I was never coming back. To this letter she paid attention."[27]

Although there were enough entanglements of the heart to disturb Haydn during the second part of his sojourn in London, they were of minor importance compared with the strain that he labored under at that time in his artistic career. The Professional Concerts twice sent a deputation to the master with the object of inducing

[25] Letter of October 13, 1791.    [26] Letter of January 14, 1792.
[27] Letter of January 14, 1792.

him by the offer of a much higher salary to go over to their camp. When they found that nothing could shake Haydn's determination to keep his word to the man who had brought him to England, they changed their tactics. Rumors began again to circulate against Haydn, to such an extent that they reached even the ears of such good Viennese friends as Hofrat von Kees and Marianne von Genzinger. Finally the bomb exploded; the English public was informed that, in view of Haydn's advanced age and inability to create important new music, the Professional Concerts had had the good fortune to engage his young pupil, the outstanding composer, Ignaz Pleyel. Musical London was tremendously stirred by this news and violent partisanships were formed. All drawing rooms rang with heated discussions as to who was the better composer, Haydn or Pleyel. Today it is not easy to envisage the "murderous harmonious war" (Haydn) between the two composers in the right light. Very few people play music by Pleyel, whom we know only as the founder of a celebrated pianoforte factory, an improver of the mechanism of the harp, and the first publisher to produce a complete edition of Haydn's quartets. In the eighteenth century, on the other hand, many people valued Pleyel's compositions very highly, especially those written in the earlier part of his life. Even Mozart wrote about Pleyel's first quartets that "they are very well written and very agreeable. It will be a happy thing for music if, when the time arrives, Pleyel should replace Haydn for us."[28] One cannot therefore blame the London public too much for taking the contest between Haydn and Pleyel seriously and awaiting the outcome with eager anticipation.

What satisfied the English sense of "fair play" was that Haydn and Pleyel remained personally on the best of terms. The day after Pleyel's arrival they dined together; they spent New Year's Eve in each other's company; they attended each other's concerts, and Pleyel, according to Haydn, displayed so much modesty that he gained his teacher's goodwill anew. But in spite of this pleasant personal relationship between the two contestants, which Haydn, worldly wise and shrewd as he was, would have kept up under any circumstances, the old master must have felt deeply hurt by the whole matter. Even if Pleyel, who perhaps had gone to London unaware of the implications of his engagement, was not to blame, it was an insult to consider the young musician worthy of entering into competition with Joseph Haydn, an insult of which Haydn was

[28] Letter from W. A. Mozart to his father dated April 24, 1784.

fully aware, though he rarely showed it. For instance there is the story told by John Taylor of a dinner with Haydn, Salomon, and Dr. Wolcot. The last was tactless enough to praise Pleyel's "genius" in the most enthusiastic terms. Haydn, at first, graciously agreed. Finally the doctor's rapture was too much for him and he remarked "with considerable warmth": "But I hope it will be remembered that he was my pupil." And once he wrote to Marianne: "Pleyel's presumption is criticized everywhere."

Pleyel had one advantage; he was an unusually prolific composer. As Haydn informed Marianne: "He brought with him a number of new compositions, which were, however, written long ago! He therefore promised to produce a new work every evening. On seeing this, I could easily perceive that a lot of people were dead set against me, so I also announced publicly that I would likewise give twelve different new pieces. In order to keep my promise and to support poor Salomon, I must be the victim and work perpetually. I do feel it, however, very much. My eyes suffer most, and I have many sleepless nights."[29] In another letter he exclaimed: "Never in my life have I written so much in one year as during the last, and it has indeed almost exhausted me."[30] There are more complaints about being quite worn out with fatigue. The amazing thing is that nothing of this weariness can be felt in the works Haydn wrote under this strain, the "Surprise" Symphony being one of them.

The London audience, in spite of the preceding venomous campaign against the composer, could not help being completely overwhelmed by these works. In the concert of February 24, two movements of the Symphony in D (No. 93) were encored and the *Morning Chronicle* declared: "The concert was exceedingly spirited and, by the overture [symphony] of the matchless Haydn, was distinguished above all common competition." Of the concert on March 16, 1792, the *Morning Herald* reported: "There has hardly ever been a more beautiful musical treat than the fifth performance of Salomon's Concert. . . . No less than six Pieces of Haydn were performed, exhibiting a richness and variety of genius that far exceed all modern Composers." On the sixth evening, the enthusiasm of the Londoners reached a climax when the "Surprise" Symphony had its first rendering. And so it went on, a series of triumphs for Haydn. On April 24 he wrote to Marianne: "In spite of the great

[29] Letter of March 2, 1792.
[30] Letter of January 17, 1792.

opposition of my musical enemies, who are so bitter against me, more especially leaving nothing undone with my pupil Pleyel this winter to humble me, still, thank God! I may say that I have kept the upper hand." When the twelve concerts for which he had contracted were over (one day before the tenth, the indefatigable composer had conducted his own most successful benefit concert), Salomon went on to add another concert on June 6 and finished the season, according to the *Morning Herald*, with the "greatest *éclat*," the instrumental pieces by Haydn being received with an "extacy [*sic*] of admiration."

Fourteen important concerts consisting to a great extent of Haydn's own compositions seem a big program for one season, but by no means did they cover all his appearances in public. He conducted Salomon's benefit concert and those for his "brother in affection" the violinist Barthélemon, for the pianist Hässler, for Madame Mara, for the vocalists, the sisters Abrams, and for many others. His creative activity was not confined to the music for the Salomon concerts and the opera. Other new works owed their origin to friendships that Haydn made in London. There was, for instance, Anne Hunter, who was married to John Hunter, the famous surgeon and anatomist. She showed him some of her poems, one of them set to music to the tune of an andante by Pleyel. This—as Marion Scott assumes[31]—may have stimulated Haydn to try his hand at these poems, the result being the charming *Six Original Canzonettas* published in 1794. Another time he heard of the financial worries of the Scottish violinist William Napier, who because of gout was unable to pursue his profession and was forced to support his numerous children as a music publisher. To help Napier, Haydn arranged Scottish folk songs for him, adding preludes and postludes, and an accompaniment of clavier, violin, and violoncello. The works brought Napier, who had been near bankruptcy, great benefit and enhanced Haydn's popularity in the British Isles. The following remarks in the *Morning Chronicle* of January 31, 1792, express the attitude of the British music lovers:

> Nothing, perhaps, can be a stronger instance of the superior genius of this great master than the facility with which he seized the wild but natural and affecting beauties of the Scots airs . . . , the taste with which he has entered

[31] Cf. Marion M. Scott, "Haydn: Relics and Reminiscences in England," *Music and Letters*, XIII/2 (1932).

into their genuine spirit, and the felicity of adaptation, with which he has harmonized, as if the original composers had possessed science enough to add the charm of harmony to their own melodies. This work will be a striking and lasting proof of how little the merit of Haydn was confined to inventing, or conquering instrumental difficulties.[32]

Finally there was a certain amount of teaching to be undertaken. Besides such nominal pupils as Mrs. Schröter and other ladies, there were the pianist Thomas Haigh and the composer John Callcott, who really did study under the master.

How Haydn managed to get all this work done, and done so brilliantly, and at the same time to lead a very active social life; how, in spite of the tremendous forces released in his creative activity he was still able to muster the emotional capacity for love and friendship, is hard to understand. Several factors may have contributed to produce the rare phenomenon of a man of sixty with the creative power and zest for living of a person half his age. During the long, undisturbed years at Eszterháza, when Haydn, in many respects, was not living to the utmost of his capacity, he stored tremendous reserves of energy for the years to come. (Other artists might have reacted differently, and probably would have aged prematurely in such an existence of unvarying routine.) Another important factor was Haydn's excellent physique. During the eighteen months he spent in England, in spite of the difference in climate, the unfamiliar food, frequent travels, and long hours, Haydn was generally in very good health. He once complained of "English rheumatism" (against which he wrapped himself from head to foot in flannel), and once he noted in his diary that he had had to be bled. But that was all. His discomforts from a polyp in the nose, inherited from his mother, were as old as Haydn himself. John Hunter almost used force to persuade Haydn to have an operation, but when the composer was seized by Hunter's strong assistants to be tied to a chair, he screamed and struggled so vigorously with hands and feet that the surgeon had to give up.

When the concert season was over, the "worn-out" composer still used every available chance to see and enjoy interesting sights in England.

On June 4, 1792, he went to Vauxhall, where the birthday of the King was celebrated, and apparently liked it very much. "The

[32] Cf. *HCaW*, III, p. 128.

place and its diversions have perhaps no equal in the world," he writes. "There are one hundred and fifty-five dining booths scattered about, all very neat, and each comfortably seating six persons. There are large alleys of trees, the branches meeting overhead in a splendid roof of foliage. Tea, coffee and milk with almonds cost nothing. You pay half a crown for admission. The music is fairly good." He also explored the country around Windsor and of Windsor itself he mentions in his notebook the "very old but splendid chapel" and the "divine view from the terrace." But while there are a few lines dealing with this subject, Haydn devotes more than six hundred words to a description of the races at Ascot Heath, which he attended on June 14. It must have warmed the hearts of his English friends to notice Haydn's eager interest in this national event. Here he saw eye to eye with them, just as he did in his passion for hunting and fishing. The following excerpt from Haydn's report shows what interested him most:

In the first heat there were three riders who were compelled to go around the course twice without stopping. They did it in five minutes. No stranger would believe it unless he were convinced by observation. The second time there were seven riders and when they approached some fell back, but never more than about ten paces and just when one thinks the one rider who is about to reach the goal will be the first, at which moment large bets are laid on him, another rushes past him with inconceivable force and reaches the winning post. The riders are very lightly clad in silk, each of a different color, to make it easier to recognize them . . . and all are as lean as greyhounds. . . . The horses are of the finest breeds, light, with very slender feet, the manes plaited into braids, the hoofs very neat. As soon as they hear the sound of the bell they dash off with the greatest force. Every leap of the horses is twenty-two feet long. These horses are very costly. A few years ago the Prince of Wales paid eight thousand pounds for one and sold it again for six thousand. But the first time he won fifty thousand pounds with it. . . . I saw five heats the first day, and in spite of a heavy rain there were two thousand vehicles, all full of people, and three times as many people were present on foot. Besides this there are all kinds of puppet plays, ciarlatanz [*sic*], conjurors, and buffoons performing during the races, and in a multitude of tents food and all kinds of wine and beer. . . .

The next day the indefatigable traveler went to Slough to meet William Herschel. Haydn was very much interested in this German musician who discovered the planet Uranus in 1781 after working on astronomy as a hobby and was now universally acclaimed as an astronomer. The main attraction for Haydn was of course Herschel's gigantic telescope. Before it was raised skyward Herschel's most prominent visitors were allowed to take a walk through the enormous tube. In 1787, King George III and his retinue did so and the monarch was delighted thus to be able to show the Archbishop of Canterbury "the way to Heaven."[33] Haydn had to content himself with gazing at the monster, the measurements of which he faithfully put down in his notebook, together with facts regarding the astronomer's very felicitous financial status. (He had married a widow with a dowry of one hundred thousand pounds.) Apparently Haydn was much impressed by Herschel's ability to "sit from five to six hours under the open sky in the severest cold weather."

Now the time for Haydn's departure was approaching, much to the distress of Mrs. Schröter, to whom "every moment of his company was more and more precious." Many other people also wanted to keep the composer in England. Haydn, while quite willing to return to London, found it imperative to go home for the time being, so that he could put his affairs in order and straighten out matters with Prince Esterházy who had summoned him to Frankfurt, where he was to attend the coronation of the Emperor Francis II.

So Haydn got his trunks ready and made various purchases for his Viennese friends, such as scissors, needles, knives, spectacles, and steel chains, the prices of which he carefully noted in his diary. He also took pains to jot down anecdotes that might amuse the people at home, such as the following: "An archbishop of London asked Parliament to silence a preacher of the Moravian creed who preached in public. The vice-president answered that it could easily be done: only make him a bishop, and he would keep silent all his life."

Until the last moment the round of social functions went on. On June 22, Haydn gave a dinner at Parsloes for the Musical Gradu-

[33] Cf. Cecil Roberts, *And so to Bath* (London, 1940).

ates' Society, and Salomon had to be invited as an interpreter, "Dr. Haydn having not made sufficient progress in the English language." Next day he attended a dinner for one hundred eighty persons that the Duchess of York gave under a tent in her garden. After that it was time for him to take leave of his numerous friends, but he promised to return before long to the country that had received him so hospitably and had given him the most exciting time of his life.

# CHAPTER EIGHT

# Vienna or London?

## 1792 – 1795

No personal documents are available about Haydn's return journey from London. We know that he again stopped at Bonn, where he had spent such pleasant hours eighteen months previously. The Elector Maximilian had already left for the coronation at Frankfurt, for which Haydn was also heading, but the Elector's orchestra invited the master to a breakfast at Godesberg, that charming village overlooking the Rhine where the residents of Bonn still like to take their guests. On this occasion Haydn had a long talk with the young Beethoven, whom he may have met on his first visit to Bonn. The musician of twenty-two showed the master a cantata (possibly the cantata on the death of Emperor Joseph II) which Haydn praised greatly. Beethoven was planning to go to Vienna to study under Haydn, and it was arranged that he should do so as soon as he could get leave from the Elector, who had undertaken to bear the expenses of his journey.

Haydn then proceeded to Frankfurt, not without some misgivings about his reception by his princely patron, since he had been forced to ignore Esterházy's earlier request for a speedy return. To his relief, however, the Prince was so engrossed in the splendors of the coronation of Francis II that he merely remarked: "Oh, Haydn, you could have saved me forty thousand florins!"

The man who arrived in Vienna in one of the Esterházy carriages on July 24, 1792, was rather different from the Haydn who had left the imperial capital only nineteen months before. He had tasted both delirious success and freedom. A highly renowned university had awarded him the degree of Doctor of Music. The Prince of Wales and other members of the highest British nobility had shown him great respect and friendliness. The newspapers, though sometimes critical in their attitude, had dealt with him and his music as providing news of importance, and he had earned a considerable amount of money. Now he had returned to the city that had witnessed his rise from the humblest beginnings. How would Vienna receive the new Dr. Haydn?

The official circles of the capital proved most disappointing. No newspaper took the trouble to mention the master's return. No concerts were arranged in his honor. The Austrian court gave no sign of recognition to the composer who had contributed so immensely to the fame of Austrian music. In contemporary diaries, which Botstiber has searched carefully, Haydn's name hardly ever appears. What a contrast to the frenzied attention given to him in London! In private life things were of course different, for his old friends were delighted to welcome Haydn home. Still, one gap, never to be filled, greatly marred Haydn's joy in his Viennese circle. Mozart was dead. The news had reached Haydn in London, and at first he tried not to believe it, for rumors of that kind were not always trustworthy. (Haydn himself had been declared dead in 1778.) When he could doubt the fact no longer, it became, even for a man of Haydn's deeply religious feeling, a trial of faith to reconcile himself to the premature passing of this genius. In January 1792 he wrote to their mutual friend, Puchberg: "I was for some time quite beside myself about his death. I could not believe that Providence should so quickly have called an irreplaceable man into the other world. Have the kindness, dear friend, to send me a list of Mozart's works not yet known here, and I will do my utmost to push them in the interest of the widow. I wrote to the poor woman three weeks ago, telling her that when her dear son was old enough, I would teach him composition without payment as well as I could, so as to replace his father to some extent." Haydn was not able to interest the British public in Mozart; at that time very few cared for him (among them, characteristically, was the Prince of Wales, who even owned the autograph of *La clemenza di Tito*). We know, however, that when consulted by the music dealer Broderip in the presence of Dr. Burney regarding the purchase of a Mozart manuscript, Haydn exclaimed with the greatest emphasis: "Do buy it by all means. He was truly a great musician. Friends often flatter me that I have some genius, but he stood far above me." Truly, Haydn suffered deeply in losing this unique artistic friend, a loss that became still more evident to him amid the old, familiar surroundings. Even with the healing influence of time, the wound inflicted by Mozart's death did not cease to hurt. As late as 1807, when some friends mentioned the name of Mozart, Haydn burst into tears, exclaiming: "Forgive me, I must ever, ever weep when I hear the name of my Mozart."

On his return to a city that in a strange way seemed to have become different, Haydn felt more than ever the need of friends who really stood close to him. His wife, of course, was not among them. Time and distance had done nothing to soften the animosity between them. Frau Haydn's letters, in which she reported poisonous gossip against her husband by people dear to him (among them even Mozart), could not improve their relationship, nor did Haydn particularly care for her suggestion that he buy her a house in Vienna that she might use as a dower residence. The house itself, which Frau Haydn insisted on showing him, pleased him well enough because of its "quiet and secluded location." As he could now afford to do so, he bought it in August 1793 after careful negotiations and had it repaired and a second story added, but he did not fulfill his wife's wishes to make her the owner of the property.[1]

No, it was not to Frau Haydn, but to Marianne von Genzinger that he turned again "for comfort." With her he felt at ease. In her home he was sure of never-failing, sincere interest. To her he played his new works; to her he described what he had seen and heard in England. Only two short notes of the autumn of 1792 have been preserved, for there was now no need for correspondence. Then, all of a sudden, a catastrophe shook Haydn's existence. On January 26, 1793, Marianne died, at the age of forty-three, leaving five children. Through her death, Haydn lost the best friend he had. None of his other old acquaintances could replace her. The composer, who had experienced the bliss of a really understanding and warmhearted friend only in his late years, now experienced a terrible loneliness that surrounded him like a wall. With Marianne's death, something never to be recaptured went out of Haydn's life. A certain sarcasm in his nature began to show, an asperity of which the diary of his second trip to London offers many instances.

The loneliness Haydn was suffering could not be dispelled even

[1] The house, situated in Vienna's sixth district, at 71 Untere Steingasse, now 19 Haydngasse, has been preserved by the city as a Haydn Museum.

by the two interesting pupils who were then constantly in touch with the master. Young Pietro Polzelli came to stay with the Haydns, and the composer, besides teaching him, helped him to get well-paying students and certainly enjoyed his company. His relation to the other pupil is not so easily described. Ludwig van Beethoven arrived in Vienna shortly after Haydn and started at once to take lessons, for which the master asked a nominal fee of eight groschen per hour. They met fairly frequently, and Beethoven's memorandum book contains such entries as "chocolate twenty-two x [kreutzer (farthings)] for Haydn and myself" and "coffee six x for Haydn and myself."

As early as 1787, Beethoven had paid a short visit to Vienna in order to meet Mozart. His great wish was to study with Mozart, but before his intention could be carried out he was recalled to his ailing mother in Bonn, and by the time he was ready to visit the Austrian capital again, Mozart had died. Thereupon Beethoven decided to study with Haydn instead, but it seems probable that he always regarded Haydn as a sort of understudy for Mozart. Such an attitude was also expressed by Count Waldstein, who wrote the following words of farewell in Beethoven's album on October 29, 1792, before the young musician's departure for Vienna:

> Dear Beethoven,
>     You are traveling to Vienna in fulfillment of your long-cherished wish. The tutelary genius of Mozart is still weeping and bewailing the death of her favorite. With the inexhaustible Haydn she has found a refuge, but no occupation, and she is now waiting to associate herself with someone else. Labor assiduously and receive Mozart's spirit from the hands of Haydn.

Haydn, a very keen observer of men, may have realized the young man's true feelings. At all events, the deep sympathy and understanding that, in spite of very different temperaments, drew Mozart and Haydn irresistibly together, were entirely lacking in the relationship between Haydn and Beethoven. The difference in their ages was not the real barrier, for Haydn loved, and was loved by, young people. But Beethoven, headstrong and prone to suspicion, was not easy to get on with and often irritated Haydn. His youthful arrogance was particularly hard to bear for a man of Haydn's age, and the older master used to refer jokingly to Beethoven as "that Great Mogul." Added to the differences in temperament was their attitude to the world-shaking political events of the time. Haydn, a loyal son of the Austrian monarchy, was filled with horror and revulsion by what he heard about the French Revolution. Napoleon was to him the archenemy, for whose downfall he fervently prayed. Beethoven saw greatness in Napoleon and initially planned to dedicate his Third Symphony to the hero. He had no hesitation in visiting the French ambassador, Bernadotte, during the latter's short stay in Vienna. More important than these tangible personal differences was the dissatisfaction Beethoven felt with the instruction Haydn provided. The young musician wanted to study counterpoint thoroughly, as he was keenly aware of the gaps in his knowledge of contrapuntal theory. Haydn set him to work on the old textbook he had studied with the greatest zeal in his youth, Fux's *Gradus ad Parnassum*. He would hand Beethoven an extract and adaptation of the text he had prepared himself and successfully used for various pupils. This time, however, success did not materialize. Haydn, absorbed in creative work, could not muster the patience to deal thoroughly with such elementary exercises. He did not give to the work of instruction the necessary attention, and he overlooked mistakes that Beethoven made. The pupil became suspicious of his teacher's competence and complained of it to the renowned pianist Abbé Gelinek who introduced him to Johann Schenk, a composer of successful Singspiels and a pedantic music teacher as well. Schenk was tremendously impressed by Beethoven's improvisations on the piano and went to call on the young genius the next day. "On his writing desk," he tells in his autobiography,[2] "I found a few passages from his first lesson in counterpoint. A cursory glance disclosed the fact that, brief as it was, there were mistakes in every key. Joseph Haydn, who had returned to Vienna, was intent on utilizing his abilities in the composition of large masterpieces, and, thus laudably occupied, he could not well devote himself to the rules of grammar. I was now eagerly desirous to become the helper of the zealous student, but before beginning my tuition I made him understand that our cooperations must be kept a close secret. In view of this I recommended him to copy every exercise that I corrected, so that Haydn would not recognize the handwriting of a stranger when the exercise was submitted to him." And so it was done. Beethoven, for the sake of appearances, continued going to Haydn for instruction, but his real teacher at that time was Schenk. The young musician could not be blamed for his duplicity;

[2] Cf. A. W. Thayer, *Ludwig van Beethovens Leben* (Leipzig, 1901–1911), I, p. 329ff.

he was eager to study counterpoint thoroughly, but could not risk offending Haydn. On the other hand, the older master's behavior is also understandable. As Schindler put it: "The eminent composer can be a good adviser on special cases, but he simply is not a teacher in the real sense of the word; that is, one who leads the student on with patience and devotion from easy to difficult problems." Nevertheless, Haydn and Beethoven outwardly kept on quite friendly terms.

An exchange of letters may throw some light on their relationship. Haydn went out of his way to intercede with the Elector in Bonn on behalf of Beethoven and wrote him as follows on November 23, 1793:[3]

> I venture to send to Your Serene Electoral Highness several pieces of music, namely, a quintet, an eight-part parthie, an oboe concerto, variations for the pianoforte, and a fugue, composed by Beethoven, my dear pupil, whose instruction has been graciously entrusted to me. I flatter myself that these will be graciously considered by Your Electoral Highness as good evidence for the industry displayed by him outside of his actual studies. Connoisseurs and non-connoisseurs will impartially infer from these works that Beethoven will eventually reach the position of one of Europe's greatest composers, and I will be proud to call myself his teacher. I only wish he could still remain for quite some time with me.
>
> As I mentioned Beethoven, I trust Your Serene Electoral Highness will allow me to add a few words about his financial status. For the past year one hundred ducats have been granted to him. No doubt Your Electoral Highness is aware that this sum was not sufficient to even cover his living expenses; probably Your Highness had good reasons for sending him with so small a sum into the great world. Under this assumption and so as not to have him fall into the hands of usurers I have partly stood security for him, partly advanced him cash, and he owes me now five hundred florins, of which not a penny was spent unnecessarily, and I would ask you to send him this amount. And as the interest on borrowed money con-

[3]Cf. Dénes Bartha, ed., *Joseph Haydn: Gesammelte Briefe und Aufzeichnungen* (Kassel, 1965), p. 297ff.

stantly increases, a situation results that is most irksome
for an artist like Beethoven. I believe, in case Your Electoral Highness should grant him for next year one thousand florins, this would be the ultimate act of graciousness
and relieve Beethoven of all worries. For the teachers that
are essential to him and the outfit indispensable for his
appearances among the highborn are so costly that from
the one thousand florins just enough for the bare neces-
sities of life would be left. Regarding the extravagance
which to a youth entering into the great world is often a
grave temptation, I believe I may answer for that to Your
Electoral Highness, for a hundred circumstances have
proved to me that he is willing to sacrifice everything to
his art. With so many tempting occasions presenting
themselves, this is quite admirable and it gives Your Serene Electoral Highness the assurance that the favors
granted to him will be refunded with interest. In the hope
Your Serene Electoral Highness will see fit to fulfill my
request henceforth to allow further help to my dear pupil
Beethoven, I remain with the most profound respect,

Your Electoral Highness' most obedient

Joseph Haydn

The Elector's reaction must have shocked Haydn, for, apart
from refusing to increase Beethoven's allowance (which was stopped
in March 1794), he stated in no uncertain, indeed, in rather rude
terms that, except for the fugue, all the compositions submitted had
been composed and performed in Bonn long before Beethoven left
for Vienna.

This put Haydn in an extremely awkward position. It was embarrassing that the Elector believed him to have conspired with
Beethoven in deceiving him, and he saw no way of proving his
innocence. On the other hand, the situation was not quite clear, for
the Elector may not have been entirely correct in his assumptions
regarding the works sent. As Bartha points out, the compositions
cannot definitely be identified nowadays. Some (the fugue mentioned by the Elector, for example) seem to be lost. The quintet
mentioned, probably Op. 4, is not a new composition but a re-
arrangement of the Octet Op. 103 composed in Bonn, which the
Elector had heard. At all events, Beethoven, in asking Haydn to

send the works to Bonn, had not been frank with his master, and Haydn was not likely to forget this.

A few years later Gelinek, after a disagreement with Beethoven, divulged Schenk's secret; yet no discernible break occurred in the relations between Haydn and Beethoven. Haydn apparently refrained from any reproaches. Maybe he told himself that his instruction in counterpoint had really not been thorough enough. Moreover, he had learned from experiences like the one with the Elector in Bonn that Beethoven was not free from duplicity in his dealings with his teacher. So they remained polite to each other. The story found in many Beethoven biographies that Haydn advised the young composer against publishing his Trio Op.1/3 because it was too bold and original is, in Landon's words, "pure fiction."[4] The work was published and probably even composed during Haydn's stay in England. Yet the report that came from Ferdinand Ries[5] may have a grain of truth. Perhaps Ries confused the trio with another work that the worldly old composer advised withholding for the time being. Beethoven, prone to suspicion, saw in such practical advice a sign of jealousy, thus totally misjudging his teacher's character. The idea of envying a composer almost young enough to be his grandson would have seemed ridiculous to Haydn who, after winning great triumphs in England, was receiving proofs of unusual admiration at home. In 1793, to the old man's tremendous gratification, Count Harrach erected a monument in the composer's birthplace to this greatest son of Rohrau, an honor hardly ever accorded to a composer in his lifetime.

No, Haydn was not jealous of the younger generation. On the contrary, he got genuine satisfaction out of its achievements and missed no opportunity to encourage its members. A charming proof of this is offered by his letter to the operatic composer Joseph Weigl, Jr., the son of his old friend, the violoncellist of the Esterházy band, Joseph Weigl:

Vienna, January 11, 1794

Dearest Godson,

When I took you in my arms shortly after your birth, and had the pleasure of becoming your godfather, I implored omnipotent Providence to endow you with the

[4] *HCaW*, IV, p. 61ff.

[5] Franz Gerhard Wegeler and Ferdinand Ries, *Biographische Notizen über L. van Beethoven* (Coblenz, 1838), p. 84ff.

highest degree of musical talent. My fervent prayer has
been heard. It has been a long time since I felt such enthusiasm for any music as for your *La principessa d'Amalfi*
yesterday: it is full of ideas, noble, expressive, in short—a
masterpiece. I felt the warmest sympathy with the well-
merited applause bestowed on it. Persevere, my dear godson, in this genuine style, that you may again show for-
eigners what a German can accomplish. Keep a place in
your memory withal for an old boy like myself. I love
you cordially, and am, dearest Weigl,

Your sincere friend and servant,

JOSEPH HAYDN

When Haydn wrote this letter, he was in the midst of preparations for a second journey to London. According to an agreement
concluded with Salomon in the summer of 1793, Haydn was to
conduct six newly composed symphonies in the English capital.
The financial terms are not known, but it seems certain that they
were at least equal to those of the first contract. It is natural that
Haydn should choose to revisit London, a city in which he had
enjoyed so much success and appreciation. There was now very
little to attract him in Vienna or in Eisenstadt, where he spent part
of the time with Prince Esterházy, for the castle of Eszterháza had
been abandoned after the death of its creator, not to be used again
for a century. But, although the Prince had no real use for him and
remunerated him insufficiently, he did not like to see his kapellmeister go, and it was difficult for Haydn to get leave again. At last he
succeeded, and the day of departure was fixed for January 19, 1794.
This time he could not rely on Salomon's help on the journey. At
first, he wanted one of his pupils, Polzelli or Beethoven, to accompany him, but after giving the matter more thought, he came to the
conclusion that neither of these young musicians would have his
welfare as much at heart as his trusted servant, Johann Elssler. So he
wisely decided to take Johann to London with him. Young Elssler,
another of Haydn's godsons, was the son of Prince Esterházy's music copyist, who helped Haydn with the first catalogue of his works
(see p. 53). Born in 1769, Johann lived with Haydn during his
youth and rendered him excellent service as a copyist, secretary,
and general factotum. It speaks in favor of both master and servant
that in spite of their being constantly together, Elssler's admiration
for Haydn was boundless. There is even a report that the factotum,

when he thought himself unobserved, censed Haydn's portrait as if before an altar. The lack of a woman's care in the aging master's life was, to a great extent, made up for by Elssler's constant devotion and thoughtfulness. To this excellent man, incidentally, a place of honor is due not only as the faithful servant, secretary, and copyist of Haydn, but as the father of the great dancer Fanny Elssler.[6]

On January 19, 1794, the two travelers set forth in a coach provided by Baron van Swieten, director of the Vienna court library, an ardent lover of music who was later to play an important part in Haydn's life. About a halt made at the well-known spa, Wiesbaden, Dies tells the following pleasant story. At the inn, Haydn heard the strains of the andante from his "Surprise" Symphony issuing from another room. He followed the sound and found a group of Prussian officers gathered around the pianoforte, enjoying the beauties of this by then very popular masterpiece. When Haydn introduced himself, the Prussians could not believe that the composer of so youthful a tune was this aged man. They were at last convinced when Haydn proudly took out of his trunk the letter bearing the signature of their own King, Friedrich Wilhelm II, which had accompanied the diamond ring so highly treasured by the composer.

About the journey no word from Haydn himself has been preserved, and our information regarding this second visit to England is altogether poor compared with that about the first journey. It should not be inferred that less happened to him or that his experiences did not seem so interesting, but the incentive to describe his impressions in letters had vanished with the loss of his most sympathetic listener, Marianne. Now there was really not a single person to whom he cared to write a detailed account of his life in England. In his notebook, he again confined himself to jotting down facts interesting to him for one reason or another, but no word of a more personal nature has come down to us. Taken as a whole, the diary of this second journey is more censorious in tone, and the comments on other artists are not very flattering.

Haydn's first appearance in London had been announced for February 3. But again, to continue the old tradition, the concert had to be postponed, as Haydn arrived on February 4, and a soloist

---

[6] That Elssler—as Larsen proved (see *Die Haydn-Überlieferung* [Copenhagen, 1939], p. 33)—made a collection of Haydn manuscripts during the composer's lifetime need not be interpreted as an act of dishonesty. It seems possible that the old and extremely forgetful composer sometimes gave his faithful factotum a manuscript without keeping the fact in mind.

engaged by Salomon, the celebrated basso, Ludwig Fischer (who had sung Osmin in the Vienna premiere of Mozart's *Die Entführung aus dem Serail*) also was late. The first concert therefore took place on February 10, and Haydn was received with the old enthusiasm and admiration, this time marred by no opposition whatever, as the Professional Concerts had been given up in 1793. There was, however, a difference in the attitude of the London audience toward the master. Haydn was greeted like an old and highly treasured friend, but the element of sensation so characteristic of his first appearance was lacking. The reporter for the *Oracle* therefore, writing about Salomon's opening night, confined himself to this comment: "We must of necessity be brief. And after all it may be best, when the chef-d'oeuvre of the great Haydn is the subject. 'Come then, expressive Silence, muse his praise.' Viotti gave a concerto, simple and affecting, like his genius. Mara sang, *c'est assez dire.*" But if Haydn did not supply as much material for the newspapers as he had three years before, the acclaim given to him was by no means less frenzied; indeed, if possible, it was even more so. A letter written on March 25 by the London correspondent for the *Journal des Luxus und der Moden* (Weimar) gives a lively description of the general reaction to Haydn's music:

> But what would you now say to his new symphonies composed expressly for these concerts and directed by himself at the pianoforte? It is truly wonderful what sublime and august thoughts this master weaves into his works. Passages often occur that render it impossible to listen to them without becoming excited. We are altogether carried away by admiration and forced to applaud with hand and mouth. This is especially the case with Frenchmen, of whom we have so many here that all public places are filled with them. You know that they have great sensibility and cannot restrain their transports, so that in the midst of the finest passages in soft adagios they clap their hands in loud applause and thus mar the effect. In every symphony of Haydn the adagio or andante is sure to be repeated each time, after the most vehement encores. The worthy Haydn, whose personal acquaintance I highly value, conducts himself on these occasions in the most modest manner. He is indeed a goodhearted, candid, honest man, esteemed and beloved by all.

This love and esteem were felt also by the members of his orchestra, who enjoyed Haydn's sense of humor and friendly ways. On the other hand, they were not above playing little jokes on him. Young George Smart, for instance (the future Sir George, a friend of Beethoven's, Weber's, and Mendelssohn's), liked to remember how he showed Haydn the "English way of playing the drums." At a rehearsal, when the drummer was absent, Smart, a violinist, volunteered to take his part, though he had never played the instrument before. Naturally he did not produce quite the desired effect. Haydn let it pass, but after the movement was finished, he went to Smart and remarked politely that in Germany the drumstick was used in such a way as not to check the vibration. Then, adopting his usual method of demonstrating his intentions on the instrument, he took the drumstick and showed himself, to the astonished orchestra, as an excellent drummer. Smart was quick to see where he had failed and exclaimed: "Oh, very well, if you like it better that way we can do it so in London too."

The Salomon series again gained added luster from the engagement of excellent soloists. The great violinist Viotti has already been mentioned. Very successful also was the blind glass harmonica virtuosa, Marianne Kirchgaessner, whom Mozart admired so much that he wrote an Adagio and Rondo for Harmonica and Instruments, K. 617, for her. (Incidentally it was in London that this unfortunate musician, who had been blind since her fourth year, was given an eye lotion that enabled her to distinguish the color and shape of objects.) Dussek again frequently appeared in the series, as did the popular singer Maria Hester Parke, who was also a good pianist. Madame Mara was engaged again, and Haydn continued to take an interest in her, though he did not always approve of her behavior, as is proved by a curious item in his notebook. It seems that the singer and her husband, Johann Mara, a talented but dissipated violoncellist, were not exactly in accord. As the oboist W. T. Parke expressed it in his *Musical Memoirs*: "Mr. Mara loved her and his bottle equally, and frequently broke the head of one and cracked the other." In writing about the singer's benefit concert on March 24, 1795, after mentioning the various artists, Haydn continued: "When the concert was over, Madame Mara gave a supper in the adjoining room. After midnight Mr. Mara stepped in quite boldly and asked for a glass of wine. Madame Mara, knowing what madness might result therefrom, appealed to her lawyer, who was sitting at the table, and this man said to Mr. Mara: 'You know our laws, you will be kind enough to leave this room, otherwise you'll have to pay two hundred pounds to-morrow.' The poor man left the party. Next day Madame Mara, his wife, traveled to Bath with her *cicisbeo*, but I think her obstinacy makes her ridiculous to the whole nation." It seems that in spite of the notorious faults of the husband, Haydn was definitely on his side.

While his feelings for the singer were of a mixed nature, Haydn wholeheartedly enjoyed the intimate friendship that he established with Domenico Dragonetti, "Il Patriarca dei Contrabassi," during this second stay in England. Dragonetti's never-paralleled mastery of his instrument fascinated Haydn, as it did everyone else. The Italian virtuoso, playing on a double bass built by Gasparo da Salò, the teacher of Amati, apparently could express anything he wished on the unwieldy instrument. Haydn must have chuckled when Dragonetti told him how, by imitating a terrific thunderstorm on the double bass, he made all the monks in a Paduan monastery jump out of their beds one night. And the fact that Dragonetti collected dolls and operatic scores with the same fervor was something that Haydn, who loved puppets so much himself, could well understand.

The English composer William Shield also was among Haydn's good friends. They spent a few days together at Taplow, and Shield declared that on this occasion he had learned more about music than he had in years of study. This shows that if Haydn did not have to follow a textbook on counterpoint explicitly, he was a pretty good teacher.

Haydn again had some real pupils and received a fee of one guinea a lesson. Some remarks he made throw a sidelight on teaching conditions at that time: "If a singer, pianoforte or dancing master asks half a guinea for his lesson, he requests before the first lesson an entrance fee of six guineas. This is done because during the winter many Scottish and Irish people, out of pride, have their children taught by the best masters, and in the end find themselves unable to remunerate them. But the entrance fee is dispensed with if the master asks for a whole guinea. This however, has to be paid at every lesson.[7]

The name of Lord Abingdon frequently appears in Haydn's notebook. This musical enthusiast was among the first amateurs who had tried to bring the master to London. He now endeavored

---

[7] This is quoted by Griesinger in his biographical sketch in *Allgemeine Musikalische Zeitung* (1809) and apparently was contained in Haydn's fourth London diary, which has disappeared. Cf. Chapter 7, n. 5.

to direct Haydn's interest toward the composition of an oratorio, suggesting to him as a possible text a poem by Nedham used as an introduction to the English translation of John Selden's *Mare Clausum*. Haydn actually started working on it, but after composing a bass aria and a chorus, gave it up, feeling that he had too little knowledge of English to justify his composing an oratorio to a text in that language. Haydn and the aristocratic lover of music even collaborated in producing *Twelve Sentimental Catches and Glees*, which, according to the title page, were melodized by the Earl of Abingdon, while the accompaniments for the harp or pianoforte were written by "the celebrated Dr. Haydn." In the privacy of his notebook, however, Haydn could not help making fun of the Earl's musical accomplishments. He quoted the following epigram, which reads in an English translation:

King Solomon and David led merry, merry lives
With many, many lady friends and many, many wives.
But when old age came creeping on, with many, many qualms,
King Solomon wrote the Proverbs and King David wrote the
    Psalms.[8]

He added: "My Lord Abingdon sets it to music, but miserably. I do it a little better." Another story connected with his friend is set down by Haydn with evident enjoyment: "Lord Abingdon had an organ built in the church on his estate. When the bishop of the diocese heard of it, he reproved the nobleman in a letter for having done so without obtaining permission, which is not allowed in England. Whereupon he received the following answer: 'The Lord gave it—the Lord can take it away.' This is very ambiguous, but very good." Through his relations with the Earl, Haydn learned how British justice functioned even in the case of high-ranking defendants. The Earl was accused of "false and scandalous" libel against an eminent attorney. He was convicted in court and sentenced to three months imprisonment and a fine of one hundred pounds.[9] This was indeed a novel experience for an Austrian accustomed to quite different treatment of the aristocracy!

In the Earl's company Haydn also visited another aristocratic music lover, Sir Walter Aston, to whom he presented a new divertimento for two flutes and violoncello.

Haydn, however, did not confine himself to intercourse with

---

[8] The German version noted by Haydn is much more outspoken.
[9] Cf. *HCaW*, III, pp. 275 and 289.

noblemen. How he became attached to a music dealer by the name of Howell is described by William Gardiner: [10]

> One morning a neat little gentleman came into his [Howell's] shop and asked to look at some pianoforte music, and he laid before him some sonatas by Haydn which had just been published. The stranger turned them over and said: "No, I don't like these." Howell replied: "Do you see they are by Haydn, Sir?" "Well, Sir, I do, but I wish for something better." "Better," cried Howell indignantly, "I am not anxious to serve a gentleman of your taste," and was turning away when the customer made it known that he was Haydn himself. Howell, in astonishment, embraced him and the composer was so flattered by the interview that a long and intimate friendship followed. [11]

Some of Haydn's friends were not connected with music at all. We read, for instance, in his diary: "Mr. March is at the same time dentist, coachbuilder, and wine merchant. He is eighty-four, keeps a young mistress, and has a daughter of nine who plays the piano quite well. I dined frequently with him. As a dentist he earns two thousand pounds a year; each carriage brings at least five hundred pounds; as a wine merchant he does not, I think, make so large an income."

But what about Mrs. Schröter? Did their friendship continue? There are no letters to help us get a clear answer to this question. It may be that at this time Haydn neglected to make copies or that they were included in his fourth notebook, which has not been preserved. Certainly the pleasant rooms Haydn occupied at this time, at 1 Bury Street, at the corner of King Street, opposite the St. James's Theatre, were near Mrs. Schröter's house. Pohl may be right in his assumption that they were chosen by the lady herself.

Furthermore, Haydn dedicated to her three of his finest piano trios (Hob. XV:24–26). The affinity of the second movement of the F-sharp minor Trio (No. 26) with that of Symphony No. 102 may be owing to the fact that this symphonic movement was a favorite of Rebecca Schröter's. [12] Her name appears again in 1800

---

[10] William Gardiner, *Music and Friends* (London, 1838–1853).
[11] Gardiner does not give a date for this occurrence and it cannot be ascertained whether it happened during the first or second visit to England.
[12] See H. C. Robbins Landon, *The Symphonies of Joseph Haydn* (London, 1955), p. 565.

among the subscribers to *The Creation*. There is no reason to assume that the feelings of either had changed in the course of years. When we hear that Haydn left the scores of his last six symphonies "with a lady in England," it seems likely that the recipient of these treasures was his fervent admirer, Mrs. Schröter. Probably she again contributed much to making Haydn's stay in the British capital a happy one.

On his second visit Haydn was again most eager to get to know various aspects of life in England. When the concert season was over, this indefatigable man of sixty-two made frequent journeys and took an avid interest in all the new sights and facts that came his way. His notebook affords much information regarding different kinds of ships, chiefly in connection with a trip to Portsmouth. He visited the palace of Hampton Court, and the beautiful park there reminded him of Eszterháza; he was conducted through the Bank of England, and later wrote a detailed report about it. When staying with Sir Charles Rich, whom he found a "rather good violoncellist," he examined the ruins of the famous abbey at Waverley and described his reaction in the following words: "I must confess that whenever I looked at this beautiful wilderness, my heart felt oppressed at the thought that all this had once belonged to my own religion." He enjoyed trips to Cowes, Newport, Winchester (whose "beautiful Gothic cathedral" he praised), and Southampton. Mentioning the Isle of Wight in his diary, he extols the "most magnificent view of the sea" from the governor's green villa. The following remark in the diary also probably refers to this lovely island: "There is a story that Julius Caesar, on his flight, came by chance to the island and exclaimed: 'This is indeed the port of the Gods!'"

No such enthusiastic words were uttered by Haydn in connection with operatic conditions in London. Griesinger reports on the basis of the lost diary: "Dr. Arnold[13] composed an opera for Drury Lane Theatre. As the backers were afraid that the work might not be successful, Dr. Arnold agreed to have it performed three times at his own expense. He spent more than seven hundred pounds on it; the backers, however, paid a crowd of people to hiss the opera off each time. Finally Arnold let the backers have the opera and the costumes for two hundred pounds, and they thereupon performed it, with some alterations—better costumes and scenery—and earned twenty thousand pounds with it in the course of one year; the pub-

[13]Dr. Samuel Arnold, composer, court organist, and conductor of the Academy of Ancient Music.

lisher alone earned some five thousand pounds, and the poor composer lost five hundred. O, what swindlers!" Haydn expressed himself in even stronger words after a visit to the Haymarket Theatre on July 29, 1794: "There they perform just as miserable trash as at Sadler's Wells. A fellow sang an aria so dreadfully and with such extravagant grimaces that I began to perspire all over my body. But he had to repeat the aria. *Oh, che bestia!*"

Any unpleasant memory of that evening was quickly dispelled by Haydn's visit to Bath, which took place only four days later and proved to be the most delightful experience of the summer. In this highly fashionable watering place lived many distinguished musicians who were eager to meet Haydn, the most desirous being the famous tenor Venanzio Rauzzini, about whom the composer Naumann said: "He sings like an angel and is also a remarkable actor." Haydn wrote a long description of the trip in his third diary, part of which reads as follows:

> On August 2, 1794, I left for Bath at five in the morning and arrived at 8 PM. . . . I stayed with Mr. Rauzzini, a very famous musician who was one of the greatest singers of his time. He has been living there for nineteen years, supports himself with Subscription Concerts in the winter, and also gives lessons. He is a very good and hospitable man. His summer house, where I stayed, lies in a very lovely site on a hill that overlooks the whole city. Bath is one of the most beautiful towns in Europe, all the houses being made of stone. The stone is quarried in the nearby hills and it is so soft that it can be cut easily into all shapes, and is very white. The longer it is out of the earth, the harder it becomes. The whole town lies on a slope, and therefore there are few coaches, but there are plenty of sedan chairs in which one can be carried a good distance for sixpence. . . . There are many beautiful squares with the most magnificent houses. I made the acquaintance of Miss Brown, an amiable, discreet person and a good pianist. Her mother is a very beautiful woman. . . .

The delight with which Haydn was received in the watering place is apparent from the welcome in the Bath *Herald and Register*: "Oh, had I Jubal's lyre, I would sweep the strings till Echo tired with repeating—Haydn treads upon Bathonian ground! Had this place, previous to his arrival, been the seat of discord, it must now be lulled into peace by the God of Harmony—while every individual who hath music in his soul must exclaim with enthusiasm: *Erit mihi magnus Apollo!*" At a later date the paper also published a French poem by a refugee in honor of the "immortal master."

Haydn had his own method of thanking his hosts for a charming reception. When Rauzzini showed him the tomb of his beloved dog Turk, in his garden, bearing the somewhat misanthropic inscription "Turk was a faithful dog and not a man," Haydn composed a four-part canon on these words (Hob. XXVIIb:45), and the grateful recipient added it to the epitaph. For the renowned musician Dr. Henry Harington, founder of the Harmonic Society of Bath, Haydn composed the music to a poem, "What Art Expresses," which the doctor had written in the Austrian master's praise.[14] This collaboration between the two musicians caused Clementi to make the following rather involved statement: "The first doctor [Harington] having bestowed much praise on the second doctor [Haydn], the said second doctor, out of doctorial gratitude, returns the first doctor thanks for all favor received, and praises in his turn the said first doctor most handsomely."

After three delightful days, Haydn went on to Bristol, which he also describes in his diary, praising the beautiful view from the hill, and remarking on the numerous churches, all in "the old Gothic style."

On returning to London in the autumn of 1794, Haydn began to make intensive preparations for the coming season. This time conditions were somewhat changed. Salomon suddenly decided not to continue his subscription series, probably because the war with France made it too difficult to secure first-class soloists. He therefore agreed to Haydn's being engaged for a new enterprise, the Opera Concerts, in which series he himself frequently appeared as a soloist. The new concerts were arranged on the largest scale known at that time. The performances took place every two weeks in the great new concert hall of the King's Theatre. Viotti was the artistic director, and Haydn shared the conductorship with Vincenzo Federici, who for three years had been accompanist at the Italian opera in London. The orchestra, led by the violinist William Cramer, was made up of no less than sixty players. The composers engaged, other than Haydn, were Muzio Clementi, Francesco Bianchi, and Vicente Martín y Soler (composer of the once successful

---

[14]The composition (Hob. XXVIb:3) has a rather strange form. The theme is first sung by a solo voice, then taken over by a mixed chorus, then followed by variations for the piano.

opera *Una cosa rara* immortalized in the second act of Mozart's *Don Giovanni*). The soloists included the greatest artists available, among them Brigida Giorgi-Banti, who had come to London in 1794. This former street singer enjoyed a tremendous success, and the words of Lord Mount-Edgcumbe reflect the general attitude: "In her, genius supplied the place of science, and the most correct ear, with the most exquisite taste, enabled her to sing with more effect, more expression, and more apparent knowledge of her art, than many much better professors. Her voice had not a fault in any part of its unusually extensive compass." Haydn wrote the concert aria "Berenice che fai?" for her, which she performed at his benefit concert, but according to Griesinger, he noted in his diary (in English) that she "song [*sic*] very scanty," which again proves that at that time very few artists earned Haydn's full approval. He also found the oboist Giuseppe Ferlendis, who made his London debut in this benefit concert, "mediocre." But even if the master did not feel quite happy about the soloists, he could not help admitting that the benefit concert was a brilliant success. He remarked in his diary: "The hall was filled with a distinguished audience. The whole society was extremely pleased, and so was I. I netted four thousand florins on this evening. This one can make only in England." Altogether the Opera Concerts were received so enthusiastically that instead of the projected nine concerts, eleven had to be given. Among other works the tenth, eleventh, and twelfth of Haydn's London symphonies (Nos. 102–104) had their first performances in this series.

During this, his last London season, Haydn was in even closer touch with the court than in preceding years. It seems surprising that the master, in spite of his outstanding success, had never been introduced to the King, but George III was so passionately devoted to Handel's works that he took little interest in contemporary music. By now, however, Haydn had become so beloved in England that the monarch could no longer ignore his presence. The oboist William Thomas Parke tells about the first meeting in his *Memoirs*:

> The Duke of York gave a grand concert of instrumental music at York House, at which Their Majesties and the princesses were present. Salomon led the band and Haydn presided at the pianoforte. At the end of the first part of the concert Haydn had the distinguished honor of being formally introduced to His Majesty, George III, by the Prince of Wales. My station at the time was so near to the king that I could not avoid hearing the whole of their conversa-

tion. Among other observations, His Majesty said: "Dr. Haydn, you have written a great deal." Haydn modestly replied: "Yes, Sire, a great deal more than is good." His Majesty neatly rejoined: "Oh, no, the world contradicts that." After his introduction, at the queen's desire, Haydn sat down at the pianoforte and, surrounded by Her Majesty and her daughters, sang and accompanied himself admirably in several of his canzonets.

From that day on, Haydn was frequently invited by the Queen to her musicales at Buckingham House. He was treated most graciously, and the Queen gave him the manuscript of Handel's oratorio in German *Der gemarterte und sterbende Jesus.* The Prince of Wales also continued to see and hear Haydn frequently. When he gave a brilliant concert and supper in honor of the King's first visit to Carlton House, the music consisted almost entirely of Haydn's works, with Haydn conducting from the clavier. According to Parke: "The magnificence of the scene on this occasion was truly fascinating. The splendor of the dresses and the elegance and beauty of the ladies all combined to strike the beholder with admiration and delight."

On April 8, 1795, the wedding of the Prince of Wales to the Princess Caroline Amalia Elisabeth of Brunswick took place. It was of course impossible for Haydn to take part in the ceremony, for it had to be entrusted to the official court musicians. He was asked only to help solve a certain problem arising from the participation of three different musicians, and he reports on it in his fourth diary as follows:

> On the twenty-first of January I dined with Dr. Parsons, and during dinner a dispute arose to which of the three doctors, Parsons, Dupuis, or Arnold, should conduct Handel's anthem at the wedding of the Prince of Wales. Dr. Parsons is master of the king's band, the other two are organists of the royal chapel. In England the organist is, however, the head in all churches, and the singers are subordinate to him. Each of the three wanted to be the principal conductor. When I was forced to express my opinion, I said: "The younger organist should play the organ, the other conduct the singers, while Dr. Parsons should conduct the instrumental performers." This did not suit them, so I left the blockheads and went home.

In spite of the negative attitude of the three musicians concerned, Haydn's advice was followed at the ceremony. Only three days later the master was invited by the newly married couple to a musical party, about which he remarks in his diary: "An old symphony of mine was given, which I accompanied on the piano; then a quartet; and later I had to sing German and English songs. The Princess sang with me and played a concerto on the pianoforte quite well." (The description recalls the musical soirée at Oatlands arranged by the newly married Duke and Duchess of York four years previously, but how much warmer had been Haydn's praise of the "sweet little lady" then! Was this his preference for the daughter of the King of Prussia or was it just another symptom of the composer's general disillusionment?)

It seems that various members of the royal house made efforts to keep Haydn permanently in England. According to Griesinger, the Queen offered him a residence at Windsor for the summer, adding, with a mischievous glance toward the King: "Then we can make music tête-à-tête." The King declared that he was not jealous of Haydn, a "good, honest German," and also extended a most cordial invitation to the composer. Nevertheless, Haydn refused, giving various reasons, among them even his attachment to his wife [*sic*], who, he said, would be unwilling to make so long a journey.

At first sight it does not seem easy to understand Haydn's attitude. England was giving him so much—much more indeed than Vienna ever had. He was the central figure of London's musical life; no other composer's works were performed so frequently or with greater applause. Respect and admiration were paid to him as the "God of musical science," while to the Viennese he was still nothing more than the court conductor of a Hungarian magnate. The income he made in England was most satisfactory too, a matter that was anything but unimportant to one who had actually known utter poverty. Personally, life in England suited him well enough, for he had a number of good friends there, probably not fewer than in Vienna, and many people seemed only too eager to make his stay in London enjoyable. If, in spite of all these advantages, he decided to return to Austria, he had good reasons for doing so.

Being the musical hero of London was gratifying, even fascinating, but also fatiguing. Haydn was living, as it were, under continuous high pressure. To produce that "electrical effect," as Burney terms it, on a large and exacting audience demanded the utmost concentration and vitality, and called for an effort that could not be maintained indefinitely. The constant demands for new works, even with their enthusiastic reception, which had inspired Haydn to his greatest achievements, would have drained him of his creative power before long. Haydn instinctively felt that now it would be better for him to stand in the limelight no longer. Age was beginning to tell, and though the man of sixty-three did not consider his creative work finished, he felt it imperative to economize his strength. A quiet life in England seemed out of the question; there was too much to do and see. Moreover, any real relaxation appeared impossible in a country where he still had a difficulty in understanding the language. The thought of his own little house in the quiet suburb of Gumpendorf drew him away; there at least he might be able to lead the secluded life, devoted mainly to his art, which he now craved.

There was yet another consideration influencing him. Prince Anton Esterházy had died a few days after Haydn's departure from Vienna. His successor, another Nicolaus, was following the tradition so gloriously established by his grandfather, Prince Nicolaus the Magnificent. He had written to Haydn that he planned to restore the former orchestra and asked the master to take over the leadership again. The composer consented, for after so many years of service for the family it was inconceivable to him that another should preside over the Esterházy orchestra. It would be wrong, however, to see Prince Esterházy's offer as the main attraction that drew Haydn back to Austria. At that time he had become independent enough in both character and financial status to choose the kind of life best suited for his art, and it will be seen that even as an employee of Prince Nicolaus Esterházy, he gave but a small part of his time and his interests to the service of his patron.

Leaving England, and this time he knew it was for good, was by no means easy, so Haydn lingered on and on. On May 4, 1795, his benefit concert took place; he directed two of his symphonies in concerts by artist friends on May 29 and June 8. After that he was free to go home, but he stayed on until August 15, eager to catch another and yet another glimpse of this English life that had become so dear to him.

His English admirers were not aware of Haydn's inner struggles; to them the matter wore a different aspect. The King had invited Haydn to take up his residence in England and the master had refused. The court was disappointed and rather offended, and, characteristically, no member of the royal family except the faithful

Duchess of York appeared at Haydn's benefit concert. The news-papers ceased to mention his name, aware perhaps of the court's changed attitude, but his personal friends remained faithful to him. Anne Hunter, who had supplied the texts for Haydn's English can-zonettas, wrote the poem "O Tuneful Voice," deploring that the composer's "accents which still vibrated in her heart" were to be heard no more. Haydn, pleased with his friend's tender words, did not hesitate to set to music the poem written in his own praise. He received various parting gifts, among them a talking parrot (which was auctioned off for fourteen hundred florins after Haydn's death), a beautiful coconut goblet from Clementi, and a silver goblet with a very respectful inscription from the Reverend W. D. Tattersall, to whose *Improved Psalmody* Haydn had contributed six melodies. The master's trunks were fairly bulging with musical compositions; ac-cording to his own list in the diary copied by Griesinger, he had written no less than seven hundred sixty-eight pages of music dur-ing his two visits to England. Nor was the money he took home a mean amount. He had once more earned twelve hundred pounds for concerts, lessons, and symphonies, and to this was added the considerable income from other works, fees for appearances at Carlton House, and other sources. Altogether he had earned some twenty-four thousand florins in the three years spent in England. This meant a sizable improvement of his financial condition, for— as he told Griesinger—when he left Vienna in 1790, his capital had barely amounted to two thousand florins. But the fruits of his stay in England cannot be expressed in figures alone. Haydn's mental outlook had been immensely widened, his self-confidence had tre-mendously increased, and if at the age of sixty-three he felt im-pelled to leave the country that had given him so much, it was not the quiet repose of old age to which he was looking forward. He now needed the seclusion necessary for starting on new artistic ventures.

# CHAPTER NINE

# On a New Path

## 1 7 9 5 – 1 8 0 1

By the end of August 1795, Haydn was back in Vienna. This time things looked more promising for him than they had on his return from London three years previously. A new head of the Esterházy family was awaiting the kapellmeister's return so that musical activities worthy of the traditions of Nicolaus the Magnificent could be arranged. Haydn had his hands full in reorganizing the orchestra and making all necessary preparations for a brilliant debut of the new *Kapelle*. The occasion was a grandiose performance on January 4, 1796, of the opera *Penelope* by Antonio Draghi. The audience was dazzled not only by excellent singers from the Vienna opera, but also by costly fireworks. The event took place in the Prince's Viennese palace. Fortunately for Haydn, his new patron, Nicolaus II, was by no means enamored of the castle of Eszterháza and much preferred spending the winter months in the imperial capital, the summer and autumn at Eisenstadt. In this respect the Prince's wishes coincided fully with those of his conductor.

However this was nearly the only point on which the Prince and Haydn saw eye-to-eye, and on the whole their relationship was not pleasant. Of the four Esterházy princes with whom Haydn was connected, the last, under whom the master served for fifteen years, was the hardest to satisfy. His predecessor had merely been uninterested in music, a state of affairs that Haydn really could not resent. With Nicolaus II, it was different. In many respects he, like his grandfather, was a passionate patron of the fine arts. He spent enormous sums in adding to his collections; he engaged well-known artists, such as the painter J. Carl Roesler and the sculptor Antonio Canova; he changed the park into the English style and rebuilt the castle (though not finishing the project), and he had excellent troupes of actors. He professed a love of music but was considered unmusical by many contemporary musicians, and he showed himself generous to some composers. It is recorded, for instance, that on a visit to Paris he gave Cherubini a ring worth four thousand thalers. But he would not have dreamed of making such a gesture to Cherubini's idol, Joseph Haydn. The truth was that he did not really care for the old composer's works. His musical interest was concentrated almost exclusively on church music. One of his favorite composers was Haydn's former "teacher," K. G. Reutter, whose outmoded compositions he could not hear too often. The Prince also admired Michael Haydn because he had written some important church music and probably thought more highly of this composer of minor abilities than of the great master of instrumental music attached to his court. On the other hand, it was flattering to his vanity to have in his employ a composer whose services made Prince Esterházy the envy of many a potentate. Therefore, of course, he kept Haydn as his kapellmeister. At first the Prince paid the composer only the old salary of fourteen hundred florins (which Haydn had received from Prince Anton without doing any work). Nor did he pretend an interest or sympathy for the master that he did not feel. Contemporaries describe the Prince's nature as worthy of an "Asiatic despot." His lack of tact and the feeling of superiority in his intercourse with composers are well revealed in his behavior toward Beethoven. At the Prince's request, Beethoven wrote his first great work of sacred music in 1806–07, the Mass in C major, which ranks among the foremost works of the kind written in that period. After the performance the Prince merely remarked to the composer, who had already proved his genius with the "Eroica" Symphony, *Fidelio*, and other works: "But, my dear Beethoven, what have you done here again?" Whereupon the outraged composer left the castle. We know from a letter the Prince wrote to Countess von Zielinska[1] that he found the Mass "unbearably ridiculous and detestable." Yet whatever his reaction to the composition, his behaviour to Beethoven reveals excessive ar-

---

[1] Cf. János Harich, "Beethoven in Eisenstadt," *Burgenländische Heimatblätter* (Eisenstadt), XXI/2 (1959), p. 173ff.

rogance. He was as complete an autocrat as his grandfather had been but lacked the latter's redeeming features, especially his genuine understanding of music. He did not, like Nicolaus I, carefully handle his immense fortune but squandered it in such a manner that Baron Mayer von Rothschild had to "be entrusted with the chaotic financial affairs of the Esterházy family."[2] This sad state of affairs was partly caused by the Prince's profligate way of life—the countless affairs carried on in his Vienna residence, with its notorious "temple dedicated to debauchery" described by Count Zinzendorf in his diary.[3]

This was the person in whose service Haydn stood in his old age. At this point in his life he felt much less prepared than he had been before to accept the despotism of a man half his age, one who in musical matters often did not understand what he was talking about. Once Haydn even went so far as to express this. When the Prince uttered some unjustified criticism at a rehearsal, Haydn burst out with: "Your Highness, it is *my* job to decide this," whereupon Nicolaus indignantly went out of the room, leaving all the musicians "horror-stricken." Nor did Haydn lose any opportunity of impressing on his patron that he felt his salary to be inadequate. This is revealed in the following letter which shows that Haydn now approached his patron without the former obsequiousness and servility. Prince Esterházy had as a housemaster in the Hungarian town of Sopron a certain Johann Alois Luegmayer, who had the good luck to be married to a niece of Haydn's. The spendthrift nephew took ample advantage of this relationship, for he liked to contract debts in the name of his famous uncle, and he was so successful in these manipulations that, according to Haydn's own testimony, Luegmayer received some six thousand florins from him in the course of several years. Eventually even Haydn, to whom the integrity of his family mattered greatly, lost patience. When informed by the Prince's administration that his account was being charged with new debts of the housemaster, he not only refused to pay them, but also boldly changed from defensive to offensive tactics. This is the way he expressed himself in an undated letter, probably written at the end of 1796 to Prince Esterházy's administrator:

> I see from the papers forwarded to me, and the enclosure from His Highness Prince Esterházy's economic

[2]Cf. *HCaW*, IV, p. 47ff.
[3]Cf. ibid., p. 46.

administration that in consequence of Luegmayer's *in-ability* to pay his debt, I am condemned to do so. Pray, why? Because I am supposed to be *able* to pay. Would to God this were the case. But I swear by the Kyrie eleison, which I am at this moment supposed to compose for my fourth Prince, that since the death of my second Prince of blessed memory I have fallen into the same state of insolvency as Luegmayer himself, only with this difference: he has descended from a horse to the back of an ass, whereas I have remained on the horse, but without saddle or bridle. I beg therefore, gentlemen, you will at least have patience till I have finished the "Dona nobis pacem," and till the Prince's housemaster Luegmayer, instead of receiving his salary from the poorly paid music director Haydn (who spent thirty-six years in the Princes' service), shall begin to get the salary justly due to him from his most gracious Prince. For surely nothing can be more sad or incongruous than that one servant should pay another servant; that is, the Kapellmeister pay the housemaster. If I should presently by my own efforts (for flatter or beg I cannot) or by the voluntary impulse of my gracious Prince be placed in a better position, I will not fail to comply with the above demand.

I am, Sir, etc. . . .

This letter apparently had two purposes. It not only stressed Haydn's insufficient salary; it was also meant to reinforce a petition dated February 7, 1797, which Luegmayer had submitted to the Prince. From it we learn that since 1793 the housemaster had received a pension amounting to sixty-eight florins and forty-two kreutzer from Haydn, and the *Naturalien*, such as rye, wine, and wood, from the Prince. He explained that on such a small income he was unable to support his wife and three small children and petitioned for an increase in salary. We do not know how the matter was settled. Usually Haydn found a better method of reaching the Prince's ear. He went to Princess Marie Hermenegild, the wife of Nicolaus II, who liked and admired the master greatly, and eventually she smoothed out matters for him. For instance, he resented not being addressed with the courtesy due a Doctor of Music of Oxford, and it was the Princess who saw to it that no one at court, not even her husband, should speak of the composer curtly as

"Haydn" without a prefix, and that official letters addressed to him were full of the flourishes accorded a person of distinction. Over the years the Princess also obtained several salary increases for the composer, as well as other favors, such as the regular delivery of wine from the princely cellars.

Altogether, Haydn, although not enjoying the work for his fourth Prince, may not have resented it too much because his duties were not particularly heavy. His main obligation was that of occasionally composing new Masses for his patron. This he did, and six masterworks were written for this purpose. Apart from that, Haydn's most important duty was to be on hand for festive occasions when the Prince wanted to show off his famous conductor, as he did when the Archduke Joseph, Viceroy of Hungary, visited Eisenstadt twice in 1797, and the Emperor and Empress once in 1800, events that were celebrated with the traditional Esterházian splendor. For the ordinary routine work there was a substitute, Johann Fuchs, a member of the orchestra, since Haydn himself felt entitled to give most of his time to occupations not connected with the service of his Prince, occupations that were to assume paramount importance during the years to come.

The composer had returned to Vienna teeming with energy, and the work to be done for his narrow-minded patron was but a poor outlet. While still in London, Haydn is said to have declared: "I want to write a work that will give permanent fame to my name in the world." The unforgettable experience of the Handel Commemoration in Westminster Abbey had convinced the composer that an oratorio was best suited to link his name indissolubly to the future. In addition to this consideration, Haydn's urge to experiment with new ways of expression drove him toward the oratorio. After writing the London symphonies, he felt that he had reached a height never to be surpassed by him in this type of music. Orchestral composition offered no further attractions to him, and though he was in his middle sixties, he felt eager to measure his strength against a new genre, one in which he had not as yet proved his mastery.

That Haydn chose the Creation for a subject is again because of England. There are various reports about it. It seems that Salomon gave the master a libretto that a man by the name of Lidley[4] had compiled for Handel from Milton's *Paradise Lost*. On the other

---

[4] Cf. D. Edward Olleson, "The Origin and Libretto of Haydn's *Creation*," *HYb*, IV (1968), p. 148ff.

hand, according to C. H. Purday,[5] the violinist Barthélemon, one of Haydn's great friends, when asked to suggest a suitable subject for an oratorio, pointed to the Bible and exclaimed: "There! Take that, and begain at the beginning." It does not seem impossible that both stories are true. Haydn, influenced by Bathélemon, may have mentioned his intention to Salomon, who then procured the libretto, which Haydn took with him to Vienna. This book was in English, and the composer, who was determined to compose a German text, needed a translator. Chance helped him to find the right man.

Vienna had among its musical amateurs of noble birth, a baron of Dutch origin whose hobby was the oratorio, especially the works of Handel. This was Gottfried van Swieten, prefect of the Vienna court library and president of the educational commission. His father, Gerhard van Swieten, had played an important part at court as the favorite physician of the Empress Maria Theresa. The son chose a diplomatic career, and from 1771 to 1777 was ambassador to the court of Frederick the Great of Prussia, where he became acquainted with north German music. There for the first time he heard the name of Johann Sebastian Bach, and his curiosity was stirred to such an extent that he traveled to visit Bach's son, Philipp Emanuel, in Hamburg and bought from him several manuscripts and copies of works by the cantor of the Thomasschule, together with some music by Emanuel himself. When he returned to Vienna, he was probably the only person in the city who owned a copy of *The Well-Tempered Clavier*. On the other hand, in 1769 the baron visited England, where he became an ardent admirer of Handel. He took home the scores of some of Handel's greatest oratorios, and thenceforth considered it his mission to propagate the music of Handel and Bach in the Sunday morning musicales that he arranged in the magnificent baroque hall of the court library. As no organ was available, the baron made one of the regular guests, Wolfgang Amadeus Mozart, reorchestrate various Handel oratorios by substituting wind instruments for the organ. Swieten also induced the young composer to arrange some Bach fugues for string trio or quartet with the addition of introductory adagios, and by drawing Mozart's attention to baroque music, exercised an important influence on the composer's artistic development. Beethoven too was patronized by the baron and repaid him by dedicating his

[5] This information was given to Carl Ferdinand Pohl by Sir George Grove, who had it from Purday's son.

First Symphony to him. Swieten was a composer himself, and though his orchestral works were "as stiff as their composer" (Griesinger), his Symphony in E-flat enjoyed the undeserved privilege of being attributed to Haydn for a long time. Altogether the baron was not what one would call a lovable person. He was obstinate, despotic, and, despite his considerable wealth, decidedly tightfisted. It was he who, when approached on Mozart's death by the destitute widow, advised Constanze to bury the master in a pauper's grave so as to save expense. Culturally his influence was sometimes anything but beneficial, and, according to Riemann, the Vienna court library suffered under his leadership greater damages than from wars or fires. He gave orders for the removal of everything that "merely gratified the imagination or was a scholastic luxury," and by so doing he had many priceless incunabula destroyed.

Nevertheless, in spite of his faults, Gottfried van Swieten was the right man for Haydn. He was much more than a mere translator, and in the chapter dealing with Haydn's last period of composition, his share in Haydn's oratorios will be pointed out. What concerns us here is the fact that van Swieten, through his influential position, gave the works the best possible start. In those times composers as a rule did not write an important work unless it was commissioned. Even Haydn, in spite of his enormous fame and secure financial position, probably would have been reluctant to do so. Had he stayed in England he might have written such an oratorio for Salomon or Gallini. To whom could he turn in Vienna, where businesslike concert enterprises in the English manner were hardly known? At this point van Swieten stepped in. He got together a group of music-loving noblemen and each guaranteed a contribution of fifty ducats to defray the expenses of performance and pay an honorarium to the composer. Thus Haydn had firm ground under his feet, and started on the composition of *The Creation*, to which he devoted most of his time and energy during the following years. The work progressed slowly, for as Haydn remarked, he spent much time over it, because he intended it to last a long time.

These years devoted to the composition of *The Creation* were among the richest and happiest in Haydn's life. He was fully absorbed by a task in which, perhaps better than ever before, he could express the innermost forces of his nature. Haydn had always been deeply religious and free from doubt and skepticism; he was really sincere when he wrote the words *Laus Deo* at the end of each of his compositions. In spite of life's darker sides, which were well known to Haydn, who had led an unsheltered life from earliest childhood, the world seemed a very good and beautiful place. To some slight extent, each of his works was a Creation, expressing praise and thankfulness to the Heavenly Father. Now he could do so on a much larger scale and with a freedom he never had had in the composition of a Mass; at the same time he had a chance to depict in sounds the beauties of nature, which delighted this passionate hunter and fisherman so much. Here he could—as was always his aim—"depict Divinity through love and goodness" and express in his own idiom the harmonious view of life, the serene affirmative spirit that filled his soul. When he worked on this oratorio, Haydn felt uplifted and in close communion with his Creator. "Never was I so devout," he said, "as when composing *The Creation*. I knelt down every day and prayed to God to strengthen me for my work." He remarked to Carpani that when he felt his inspiration flagging, he "rose from the pianoforte and began to say his rosary." He "never found this method to fail."

The effect that Haydn wanted to achieve with this work cannot be better expressed than in the words that Princess Eleonore Liechtenstein used in a letter to her daughter about *The Creation*: "One has to shed tender tears about the greatness, the majesty, the goodness of God. The soul is uplifted. One cannot but love and admire."[6]

April 29 and 30, 1798, were exciting days for the Viennese. Although only invited guests were admitted to these first performances of *The Creation* at the palace of Prince Schwarzenberg, a tremendous crowd of onlookers gathered outside the building. The market stalls on the Neuer Markt (formerly the Mehlmarkt), where the palace (demolished in 1893) was situated, had to be removed, and twelve policemen and eighteen mounted guards were stationed to keep order in the approaches to the house. The privileged who were allowed to enter consisted mostly of the nobility, among them, as Princess Liechtenstein records, "all the elegant Polish, English, and Viennese ladies." Carpani also relates: "I was present, and I can assure you I never witnessed such a scene. The flower of the literary and musical society of Vienna was assembled in the room, which was well adapted to the purpose. The most profound silence, the most scrupulous attention, a sentiment, I might almost say, of religious respect prevailed when the first stroke of the bow was given." On this occasion the composer was not his usual placid

[6] See Carl Ferdinand Pohl and Hugo Botstiber, *Joseph Haydn* (Leipzig, 1927), III, p. 130.

self. "One moment," he said later, "I was cold as ice, the next I seemed on fire. More than once I was afraid I should have a stroke." The musicians were of the first rank. Haydn himself conducted in the modern way with a baton, as was customary for choral performances. At the piano sat the court composer, Salieri. The soprano part was sung by Christine Gerardi, aged twenty-one, whom a contemporary critic described as follows: "Flexibility and beauty of voice, a lovely figure, expressive features, and lustrous eyes give vigor to each of her words and grace to every sound rising from her throat."[7] The male soloists were Ignaz Saal, bass of the court opera, and Mathias Rathmayer, professor of the Theresian Academy, whose beautiful tenor voice Princess Liechtenstein praised. Success was overwhelming and far beyond expectation. Most of the listeners may have felt like the Viennese correspondent of the *Neuer teutscher Merkur*, who wrote: "Three days have gone since that enrapturing evening, and still the music sounds in my ears and in my heart; still the mere memory of all the flood of emotions then experienced constricts my chest."

Furthermore, Haydn had good reason to be well satisfied with the material success. Not only did his aristocratic patrons pay him the agreed honorarium of five hundred ducats, to which Prince Schwarzenberg, after the first rehearsal, added a roll containing another hundred ducats,[8] but in addition they presented him with the entire receipts from the admission fees. However, this was only the beginning. For years *The Creation* was to prove so unfailing an attraction that the proceeds from it, mostly given to charitable institutions, by far surpassed even the receipts from the London benefit concerts that had once seemed so extraordinary to Haydn.

As early as May 7 and 8 of the same year, the work was again played at the Schwarzenberg Palace. Suddenly, however, the exertion of these last years made itself felt: Haydn broke down and had to spend some time in bed. Though his absorption in the congenial task of composing the oratorio brought him the greatest happiness, it also imposed a tremendous strain. On many occasions physical weaknesses checked the flow of his inspiration and caused Haydn to despair, and when he had recovered and could go on with his work, a certain lack of confidence in what he was doing taxed his strength as the writing of symphonies or string quartets never had. A letter

[7] In the *Neuer teutscher Merkur* (May 3, 1798).
[8] Cf. C.-G. Stellan Mörner, in "Haydniana aus Schweden um 1800," *H-St*, II/1 (Mar. 1969), p. 28.

that he addressed to the publisher C. G. Breitkopf on June 12, 1799, is very significant in this respect. Although written one year after the memorable first performance of *The Creation*, the excerpts herewith reproduced reflect the strain of the past years of composition and show that Haydn was not certain even then how the more conservative critics would receive the work that was now to be circulated in print throughout the musical world:

> . . . My business unhappily expands with my advancing years. The world daily pays me many compliments, even on the fervor of my latest works; but no one can believe the strain and effort it costs me to produce them, inasmuch as time after time my enfeebled memory and the unstrung state of my nerves so completely crush me to earth that I fall into the most melancholy condition. For days afterward I am incapable of formulating one single idea, till at length my heart is revived by Providence, and I seat myself at the piano and begin once more to scratch away. Enough of it! . . . *I only wish and hope that the critics may not handle my* Creation *with too great severity and be too hard on it. They may possibly find the musical orthography faulty in various passages and perhaps other things also, which for so many years I have been accustomed to consider as minor points, but the true connoisseur will see the real cause as readily as I do, and willingly ignore such stumbling blocks. Nulla Regola s[enza] e[ccezione].*[9]

Writing a full-sized oratorio with such painstaking care would be a heavy task for any artist in his late sixties, but Haydn by no means confined himself to this work. During these same years he wrote two large Masses, a vocal arrangement of *The Seven Last Words*, a concerto for keyed trumpet, some of his very best string quartets, three trios with piano, and his own favorite, the national hymn "Gott erhalte," which more than anything else enhanced his popularity in his own country. The impulse to compose the Austrian hymn also came from England. Noticing the deep impression produced in London whenever "God Save the King" was played, Haydn felt that in the distressed times of the Napoleonic Wars Austria needed a patriotic song. Here, too, van Swieten proved of ser-

[9] The final part of the letter beginning with "I only wish and hope . . ." was underlined by Haydn.

vice in the realization of the master's idea. He discussed it with the imperial chancellor, Count Saurau, who gladly took up the project and commissioned a poet by the name of Leopold Haschka to write a suitably patriotic text.[10] In January 1797, Haydn set it to music and on February 12, on the Emperor's birthday, the anthem was sung in all the theaters of Vienna and the Austrian provinces. The enthusiasm aroused by the new hymn was tremendous, and the following little story throws a sidelight on its fast-growing popularity. A wealthy Englishman, who seemed to have stepped out of a fairy tale, offered to provide trousseaux for twenty-four engaged couples in Vienna who did not have enough money to be married, and thus make their marriages possible. The fortunate young people all were married simultaneously at St. Stephen's and then liberally entertained at Jahn's, the court caterer. Music was provided by a military band which, upon urgent request, had to play three times in succession the national hymn introduced to the Viennese only two days earlier.

Haydn received from the Emperor a gold box with the monarch's portrait and a substantial gratuity. The composer may have considered a state decoration a more appropriate gesture of thanks for this national hymn that so greatly built up the public morale at a time when it was sorely needed. But even though the Emperor Franz and his second wife, another Maria Theresa, felt much more friendly toward the master than their predecessors on the Habsburg throne, it simply did not occur to them to grant such an honor. In spite of the innumerable tributes of admiration that Haydn received in his old age, the award of a decoration from court was not among them.

But other honors were bestowed on him. One came from Sweden, when the Austrian composer was made a member of the Royal Music Academy. Another one, awarded in Vienna, had a symbolic significance, as it annulled an injustice under which Haydn had long smarted. The Viennese Tonkünstlersocietät had coolly rejected Haydn's application in 1779, but now offered him membership as "perpetual assessor" with exemption from any admission fees. This was a very unusual procedure, as the Societät, whose

[10] A somewhat divergent account of these events was reported in a letter from Count Saurau to Count Dietrichstein, the director of court music. Saurau claimed that the idea of a national anthem had originated with him and that he had then turned to Haschka and subsequently to Haydn with a request that the composer set Haschka's verses to music. Cf. *HCaW*, IV, p. 241.

main function was to insure musicians and their families, naturally was dependent on the payments of its members. The musicians, however, felt it imperative to make an exception in the case of Haydn, in order to obliterate their former shortsightedness. In doing so they not only gave great pleasure to the old master, but also brought important material benefits to the institute. From that time on Haydn showed himself most generous to the Societät. Shortly after his election he gave them the music to his new vocal version of *The Seven Last Words* and himself conducted two successful performances, thus assuring unusually high receipts. How little Haydn spared himself when there was a chance of helping the Societät is revealed in his calendar for March 1799. This month was devoted mainly to rehearsals of *The Creation*, which was to be performed for the first time in a theater open to the general public on March 19. In addition to this task, the burden being increased by two performances of the oratorio on March 2 and 4 at the Schwarzenberg Palace, Haydn conducted performances of *The Seven Last Words* for the Societät on March 17 and 18, the two days immediately preceding the great event. Nevertheless, on March 19 he showed no signs of fatigue, and the first public performance of the oratorio brought him sensational success. Indeed, so thrilled were the Viennese about the event (it drew the greatest crowd ever seen in the Burgtheater) that they hardly seemed to notice the Russian army under Suvarov that was passing through the capital on the same day. The correspondent for the Leipzig *Allgemeine Musikalische Zeitung* wrote as follows:

> On the nineteenth I heard Haydn's *Creation*. Not to report to you about this good fortune (for this is what it was) would reveal either too little feeling for art or for friendship. The crowd was immense and the receipts amounted to 4088 fl. 30 kr., a sum never before collected by a Viennese theater. Moreover, the nobility paid for all the not inconsiderable expenses of production. One can hardly imagine with what quiet and reverence the whole oratorio was received, only gently interrupted by soft exclamations at the most striking passages, and what enthusiastic applause sounded at the end of each piece.

The soprano singer was the seventeen-year-old Therese Saal, whose father, Ignaz Saal, performed the bass solos. One critic wrote of her performance: "The part of Eve in Haydn's *Creation* will hardly ever be sung again with such warmth, delicacy, and devout simplicity."

As a Christmas present for the Societät, Haydn conducted two performances of *The Creation* on December 22 and 23, 1799, and thereby again greatly improved the institute's financial status. On this occasion a critic for the *Allgemeine Musikalische Zeitung* wrote: "Haydn's gestures were most interesting to me. With their aid he conveyed to the numerous executants the spirit in which his work was composed and should be performed. In all his motions, though anything but exaggerated, one saw very clearly what he thought and felt at each passage." From that time forward it became the custom for Haydn to let the Societät perform his great oratorio, usually under his own direction. In a letter that the publisher George Thomson wrote to Haydn's friend Mrs. Hunter, he remarked: "Haydn wrote me lately that in three years forty thousand florins had been raised for the poor families of musicians by the performances of *The Creation* and *The Seasons* in Vienna."

One year after the first public performance in Vienna, *The Creation* was heard in London, and in this event the rivalry between competing impresarios played an important part. This time it was a race between Salomon and Ashley,[11] both having ordered the score from Haydn. The unlucky Salomon decidedly came out second. Not only did he have to pay the outrageous sum of £30.16.0 for postage, whereas Ashley's expenses for delivery through the courier of the British Legation amounted to only £2.12.6, but also, what was worse, Ashley was far quicker in presenting the oratorio. *The Creation* was performed by him in Covent Garden on March 28, 1800, only six days after receipt of the score, while Salomon followed on April 21. The amazing speed of Ashley's production was due mainly to the excellent organization of the copyist, Thomas Goodwin, who had to get one hundred and twenty parts copied out in so short a time. When praised for his efficiency, Goodwin remarked: "Sir, we have humbly emulated a great example; it is not the first time that the Creation has been completed in six days." Salomon followed with several performances through April and May up to June 4. By and large the reception given to Haydn's masterwork was lukewarm and in striking contrast to the attitude

[11] Ashley directed the Lent oratorios at Covent Garden inaugurated by Handel. He began directing them in 1795.

of the British audiences toward the composer's symphonies. Comparisons with Handel's "sacred inspiration" seemed inevitable to English friends of music and generally turned out to Haydn's disadvantage. Especially Haydn's bold stroke of genius in evoking the chaos in the instrumental prelude seemed too dissonant to be acceptable to the listeners.

Paris followed London's example a few months later. Interest in Haydn's compositions had been steadily increasing there, and the French friends of music desired that the composer himself conduct his oratorio. This attitude was rather remarkable in view of the almost continual state of war in those years between France and Austria. However, if the French were magnanimous enough to forget political controversies for the sake of good music, the Austrian police definitely did not adopt this attitude. When Pleyel, who had settled in Paris and become a French citizen, was sent to Vienna by the Opéra in the summer of 1800 to present the French invitation to Haydn in person and possibly carry him off as Salomon had done ten years previously, the Austrian authorities did not allow the musician, lest he might be a spy, to cross the border from Germany. All the endeavors of Haydn and the publishing house of Artaria proved of no avail, and Pleyel had to return to Paris without having accomplished his mission. At first Haydn felt greatly tempted to go to Paris, for he had not forgotten how delightful it was to travel in a foreign country. In the end, however, he decided against it, and the Paris performance took place on December 24, 1800, under Steibelt's direction. Unfortunately the attention of the audience was greatly distracted by the news that Bonaparte, then First Consul, who was attending the concert, had just escaped a bomb attempt on his life in the rue Nicaise. In spite of this drawback the musicians were so enthusiastic about *The Creation* that they had a large gold medal engraved in commemoration of the event. This medal, designed by Gatteaux, was presented to Haydn one year later and gave him immense pleasure.

Although Haydn would certainly have enjoyed a visit to Paris, he was wise not to yield to the temptation. His physical strength might have been unequal to the exertion, for since the spring of 1800 his health had not been satisfactory. Early in April he had been seized by a "rheumatic fever of the head" that kept him in bed and at first looked so serious that, according to a letter from the British embassy, the Viennese "were not altogether devoid of alarm in regard to his recovery." Although Haydn was allowed to get up by the end of April, his convalescence proceeded very slowly. Throughout the summer at Eisenstadt he was tired and dispirited, and it was not until August 2 that he was able to write to Luigia Polzelli that he was feeling better.

This breakdown, far worse than the one two years before, was not surprising. Indeed it is rather remarkable that it had not occurred earlier. Haydn had been absorbed in too many activities. He had even, for the first time, tried his hand in business by being his own publisher. In so doing he apparently followed the advice of van Swieten, who considered the publication of *The Creation* through a business firm "not honorable." Haydn collected the subscriptions for the score of the oratorio himself and, with his characteristic politeness, in many cases took pains to write detailed answers. The subscribers' list to be found in this first edition of the oratorio is illuminating in many respects. That both Austria and England claimed Haydn for their own is shown by the illustrious names heading the list: the Austrian Empress and various archdukes of the House of Habsburg, the King and Queen of England, the Prince and Princess of Wales, the Duchess of York, and the Princesses Augusta, Elisabeth, Maria, Sophia, and Amalia. About half the remaining subscriptions came from England. Among them were the names of many persons who had become Haydn's friends during his stay in the British capital: Bartolozzi, Barthélemon, Salomon, Mrs. Schröter, the Misses Abrams, Sir Patrick Blake, Lady Rich, and Haydn's colleagues in the Doctorate of Oxford, Dr. Arnold, Dr. Aylwood, and Dr. Ayrton. In addition there was a surprisingly large number of members of the British nobility; characteristically, many of the subscribers were women. Apparently the memory of Haydn's earlier social success still was very much alive. Among the Austrian subscribers we also find many aristocratic music lovers, names like those of the Princes Lichnowsky, Kinsky, and Liechtenstein, all familiar to us from Beethoven's dedications. Germany too was represented by various princes and duchesses. Looking over this imposing list, the son of the modest wheelwright must have felt great satisfaction. But when the preparatory work was done and the score of the oratorio securely launched, Haydn entrusted the firm of Artaria with the distribution of the work, recognizing that his time might be spent in a more congenial way.

The constant awareness of "so much to be done" drove the old master on inexorably, heedless of his diminishing physical strength. He was now almost exclusively absorbed in creative work. An interesting document preserved in the Mozarteum at Salzburg and entitled *Daily Schedule of the late Herr v[on] Haydn*[12] (possibly writ-ten by Elssler) gives some details of the composer's way of life. It reads as follows:

In the summertime he rose at 6:30 AM. First he shaved, which he did for himself up to his seventy-third year, and then he completed dressing. If a pupil was present, he had to play his lesson on the piano to Herr von Haydn, while the master dressed. All mistakes were promptly corrected and a new task was then set. This occupied an hour and a half. At eight o'clock sharp, breakfast had to be on the table, and immediately after breakfast Haydn sat down at the piano, improvising and drafting sketches of some com-position. From eight to eleven-thirty his time was taken up in this way. At eleven-thirty calls were received or made, or he went for a walk until one-thirty. The hour from two to three was reserved for dinner, after which Haydn imme-diately did some little work in the house or resumed his musical occupations. He scored the morning's sketches, devoting three or four hours to this. At 8:00 PM Haydn usually went out, and at nine he came home and sat down to write a score or he took a book and read until 10:00 PM. At that time he had supper, which consisted of bread and wine. Haydn made a rule of eating nothing but bread and wine at night and infringed it only on sundry occasions when he was invited to supper. He liked gay conversation and some merry entertainment at the table. At eleven-thirty he went to bed, in his old age even later. Wintertime made no difference to the schedule, except that Haydn got up half an hour later.

Griesinger amplifies this schedule by telling us that every evening Haydn carefully went through the household accounts in order to keep his servants in bounds. On the other hand, he liked to play cards with them in winter evenings, and got much amusement from seeing their delight when they won a few pence from him. Haydn, fully absorbed in creative work, probably enjoyed inter-course with such simple people as a relaxation. On the whole, this way of life left but little scope for close relationships of any kind,

[12] It was customary in the Austrian Empire to employ the word "von" (abbreviated "v.") in addressing every person of good standing, although it was rightfully con-fined to the nobility.

and indeed there is not much to relate about Haydn's personal activities during these years. From 1797 he lived in his own house, doubly enjoyable because his wife was hardly ever there. Frau Haydn, who was suffering from severe rheumatism, spent most of her declining years at the sulfur springs of the little town of Baden, where she died on March 20, 1800. The event probably meant little to her husband, for he had become used to a sort of bachelor existence and was well looked after by Elssler and the cook, Anna Kremnitzer. There was one person, however, who was sent into a flurry of excitement by the news of Frau Haydn's death. Luigia Polzelli again was living in Vienna, although not in the service of Prince Esterházy, for Haydn apparently did not attempt to obtain an engagement for her. Luigia lost no time in reminding Haydn of his former promise to marry her when he was free. The old composer did not like the idea at all; he felt too settled in his ways for any further matrimonial experiments. All that mattered to him was to pass the remainder of his life in a smoothly ordered routine that would be instrumental in conserving his creative powers. When Luigia found it was impossible to change his attitude, she made him sign the following document:

> I, the undersigned, promise Signora Luigia Polzelli, in case I should marry again, to take nobody else for wife other than the above-mentioned Luigia Polzelli; and if I remain a widower, I promise to leave the above-mentioned Luigia Polzelli after my death a pension of three hundred florins in Vienna currency for so long as she lives. Valid before any judge, I sign
>
> JOSEPH HAYDN
>
> *Maestro di Cappella to his Highness*
> *the Prince Esterházy*

Vienna, May 23, 1800

Luigia, on her side, did not promise anything. Thus, with Haydn's pledge safely in her pocket, she saw no reason for remaining single. She therefore married an Italian singer, Luigi Franchi, and they went to Italy. The old master, while not feeling jealous, did not like to be imposed upon, and therefore in his will he reduced the pension to half the promised amount.

So Luigia Polzelli gradually faded from Haydn's life, and no other woman appeared to take her place or that of Marianne von Genzinger. As the above-mentioned *Daily Schedule* testifies, Haydn still had some pupils. He had lost the one of whom he had been particularly fond. Pietro Polzelli, Luigia's eldest son, died in 1796, at the early age of nineteen. His place was taken to some extent by Sigismund von Neukomm, who worked for seven years under Haydn and became attached to him. In 1799 Anna Milder (the first to sing the part of Leonore in Beethoven's *Fidelio*) also became a sort of pupil. Haydn found that the girl of fourteen had a voice "as big as a house" and handed her over for instruction to Neukomm, while taking an active interest in the singer's development. When she won her first laurels in 1803, Griesinger worte: "Her voice sounds like pure metal and as her teacher Neukomm is schooled by Haydn, she produces long vigorous notes without flourishes and exaggerated ornaments." The name of Griesinger (cf. p. 12n.) frequently occurs in our report. From 1799 he was in close contact with Haydn, whom he described to the firm of Breitkopf and Härtel after his first visit as "a cheerful and still well-preserved man, and to all his colleagues a model of modesty and simplicity." Haydn immediately took a fancy to the young man, who understood how to humor him and thus obtained important contracts for the Leipzig publisher. (On the other hand, presents from Breitkopf and Härtel, such as a diamond ring, handkerchiefs of Indian silk, waistcoats of English cashmere, and colored silk hose pleased the old man immensely.)

Another publisher who also used a personal emissary was George Thomson of Edinburgh, who asked Mr. Straton and subsequently Mr. Stuart, both of the British Legation, to negotiate with Haydn for arrangements of Scottish folk songs to be published by him. Haydn approved the suggestion and in the course of years supplied some two hundred fifty airs to Thomson, for which, according to the publisher's statement, he received £291.18.0. No friendship, however, developed between Haydn and Straton, who apparently did not have much use for musicians. The following passage in a letter from Straton to Thomson[13] reveals a feeling of superiority that made impossible a closer relationship with the composer:

> Haydn called here yesterday and mentioned that he
> had already written to you and also begun the composition

[13] Cf. Pohl and Botstiber, *Joseph Haydn*, III, p. 159.

of the accompaniments to the Scotch airs (fifteen in number) that you had sent him through me. He seemed desirous of having rather more than two Ducats for each air, but did not precisely insist upon this point, which I therefore left undecided exhorting him to proceed with his composition as speedily as its nature as well as that of his other occupations will admit of. This he solemnly promised but said that he could not possibly determine a period for finishing the airs in question. Upon the whole he appears to be a rational animal, whereas all that can be said of the other, I mean Koz[eluch],[14] is that he is a Bipede without feathers.

Similar work was done by Haydn for the publisher William Whyte of Edinburgh, the Viennese firm of Artaria serving as intermediary. Whyte published sixty-five arrangements of Scottish folk songs, paying Haydn twenty florins for each. This undemanding task, in which Haydn may have received help from his pupils, seems to have given him satisfaction and also provided pleasant additional income.

In 1800, Haydn met two English people of great renown. Early in the fall, Admiral Nelson and Lady Hamilton paid a visit to the Esterházys at Eisenstadt. Haydn asked his publisher Artaria to send him a copy of his cantata *Arianna a Naxos* because Lady Hamilton wanted to sing it. Griesinger reports about the event to Breitkopf: "In Lady Hamilton, Haydn found a great admirer. She visited the Esterházy estate in Hungary, but paid little attention to its splendors, and for two days did not budge from Haydn's side." She sang various compositions by the composer. There is also an unconfirmed report from Griesinger that Nelson asked for the worn-out pen Haydn had used when writing his *Nelson Mass* (cf. p. 346f.), and in exchange gave the master his valuable gold watch.

In the same year the Bach biographer and musicologist Johann N. Forkel visited the composer and brought him a poem that the famous poet Christoph Martin Wieland had written on hearing *The Creation*.

Haydn was happy to be reminded of the years in London by visits from his good friends Domenico Dragonetti, the double-bass virtuoso, and the young Johann Baptist Cramer. Michael Haydn's

---

[14]Leopold Anton Koželuch, serving as Viennese court composer, also arranged Scottish airs for Thomson.

short visit to Vienna also gave both brothers much enjoyment. To Michael, who had lived in Salzburg since 1762, a trip to the capital was about as exciting and important as the London visits had been to his brother. He kept a diary of all he saw and did, and after the lapse of a year he tried to revive the memory of all those delightful experiences by rereading his notebook.[15]

Although Joseph enjoyed such pleasant episodes, his main interest always lay in composition. The year of the first performance of *The Creation*, 1798, also saw the completion of the *Nelson Mass*; 1799, that of the *Theresa Mass*. During these same years Haydn composed two string quartets, Op. 77, for Prince Lobkowitz, and small vocal works such as the thirteen vocal duos, trios, and quartets, written, according to the composer's words to Griesinger, "*con amore* in happy hours, without being commissioned."[16] All this happened, as it were, on the fringes of his creative life, the center of which was fully occupied after the completion of *The Creation* by another oratorio, *The Seasons*. The impulse for the composition of this oratorio came from van Swieten, who, after winning so many laurels with Haydn, was eager to continue on this path. He translated James Thomson's epic poem "The Seasons" and adapted it as a libretto for an oratorio, giving Haydn minute instructions as to the sequence of the arias and recitatives. In his translation he made use of the German text presented by the poet B. H. Brockes in 1745. Haydn, though he considered the guidance of the composer by the poet to be quite in order, did not feel so happy as when he had composed *The Creation*. The somewhat verbose and philistine text did not inspire him as strongly as van Swieten's earlier libretto. Griesinger reports that when he had to compose the words in praise of industry, Haydn observed that though he had always been very industrious himself it had never occurred to him to set industry to music. On the other hand, Dies stresses Haydn's doubts about van Swieten's advice to insert tone pictures wherever possible. The imitation of natural sounds and voices, such as the song of birds and the roll of thunder, which had long been familiar in music, gradually had become unacceptable to certain aesthetic circles. Their rejection of such devices made the old master feel uncertain when composing music to a libretto that seemed urgently to call for

[15] This is mentioned in a letter from Michael to Joseph Eybler, dated November 5, 1799. See Pohl and Botstiber, *Joseph Haydn*, III, p. 133. Joseph Eybler was an intimate associate of both Haydn and Mozart and studied under Albrechtsberger.
[16] Cf. Edward Olleson, "Georg August Griesinger's Correspondence with Breitkopf and Härtel," *HYb*, III (1966), p. 29.

them. Haydn naturally blamed van Swieten for any passages in his
score that seemed to savor of such devices, and there are records
about various disparaging remarks that he made about the libretto.
When correcting the proofs of the pianoforte adaptation of the
work, he wrote on December 11, 1801, to A. E. Müller, author of
the piano score, regarding No. 76: "This whole passage imitating a
frog has not flowed from my pen. I was forced to write down this
Frenchified trash. With the whole orchestra the wretched idea
easily disappears, but it must not be included in the piano score."
Unfortunately, through an indiscretion, the German critic Johann
Gottlieb Spazier got hold of Haydn's own comments and used them
in his review as an argument against van Swieten's text. The baron
was furious and promised to rub this remark into Haydn with "salt
and pepper." Two weeks later, however, Griesinger was able to report to Breitkopf and Härtel that the storm had passed. After all,
van Swieten was too happy basking in the sunshine of Haydn's
successes to sever so important a connection.

In point of fact, *The Seasons* achieved a triumph. Amazingly
enough, the completed work, in its freshness of inspiration, revealed no trace of the physical handicaps and difficulties that the
composer had suffered while writing it. Haydn won the battle, but
the price he had to pay was tremendous. His health was now definitely shattered, for, as he said himself, "*The Seasons* has finished
me off." Still, stubborn like so many of his forefathers, Haydn dog-
gedly continued doing what he felt to be essential, and the very
months before the first performance of the work show him trying
to continue his active life in the face of increasing physical failings.
In January 1801, when war was again ravaging unhappy Austria,
Haydn helped to raise money for the wounded. A performance of
*The Creation* conducted, according to Rosenbaum,[17] by the composer "with youthful fire," netted 7183 florins for the good cause,
and a concert in which Haydn and Beethoven cooperated with
Christine Gerardi, who first sang the part of Eve, brought in as
much as 9400 florins. But in February 1801 Haydn was again laid
up with "rheumatic head fever." This kept him inactive until the
middle of March. Still, on March 29 and 30 he again conducted *The
Seven Last Words* for the Societät, and, above all, he was burdened
with the exacting preparations for the production of *The Seasons*.

[17]J. C. Rosenbaum, official in the service of Prince Esterházy, kept a diary that affords much interesting information about Haydn after his return from London. (Cf.
p. 9.) Rosenbaum was married to Haydn's godchild, a singer at the Vienna opera,
Therese Gassmann.

Again, Prince Schwarzenberg had the privilege of hosting this important event, which took place on April 24, 1801; the oratorio was repeated on April 27 and May 1. The soloists were the singers who participated in the first public performance of *The Creation* and again produced a great effect. The correspondent for the *Allgemeine Musikalische Zeitung* described the reaction of the listeners with these words: "Silent reverence, amazement, and loud enthusiasm alternated for the powerful appearance of colossal visions; the immeasurable abundance of splendid ideas surprised and overwhelmed the boldest expectations."

Shortly afterward, the Empress Maria Theresa insisted on having a performance of *The Seasons* at court, to be followed the next day by *The Creation*. In both oratorios the Empress sang the soprano solos "with much taste and expression, but a small voice," according to Haydn. These events occurred on May 24 and 25, and four days later the first public production of *The Seasons* took place in the Redoutensaal. Haydn had reason to be well satisfied with the financial result for, in addition to the receipts of 3209 florins, he was presented with an honorarium of six hundred ducats by a group of aristocrats who also paid all the expenses. But it is doubtful whether the composer was much impressed by this fact, though as a rule he showed an increasing eagerness to earn large sums of money in his old age. He was now too weary, too exhausted from the unending struggle between his urge to create and his worn-out body. His thoughts were moving more and more toward the ultimate goal, and on June 5, 1801, Griesinger wrote to Leipzig: "Haydn has just drafted his last will."

# CHAPTER TEN

# Retiring from Life

## 1 8 0 1 – 1 8 0 9

Haydn's last will, which he worked on from May to December 1801, is an interesting document, for it throws light on his character. It is the testament of a man of means, for when Haydn died he left bonds in the value of 14,800 florins; property that, when auctioned off, brought 23,163 florins; and a house that was sold for 17,100 florins—a total equivalent to 27,000 dollars, which of course meant much more at that time than the same amount would today. But the man who had risen so high in the world did not forget his humble origin. Although he had left his father's house at the age of five, and never since had been more than an occasional visitor to it, he retained a deep-rooted attachment to his widely branched family. For a man who hardly knew what it was like to grow up in the midst of brothers and sisters, such an existence was imbued with a certain nostalgic fascination. Possibly he felt close to his relatives because he had never been obliged to live with them, had never suffered the fate of other growing artists, that of being hampered by a family's narrow-mindedness and lack of understanding. He had always relied on himself alone. Throughout his life he hardly ever received a favor from any relative, though he had assisted dozens of them materially. In many villages near Eisenstadt and Eszterháza there dwelt nephews and nieces of Haydn who had settled in the neighborhood mainly because of their generous uncle. Haydn loved visiting them, and again and again became the godfather of their children and helped one or another of them to set up business or get good training in a trade. A charming instance of Haydn's family sentiments is recorded by Carpani.[1] Once a year, he reports, Haydn invited all his relatives of the neighboring villages to the little town of Bruck an der Leitha, where he gave them a feast in the best inn, presented each with a small sum of money, and on parting embraced each and extended a cordial invitation for the next year. "Haydn called this family gathering his day of grandeur and went to it happily and proudly." While writing his testament, he saw himself as if again presiding over such a family gathering and made the greatest effort to remember everyone and to distribute his riches fairly. So the last will of the world-famous composer provided, for the most part, legacies to hardworking artisans. A shoemaker, a blacksmith, a silversmith, two seamstresses, a saddler's widow, and two lacemakers were among the legatees.

On the other hand, various bequests to women not related to him point to the master's interest in the fair sex. It is much to be regretted that it seems hardly possible to follow up these interesting clues. The only legatee whom we know even a little about is the singer "Babett," or Barbara, Pilhofer, first soprano at the Esterházy court. But there are also legacies to Mesdemoiselles Anna and Josepha Dillin, to the blind daughter of the choirmaster at Eisenstadt, to the four daughters of the wigmaker Sommerfeld of Pressburg, to the daughter of the bookkeeper Kandler, and others. Most tantalizing is the provision of a thousand florins for Mademoiselle Catharine Csech, waiting woman to Princess Grassalkovics. The Princess was the daughter of Prince Nicolaus the Magnificent, and it seems possible that she employed a girl from her father's estate as a waiting woman who might have known Haydn well. (Was she the predecessor of Luigia Polzelli?) The entry, however, was subsequently crossed out by Haydn, just as he canceled the bequest to his first love, the sister of his late wife (see p. 39). Whether Haydn acted thus because he believed these women to be dead is not known. In the case of his sister-in-law, Josephine Keller, he would have committed an error, for she died ten years after Haydn, at the age of eighty-six. The legacy to Luigia Polzelli has been mentioned. Haydn left her an annuity of one hundred and fifty florins and remarked: "I hereby revoke the obligation in Italian, signed by me, which may be produced by Madame Polzelli, otherwise so many of my poor relations with greater claims would receive too little."

[1] Giuseppe Carpani, *Le Haydine* (Milan, 1812), p. 15.

After her death the amount was to be divided. Half was to be used for maintenance of the Haydn monument at the Harrach Castle as well as of a statue that Haydn's father had placed at the door of the sacristy in the Rohrau church; the other half was to be given to the two poorest orphan boys in Rohrau for their education and, on their coming of age, to the next two most deserving orphans.

Other important legacies were left to the master's faithful servant, Johann Elssler, to the cook, and to the housekeeper. But it was to Haydn's two brothers, Michael and Johann, that the two largest sums of four thousand florins each were bequeathed. Of these brothers, Johann was probably nearer to the composer's heart because it had fallen to Haydn to look after him; after the death of their father, Johann had joined his brother in Eisenstadt. Although trained as a wheelwright, Johann became a tenor singer in the church choir, but his musical accomplishments seem to have been very modest, for in spite of his brother's influence, he never rose from this inferior position during forty years of service. As his salary was very small, he was mainly dependent on Joseph, and his distinguished brother helped him continually, found pupils for him, and for twenty-five years sent him every summer to the sulfur springs of Baden near Vienna, where Johann had to take the cure.

Thus to set his house in order was no sad task for Haydn. Rather it afforded him satisfaction, for his heart was warmed by the thought of how much his financial assistance would mean to some of these humble people. His health improved while he was engaged in the task; indeed, it seemed in those summer days of 1801 as if he had recovered from the "terrible worry and torture" of composing *The Seasons*. He went again to Eisenstadt and was industriously working on a new composition for his Prince, the so-called *Creation Mass*. On September 11 he wrote to Thaddäus Weigl, son of the cellist: "Poor old boy that I am, I have just come to the end of my new Mass which is to be produced the day after tomorrow." Again this splendid work reveals no signs of fatigue, and in addition to its composition Haydn continued to deliver Scottish songs to Thomson.

His contented state of mind was also due to various proofs of worldwide recognition that reached him during this year. From Amsterdam came a letter announcing that the Society Felix Meritis had made him an honorary member. From Paris arrived Gatteaux's beautiful medal accompanied by a most enthusiastic letter signed by one hundred forty-two musicians who had taken part in the performance of *The Creation* on December 24, 1800. The message from Paris was transmitted to Haydn by the Austrian ambassador, Count Kobenzl, who addressed the composer in an equally flattering letter. Haydn cherished the gift from France immensely and told his Prince that he would bequeath the medal to him, provided he could be assured that it would be kept in the Esterházy treasury. Nor was this the only tribute that the master received from France in 1801. In December he was elected an *associé étranger* to the class of fine arts of the Institut de France, and this time a medal was engraved by Dumarest. This great honor caused some disappointment and bitter remarks in England, for Sheridan had been an unsuccessful candidate for membership. It would be wrong, however, to deduce from outbursts of indignation in some parts of the press, a changed attitude among British music lovers toward Haydn. When, at about the same time, the sculptor Grassi made busts of the composer in two different sizes, five of each size were immediately ordered from England.

While the entire world was paying homage to Haydn, there were still fellow countrymen who did not even know him by name. This is revealed by a rather absurd episode that happened in July 1801. The little town of St. Johann in Bohemia wanted to hear *The Creation*. Rehearsals were started under the auspices of the music-loving pastor, who applied to the Prague consistory for permission to perform the oratorio in an old unused church. Strangely enough the reply was negative. The indignant citizens then tried to build an improvised concert hall, but when this plan proved to be impracticable, they decided to hold the performance in the old church in spite of the prohibition issued by the authorities. The good pastor was abducted in a carriage, so he would not be held responsible for the violation of the decree from Prague, and the citizens duly had their performance of the oratorio. Another pastor, hearing about the matter, delivered a fulminating tirade against the desecration of the church by the performance of the work of a "heathen" (the German word for "heathen" having the same sound as the name of the composer). Naturally the pastor of St. Johann became worried about the reaction in Prague and appealed to Haydn. The master, in a reply[2] written to the pastor, said that the whole strange story "did no credit to the head and heart of those responsible," and continued: "At all times the story of the Creation has been considered the loftiest, most awe-inspiring one for mankind. To accompany this great work with suitable music could certainly have

[2] The letter is dated "Eisenstadt, July 24, 1801."

only the effect of increasing the holy emotions in man's heart and making him more sensible to the goodness and power of the Creator. How could this stirring of divine emotions be a desecration of the church?" Finally Haydn promised to intercede, if necessary, with the Emperor, who had always listened to the oratorio with the deepest emotion. We do not know the outcome of this storm in a teacup, but it is to be assumed that the persons responsible for it did not persist in their ridiculous persecution.

The report of a performance of *The Creation* in another little circle was likely to make Haydn forget the annoying incident. In the small German town of Bergen on the North Sea island of Rügen, enthusiastic music lovers got together and performed Haydn's oratorio with a very modest number of players. So great was their delight and gratitude that they felt bound to express them to the composer. Coming from the heart, this expression moved Haydn deeply, and he answered with one of the most charming letters of thanks he ever conceived:

Vienna, September 22, 1802

Gentlemen:

It was indeed a most pleasant surprise to receive such a flattering letter from a place where I could have no idea that the fruits of my poor talents were known. When now, however, I see that not only is my name familiar to you, but that my compositions are performed by you with approval and satisfaction, the warmest wishes of my heart are fulfilled: to be considered by every nation into which my works penetrate as a not wholly unworthy priest of this sacred art. You reassure me on the point so far as regards your fatherland, but even more, you give me the pleasant conviction (which cannot fail to be a most welcome consolation in my declining years) that I am often the enviable source from which you, and so many families susceptible of true feeling, derive in their homely circle, pleasure and enjoyment. What happiness does this thought cause me! Often, when contending with obstacles of every sort that interfered with my work, often when my powers both of body and mind were failing and I felt it a hard matter to persevere in the course I had entered on, a secret voice within me whispered, "There are but few contented, happy peoples here below; everywhere grief and care prevail; perhaps your labors may one day be the source from which the weary and worn, or the man burdened with affairs, may derive a few moments' rest and refreshment." What a powerful motive for pressing onward! And this is why I look back with heartfelt and cheerful satisfaction on the work to which I have devoted so long a succession of years and such persevering efforts and exertions. And now in the fullness of my heart I thank you for your kindly thoughts of me, and beg you to forgive the delay of my answer. Feeble health, the inseparable companion of the gray-haired man of seventy, and likewise pressing business, have until now deprived me of this pleasure. Perhaps nature may yet accord me the gratification of composing a little memorial for you from which you may gather the feelings of a gradually dying old man who would fain, even after death, survive in the charming circle of which you draw so pleasing a picture. I have the honor to be, with the highest consideration,

Your obedient servant,

Joseph Haydn

The references in this letter to declining years, feeble health, and death are very significant. At that time Haydn was already prone to stress these points, a tendency that was to increase in the years to come. While up to the time of his return from England the composer had felt younger than his actual age, the opposite was becoming his state of mind now. He did not let any opportunity go by to refer to his advanced age (he occasionally pretended to be older than he was). It is also significant that on receiving letters he did not care to answer, he merely sent the respective person his musical visiting card bearing his name and above it a quotation from his four-part song "Der Greis" which reads, in English translation: "Gone forever is my strength, old and weak am I." Yet he did not stop working. Indeed, the summer of 1802 saw him "laboring very wearily" (as he termed it) on his last Mass. In addition, he was engaged on the Quartet Op. 77, No. 3, and supplied Scottish folk songs to Whyte of Edinburgh. Official duties kept him busy as well, and documents in the Esterházy archives contain various reports by him on engagements of new musicians, on dismissals, and on the examinations of singers. But old age was beginning to bear heavily on this man who had led so extremely industrious a life. He was not really ill, except for the discomfort caused by his old enemy, a nasal polyp which, according to Griesinger, made him "grumpy and uncomfortable." (Now he probably regretted having refused so vehemently the help offered him by the celebrated surgeon John Hunter in London.) But he grew increasingly weary, and fits of dizziness often prevented his working at the piano. The Prince, aware of the state of affairs, began to look for an adequate substitute, and since he was mainly interested in church music, he sought an expert in this kind of composition. His choice fell at last on Michael Haydn who, through the occupation of Salzburg by the French in 1800, had been robbed of all the valuables and cash in his possession and appeared willing to leave his old post. Brother Joseph thereupon lent a helping hand, sent him a golden watch to replace the silver one Michael had lost, promised him money as soon as the interests on his savings were due, and, on Michael's visit to Vienna in 1801, seems to have been instrumental in the negotiations with Prince Esterházy. Michael was offered a yearly salary of fifteen hundred florins, more than twice the stipend he received in Salzburg. The Prince apparently counted on Michael's arrival, but the musician, after long hesitation, felt more inclined to remain in Salzburg and to work there under its new ruler, Grand Duke Ferdinand III of Tuscany. A draft of Joseph's answer to his brother's notification dated January 22, 1803, has been preserved, and is noteworthy because it throws light on Joseph's opinion of his patron:

> Your action regarding His Royal Highness the Archduke
> and my Prince was carefully considered and courageous.
> Though I and the whole world must regret it, neither side
> can reproach you in any way. Both patrons are great, but
> the Grand Duke's love for and understanding of music
> surpass that of my Prince. Your heart and mind must
> decide whom to give the preference. Meanwhile I wish
> you happiness for whatever position you choose and hope
> to hear as quickly as possible about your final decision.

Michael remained in Salzburg and Prince Esterházy had to find another man. Abandoning his search for the moment, he appointed Johann Fuchs, who really had done the work for the past years, as vice-conductor, while Tomasini was to be responsible for the chamber music in Haydn's absence. At last, in 1804, at Haydn's recommendation, he engaged as concertmaster and composer Jo-

hann Nepomuk Hummel, Mozart's pupil, who had also received
some instruction in organ-playing from Haydn, and it was Hummel who actually took over the master's duties. Moreover, since
1807 Haydn's pupil Antonio Polzelli served as "substitute concertmaster and director."

Even after Haydn had ceased working with the Esterházy musicians, they maintained their loyalty to their fatherly friend. That
they honored him on his name day is revealed in a charming letter
to Antonio Polzelli which Haydn dictated and signed on March 20,
1808:

> The true filial feelings expressed by you and all the
> members of the princely Esterházy band on the occa-
> sion of my name day have made me shed scalding tears.
> Deeply moved I thank you and the others with all my
> heart and ask you to tell all members on my behalf that I
> regard them all as my dear children whom I ask to show
> patience and forbearance with their old, infirm father. Tell
> them that I am attached to them with fatherly love and
> that there is nothing I wish more than to have strength
> enough to experience once more the harmony at the side
> of these worthy men, who made the fulfillment of my
> duties so pleasant. Report to them that my heart will
> never stop remembering them and that it is my greatest
> pride to stand—thanks to the grace of my serene Prince—
> at the head of great artists who are noble and grateful
> human beings as well.

The release from official duties after 1802 caused Haydn's physical condition to remain for a while comparatively stationary, with
occasional periods of well-being. In June 1803 he started on his last
quartet. However, only two movements were ever completed.

In the same year the master made his last appearance as a conductor when he performed *The Seven Last Words* for the benefit of
the civic Hospital of St. Marx, a charitable institution in which he
took a great interest. From then on he was more and more confined
to his house and was hardly ever seen in public. Even when special
homage was to be paid to him on his seventy-third birthday (in
1805), he could not attend the celebration. The scene was the first
public appearance of Wolfgang Mozart *fils*, who was to perform
among other works a cantata he had composed to words by Griesinger in honor of Haydn's birthday. It was planned that Haydn

should introduce the young musician to the audience, but finally the project had to be abandoned: it was feared the excitement would be too much for the invalid master.

Short walks, which were all Haydn could manage with his badly swollen legs, were taken in his own little garden, supported and almost carried by the faithful Elssler. Once the actor August Wilhelm Iffland saw Haydn returning from a stroll in his garden with flowers in his hands, and the old man, who "clearly took comfort in their fragrance," remarked to his guest that "he had attended to his devotions in nature."

Now that the composer definitely felt that the period of his creative work was over, he liked to look back on his former achievements and was eager to see a catalogue of his life's work prepared. With the help of earlier lists, the thematic catalogue intended to embrace all the works composed by Haydn in the last fifty-five years was compiled in 1805 and written out by Elssler. It seems to have been preceded by two brief summary catalogues, one written by Haydn and the other by Elssler, which Landon ascribes to the years from 1794 to 1804.[3] Elssler was also given the task of writing a catalogue of Haydn's music library, while the composer himself produced a list of the operatic librettos he owned.

Haydn spent his last years in increasing bodily discomfort, and they cannot be called happy ones. They differed too completely from his former way of life to satisfy him, and forced inactivity weighed heavily on him. For instance, Carpani describes his mood as a "habitual state of sadness" and an "absorption in the melancholy sentiment that life was escaping him." Still, there were brilliant patches even in this shadowy existence. Haydn was fortunately spared the tragic fate of other aging masters who were forgotten in their own lifetimes. On the contrary, evidence of his outstanding reputation again and again broke the dreary monotony of an invalid's life. He even experienced the strange sensation of reading obituary notices about himself. In 1805 the rumor spread over Europe that Haydn had died. In England the *Gentleman's Magazine* announced the master's death (at ninety-seven years of age!) and the publisher Thomson wrote a letter of condolence to the Viennese bankers, Fries and Company, who had handled his business with Haydn. In Paris the greatest consternation prevailed. Cherubini wrote a cantata on Haydn's death and Kreutzer composed a violin concerto based on themes from Haydn's works. A

[3] Cf. *HCaW*, V, p. 325ff.

special memorial concert with these works and Mozart's *Requiem* was planned for February 1805, but good news from Vienna put a stop to the undertaking.

Haydn was rather amused by the whole matter. He signed a letter to Thomson "to prove that he was still of this base world," and when he heard about the plans in Paris, he remarked: "The good gentlemen! I am greatly indebted to them for the unusual honor. Had I only known of it in time, I would have traveled to Paris to conduct the *Requiem* myself."

High tribute was projected to be paid to the dead composer, nor was this surprising. After all, it has always been so. It is far more rare to see a living composer as greatly honored as Haydn was. In 1803 he had been awarded the gold Salvator Medal by the city of Vienna, and one year later the city named him an honorary citizen. The French, in spite of the honors previously awarded, still felt that they had not done enough for so great a master. In 1805 a diploma of membership was handed him from the Paris Conservatory, another in 1807 from the Société Académique des Enfants d'Apollon, both accompanied by gold medals. In the following year the Philharmonic Society of St. Petersburg followed the example of Paris. It is not surprising that the old master, when he was feeling particularly low and depressed, should have taken out the box holding his medals, drawing encouragement from these visible signs of his success.

Of course, he derived an even greater pleasure from displaying them for his guests, and this was usually part of the ceremonial observed with visiting strangers whom the name of Haydn had drawn to the little house in the quiet Viennese suburb. These visits meant much to the invalid, and although they sometimes tired him greatly, he would not have missed them for anything. He was always ready to receive anyone who might drop in unannounced. He once remarked to Dies: "You seem to be surprised that I am fully dressed, though I am ailing and weak and cannot go out. My parents trained me strictly as a child to be clean and orderly, and these two qualities have become second nature to me." But the simple wheelwright and Count Harrach's cook would never, in their wildest dreams, have thought of seeing their Sepperl attired on an ordinary working day in the manner that the Czech musician Johann Wenzel Tomaschek describes: "Haydn sat in an armchair, very much dressed up. A powdered wig with sidelocks, a white neckband with a gold buckle, a white, richly embroidered waistcoat of heavy silk, in the midst of which shone a splendid jabot, a dress coat of fine coffee-colored cloth with embroidered cuffs, black silk breeches, white silk hose, shoes with large silver buckles curved over the instep, and on the little table next to him a pair of white kid gloves made up his attire."[4]

The year 1805 was particularly rich in interesting visitors. On November 5, 1805, an English physician, Dr. Henry Reeves,[5] called on him, affording the old composer a pleasant opportunity for reminiscing about the good time he had had in England. On this occasion he remembered the charming compliment he had paid Mrs. Billington regarding the Reynolds portrait of her as St. Cecilia (cf. p. 117), for which she had given him a kiss. The pianist Marie Bigot (to whom Beethoven gave the autograph of his Sonata Appassionata) delighted Haydn so much with her interpretation of his own works that he exclaimed: "My dear child, you have not only played this, you have composed it." The visit of the violinist Pierre Baillot may have left a less pleasant memory, for when the friendly host opened his arms, the impetuous Frenchman embraced him with such violence that he almost knocked out the old master's last two teeth. Another visitor from France was Haydn's former pupil and later competitor, Ignaz Pleyel, now a successful publisher. He had greatly pleased the master by his edition of Haydn's complete string quartets. Pleyel was accompanied by his son, Camille, who described the visit as follows in a letter to his family dated June 16, 1805:[6]

> We found him very weak; the face, it is true, has
> hardly changed, but he can scarcely walk, and when he
> speaks for some length of time, he completely loses his
> breath. He told us that he was only seventy-four years old
> [as a matter of fact, Haydn was seventy-three], and looks
> as if he were eighty, so weak is he. We found him holding
> a rosary in his hands, and I believe he passes almost the
> whole day in prayer. He says always that his end is near,
> that he is too old, and that he is useless in this world. We
> did not stay long because we saw he wished to pray. I
> embraced him and kissed his hand, which gave him great

[4] See Carl Ferdinand Pohl and Hugo Botstiber, *Joseph Haydn* (Leipzig, 1927), III, p. 260.
[5] Dr. Reeves's memoirs (published by his son, London, 1877) were recently consulted by Landon (cf. *HCaW*, V, p. 494). He found there a confirmation of the anecdote regarding Mrs. Billington previously reported only by Carpani.
[6] Cf. *Monthly Musical Record* (Sept. 1, 1885).

pleasure. He has a very pretty and well-furnished house, but it seems that he does not see anyone. [Here Camille was definitely mistaken.]

The most welcome of all his guests from France proved to be Luigi Cherubini, who took the opportunity of calling on his beloved "Father" when he was invited to produce his operas in Vienna. They spent many happy hours together. Haydn found Cherubini a "handsome little man full of distinction" and gave him the autograph of his Symphony No. 103 (with the Drum Roll). He wrote under his name 'Giuseppe Haydn' the words: *Padre del Celebre Cherubini ai 24tro di Febr. 806.*

Viennese friends of course continued to visit Haydn, above all Griesinger, who, as he wrote to Breitkopf, could not bear to give up these visits, though the old man was growing weaker from day to day. He tried to get whatever information he could from the composer for his proposed book, and the same was done by a new friend, the painter Albert Christoph Dies, who paid thirty calls and set down the contents of his conversations in his *Biographische Nachrichten von Joseph Haydn*, published in 1810. Haydn did not object to the inquisitiveness of his friends. He lived more in the past than in the present and evidently enjoyed looking back on the struggles of his childhood and youth.

Another welcome visitor was Magdalena von Kurzböck, an excellent pianist, to whom Haydn's last piano sonata (Hob. XV:52) and his last piano trio (Hob. XVI:31), both in E-flat, are dedicated.

Sometimes Haydn had the pleasure of seeing his dear Princess Esterházy in his house. It was she, for instance, who brought the deeply moved master the sad news of the death of his brother Johann in May 1805. She was, as Haydn said, like a good angel to him, and thanks to her influence, her husband now showed himself much more gracious to the invalid composer and increased his salary in 1806 to twenty-three hundred florins. Moreover the Prince offered him the use of his carriage and paid the accounts of his Viennese doctor and apothecary which, because of the inflation, amounted in one year to no less than 1,017 florins.

On no other occasion did the love and respect shown to the composer become more apparent than at the remarkable performance of *The Creation* in Italian on March 27, 1808. The concert was planned in celebration of Haydn's approaching seventy-sixth birthday. The master was formally invited, and in view of the mild weather, his physician allowed him to leave the house. Prince Esterházy was prevented from attending the performance because of important business, but he sent his carriage, and Haydn rode slowly to the university with Magdalena von Kurzböck. A huge crowd, which had to be kept in order by military guards, had gathered in front. Members of the high nobility, as well as distinguished musicians—among them Beethoven, Salieri, Hummel, and Gyrowetz—received the master, who was carried in an armchair into the beautiful lecture hall. On his appearance, a flourish of trumpets and drums was sounded, mingled with jubilant exclamations: "Long live Haydn!" The master was seated with the highest aristocracy, next to Princess Esterházy, who wrapped the old man in her own shawl when she noticed him shivering a little. Many other ladies followed her example, and soon Haydn was covered with the costliest of garments. The French ambassador, noticing with pleasure that Haydn was wearing the gold medal from the Concerts des Amateurs on his coat, exclaimed: "This medal is not enough; you should receive all the medals that are distributed in the whole of France." Poems in German and Italian were written for the occasion and were handed to the master by his friends Magdalena von Kurzböck and the Baroness Spielmann. The conductor was Salieri; at the leader's desk sat the famous virtuoso Franz Clement, who thus repaid Haydn for having conducted the benefit concert for the boy of eleven in London. The audience was in an unusually receptive state of mind. When thunderous applause followed the words "Let there be light—and there was light," Haydn lifted his hands upward, as though to say: "Not from me, from thence comes everything." The reception given to him and his work moved the master indescribably. Indeed, he was so shaken that it was thought advisable not to let him stay on after the intermission. Everybody present realized that the frail old man's days on earth were numbered. The people thronged around him with tears in their eyes, shaking his hands and embracing him. Only in broken sentences could Haydn express his thanks and good wishes, but before he was carried out, he lifted his hand as if to bless the whole assembly.

Princess Esterházy had the scene painted by Balthasar Wigand and mounted on a costly box which she gave to the delighted composer. It contained a sumptuous album with the most cordial inscriptions from the princely family and was furnished with elegant writing equipment and all kinds of useful instruments in fine English steel and gold. After Haydn's death, the princess acquired the box again for the sum of four hundred florins and later gave it to Franz Liszt. Eventually it became the property of the Museum of the City of Vienna. During the turbulent events of 1945 the relic was destroyed, however, and only a few tiny parts of it have been rescued.[7]

Although the admiration of the Viennese for Haydn had reached its greatest intensity, it never succeeded in pervading the official court circles. Right after the memorable performance of *The Creation*, Count Chotek, minister of state, wrote to the Emperor:[8]

> I have just come from the University Hall, from Haydn's triumph with *The Creation*, heard with solemn, holy emotions in his presence among the irrepressible acclaims of a gathering of the first of Your Empire and the most august friends of music. On this occasion, the most blissful feelings, which only Virtue and Religion call forth, and which Haydn so powerfully and ardently depicted in this and his other immortal works, took hold of all hearts and were expressed so loudly in thanks for the composer that he, conscious of his infirmity, felt obliged to leave the circle of his admirers. At this occasion soft wishes were uttered to me that this ever righteous and greatly respected man, who wrote works inspiring us to goodness, works—one might say—that are holy, should before his demise be honored by his gracious monarch through the conferment of the Leopold order.

This letter, dated March 28, 1808, reached the monarch only on November 26, 1814, when Haydn was no longer on this earth. The file contains a remark that the delay was insignificant as the Leopold order was intended only for excellent service in church, state, or military matters, as well as for outstanding patriotic merits in connection with charitable activities, and therefore could not have been conferred on the composer of *The Creation*. (The fact that Haydn had composed the Austrian national anthem was not thought worthy of mention.) The Emperor confirmed his agreement with this attitude by signing the act.

Haydn, who had heard of the minister's suggestion, is reported

[7] See Leopold Nowak, *Joseph Haydn*, 2d ed. (Vienna, 1959), p. 454.
[8] Cf. Ferdinand Pfohl, "Joseph Haydn, der Leopolds Orden und die sancta simplicitas," *Zeitschrift für Musik*, CIV/1 (Jan. 1937), p. 66ff.

to have been "as happy as a child" about it and to have prepared what to reply in an audience with the Emperor. It is good to know that he never became aware of the court's attitude.

The performance of *The Creation* at the university proved to be Haydn's last public appearance. Before long, political conditions made festivities of the kind impossible, as Austria again became the scene of a devastating war. Decisive battles were fought in the spring of 1809, and the French army came nearer and nearer to Vienna. These were indeed dark days for the invalid master. His greatest concern was in the revision and alteration of his last will. In the years that had passed since he first drafted it, Haydn's two brothers, Johann and Michael, had died (in 1805 and 1806 respectively). The master, while bequeathing one thousand florins to Michael's widow but leaving most of the legacies unaltered, made his only surviving nephew, Mathias Frölich, his principal heir. Mathias, who had been trained as a blacksmith at Haydn's expense, lived in the village of Fischamend, near Vienna. One year after his uncle's death he settled down in Rohrau, where he stayed for the rest of his life serving the Counts Harrach. He had the pleasure of witnessing, in 1841, the first Haydn Commemoration, which took place in the Rohrau church on Haydn's birthday. Whether Mathias was worthy of his uncle's inheritance is open to doubt. Schmid's information that he kept a piano owned by his uncle in a loft and used it as a flour bin does not impress us favorably. Be that as it may, Mathias did not derive from his uncle's rich bequest the benefit that Haydn fondly imagined. Haydn had left behind an estate worth 55,713 florins (or 5,571 pounds sterling at the 1809 rate of exchange); and even after all the bequests provided in the will were paid, a considerable amount was left to the blacksmith. However, owing to the inflation following the Napoleonic Wars, the money that Mathias inherited lost its value almost entirely and the principal heir of the wealthy composer died a poor man.

Six weeks before his death, Haydn called his servants and his grandniece, Ernestine Juliane Loder, who was looking after him, into his room and read them his will, for he wished to know whether they were satisfied with its provisions. Ernestine was especially favored as, apart from one thousand florins, she was bequeathed furniture to equip a room. All of them heartily thanked him with tears in their eyes. By the beginning of May the French had captured some of the western suburbs of Vienna and made the castle of Schönbrunn their headquarters. Haydn's house was perilously near the enemy and Magdalena von Kurzböck entreated him to move to her house in the center of the city. Haydn refused, for he felt unequal to coping with any change in his life. On May 12 the great bombardment of the city started, and a cannon fell with a tremendous noise quite near Haydn's house. The house shook as in an earthquake and the members of Haydn's entourage were scared out of their wits. Not so the old invalid, who exclaimed above the uproar: "Children, don't be frightened; where Haydn is, nothing can happen to you." (Marion Scott very aptly called this "sublime illogicality" the "Nelson touch in Haydn.") For twenty-four hours the bombardment went on, shattering the poor man's nervous system. When Vienna capitulated and quiet was restored, the invalid, at whose doorstep Napoleon had placed a guard of honor, was unable to recover. He suffered no pain, but his strength was ebbing away. On May 26 kind fate allowed him one great joy. A French officer of hussars, by the name of Clément Sulemy, called and after conversing with the master about *The Creation*, sang to him the aria "In native worth." According to a letter from Andreas Streicher[9] (who got the report from Elssler), he sang in "so manly, so sublime a style, and with so much truth of expression and real musical sentiment that Haydn could not restrain his tears of joy and assured the singer as well as the people in his house that he had never before heard the aria sung in so masterly a manner. After half an hour's visit the officer mounted his horse in order to go against the enemy." (Schnerich asserts that Sulemy fell soon afterward in the battle of Aspern.) On the same day, Haydn called his people to the piano and played for the last time his favorite, the Austrian hymn. In those days of Austria's collapse, the act had an unusual significance. Haydn, playing it three times in succession, put into the immortal tune all he felt for his unhappy country, and although his strength nearly failed him, he achieved an "expressiveness that surprised even himself."[10] But on the next day he could rise no more. A second doctor was called in for consultation, but was unable to suggest anything to combat the quickly progressing exhaustion. The master seemed to be quite happy, and when asked how he was feeling, whispered: "Children, be comforted, I am well." Nevertheless the periods of unconsciousness increased and on May 31, 1809, shortly after midnight, he went "blissfully and gently" to sleep, to wake no more.

Austria, in the throes of a deadly struggle, could not pay the

---

[9] Streicher's letter to Griesinger is dated July 2, 1809.
[10] Elssler's letter to Griesinger dated June 30, 1809.

departed the honors that unquestionaly would have been extended
to him in normal circumstances. Indeed, there was so great an up-
heaval in the town that the news of Haydn's death was hardly circulated before the funeral. Thus the obsequies, which took place to
the sound of Michael Haydn's *Requiem*, were of the simplest kind.
Carl Rosenbaum, ex-secretary of Prince Esterházy, commented in
his diary on the event as follows: "Haydn lay in his large room,
dressed in black, not disfigured at all. At his feet were placed the
seven medals from Paris, Russia, Sweden, and Vienna. After five
o'clock he was borne in an oak coffin to the Gumpendorf Church,
carried around it three times, blessed, and carried to the Hund-
sturm Cemetery. Not a single Viennese conductor accompanied
him." However, Rosenbaum could not deny that the official obsequies, which took place on June 15, were "very solemn and worthy
of Haydn." Members of the French army alternated with grenadiers
of the municipal militia to form a line around the catafalque. The
medals were placed in front of it, among them the little ivory tablet
with Haydn's name which had been handed to the master as a free
pass to the London concerts.[11] High-ranking French generals, officials, and officers, as well as the whole cultured world of Vienna,
were present. The music was chosen very fittingly for the occasion,
for it was the *Requiem* by his beloved Mozart that Vienna's musicians played on taking leave of Joseph Haydn.

[11] According to Griesinger, Haydn was particularly impressed by this courtesy and
stressed the fact that nothing of the kind had ever been shown him in Vienna.

# CHAPTER ELEVEN

# An Incongruous Postlude

In the year of Haydn's death, Prince Esterházy applied for permission to have the body exhumed and moved to Eisenstadt. But presently the whole matter slipped his memory, and though he received the permission, no action was taken. Haydn's tomb remained neglected until in 1814 the master's devoted pupil, Sigismund Neukomm, on returning to Vienna from France, had a simple marble tablet erected bearing as an inscription Haydn's favorite quotation from Horace, *non omnis moriar*, set as a five-part riddle canon. The Prince continued to ignore the question of Haydn's last resting place until in 1820 he was reminded of his obligations by Adolphus Frederick, Duke of Cambridge. This distinguished visitor observed, after attending a gala performance of *The Creation* given in his honor at Eisenstadt: "How fortunate was the man who employed this Haydn in his lifetime and now possesses his mortal remains." Prince Esterházy did not care to contradict his guest's assumption, but he gave orders immediately for the body to be brought to Eisenstadt for burial in the Bergkirche, where Haydn had so often performed his own Masses. When the coffin was opened for identification, the horrified officials found no head on the body, but only the wig. Inquiries soon brought an explanation of the mystery. Two students of Gall's and Spurtzheim's work on phrenology, namely Haydn's friend C. Rosenbaum, and J. N. Peter, the administrator of a penitentiary, had bribed the gravedigger and stolen Haydn's head after the funeral in order to "protect it from desecration." Peter had a black wooden box made, with a golden lyre at the top and glass windows. In it the skull was placed on a white silk cushion trimmed with black. When Haydn's body arrived in Eisenstadt without the head, the Prince was furious and sent the police to Peter, who said that he had given the skull to Rosenbaum. A search in the latter's house did not yield any result, since Rosenbaum's wife, the singer Therese Gassmann, hid the skull in her straw mattress and lay down on the bed. The Prince now tried bribery, and his emissary promised Rosenbaum a large sum if he would deliver the skull, whereupon the skull of an old man was handed to the Prince and buried with Haydn's body. Not unnaturally, Prince Esterházy did not keep his promise of a reward, but neither had the wary ex-secretary acted honestly, since he had not delivered the right skull. On his deathbed Rosenbaum gave Haydn's skull to Peter and made him promise to leave it in his will to the museum of the Gesellschaft der Musikfreunde in Vienna, the owner of a great number of valuable Haydn relics. There the skull found its resting place from 1895 until 1954.[1] In 1932, Prince Paul Esterházy had a Haydn mausoleum erected in the Bergkirche with a marble sarcophagus surrounded by four stone figures representing the seasons. But twenty-two years had to elapse before the skull was united with the other remains. Since 1954 Haydn has been buried in the little town of the Burgenland which played so important a role in his artistic growth.

[1] The authenticity of the skull at the Society of Friends of Music was proved beyond any doubt by Joseph Tandler in "Über den Schädel Haydns," *Mitteilungen der anthropologischen Gesellschaft* (Vienna), XXXIX (1909).

# PART TWO

# Works

# *The Sources*

The music lover eager to acquaint himself with the prodigious output of Joseph Haydn faces a rather peculiar situation. Collected editions have been published of the works of Bach and Handel, Mozart and Beethoven, Schubert and Chopin, Berlioz and Brahms, as well as many other great composers. In several cases a second, improved and updated version of a previously printed edition has even been produced. However, a complete collection of the works by the author of the "Clock" and "Surprise" symphonies, *The Creation* and *The Seasons* is not yet available. Again and again attempts have been made to reach this goal, but complete success has still not been achieved.

Between December 1799 and December 1806, the great publishing house of Breitkopf and Härtel in Leipzig issued twelve installments of the so-called *Oeuvres complettes*. This edition, to which the old composer himself contributed a brief preface, was, however, not a collected edition in the modern sense. It contained only compositions for solo piano or works with piano, such as songs and piano trios, and even these types of compositions were by no means complete.

Haydn's former pupil, Ignaz Pleyel, supplemented the Breitkopf editions by simultaneously publishing a *Collection complète des Quatuors d'Haydn* in Paris. This edition, which was considered a model of its kind for a long time, does not deserve its designation either. An early quartet, known as No. 0, is missing. Moreover, Pleyel included arrangements of other works not originally written for string quartet, and even pieces which in all likelihood were not composed by Haydn at all. Today it seems certain that Haydn did not compose eighty-three original string quartets, as Pleyel assumed, but only sixty-eight.

It was almost a century after Haydn's death before attempts were made to present a regular collected edition of his compositions. In 1907 Eusebius Mandyczewski, curator of the archives of the Gesellschaft der Musikfreunde in Vienna, presented a thematic list of one hundred and four Haydn symphonies, and published the first forty-nine of these works. Gradually the collected piano sonatas and songs, *The Creation* and *The Seasons* followed in this series, which was published again by Breitkopf and Härtel in Leipzig. However, after the first world war, publication came to a complete stop. Thanks to the initiative of twenty-four-year-old H. C. R. Landon, a new enterprise was started in 1950 by a group of Haydn enthusiasts in Boston, Massachusetts. Under the leadership of the renowned Danish Haydn scholar J. P. Larsen, the Haydn Society, as the new association was called, issued symphonies Nos. 50–57 and 82–92, as well as four Masses, whereupon financial difficulties forced it to relinquish the plan. Ultimately the Joseph Haydn Institute of Cologne, West Germany, took over this task, with J. P. Larsen serving once more as the general editor. In 1960 he was succeeded by the brilliant G. Feder, who has held the leading position since that time. Everything points to full success for this latest venture, which is being carried out with scholarly thoroughness. So far more than fifty volumes have been issued, but a great deal remains to be done before this edition, published by G. Henle Verlag in Munich, can furnish a complete picture of the composer's output. In the meantime, a significant supplement has been provided by the numerous publications of Haydn's works that Landon has offered. They include the composer's collected symphonies, piano trios and string trios, as well as a number of concertos, overtures, divertimenti, arias, cantatas, masses, and operas, issued mainly by Doblinger or Universal-Edition in Vienna. The late Christa Landon edited the complete piano sonatas, also published by Universal-Edition.

Unsolved problems also plague a thematic catalogue of Haydn's works. Around 1765 the composer himself started on a thematic list of his works, the *Entwurfkatalog* (draft catalogue), which is of great significance, especially for the period up to 1777. This list, which is the property of the Deutsche Staatsbibliothek, Berlin, is mostly in the composer's own hand and provides an invaluable tool for authenticating early compositions. Unfortunately it is by no means complete, and certain categories of compositions, such as the piano sonatas or the songs, are badly neglected. Much more extensive is the *Verzeichnis aller derjenigen Compositionen welche ich mich beyläufig erinnere von meinem 18ten bis in das 73ste Jahr verfertiget zu haben* ("A list of all those compositions that, as nearly as I can remember, I composed from my 18th to my 73rd year"). This compilation was made by Haydn's faithful amanuensis, Johann Elssler, in collaboration with the composer. Formerly the property of Prince Esterházy,[1] it contains many hundreds of themes of Haydn's works presented in systematic order on one hundred thirty-two pages. The catalogue is indeed an important document, and at first sight it creates the impression of real completeness. Unfortunately, however, the memory of the man of seventy-three left much to be desired, and all the friends who visited him in 1805, the year of the completion of this catalogue, agreed that Haydn's recollections were far from trustworthy. He and Elssler used the best sources at their disposal for this work, the above-mentioned *Entwurfkatalog*, autographs and other manuscripts from Haydn's collection, as well as various printed editions authorized by the composer himself. But in spite of these great efforts, the catalogue contains quite a few mistakes. A work called *L'infedeltà fedele* (Faithful Unfaithfulness), for instance, is listed among the operas. Actually Haydn never wrote any work by that name, and the title should not have been included.[2] Similarly, among the Masses the so-called *Little Organ Solo Mass* is quoted twice: once with measures three and four of its beginning, as Mass No. 4, and then with measures one and two, as Mass No. 13. In the list of symphonies, Haydn and Elssler quote as No. 17 the first movement and as No. 91 the second movement of the same symphony (Hob. I/34). Similarly, they designate as No. 32 the slow introduction and as No. 100 the following presto of the same symphony (Hob. I/54). The confusion about Haydn's string quartets caused by Pleyel's edition is not corrected, as the *Haydn-Verzeichnis* adopts the publisher's complete list without attempting any improvements or changes. Finally, no less than sixty-

---

[1] The catalogue was lost around 1945 but is preserved in a facsimile edition. (See p. 198 n.4.)

[2] Dénes Bartha and László Somfai, *Haydn als Opernkapellmeister* (Budapest, 1960), p. 95, point out that the libretto of Cimarosa's opera *L'infedeltà fedele* was used as a model for Haydn's *La fedeltà premiata*, a work listed among the operas in the catalogue.

four pages of the Haydn-Elssler catalogue are devoted to a listing of three hundred sixty-five arrangements of Scottish, Irish, and Welsh folksongs, which Haydn had turned out in a somewhat mechanical manner, partly with the help of his pupils. Added to the shortcomings of the *Haydn-Verzeichnis* is the fact that many of the works listed in the catalogue are not to be found in any library; they were probably lost during one of the fires that ravaged both Eszterháza and Eisenstadt. On the other hand, a number of Haydn's compositions whose authenticity cannot be doubted are missing from the Haydn-Elssler catalogue. Especially for the period before 1765 and for such occasional compositions as the little pieces for musical clocks or the lira concertos, the 1805 list is not a reliable source.

In the second half of the nineteenth century, the Haydn biographer C. F. Pohl conducted extensive research on a thematic Haydn catalogue, but he presented only a fraction of his material as an appendix to the second volume of his book.[3] Shortly before the outbreak of the Second World War, J. P. Larsen made a highly significant contribution by carefully investigating all of the source material and publishing both the draft catalogue and the Haydn-Elssler list of 1805 in facsimile.[4] Larsen's work also includes the "Kees catalogue," a list of Haydn's symphonies that belonged to the composer's friend Hofrat von Kees and constituted the basis for the enumeration of the symphonies in the Haydn-Elssler list. Anthony van Hoboken built all this extensive material into a monumental thematic catalogue, the first volume of which appeared in 1957, and the third and last in 1978, when its author had reached the biblical age of ninety-one.[5] Thanks to indefatigable research carried out over several decades in the libraries of Europe and America, the author was in a position to present an enormous amount of valuable material in well-ordered form.

Hoboken's work is of the utmost importance for Haydn research, yet, for obvious reasons, it can offer only partial solutions to the vast problems encountered. Despite its enormous proportions, the catalogue is not quite complete and scarcely attempts to offer any new answers to the numerous questions of authenticity and chronology facing Haydn scholars. Eventually a new edition of

[3] Carl Ferdinand Pohl, *Joseph Haydn* (Berlin, 1875 and 1882).
[4] Jens Peter Larsen, *Die Haydn-Überlieferung* (Copenhagen, 1939). *Drei Haydn Kataloge in Faksimile* (Copenhagen, 1941). Second facsimile edition, with a survey of Haydn's oeuvre (New York, 1979).
[5] A. van Hoboken, *Joseph Haydn, thematisch-bibliographisches Werkverzeichnis*, 3 vols. (Mainz, 1957–1978).

the catalogue will have to be issued, incorporating the important results of recent research.

The reason for this situation is no less fantastic than the situation itself. It can be expressed in a brief sentence: Haydn was too famous. During the last part of the eighteenth century and the beginning of the nineteenth, there was a continual demand from amateurs and professional organizations all over the world for new compositions by Haydn. The composer did all in his power to satisfy these urgent calls, but his creative output was never able to keep pace with the unending stream of orders. Haydn often sold the same work both to private persons or organizations and to publishers of different countries. The Paris symphonies, for instance, were sent to Paris for performances in the Concerts de la Loge Olympique and were later sold to the publishers Imbault in Paris, Artaria in Vienna, and Forster in London. Somewhat different is the case of the symphonies written for Prince Ernst of Öttingen-Wallerstein. In 1787 this ardent music lover asked Haydn for three symphonies that "besides himself nobody else must own." When the music was delivered, the delighted prince sent the master a heavy gold snuffbox filled with fifty ducats. Soon after, however, these same symphonies mysteriously found their way to different publishers, such as Hummel in Amsterdam, André in Offenbach, Le Duc in Paris, and Forster in London. We cannot avoid the suspicion that Haydn secretly connived at these publications. If so, he was but following a custom usual in the eighteenth century. One of the most puzzling problems created by the enormous demand for Haydn's music is that of the Piano Trio in C major (Hob. XV:3). The composer sold this work to Forster in London in 1784, and it was also printed by Artaria in Vienna. Nevertheless, in 1803 the master rather surprisingly informed Breitkopf and Härtel that this trio was not his own work but a composition by his brother, Michael. This is a case of Haydn versus Haydn, and it seems not unlikely that the composer, hard pressed for new compositions, sent the publishers a work by his younger brother.[6]

But with all his shrewdness, and even with the use of petty devices, Haydn was never able to satisfy all the publishers. Soon these disappointed men found an easy way out of their difficulties. They produced their own Haydn compositions. The number of works by other composers published during Haydn's lifetime under his name is excessive. Jens Peter Larsen points out that the so-

---

[6]Cf. Hoboken, I, p. 685f.

called Haydn symphonies in his Op. 9, 12, and 13, printed in Paris, contain sixteen works of which only three are authentic Haydn compositions.[7] The case of his string quartets is even worse. Op. 18, 21, and 28 contain eighteen pieces, of which nòt one is genuine. It is known that Forster in London, though a personal friend of Haydn, printed authentic and spurious Haydn symphonies indiscriminately. The Czech composer Gyrowetz tells us in his autobiography[8] that when he arrived in Paris in 1789 he was surprised to find his own Symphony in G major printed under Joseph Haydn's name (see p. 84). In this case the publishers excused themselves by saying that they had bought the symphony from the violinist Tost, a member of the orchestra at Eszterháza. Probably they acted in good faith, as they knew of Tost's connection with Haydn's orchestra and the violinist had sold them genuine symphonies together with the counterfeit one.

It is not easy to determine in every case who was really responsible for the fraudulent use of Haydn's name. Very often the publishers were the culprits; sometimes, however, the copyists in Vienna, or even members of Haydn's orchestra, were approached, and these men were often more interested in gaining substantial fees than in scrupulously observing the truth. It was much easier to take a composition by Vanhal, Dittersdorf, Gyrowetz, or Michael Haydn and change the name on the title page than to obtain a new work from Haydn himself, who had the inconvenient habit of disposing of every composition even before it was put on paper.

Neither the dubious nor the outright false compositions of Haydn were always printed. Before 1780 in particular, music was often produced by professional copyists. How important this form of reproduction was is shown by the fact that between 1760 and 1787 the publishing house of Breitkopf and Härtel issued no less than twenty-five thematic catalogues of "musical works that have not been made public through printing" and were "now to be had in correct manuscript copies."[9] The name of Haydn appears frequently in these catalogues, but they are a source both of information and of confusion, for again only some of the compositions listed under the master's name were really written by him. Haydn, however, may have felt a certain consolation in the fact that he was

[7]Larsen, *Die Haydn Überlieferung*, p. 99.
[8]Cf. p. 88.
[9]These very important catalogues were presented in a facsimile edition by Barry S. Brook (New York, 1966).

by no means the only composer whose name was falsely used. In his article on Sammartini, Georges de Saint-Foix proved that of the four symphonies listed under the name of Sammartini in the Breitkopf catalogue of 1762 only two were by the composer himself, the third and fourth being by Martinelli and Pergolesi respectively.[10]

The twentieth century made its contributions to the confusion. Adolf Sandberger, known for his important work in various fields of Haydn research, startled scholars in 1932 by declaring that Mandyczewski's list of Haydn's symphonies omitted at least seventy-eight works.[11] According to Sandberger, a number of the symphonies that Mandyczewski considered dubious or false are clearly genuine, whereas other authentic Haydn symphonies were not even known to Mandyczewski. One of the foundations of Haydn research, erected slowly and painstakingly by Pohl and Mandyczewski, seemed about to collapse. Ultimately Sandberger's claims were completely disproved. Nobody was much surprised when, in 1938, under the auspices of the eminent Sir Donald Tovey, a "rediscovered" symphony was printed under the name of Joseph Haydn, though an autograph score clearly proved that all movements but one were by Michael Haydn.[12]

Another case of mistaken identity took a rather surprising turn. In 1936, Ernst Fritz Schmid edited the Göttweig sonatas, which he considered to be unknown pianoforte sonatas by Joseph Haydn; but in the very next year he had to confess that instead of Haydn, one of his lesser contemporaries, the publisher Franz Anton Hoffmeister, was the real author of these compositions. Also, the *Requiem* edited by Schmid under Haydn's name turned out to be the work of a minor composer.

Thus it is certainly not easy to form a correct idea of what Haydn actually wrote; yet some sources are above suspicion. Among the best are Haydn's autographs. If a work is in the master's own script, written with his characteristic thin, energetic notes on a sheet of paper showing one of the familiar watermarks, there is hardly any room for doubt. This is especially so if one finds written

[10] Georges de Saint-Foix, "La chronologie de l'oeuvre instrumentale de J. B. Sammartini," *Sammelbände der Internationalen Musikgesellschaft* (1914).

[11] Adolf Sandberger, "Zu den unbekannten Sinfonien von Joseph Haydn," *Acta Musicologica*, VII (1937), pp. 5–25.

[12] See Marion M. Scott, "Mi-Jo Haydn," *The Monthly Musical Record* (Mar.–Apr. 1939).

at the beginning the typical *Di me Giuseppe Haydn*, together with the date of the composition, and at the end *Finis. Laus Deo* (The End. Praise the Lord).

Altogether, perhaps two hundred autographs of Haydn are accessible, a not inconsiderable quantity, though woefully small compared with the composer's whole output. The majority of these autographs are to be found in the National Library, Budapest, which took them over from the archives of Prince Esterházy. The large collection of Haydniana that was built up through the composer's long service for the princely family was vastly increased by the purchase of autographs after his death. A smaller, though still important amount of Haydniana is to be found in the two Berlin libraries that have possession of the former Prussian State Library— the Deutsche Staatsbibliothek in East Berlin and the Staatsbibliothek Preussischer Kulturbesitz in West Berlin. Also highly significant are the collections of the Österreichische Nationalbibliothek and the Gesellschaft der Musikfreunde in Vienna; the Bibliothèque Nationale in Paris; the British Library in London; and the Library of Congress in Washington, D.C. All these contain not only autographs, but also vast amounts of contemporary prints and copies of Haydn's works. They are supplemented by the libraries of monasteries and aristocratic families that maintained contact with Haydn. Research in these archives, located in the territory of the former Austro-Hungarian monarchy, is proving eminently fruitful.

Authentic contemporary editions also furnish important sources of information about Haydn's music. Not all the publishers and copyists were pirating Haydn. Many of them were authorized by the master himself, and in some cases we know that he personally supervised the publication of the music. Early editions of this type must certainly be considered fully reliable. Among these authentic prints, the editions of the Viennese publishers Artaria and Company are of special importance.[13] Between 1780 and 1790 one hundred fifty-seven works by Haydn, both original compositions and arrangements, were published by Artaria. Of equal rank are the editions of the Paris symphonies by Imbault, Paris, for which Haydn furnished the autographs. After Haydn visited England, business connections with London publishers predominated. He worked with William Forster, Longman and Broderip, John Bland, William Napier, George Thomson, and others. The important relation to the German publishers Breitkopf and Härtel took quite

---

[13] Cf. Larsen, *Die Haydn Überlieferung*, p. 98ff.

some time to establish, since the master did not at first answer the firm's written inquiry concerning whether or not he would agree to the publication of a substantial number of works. But when Georg August Griesinger (cf. p. 12n.) offered to serve as Breitkopf's agent and called on the old composer, Haydn gladly gave his consent.

The authentic manuscript copies of his compositions are a final source of information on the extent of Haydn's work. If the work of a copyist is supplemented by Haydn's own writing—for instance in his corrections or signature—there can be no doubt that the master approved of it.[14] The same may be said of those manuscripts that display the familiar handwriting of the master's copyists such as Joseph and Johann Elssler or Radnitzky. Even if the identity of the writer is unknown, the mere fact that an eighteenth-century manuscript can be traced back to Haydn's own library or that of Prince Esterházy makes its authenticity appear highly probable.

The present book does not propose to enter the gray territory of works whose authenticity is not fully confirmed. It attempts to offer a survey of Haydn's well-documented output, to discuss compositions that characterize his artistic personality, and to deal at greater length with some of the masterworks that represent the culmination of his creative genius.

[14]Thus the Haydn House at Eisenstadt possesses a score of Haydn's opera *Armida* written by a copyist but containing many annotations and corrections by Haydn himself.

# CHAPTER TWELVE

# $\mathcal{Y}outh$

## THE FIRST PERIOD
## 1750 – 1760

Like the work of other great masters, the creative output of Joseph
Haydn can be divided into several periods clearly distinguished
from each other. As lines of demarcation we may consider the end
of the decades constituting the second half of the eighteenth century. Thus the period of youth would reach from 1750 to 1760, the
preparatory period from 1761 to 1770, the middle period from 1771
to 1780, full maturity from 1781 to 1790, and the period of supreme
mastery from 1791 to 1803.[1]

There is nothing sensational about Haydn's early compositions.
Unlike the precocious geniuses of the eighteenth century—a Pergolesi or a Mozart—who died at an early age, or the masters of the
romantic period, who wrote some of their best works at the beginning of their careers, Haydn developed with the utmost slowness.
If an accident had caused his death when he was thirty-one, the age
at which Schubert died, he would not have written a single work
capable of bringing him lasting fame. Like Handel and Verdi,
Haydn composed his greatest masterpieces during the later part of

[1] Jens Peter Larsen divided Haydn's creative output into eight periods instead of this
author's five periods. See his "Zu Haydns künstlerischer Entwicklung" in *Festschrift
Wilhelm Fischer* (Innsbruck, 1956), p. 123. He also considers the years 1750, 1760,
and 1790 significant turning points. H. C. Robbins Landon's monumental Haydn
biography is divided into five volumes (1732–1765, 1766–1790, 1791–1795, 1796–
1800, 1801–1809), thus assigning the largest number of works to the second volume.

his life. He was nearly sixty when he wrote his first London symphony and close to seventy when the two great oratorios, *The Creation* and *The Seasons*, were completed.

Hardly any of the young musician's first attempts pointed to future greatness. His first period is characterized by youthful immaturity and dependence on the models of other composers. It starts approximately at his eighteenth year, when, according to the testimony of the Elssler catalogue, he began to compose. To the first years belong the keyboard sonatas, various chamber music pieces and divertimenti (among them the very important early string quartets), organ concertos, symphonies, and compositions for the church and for the stage. In these works Haydn adopted the tenets of the "preclassical" school, creating light, playful, gay compositions. He was just one of the many exponents of the *style galant*, and by no means the most important.

In order to understand the position of the young composer, it is necessary to look back at the general evolution of music during the second quarter of the eighteenth century.

Even before Johann Sebastian Bach wrote his most important works, a strong reaction had set in against the style of the great old master of baroque music. "The essence of the new artistic creed was," as Paul Henry Lang points out, "an urge for liberty; liberation from the rules that had become stereotyped, from the stylistic conventions that had become rigid, from the artistic forms that had become immutable."[2] The new rococo period tried to supplant majestic splendor with graceful delicacy. Whereas baroque art had striven toward a powerful unity of form, the younger generation preferred looseness and variety. Music had changed the buskins of pomposity for the dancing slippers of the *style galant*.

This revolutionary movement originated mainly with Italians, Austrians, and Bohemians born during the first quarter of the eighteenth century. The "preclassical" composers, as they are frequently called, stood midway between the baroque and the classical masters. They were from fifteen to thirty years younger than Bach and from fifteen to thirty years older than Haydn. This "preclassical" school disliked every type of polyphonic writing. Strict counterpoint was practically eliminated and even though *sonata da chiesa* elements (a slow movement preceding a fast one at the beginning of a composition) frequently may be observed, they are usually stripped of contrapuntal complications. On the other hand the sin-

[2] Paul Henry Lang, *Music in Western Civilization* (New York, 1941), p. 533.

fonia, the artless curtain-raiser of the Italian opera, consisting of a fast, a slow, and another fast movement, now came into frequent use as a separate instrumental piece. Its popularity was matched only by the suite, a set of pieces of dance character. Both these forms exhibit the easy gaiety and the colorful variety so dear to the rococo period.

Soon the sinfonia and suite began to attract and influence each other. A great number of hybrid forms resulted from their combination, one of which was to become of outstanding importance. About 1740 the Viennese composer Matthias Georg Monn wrote a sinfonia consisting of an allegro, a slow aria, and a final allegro; between the last two movements he inserted a minuet taken from the suite of dances. But the possibilities of the newly created form were not realized immediately, at least in Vienna. Monn and his contemporary, Georg Christoph Wagenseil, still preferred the sinfonia in three movements to the cycle of four movements.

Even more important than the shaping of the new instrumental form was the development of its first movement into the so-called sonata form. The beginning of this process was to be observed as far back as the baroque period and was not completed until about the year 1770. The aim of this evolution was to create, as an analogy to the three movements of the sinfonia, three sections in its first movement. An "exposition" displayed the themes, a "development" treated them in a varied way and modulated to distant keys, and a "recapitulation" brought a restatement of the first section. Even the exposition itself was in three parts, for between the main theme at the beginning and the closing theme (codetta), a subsidiary theme was inserted. These transformations were made with a view to giving greater solidity and poise to the levity of the sinfonia form. For no sooner had the massive grandeur of the baroque style been overcome than a new process of complication set in, and it is significant of the German mentality that German composers took the lead in this movement. Joseph Haydn's work carried the development to a climax, but he was only continuing a process begun by the preceding generation.

This leads to the question, who were Haydn's immediate predecessors? Hugo Riemann[3] tried to prove that Haydn was a disciple of such Bohemian and Austrian composers as Franz Xaver Richter (b. 1709), Ignaz Holzbauer (b. 1711), and Johann Stamitz (b. 1717),

[3] See Hugo Riemann, *Handbuch der Musikgeschichte* (Leipzig, 1922), II, p. 3, and Prefaces to *Denkmäler deutscher Tonkunst in Bayern*, second series, III, p. 1; VII, p. 2; VIII, p. 2.

living at Mannheim in southwestern Germany. Fausto Torrefranca[4] and Robert Sondheimer,[5] on the other hand, considered that certain Italian composers, especially Giovanni Battista Sammartini (b. 1701), exercised a decisive influence in the development of the classical style. But it is hardly to be doubted that Guido Adler and Wilhelm Fischer[6] were correct when they stated that Haydn carried on from where such Viennese composers as the younger Georg Reutter (b. 1708), Georg Christoph Wagenseil (b. 1715), and Georg Matthias Monn (b. 1717) left off. Haydn may have known of the Mannheim group and of various Italian composers, but as their style differed so little from that of the Viennese masters, he had no need to draw from foreign sources what he was able to find at home. It is true that young Haydn used the Mannheim *Walze* (steam roller), a melody rising by steps with a simultaneous crescendo and the accompaniment of a pedal point; he liked sudden changes from forte to piano, from strong sections in unison to soft harmonized sections. He employed subsidiary themes in the minor with their characteristic imitations, and the "rocket" themes that suddenly rise from a low to a high range. But all these devices were the general property of the time and Haydn had no need to go to Mannheim or Milan to become acquainted with them; he found them right on his doorstep, in the city where he grew up. In those few cases, however, in which Viennese "preclassical" composers differed from their contemporaries, Haydn always tended to identify himself with the Austrian tradition. Like Monn and Wagenseil, the young composer in turn wrote symphonies in three and in four movements; like those Austrian composers, he used recapitulations that brought in a complete restatement of the material of the exposition. On the other hand, Haydn did not follow Stamitz and other early symphonists in their penchant for incomplete recapitulations.

While in his orchestral music young Haydn favored the sinfonia form with slight influences from the suite, his works for clavier and his chamber music were based on the suite form with slight influences from the sinfonia. The composer employed here the divertimento, the partita, or the cassazione, sets of pieces in which the use of the same key and dance character prevailed, with one or more

[4]Fausto Torrefranca, "Le origini della Sinfonia," *Rivista Musicale Italiana* (1913).
[5]Robert Sondheimer, "G. B. Sammartini," *Zeitschrift für Musikwissenschaft*, III (1920–1921).
[6]See Guido Adler's and Wilhelm Fischer's works in the Bibliography. Cf. also Jens Peter Larsen, "Towards an Understanding of the Development of the Viennese Classical Style" in *International Musicological Society. Report of the Eleventh Congress, Copenhagen, 1972*, (Edition Wilhelm Hansen), p. 23, and *HCaW*, I, p. 83ff.

movements displaying simple sonata form. In these pieces Haydn closely followed the "preclassical" style. His minuets, for instance, with their typical motion in triplets and formalistic cadences, clearly show the rococo spirit.

In discussing the works in such an order as to begin with the compositions written for small ensembles and gradually proceeding to those written for bigger groups of instruments, we must first deal with the sonatas for keyboard instruments. It should be emphasized here that in his early compositions Haydn probably employed the predecessors of the piano: the harpsichord, the virginal, and the clavichord. On the other hand, from about 1770 the pianoforte seems to have been in Haydn's mind for his keyboard compositions. The words *per il cembalo* or *pour le clavecin* on some of the old manuscripts or printed editions must not lead us to believe that the composer actually wrote these compositions for the harpsichord. *Pour le clavecin ou fortepiano* was a standard indication on clavier compositions of the period and is found even on a number of Beethoven's piano sonatas.[7] However, Haydn's pianoforte should not be imagined as the instrument used in the nineteenth century. The piano of the romantic period, with its cast-iron frame, repeating action, and heavy strings, was very different from the lighter, smaller Haydn clavier with its weak tone, thin strings, and small hammerheads producing transparent, clear sounds.

• • •

Haydn wrote compositions for a keyboard instrument from his early youth to old age. The fifty-odd works that he contributed to the form cover a period of about four decades. It is impossible to determine with certainty which of these compositions were written before 1760, but it seems quite likely that the sonatas Hob. XVI:1, 2, and 4 were created at such an early date.[8] The first sonata shows the composer completely absorbed in the Austrian art of Georg Christoph Wagenseil. The use of the same tonality in all three movements, the name *partita*, the inclusion of a minuet with a trio in the minor key, the Alberti basses, the occurrence of melodies that seem to have been conceived first for the violin and later arranged

[7] The fact that during the last years of his life Haydn owned a precious English harpsichord made by Burkat Shudi and John Broadwood has no connection with his clavier compositions. From this harpsichord the master may have conducted symphonies or other large ensemble works, but it was not used as a solo instrument for his sonatas.

[8] The authenticity of Nos. 1 and 2 could not be definitely established, but it seems likely that these two works are genuine.

for the pianoforte, and the clear separation of the three themes in the exposition of the first movement are typical of the Viennese piano style of the rococo period. On the other hand, the second sonata shows some marks of the influence of Philipp Emanuel Bach, which was to assume much larger proportions in the years to come. The syncopations and unison passages, the passionate and quite personal character of the largo, with its sudden contrasts of mood, are unmistakably of north German origin. But there is no doubt that at this early age Haydn's art grew primarily out of the soil of his native country. Although in the fourth sonata some technical details, such as the division of passages between the two hands, still remind us of Bach, the predominantly Austrian character, especially conspicuous in the minuet and trio, shows the true origin of the work.

• • •

Haydn's keyboard trios for harpsichord, violin, and violoncello (or a larger bowed string instrument) are offspring of the baroque trio sonata. As early as the first half of the seventeenth century, tendencies were noticeable to transform the trio sonata for two melody instruments and bass into a duo for harpsichord and a single melody instrument.[9] In this new combination, the right hand of the keyboard player took over the part of the second melody instrument, and his left hand that of the bass. This progressive version reached a climax in the works of J. S. Bach, who wrote quite a number of such works. Towards the middle of the eighteenth century a kind of reaction set in, however, which is also noticeable in Haydn's early keyboard trios. These trios repeatedly contain brief sections in which the harpsichord is treated as a mere continuo instrument. Only the bass of the keyboard part is written out, while there are no notes for the right hand, which is expected to improvise an accompaniment. Moreover, throughout the trios the cello is used only to reinforce the left hand of the clavier and is never accorded a solo passage, a feature that can also be observed in Haydn's later trios. According to a valuable study by Georg Feder, the following eight trios belong to the first period—Hob. XV:34, 36, 37, 38, 40, 41, C1, F1.[10]

[9] Cf. Arnold Schering, "Zur Geschichte der Solosonate in der 1. Hälfte des 17. Jahrhunderts," in *Riemann Festschrift* (Leipzig, 1909).
[10] Georg Feder, "Haydns frühe Klaviertrios," *H-St*, II/4 (Dec. 1970), p. 314. Haydn's collected clavier trios were edited by H. C. Robbins Landon for Doblinger (Vienna, 1970). Moreover, the trios, written during the first four periods of composition were edited by W. Stockmeier in *JHW*, XVII/1 and 2.

These compositions, which are largely unknown to music lovers, must be counted among the most attractive works from Haydn's youth. Landon points out that their violin part is more interesting and challenging than that of Haydn's late trios, which were intended primarily for amateurs. He suggests therefore that the composer wrote the violin part for himself, while the beautiful Countess Morzin played the harpsichord.[11] Attractive stylistic variety can be observed among the trios. Apart from the common keys of C, G, and F major, Haydn also chose less popular signatures for these compositions, such as B-flat, E-flat, and E major, as well as F minor. The traditional three-movement form, fast-minuet-fast, is repeatedly modified. Thus in No. 36 the minuet is replaced by a spirited polonaise, while in C1 an adagio with six variations serves as finale. Number 37 starts, like a church sonata, with an adagio, which also offers an opportunity for the insertion of a cadenza for violin and harpsichord. It is followed by an allegro molto and a minuet with trio. Number 41 even anticipates future formal developments as it consists of four movements: two brisk allegros surrounding a minuet with trio and a richly ornamented adagio. The overall mood in these early trios is closer to serious expressiveness than to the carefree gaiety prevalent in compositions of the time. Even at this early stage of Haydn's artistic development, the strongly emotional trends dominating the composer's music around 1770 announce themselves.

• • •

Among Haydn's chamber music, no other compositions can equal the importance of his compositions for strings alone. The earliest of these works, the trios for two violins and cello, are obviously again descendants of the baroque trio sonata for two violins and bass. The fact that many of these trios start with an adagio, followed by an allegro, likewise points to models in earlier music. Section V of Hoboken's catalogue enumerates no less than eighty string trios attributed to Haydn. The first twenty-one of this group are listed in Haydn's draft catalogue and in the Haydn-Elssler catalogue of 1805. To these undoubtedly authentic compositions, Landon, who has prepared a collected edition of the trios, added thirteen more compositions that he considers genuine Haydn works.

The rather thin texture of the trios Hob. V:15–20 and the oc-

[11] *HCaW*, I, p. 263.

casional crossing of the violin part with that of the bass indicate that the composer, in writing these trios, had not quite overcome the influence of the past. Apparently he expected a keyboard instrument to double the part of the violoncello at the lower octave. Most of Haydn's unassuming string trios display the simple, cheerful character of the *style galant*. Thus it is not surprising that music-loving amateurs quickly took to them. They were frequently copied by hand and printed by Austrian, German, French, and English publishers.

• • •

Far more important than Haydn's string trios are his quartets for two violins, viola, and violoncello. In his valuable *Studien zur Geschichte des Streichquartetts*, Ludwig Finscher offers a survey of the numerous sinfonie, sonatas, concertini and concerti a quattro, the cassazioni, divertimenti, and quadri in use during the first half of the eighteenth century.[12] These were eventually condemned to oblivion while Haydn's early quartets were prodigiously successful. In our own time, whenever the master's music is mentioned, we like to think of his quartets, and there is every reason for doing so. Although Haydn wrote a great many of them, all are interesting, and most of them unquestioned masterpieces; they were declared unequaled by Goethe, who was not even particularly interested in Haydn.

There is still another reason why the string quartet plays so important a role in Haydn's musical evolution. The composer was in his twenties when he wrote his first quartet, and he had passed his seventieth birthday before he began to work on the Quartet Op. 103,[13] which proved to be the last significant composition he was ever to write. No other form of music occupied the composer for an equal length of time.

The exact number of Haydn's string quartets is not easily established. Eighty-three are enumerated in the Haydn-Elssler catalogue of 1805, which in turn was based on the thematic list presented in 1801–02 by I. Pleyel in his collected edition of the string quartets (cf. p. 195). These quartets include the adaptation of an early symphony in three movements (Hob. III:5, based on I:107), of two divertimenti for string quartet and two horns (Hob. III:9 and 11,

---

[12] Ludwig Finscher, *Studien zur Geschichte des Streichquartetts*, vol. I: *Die Entstehung des klassischen Streichquartetts* (Kassel, 1974).
[13] It is customary to refer to Haydn's string quartets—but to hardly any other group of his compositions—by opus numbers.

based on II : 21 and 22), as well as seven arrangements of Haydn's highly successful composition *The Seven Last Words* (see p. 302ff.). Moreover, the authenticity of six of the quartets (Hob. III : 13 – 18) is quite doubtful. It is now generally assumed that these works, known as Haydn's "Op. 3," were composed by P. Romanus Hoffstetter, a Benedictine monk who imitated Haydn's style.[14] On the other hand, Haydn and his amanuensis omitted at least one work, written in the composer's youth, the Quartet in E-flat major, No. 0 (Hob. II : 6), which was erroneously listed among the *Divertimenti auf verschiedene Instrumenten.*[15] Thus, as mentioned before, not eighty-three, but rather sixty-eight original string quartets by Haydn exist.

Just as uncertain as the exact number of the early quartets are the dates of their composition. Haydn's friend Griesinger contends that the master's first quartet was written in 1750. Pohl, the great Haydn scholar, considers this too early and assumes that the quartets Hob. III : 1 – 18 (known as Op. 1, Nos. 1 – 6; Op. 2, Nos. 1 – 6; and Op. 3, Nos. 1 – 6) were written about five years later. While this is not quite acceptable either, there is no doubt that the quartets Hob. II : 6, III : 1 – 4, 6, 7, 8, 10, and 12—usually designated as No. 0, Op. 1, Nos. 1 – 4 and Op. 2, Nos. 1, 2, 4, and 6—reflect the earliest phase of Haydn's contributions in this field. Landon assumes that the first six of these ten compositions were written ca. 1757 – 58, the last four between 1759 and 1761.[16] As they form a rather homogeneous entity, these ten quartets will be discussed here together.

The quadri and cassazioni, as the Breitkopf catalogue calls the earliest quartets, or the quartet-divertimenti, as Finscher calls them,

---

[14] Cf. Alan Tyson and H. C. Robbins Landon, "Who Composed Haydn's Op. 3?," *Musical Times*, CV/1457 (July 1964), p. 506ff; László Somfai, "Zur Echtheitsfrage des Haydn'schen Opus III," *HYb*, III (1966), p. 155ff; O. Eckhoff, "The Enigma of Haydn's Opus 3," *Studia musicologia norvegica*, 1978, p. 9ff.

[15] Early editions of Haydn's six string quartets forming Op. 1, such as those printed by J. J. Hummel, Amsterdam; Longman and Broderip, London; and Bremner, London, include this quartet "No. 0" together with the quartets Hob. III : 1 – 4 and 6. Later editions, however, such as that of La Chevardière, Paris, omitted the quartet in E-flat major, replacing it with the aforementioned adaptation of an early symphony in three movements (Hob. III : 5), which was designated as quartet, Op. 1, No. 5. The score of the orchestral version of this symphony, including oboes and horns, was edited by H. C. Robbins Landon as an appendix to his work *The Symphonies of Joseph Haydn* (London, 1955). Score and parts of quartet "No. 0" were edited in 1932 by Marion Scott for Oxford University Press (London) and independently from it by Karl Geiringer for Nagel's *Musikarchiv* (Hanover, now Kassel). At present, critical editions of the quartets Hob. III : 1 – 4, 6 – 8, 10, 12, and II : 6 are offered by Georg Feder in *JHW*, XII/1 (Kassel).

[16] *HCaW*, I, p. 254.

PLATE 1   Joseph Haydn, by T. Hardy. London, 1792.

PLATE 2   The house in Rohrau, Lower Austria, where Haydn was born.

PLATE 3    St. Stephen's Cathedral, Vienna.

PLATE 4  Vienna around 1740.

PLATE 5  Joseph Haydn in the uniform of an Esterházy court officer.

PLATE 6 Prince Nicolaus Esterházy (the Magnificent).

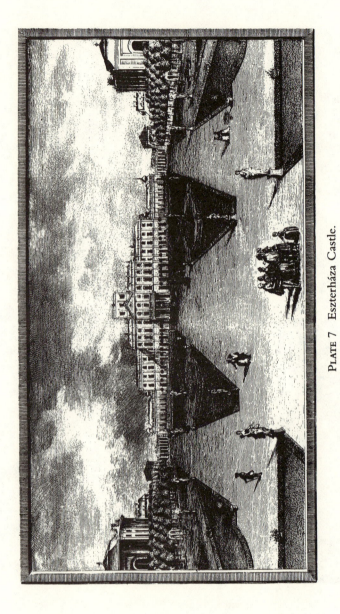

PLATE 7  Eszterháza Castle.

PLATE 8   An opera performance, supposedly at Eszterháza Castle.
The composer is conducting from the harpsichord.

PLATE 9   Haydn's square piano, his baryton, and his bust (without a wig) by A. Robatz.

PLATE 10   J. Haydn, beginning of the String Quartet, Op. 74, No. 3. Autograph.

PLATE 11  Prospect of London in the eighteenth century by Bowles.

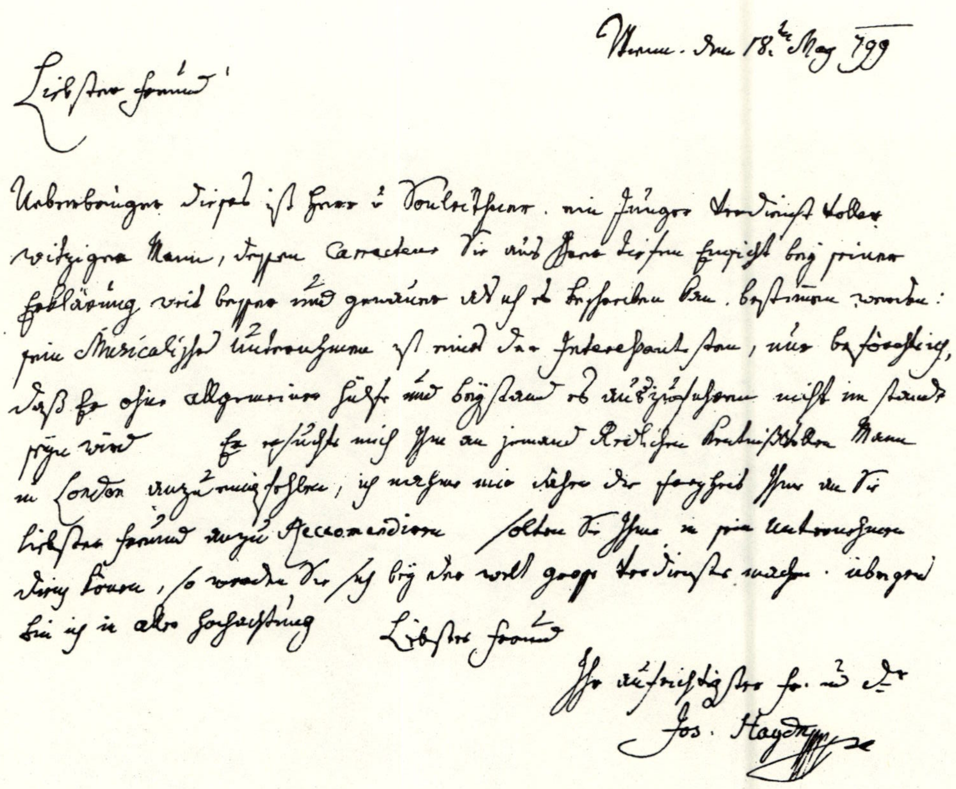

**PLATE 12** Autograph letter of Haydn to J. P. Salomon, dated May 18, 1799.

PLATE 13    Title page of the original edition of Haydn's *The Seasons*.

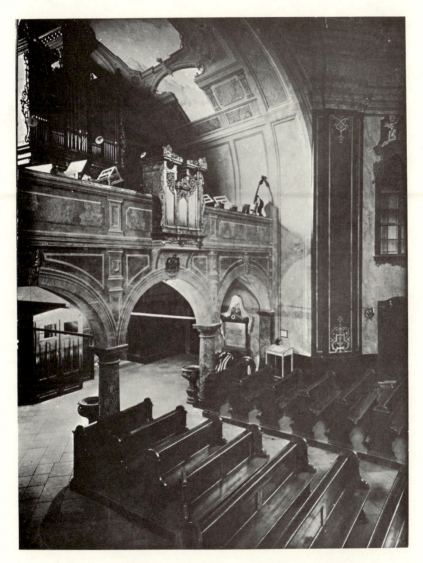

PLATE 14    The Bergkirche in Eisenstadt where Haydn's last
masses had their first performance. A monument to
the composer is visible under the choir, at left.

quite clearly show the influence of the suite. They are always in the major key and contain five movements, two of them minuets. The order of the movements is well balanced and symmetrical: allegro, minuet, adagio, minuet, presto (or allegro molto). Slight variations of this scheme are to be found in Op. 1, No. 3, and Op. 2, No. 6, in which the first and third movements change places. The majority of the movements in each quartet preserve the same key except that for the trios of the minuets, in compliance with the Viennese tradition, the tonic minor is preferred, while the slow movements are written in the subdominant, the dominant, or again in the tonic minor. Within this rigid scheme, however, Haydn displays a surprising variety of details, indicating both the richness of his imagination and the rather immature state of his technical knowledge. The treatment of the sonata form differs in practically all of the first movements, sometimes two, sometimes three, or even four themes being introduced. A genuine development of themes, in the manner of Haydn's mature style, is not to be found in any of these early compositions. But the composer conscientiously tried to make a choice of themes for the second parts of his sonata forms, usually giving preference to the second or third melody over the main theme.

These early string quartets need not necessarily be performed by four players only; the execution by a small orchestra of stringed instruments is correct, as the difference between chamber and orchestral music is not manifest in this first period. Nevertheless, the first signs of a genuine string quartet style already are to be noticed. It is true that the viola frequently uses the same rhythm as the violoncello, and even plays in octaves with that instrument; the composer occasionally concentrates the whole of the melodic life in the first violin part, so that the adagio of Op. 2, No. 2, for example, with its six-four chord for the cadenza near the end, resembles a concerto rather than a quartet. There are also many dialogues between the two violins, reminding us of the technique of the old trio sonatas. At the same time, the transparent style of the third movement of Op. 1, No. 3—in which all four instruments are granted an equal share of the thematic material—gives a fair promise of future achievements.

The contents of the quartets are simple and cheerful, with a preference for melodies resembling folk songs of Austrian character. An exception is found only in the adagio of Op. 2, No. 4, the passionate ardor of which reminds us of the north German art of Philipp Emanuel Bach, with which Haydn had just become acquainted. A movement of similar character is the above-mentioned largo of the second piano sonata, which was probably written about the same time.

During his first period of composition, Haydn also composed a Quintet for Strings in G major (Hob. II:20). This is probably a work that, according to Griesinger, the young musician wrote for the nocturnal serenades in which he frequently participated. The six movements of the composition again show the character of the suite. Most of the movements are in the same key, simple in form, and of a light and graceful character including folksonglike elements.

•   •   •

The next group comprises a number of smaller works for either string and wind instruments or wind instruments alone. Of particular significance are the so-called *Feldparthien*, small compositions that Haydn wrote primarily for the wind band of Count Morzin in Lukavec. They were at first scored for two oboes, two horns, and two bassoons, while clarinets, trumpets, and English horns made their appearance in later pieces. These compositions, as well as some suitelike chamber music works for both string and wind instruments, mark the transition toward symphonic music. Haydn listed them in the catalogue of 1805 as *Divertimenti auf verschiedene Instrumenten*.

Characteristic of the compositions in this class is an inexhaustible interest in sound effects; musical color is so important for the composer that for a short time it even obscures his interest in form. These divertimenti provided Haydn with a training ground for the use of orchestral instruments, particularly the winds. At first, however, his experiments produced scanty results; for example, in the two sextets for two violins, viola, violoncello, and two horns (Hob. II:21 and 22), the horns are used primarily as filling voices. In the slow middle movements, as in Haydn's first symphonies, they are omitted altogether. This might have induced some musicians to perform the sextets without wind instruments and thus to transform the compositions into string quartets (Op. 2, Nos. 3 and 5).

A change is noticeable in the little *Feldparthie* in F major for two oboes, two horns, and two bassoons (Hob. II:15), composed in 1760. Here, significant roles are given to the horns both in the adagio and in the presto finale. Similarly in the Divertimento in F major, scored for the same instrumental combination (Hob. II:23), the musical ideas seem to grow out of the technical potentialities of the horn.[17]

As for the woodwind instruments, the octet for two horns, two English horns, two violins, and two bassoons of 1760 (Hob. II:16) exploits with rare skill the colorful quality of the gentle, melancholy English horn. Sound effects of great beauty are realized, particularly in the adagio of this piece (Ex. 1).[18]

EXAMPLE 1   Divertimento in F for two English horns, two bassoons, and two horns, and two violins

A favorite form of these divertimenti is the variation. Haydn liked to entrust the melodic line of each variation to a different instrument. A good example of this procedure may be found in the popular divertimento *Der Geburtstag* (The Birthday) with the andante *Mann und Weib* (Husband and Wife), written before 1760

---

[17] Critical editions of Hob. II:15 and 23 have been presented by H. C. Robbins Landon for Doblinger (Vienna, 1959).
[18] Edited by Janetzky for Hofmeister (Leipzig, 1954).

(Hob. II: 11). It is scored for flute, oboe, two violins, violoncello, and bass.[19] The finale gives the lead to the first violin in the theme, to the violoncello in the first variation, to the flute in the second, to the second violin in the third, to the oboe in the fourth, and again to the first violin in the fifth; however, in the last three variations the instruments more or less blend together, with no one entirely taking the lead. The eighth variation may have been a favorite of Haydn's or of Prince Esterházy's. The composer used it again as a basis for the second movement in his symphony Hob. I:14.

We do not know for which specific birthday this divertimento was written. However, the reason for the andante's designation, *Mann und Weib*, is obvious. The melody is presented here in solid octaves, clearly expressing the firm union of the couple.

The soloistic employment of instruments in certain divertimenti brings elements of the concerto into the form. This is revealed with particular clarity in the Divertimento in G major for flute, oboe, two violins, violoncello, and bass (Hob. II:1). It frequently shows, as in a concerto grosso, a real concertino of flute, oboe, and first violin, to which even a proper cadenza is entrusted in the slow movement.

A similarly brilliant character is displayed in the nonet for two oboes, two horns, two violins, two violas and bass (Hob. II:20), probably written before 1757.[20] This composition has the same arrangement of its five movements as the early string quartets. In a manuscript of the National Museum in Prague, the work is called a concertino, since the composer shows a marked tendency to let each of the nine instruments have an interesting and independent part; to the oboes, in particular, attractive passages are assigned.

Haydn's real concertos of the first period were written primarily for organ or harpsichord and small orchestra. In his draft catalogue, the composer listed four concertos with their incipits and two additional ones without incipit. However, according to subsequent research, he composed a considerably larger number of such works.[21] Hob. XVIII lists eleven additional keyboard concertos, several of which are probably authentic.

Landon points out that it was the custom in Austria, Bohemia,

[19] Edited by Lemacher and Mies for Tonger (Cologne, 1932).
[20] Critical edition by H. C. Robbins Landon for Doblinger (Vienna, 1962).
[21] Cf. Georg Feder, "Wieviel Orgelkonzerte hat Haydn geschrieben?" *Musikforschung*, XXIII/4 (Oct.–Dec. 1970), p. 440ff. On the basis of an investigation of the range of the keyboard parts, the author assumed that the concertos were primarily meant for the organ.

and southern Germany to perform organ concertos in the middle of the Mass on small organs without pedals.[22] Haydn's organ concertos may have been written for such a purpose. At the same time, the composer was not averse to the secular use of his music, which accounts for the fact that in old manuscripts, and even in the draft catalogue, these works are occasionally listed as harpsichord concertos.

The musical form is remarkably well developed in the keyboard concertos. However, little technical brilliance is noticeable in the soloist's part, which might be due to the intended ecclesiastical use of these works. The origin of the keyboard concerto from the violin concerto, so clearly shown in Bach's compositions, is also noticeable in Haydn's works. As a rule, the left hand of the solo instrument doubles the bass, and only the right hand is melodically independent. Sometimes both hands participate in brilliant scale runs or triad passages. The Organ Concerto in C major (Hob. XVIII:1) of 1756 is typical of these early works. The composer lists it in his draft catalogue as *per il clavicembalo* while it is headed in the autograph as *Concerto per l'Organo*. Here the baroque ambiguity in the use of the term *clavier* is evident; one is reminded of Bach's nomenclature *Clavierübung* applied to music for both the organ and stringed keyboard instruments. However, in Haydn's concerto the fast runs seem to be much better suited for a harpsichord than for the serious church instrument. In this concerto, the importance of the solo instrument is still diminished by a comparatively large orchestra (strings, two oboes, two trumpets); the composition is much more like a piece of ensemble music than a real concerto.[23]

Similar in character is another C major organ concerto (Hob. XVIII:8). Although its accompanying orchestra dispenses with oboes, it entrusts significant tasks to the brass instruments (two trumpets or two horns). The work, the authenticity of which is not certain, may have originated somewhat later than the first organ concerto.[24]

A concerto in F major for clavier and violin solo with strings (Hob. XVIII:6) also belongs to Haydn's early works in this field. It points to the origin of such compositions in the baroque double concerto for two violins. The thematic material is distributed be-

[22] *HCaW*, I, p. 198.
[23] Edited by Schneider for Breitkopf and Härtel (Wiesbaden, 1953).
[24] Edited by H. C. Robbins Landon for Doblinger (Vienna, 1960).

tween solo violin and keyboard instrument, the clavierist's right hand assuming leadership; here too the left, in the manner of a continuo instrument, strengthens the bass and supplies filling notes.

Closely related to these early concertos are several divertimenti for keyboard instrument and strings (Hob. XIV:1–13) mostly written in the fifties or early sixties. These pieces, which appear in old manuscripts under varying designations and, as is customary in Haydn's early works, in different instrumentations, stand once more on the borderline between concerto and chamber music. A good example is supplied by the little C major Concertino in three movements (Hob. XIV:11). The short, simple work, which Haydn composed in 1760, is scored for cembalo, two violins, and bass, without viola and wind instruments, and assumes the character of a quartet with obbligato clavier rather than that of a concerto.

•  •  •

In discussing Haydn's symphonies we can use as a basis the excellent list of one hundred four works provided by Eusebius Mandyczewski in 1907 (cf. p. 196) and printed in the symphony volumes of both the Breitkopf and Härtel and the Haydn Society collected editions.[25] The catalogue of Haydn's symphonies in section I of Hoboken's catalogue still uses the Mandyczewski numbers, adding, however, four works, the concertante symphony of 1792 (I:105), the orchestral version of the String Quartet Op. 1, No. 5 in B-flat (I:107), the so-called Partita in B-flat (I:108), and a Symphony in D lost today (I:106). The main corrections needed in the old list concern the chronological order. New research established that a substantial number of symphonies were entered by Mandyczewski in the wrong places. Thus for instance, Symphony No. 40, according to the original manuscript, was written in 1763 and therefore belongs to symphonies Nos. 13 and 14 from the same year. Number 49 was composed in 1768 and ought to be placed between Nos. 38 and 39. Number 72 should, for stylistic reasons, be assigned to the first half of the 1760s, possibly after No. 20; the Paris symphonies Nos. 83 and 87 were written in 1785, and accordingly should be inserted between Nos. 81 and 82.

It is not quite clear how many of Haydn's symphonies were

---

[25] This edition, which was partly based on insufficient source material, is superseded by the *Critical Edition of the Complete Symphonies*, edited by H. C. Robbins Landon and published by Universal-Edition and Doblinger (Vienna, 1963–1968). Of great value also is the edition (*JHW*) of the Haydn Institute in Cologne, published by Henle Verlag (Munich). As of 1981 it comprised about a quarter of the symphonies.

created before the composer entered the service of Prince Esterházy. A collection of authentic copies of Haydn's early symphonies was recently discovered in the Hungarian castle of Keszthely (cf. p. 38n.). The title pages of the individual works are numbered in the composer's own hand, indicating a chronological order.[26] Unfortunately, however, several works out of this series are lost. Robbins Landon undertook the difficult task of supplementing the missing items. He produced the following list of nineteen symphonies in which the numbers in parentheses represent the scholar's substitutions:[27] Hob. I:1, 37, 18, (19), 2, (108), (16), (17), 15, 4, 10, 32, 5, 11, 33, 27, (107), 3, (20). This list is, as the author himself admits, partly hypothetical, but both external and stylistic reasons seem to indicate that it conveys an approximately correct picture of Haydn's symphonic output during the Morzin years.

In the symphonies Hob. I:1 and 2, which may be considered representative of the earliest group, Haydn certainly did not establish himself as a great innovator. Both works are in three movements without minuet. Number 1 begins with the fashionable "steam roller," which Haydn may have borrowed from a symphony by Stamitz (cf. p. 207), and introduces a subsidiary theme in the minor key with imitations, typical of the Viennese "preclassical" composers. The wind instruments (two oboes and two horns) are employed mainly to increase the sonority of the full orchestra; no use is made of them in the piano passages or in the slow middle movements. A continuo instrument, such as a harpsichord, is essential for filling the occasional gaps between the melody and the bass. This is particularly noticeable in the andante of No. 2; since only the melody and the bass are written out, the cooperation of a harpsichord is necessary.

Similarly, the partita, I:108, starts with a steadily moving bass in eighth notes that we would rather expect to find in a work of Bach's than in a composition of Haydn's. It is also characteristic that eighteenth-century publishers considered the wind instruments (two oboes, two horns, and one bassoon) as superfluous. The partita was printed in 1768 by Chevardière in Paris and in 1785 by his successor Le Duc as a simple string quartet—this in spite of the fact that a few significant solos were entrusted by the composer to the wind instruments.

In some of these early works, four movements, instead of the

[26] See *HCaW*, I, p. 240.
[27] Ibid., p. 280ff.

traditional three, can already be observed. We find them, for instance, in the partita and in I:3, which also displays a subsidiary theme in the dominant major. In this work, the light rococo spirit of previous compositions is replaced by a rather rigid and polyphonic style. The first movement shows a strong contrapuntal tendency; the minuet furnishes canonic imitations, and the finale shows a real double fugue. Hob. I:32 and 33, both in four movements, assume a particularly brilliant character as two trumpets and timpani join the traditional oboes and horns in the wind section. The principle of the 1780s, providing each musical instrument with a fair share of the thematic development of the musical material, is foreshadowed in the beginning of Symphony No. 37. There are also early signs of the *Empfindsamkeit* (sensibility) of the following period. Number 16 has as a main theme a sequence of wailing "sighs," prepared dissonances introduced on the strong beat and resolved by stepwise progression downward on the weak beat. To emphasize the unusual character of these "sighs," Haydn introduces them in the bass.

● ● ●

In his works for the stage, Haydn began his career as a close adherent to the Viennese tradition, and Joseph Felix Kurz-Bernardon, the Viennese actor and author of farces, became his librettist when the composer was only nineteen. A truly Austrian book, filled with merry gaiety and coarse realism, delightfully ridiculing the stilted style of the serious opera, was used by the composer in his first work for the stage, a Singspiel entitled *Der krumme Teufel* (based on Lesage's *Le Diable boiteux*). The work (Hob. XXIXb:1) seems to have been successful, but no trace of it can be found. It was probably revived around 1758 in a new version as *Der neue krumme Teufel* (Hob. XXIXb:1b). The libretto has been preserved, but Haydn's music seems to be definitely lost. In an interesting study Robert Haas expressed the assumption that young Haydn kept up the connection with Kurz-Bernardon during the 1750s, occasionally writing music to other comedies by the poet-actor.[28] If this theory is correct, it may be presumed that a collection of *Teutsche Comoedie-Arien* in the Vienna National Library, containing texts by Kurz-Bernardon from the years between 1754 and 1758 and set to music by anonymous composers, contains pieces by Haydn.

[28] Robert Haas, "Die Musik in der Wiener deutschen Stegreifkomödie," *Studien zur Musikwissenschaft*, XII (1925).

Volumes 64 (1926) and 121 (1971) of the *Denkmäler der Tonkunst in Österreich* offer valuable selections from this collection. The arias, duets, trios, and quartets presented here are imbued with a healthy earthiness and keen wit, displaying a surprising sense of musical form, so that it does not seem altogether unlikely that young Haydn contributed his share to the collection. It is particularly remarkable that one of these *Comoedie-Arien* contains a quotation from Haydn's *Salve Regina* in E major and from other works of the young composer.[29]

•   •   •

To Haydn's earliest dated compositions, besides the Organ Concerto in C major, belongs the *Salve Regina* in E major (Hob. XXIIIb:1) just mentioned. Both these works, according to their autographs, were composed in 1756. The *Salve Regina* is scored for soprano solo and four-part chorus, two violins, organ, and bass. It is a short piece in three movements, showing in its typically Italian melodies and coloratura for the soloist the influence that Haydn's new teacher, Porpora, exercised on the responsive mind of the young composer. On the other hand, the choral numbers are simple and forceful, and the insertion of the solo part is very skillfully handled.

In his settings of the Mass, Haydn naturally followed models that he had studied as a choirboy at St. Stephen's. They were by such composers as the two Reutters, father and son, Antonio Caldara, and Johann Joseph Fux, the great master of counterpoint; possibly also by older musicians like Johann Stadlmayr and Christoph Strauss. The style of these composers had its roots in Italy. The solid texture and the tendency to assemble solo voices, vocal tutti, and orchestral instruments in individual choirs used alternately, point to the styles of Venice and Rome. The display of arias and duets with brilliant coloratura and the use of operatic effects, however, show the influence of Neapolitan music, but these devices of southern Italian art had been used in Austria for over a century, with the result that by Haydn's time their origin was all but forgotten.

The little Mass in F major (Hob. XXII:1), written around 1749, is one of the most important works of Haydn's early youth. It is a so-called *missa brevis*, a concise composition of the Mass text,

---

[29] Eva Badura-Skoda's valuable article "Teutsche 'Comoedie-Arien' und Joseph Haydn," in *Der junge Haydn* (Graz, 1972) provides a piano score of this aria.

using a very small accompanying orchestra. This work is written
for two solo sopranos, a four-part chorus, two violins, organ, and
bass (an ensemble very similar to that used for the *Salve Regina*).
The words are crowded together as much as possible, and in order
to abbreviate the composition, occasionally the four voices simultaneously sing different sections of the liturgical text. Only in the
Benedictus given to the two solo sopranos is the melodic impulse
allowed to develop freely. This little duet and the coloratura of the
solo voices display the influence of the Neapolitan school. Remarkable is the composition of the Kyrie, which, as in later Masses by
Haydn and in Beethoven's first Mass, is also used for the "Dona
nobis pacem." The words of the Kyrie eleison (Lord have mercy on
us) were set to a melody with a folk song character (Ex. 2), the

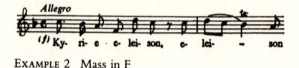

EXAMPLE 2    Mass in F

music showing so carefree and cheerful an attitude that it hardly
seems appropriate to the solemn words of the prayer. This brings us
to an important feature of Haydn's church music, which must
be understood in order to appreciate the master's sacred works.
Haydn's "attitude toward religion was not gloomy and repentant,
but gay, reconciled, and trustful, and this character is also to be
found in his compositions for the church" (Griesinger). To Haydn's
pious optimism a prayer for mercy seemed to involve a grant of this
request, and he felt justified in beginning and ending his Mass in a
spirit of happy confidence. Haydn made hardly any distinction between sacred and secular music. As a painter of the Renaissance
period did not hesitate to give to the Madonna the features of some
girl he knew personally, so Haydn applied the principles of instrumental music to his Mass by starting and ending with an allegro.
As Alfred Schnerich, the champion of Haydn's church music, explains, this can also be defended from a liturgical point of view,
since on a festive day the congregation ought to be received as well
as dismissed in a spirit of joyousness.[30]

   Haydn himself was always fond of this work of his early youth,
and as an old man he took it up again, having wind instruments

[30] See his *Messe und Requiem seit Haydn und Mozart* (Vienna, 1909).

(flute, two each of clarinets, bassoons, and trumpets, as well as timpani) added to the modest score in order to present it to Prince Nicolaus II Esterházy.[31] "What I like particularly in this little work," he confessed to the painter Dies, "is its tunefulness and a certain youthful fire." No modern critic can be so sophisticated as not to acknowledge these merits in the unpretentious composition.

At about the same time, or somewhat earlier, originated the Mass in G major (*Rorate coeli desuper*) (Hob. XXII:3). Its title, derived from Isaiah 45:8, is to be found in the introit for the fourth Sunday in Advent, and a part of this Gregorian chant is used in the Kyrie. The work, written for four-part chorus, two violins, organ, and bass, was rediscovered in 1957 by H. C. R. Landon in the Austrian monastery of Göttweig.[32] This is again a typical *missa brevis*, allotting not more than thirteen measures to the Kyrie, eleven to the Sanctus, and less than nine to the Gloria. Several mistakes in part-writing prove it to be the work of an inexperienced, budding composer.

[31] This arrangement was probably merely supervised by Haydn. The manuscript of the later version in the Esterházy library shows the parts of the original composition written by Haydn's copyist, Elssler, and those for the wind instruments inserted by his pupil, Polzelli.
[32] The Mass was edited in 1957 by H. C. Robbins Landon for Haydn-Mozart Presse, Vienna. Although the incipit is quoted in both Haydn's draft catalogue and the list of 1805 (in the latter, however, with a slight deviation from the version of the score), the authenticity of the work has been doubted. No autograph of the Mass has yet been found and Haydn's name does not appear on any eighteenth-century copy, while, on the other hand, old manuscripts attribute the composition to Georg Reuter, Jr., or F. P. F. Arbesser. Moreover, the entry in the draft catalogue was made in the 1790s when Haydn's memory was possibly no longer reliable.

# CHAPTER THIRTEEN

# A Phase of Transition

## THE SECOND PERIOD
## 1761 – 1770

It is a new Haydn that we meet after the composer becomes conductor for the Princes Esterházy. The Haydn of the 1760s is a successful man occupying an important position and held in high esteem by his subordinates and even by his patron.

Now Haydn could work regularly with a group of well-trained singers and players. He could study at the closest range the possibilities of each instrument and the human voice. He could hear each of his compositions almost before the ink on the manuscript was dry, a state of matters that should appear enviable to young composers of our present time, who almost despair of ever hearing their symphonies and operas performed.

Gradually Haydn succeeded in finding a way toward the expression of his true self. During the first years of his appointment at the court of Prince Esterházy he continued to master the overpowering influences of the past. There was, to be sure, no deliberate effort to break with tradition. But while on the whole preserving the musical language of the "preclassical" composers, Haydn became increasingly able to imbue it with his own artistic personality. The playful grace of the *style galant* was more frequently replaced by a leaning toward serious baroque means of expression, and at the end of the decade an increasing number of stylistic features pointed to the passionate subjectivity of the following period. The sixties of the eighteenth century were for Haydn essentially a phase of transition. Old and new elements were more closely interwoven than in any other period of his artistic evolution; and while the man of thirty was discovering himself, the world was slowly becoming aware that a genius was living and maturing in the remoteness of the Hungarian plains.

• • •

To the keyboard sonatas of the second period belong, in all likelihood, the following eighteen compositions: Hob. XVI:3, 5–10, 12–14, 18, 19, 44–47, G1 and XVII:D1. Georg Feder rightly points out that the early works are clearly divided into two groups: short and technically easy compositions (such as Hob. XVI:3, 4, 7–10) meant for educational purposes and amateurs, as well as longer, technically more demanding works (such as Hob. XVI:5, 6, 12–14) intended for professional players.[1]

In the sonatas of the sixties the influence of the *style galant* is still quite strongly noticeable. The character of the suite is predominant, a minuet is hardly ever missing, and in most sonatas the same tonality is preserved in all movements[2] (cf. Hob. XVI:5, 7–10, 12–14, 44). It might be considered as experimental features that the sonatas Nos. 18 and 44 are in two movements only, while, on the other hand, Nos. 6 and 8 make use of the four-movement form (with minuet and slow middle movement) usually reserved for larger ensembles.

These keyboard sonatas are obviously influenced by Haydn's ensemble music. Many sections seem really meant for violin and figured bass, and it is not at all surprising that some of these sonatas were also printed "with the accompaniment" of a violin or a violin and violoncello. Some passages are definitely inspired by the technique of the violin, and the frequent changes from high to low registers suggest the arrangement for pianoforte of an orchestral composition.

At the same time, these sonatas do not lack indications of future trends. In addition to violinistic features, one finds here freely modulating passages, especially in the development sections, which exhibit a definitely pianistic character (see the first movement of No. 5). Still more important is the fact that Haydn was already striving toward the unity and concentration of form so characteristic of the best among his mature compositions. In the first movement of No. 3, the continuous use of triplets, sometimes in the bass

[1]*JHW*, XVIII/1, p. viii.
[2]However, the trios of the minuets are, as a rule, in the parallel key.

and sometimes in the treble, gives the work considerable uniformity. In No. 10 the second subject is closely related to the first, and it remains for the third to bring in new melodic material, a procedure that was to become important in Beethoven's compositions.

The closer we come to Haydn's third period, the clearer become the indications of the influence of Philipp Emanuel Bach. Number 46, written between 1765 and 1768, contains a wide-contoured adagio in D-flat major, testifying, with its pathos and sudden changes of mood, to the impact of the north German master's music on Prince Esterházy's conductor. Number 19, of 1767, was even considered by an English periodical[3] to be a parody of the style of the Hamburg master. According to the author of the article, Haydn wanted thus to revenge himself for the unfriendly attitude that Bach had assumed toward him. A refutation of this statement was made by Bach himself when he declared most emphatically in an article for a Hamburg paper[4] that he and Haydn were the best of friends and that all assertions to the contrary were to be considered mere lies. But it cannot be denied that a certain similarity exists between Haydn's Sonata No. 19 and Emanuel Bach's piano compositions. The transparency of the two-part writing in the work of the younger composer, the accompaniment of melodies in high register by low-pitched basses introducing rests on accented beats of the measure, the dramatic development in the first movement, the broad baritone melody of the subsidiary theme in the second movement, and, most of all, the unrelenting intensity of feeling permeating the whole work all show Haydn as a diligent disciple of Johann Sebastian's great son.

Two shorter keyboard compositions were likewise written during this decade. A set of twenty variations (Hob. XVII:2) seems to have been conceived in G major but later transposed by the composer himself to A major. The arietta serving as its theme, as well as twelve of the variations, was printed in 1789 by Artaria in Vienna. This is stylistically a rather conservative composition, apparently intended for the harpsichord and strictly following the traditional chaconne form.[5] Like several other early keyboard works by Haydn, it may have been written for the composer's pupils.

Rather different in character is the Capriccio in G major (Hob. XVII:1), published by Artaria at about the same time. In the tradi-

---

[3] *The European Magazine* (London, October 6, 1784).
[4] *Hamburger Unpartheiische Correspondenz*, no. 150 (1785).
[5] Cf. the edition of Haydn's smaller clavier compositions, edited by F. Eibner in *Wiener Urtext Ausgaben* for Universal Edition (Vienna), preface, p. xix.

tional manner, the old print offers the alternative *pour le clavecin ou pianoforte*, but the humorous composition, implying finely differentiated dynamics, seems better suited to the modern piano. This is a fantasy in loosely constructed rondo form. Its original manuscript has survived and bears in the composer's hand the heading: *Capriccio Acht Sauschneider müssen seyn del Giuseppe Haydn m[anu prop]ria [1]765*. The author uses as a basis of the piece the rather vulgar folk song "Acht Sauschneider" (Eight men castrate a single boar).[6] It is interesting that in the following year, Mozart, at that time aged ten, was attracted by the same tune and inserted it in his *Gallimathias Musicum* (K. 32).

Unlike Mozart, Haydn showed little interest in music for piano duet. A piece of this kind, probably written in the sixties, seems to make fun of the educational aims that as a rule were responsible for the composition of such works. *Il maestro e lo scolare* (Hob. XVIIa:1) consists mainly of an andante with seven variations. The instructor plays a short phrase, and the pupil immediately repeats it two octaves higher. This simple game is continued throughout the set of variations, eventually becoming tiresome. A plain *tempo di menuetto*, fortunately without imitation, serves as a coda.

•  •  •

The six sonatas for violin and viola (Hob. VI:1–6) were probably written in the late sixties. Here Haydn revived the old style of solo sonata with *basso continuo*. The whole melodic life is concentrated in the violin part, the viola providing the basis for the harmonic support. The violin displays inventive power and a brilliant conception, and were it not for the poor treatment accorded the viola part, these sonatas would have to be counted among Haydn's representative compositions of the sixties. It might be worthwhile to use the viola part as the bass for a newly made piano accompaniment; a set of rather interesting violin sonatas could thus be produced that might easily take the place of the inferior arrangements for violin and piano published in our time under Haydn's name (see p. 317).

While Haydn wrote a comparatively large number of keyboard sonatas during the sixties, his interest in the clavier trio proportionately decreased. Feder assigns only three works (Hob. XV:1, 35, and 2) to this period.[7] A stylistic advance over the works of the first

---

[6]Critical edition by S. Gerlach for Henle Verlag (Munich).
[7]Georg Feder, "Haydns frühe Klaviertrios," *H-St*, II/4 (Dec. 1970), p. 314.

period is hardly noticeable, since the character of the suite is still prevalent. Thus, No. 2 in F major is in three movements, all in the same key, the second is a minuet, the third a set of variations. Certain passages in the first movement still require the realization of a continuo, and the curious entanglement of the two hands in the same movement indicates that the composer wrote these phrases with a two-manual harpsichord in mind. Altogether, these trios were obviously conceived for the traditional cembalo, whereas Haydn's keyboard sonatas of the sixties gradually move towards a pianistic technique. The introductory movement of the G minor Trio No. 1 provides opportunities for both harpsichord and violin to exhibit technical skill. Similarly the etudelike capriccio opening the A major Trio No. 35 offers gratifying tasks to the two main instruments. Although dynamic signs are missing throughout these early trios, the finale (presto) of No. 1 introduces attractive examples of forceful statements in unison, alternating with delicate answers in a higher octave—a kind of echo effect particularly well suited for a two-manual harpsichord.

Closely related to the clavier trios is the Quintet in E-flat major (Hob. XIV:1). This attractive divertimento, which is scored for two horns, violin, string bass, and cembalo, assigns to the wind instruments not only a filling part but also little solo passages. Unfortunately this is the only work of its kind; the composer never repeated this very successful experiment.

Among the trios for two violins and violoncello, Hob. V:1–4, 8, 10, and 12 might belong to the second period. They are musically more interesting than the earlier works of this type, and were probably written after Haydn had entered the service of Prince Esterházy. The first violin parts, which ascend nearly up to $c^4$ and frequently introduce double stops, seem to indicate that the composer had the brilliant violinist Tomasini in mind when he wrote these movements. But the substance of the trios has also changed. The pastoral character of the deeply felt adagio in No. 2, the ardent passion in the adagio in B minor in No. 3 (Ex. 3) and the frequent daring modulations all show that Haydn had begun to outgrow the superficiality of the rococo style.

EXAMPLE 3   Divertimento for two violins and bass, B minor

These trios for two violins and violoncello were succeeded by trios for baryton, viola, and violoncello, which Haydn wrote for Prince Nicolaus Esterházy, an enthusiastic devotee of the baryton. This unusual stringed instrument is a relative of the bass viola da gamba. As a rule, six or seven gut strings extend over its finger-board, and about twice as many metallic strings are stretched behind the neck, and consequently cannot be reached by the bow. These metallic strings can be plucked by the thumb of the left hand, the neck of the instrument being open in the back. Pizzicato and arco notes are at times sounded simultaneously, which makes any performance on the instrument rather difficult. In consequence the baryton never attained great popularity, and its use was always confined to a small circle.

Contemporary sources vary in their estimates of the merits of the instrument. Friedrich August Weber, a physician who was one of the most spirited musical writers of the time, praised it, saying, "One seems to hear the gamba and the harp at the same time," and confessed that he was "moved to tears" by its sounds.[8] Dr. Burney, discussing the performance of the baryton virtuoso Andreas Lidl, who had been in the service of Prince Esterházy before going to London, writes: "Mr. Lidl, indeed, played with exquisite taste and expression upon this ungrateful instrument with the additional embarrassment of base [*sic*] strings at the back of the neck with which he accompanied himself, an admirable expedient in a desert, or even in a house, where there is but one musician; but to be at the trouble of accompanying yourself in a great concert; surrounded by idle performers who could take the trouble off your hands, and leave them more at liberty to execute, express, and embellish the principal melody, seemed at best a work of supererogation."[9]

Haydn wrote more than one hundred and sixty baryton pieces for his patron. About one-tenth of these compositions seem to be lost.[10] Among the others, the one hundred twenty-six baryton trios form the largest and most important group.[11] The earliest of these

---

[8] *Musikalische Zeitung* (1788).
[9] See Charles Burney, *A General History of Music* (London, 1776–1789), II, p. 1020 (Reprint by F. Mercer, New York: Dover, 1957).
[10] This fact ought to be stressed, for in 1904 William Henry Hadow wrote in the *Oxford History of Music* (V, p. 41) about Haydn's baryton compositions: "This vast mass of music has wholly disappeared, except for three divertimenti and a few inconsiderable fragments."
[11] The trios Hob. XI:25–126 were presented in *JHW*, XIV/2–5 by H. Unverricht, M. Harting, and H. Walter. Cf. also William Oliver Strunk, "Haydn's Divertimenti for Baryton, Viola, and Bass," *Musical Quarterly*, XVIII/2 (Apr. 1932), p. 216ff.;

pieces were created in 1762 when Nicolaus the Magnificent became the ruling prince, but Haydn seems at first to have displayed a rather lukewarm attitude toward this form. When, however, he received in 1765 his patron's energetic command to apply himself to composition of pieces playable on the baryton, of which but few had been supplied so far (see p. 61), he acted accordingly: through the following decade a steady flow of new works for the baryton may be observed. Only around 1774 did the Prince's interest in the instrument wane when he became engrossed in operatic productions that kept his conductor more than busy.

The first ninety-six trios were originally entered in four volumes, each of which contains twenty-four works. There is good reason to assume that Hob. XI: 1–48 were composed between 1762 and 1767, Nos. 49–72 in 1767 and 1768, Nos. 73–96 between 1769 and 1771, and Nos. 97–126 between 1771 and 1775.

The form of the baryton trios shows a certain resemblance to that of the trios for two violins and violoncello. The pieces for baryton, viola, and violoncello are mostly in three movements, with a minuet in the middle or at the end, and the second movement usually in a key closely related to that of the other movements. A number of fine specimens are to be found in this collection, showing that Haydn gave of his best even when he did not expect his compositions to be heard outside the court of his prince. Nearly every trio has an interesting little detail, such as the charming melody for baryton in the adagio of No. 1, the attractive changes of dynamics in the minuet of No. 34, and the pretty variations in No. 38.[12] The humorous minuet *alla zoppa* (limping minuet) in No. 52,[13] the remarkable changes between plucked and bowed baryton passages, with an occasional combination of the two effects in the adagio of No. 56, the pizzicato of the baryton in the trio of the minuet in No. 61, and the succession of wailing appoggiaturas in the trio of the minuet in No. 82 (entitled *Das alte Weib* [The Old Woman]) are additional examples. The august baryton player also must have enjoyed the quotations from operas Haydn inserted, such as the tune of the aria "Che farò senza Euridice" from Gluck's *Orfeo ed Euridice* in No. 5, or a melody from Haydn's own comic opera *La*

---

Hubert Unverricht, "Zur Chronologie der Barytontrios von Joseph Haydn," in *Symbolae Historiae Musicae* (Mainz, 1971), p. 180ff.; and Hubert Unverricht, *Geschichte des Streichtrios* (Tutzing, 1969), p. 127ff.

[12] The theme of these variations appears also in the piano duet *Il maestro e lo scolare*.

[13] This piece and the ensuing trio also appear in Haydn's Symphony No. 58.

*canterina* in No. 29. Although the best baryton trios were written during Haydn's third period, these earlier pieces certainly do not lack charm.

• • •

Haydn's string quartets of the 1760s are probably the only compositions of this period that still enjoy a certain amount of popularity, at least with ambitious amateurs.

The quartets, known as Haydn's "Op. 3" (Hob. III:13–18) probably slipped by mistake into Pleyel's collected edition of the composer's string quartets, and from there into the Haydn-Elssler catalogue of 1805 (cf. p. 197). The fact that these six pieces were not mentioned in Haydn's draft catalogue and were first published as late as 1777 (by Bailleux, Paris, a firm known to have issued spurious Haydn works) casts grave doubts on their authenticity. The individual quartets in the "Op. 3" certainly differ from the rest of Haydn's early quartets. No. 2 consists of a slow set of variations, a minuet with trio, and a presto finale. In No. 4 there is no minuet, and the central adagio has shrunk to a few measures so that the piece consists basically of two fast movements only. In the well-known serenade of No. 5 the innocent tune, carried from beginning to end by the first violin, is accompanied by a pizzicato of the other three instruments, whose monotonous simplicity appear foreign to Haydn's inexhaustible inventiveness. Thus the theory that not the composer himself, but a skillful imitator—the monk P. Romanus Hoffstetter (1742–1815)—wrote these quartets, seems fully convincing.[14]

The following authentic series of six quartets (Hob. III:19–24), known as Op. 9, was composed around 1769. In this cycle, four movements, with a minuet as the second one, have become the rule. In the movements in sonata form, the development section assumes increasing importance. Whereas in earlier compositions the exposition is apt to be more than twice as long as the development, these two sections in Op. 9, No. 2, are almost equal in length. At the same time, the developments begin to outgrow the traditional sequences and modulations; they show—for example, in the first movement of Op. 9, No. 4—a subtle sense of discrimination between ideas more and less suitable for elaboration. Moreover, the composer now tries to express greater intensity of feeling. The fervent ardor that seemed like an episode in the adagio of Op. 2, No.

[14]Cf. n. 14 on p. 212.

4, attains increasing importance in the quartets of Op. 9. There can
be no doubt that these works foreshadow the master's *Sturm und
Drang* period. Some aspects of this may be found in the first movement of No. 1, with its use of the minor key and of syncopations in
the subsidiary group of themes and with the surprising hold over
the six-five chord. These tendencies are still more obvious in the
impassioned introduction to the slow movement of No. 2 (Ex. 4),

EXAMPLE 4    String Quartet, Op. 9, No. 2

where they create a mood of tension and pathos to be resolved in
the ensuing poignant cantabile.

This applies also to the first movement of the dramatic Quartet
No. 4 in D minor; the chromaticism, syncopations, and pauses
seem like a challenge to the levity of the rococo period. In the ardent minuet of this quartet, the grand pause on the first beat of the
third measure is easily recognizable as one of Philipp Emanuel
Bach's favorite means of expression. But the antithesis of this
mood, uncontrollable mirth, also is beginning to gain in importance. The same D minor Quartet contains in its finale certain sections that foreshadow Beethoven's scherzos.

A peculiarity of this cycle, as well as of the next six quartets, is
the brilliant character of the first violin part, with its difficult runs
and double stops and its predilection for the highest registers. An
explanation for this tendency is easily found in the fact that Haydn

then had at his disposal a player of unusual technical gifts, Luigi Tomasini, first violinist of the Prince's orchestra. It must not be overlooked, however, that the personal and somewhat rhapsodical character of the music really calls for a certain display of virtuosity. Looking at the problem from this angle, it would seem that Tomasini was the ideal interpreter rather than the instigator of the brilliant parts for the first violin.[15]

Among the chamber music compositions for string and wind instruments written in this period, two are of particular significance. One is a *Divertimento a nove stromenti* (Hob. II:17), which dates from the beginning of Haydn's service at the court of Prince Esterházy. It is scored for two clarinets (instruments rarely used in Haydn's early works), two horns, two violins, two violas, and bass, and consists of no less than nine movements. A march in *tempo adagio* serves as a rather unusual introductory movement. It is followed by a brisk, effectively orchestrated allegro. The fourth movement is an instrumental recitative, reminding us of a similar section in the symphony "Le Midi" (Hob. I:7) from the year 1761. In the eighth movement the composer introduces a folk-song melody, "The Night-Watchman's Song," which he liked to utilize in instrumental compositions.[16] Throughout, slow movements, fast movements, and minuets with trio effectively alternate, making this one of the most entertaining works by the young Haydn.

Quite different in character is the trio for horn, violin, and violoncello (Hob. IV:5) of 1767. It consists of only two movements, including a very effective theme and variations. Here the horn has some really interesting technical problems to master, and occasionally the instrument's role as the ardent singer of German romanticism is foreshadowed.

The lack of technical brilliance noticeable in the keyboard concertos of Haydn's youth is to be observed in this period too. Thus the Concerto (divertimento) in C major of 1764 (Hob. XIV:4), written for clavier, two violins, and bass, is really a keyboard sonata with doubling and accompanying string parts. In early English editions it was published as a "Lesson for the harpsichord," omitting the insignificant parts for the other instruments.[17] Close to the spirit of a real concerto comes Hob. XVIII:3 in F major, composed

---

[15] A critical edition of the string quartets Op. 9 was presented by Georg Feder in *JHW*, XII/2.
[16] Cf. Geoffrey Chew, "The Night-Watchman's Song . . . ," *H-St*, III /2 (Apr. 1974), p. 106ff.
[17] Forster (London, 1783–1784); Cooper (London, after 1800). The original version was edited by G. Wertheim (London, 1955).

around 1765. This cembalo concerto is, however, rather conventional in musical language and old-fashioned in its technique, thus revealing the composer's moderate interest in the form.

Closer to the modern concerto spirit is the G major Clavier Concerto (Hob. XVIII:4),[18] probably written around 1770. The increased impetus of the passages and the occasional use of full chords show Haydn's effort to endow the part of the soloist with at least a moderate amount of brilliance. The expression of heroic defiance in the first movement proves the closeness of this work to the "romantic crisis." The final rondo brings the entrances of the tutti-ritornello on different degrees of the scale, thus displaying a certain affinity with the form of the Vivaldi concerto, and it surprises us by both its bold modulations and the inexhaustible imagination that continually finds new ideas for the retransitions to the main theme.

Among the violin concertos,[19] the G major (Hob. VIIa:4), listed in the Breitkopf catalogue of 1769, is probably an earlier work. The concentration of the thematic life in the parts of the accompanying orchestra and the small share accorded to the solo instrument in the development of the main ideas seem to prove this. More significant still is the very simple technical equipment of the violin part, which hardly ever oversteps the first three positions, and a certain austerity in the melodic idiom, combined with a predilection for subsidiary themes in the minor. Quite different are the two concertos in C major (Hob. VIIa:1) and A major (Hob. VIIa:3), one written around 1765, the other before 1770, and both apparently intended for Haydn's favorite violinist, Luigi Tomasini. In these the violin competes with the orchestra in the elaboration of the themes; and double stops, big skips, fast runs, and melodies in the highest register offer a more gratifying task for the skill of the soloist. Tomasini seems to have given good advice to the composer as far as violinistic technique is concerned. Moreover, the concertos are imbued with a warmth of expression rarely to be found in Haydn's early concertos.

The Violoncello Concerto in C major (Hob. VIIb:1) is listed in both Haydn's *Entwurfkatalog* and the *Haydn-Verzeichnis* of 1805. The music itself, however, remained unknown until 1961 when O. Pulkert discovered it in the National Museum of Prague.[20] The

---

[18] Edited by K. Schubert (Hanover, 1932).
[19] The concertos Hob. VIIa:4 and 1 were edited by W. Davisson for Breitkopf and Härtel (Leipzig, 1909), and Hob. VIIa:3 by H. C. Robbins Landon for Haydn-Mozart Presse (Vienna, 1952).
[20] Pulkert also edited the work in a critical edition for Artia (Prague, 1962).

composition was apparently written before 1765 for Haydn's friend, the excellent cellist Joseph Weigl. It is one of the most significant works from this period, a broadly conceived, festive piece, offering the soloist opportunities to display substantial technical skill. Virtuosos of our day have quickly availed themselves of this welcome addition to their repertoire. In recent years the work has frequently appeared on concert programs and has been recorded repeatedly.

In Haydn's concerto for the French horn of 1762 (Hob. VIId:3), the technical problem of writing a concerto for a brass instrument that was not yet equipped with valves seems to have inspired the master. The many gaps between the notes of the horn are barely noticeable; the melodies are adapted to the possibilities of the instrument, and the expressive music displays all shades of emotion, from powerful energy to tender longing.[21]

• • •

During the 1760s Haydn seems to have written over thirty symphonies (Hob. I:6–9, 12–14, 20–26, 28–31, 34, 36, 38–41, 43–44, 47–49, 58, and 59),[22] more than during any other decade of his life. The pleasure he found in the new experience of working regularly with a select group of musicians apparently stimulated his creative powers.

To a kind of preparatory stage belong the six *scherzandi* for flute, two oboes, two horns, two violins and bass (Hob. II:33–38). They are little pieces, in the keys of F, C, G, D, A, and E major. Each of these sinfoniettas consists of four short movements (allegro, minuet, andante or adagio, presto). They might not even have been attributed to Haydn if the master himself had not listed one of them (the Scherzando in A major) on the first page of his draft catalogue.

On quite a different level are the full-sized symphonies from this period. Of special importance here are the composer's attempts

[21] A flute concerto in D major mentioned in the draft catalogue (Hob. VIIf:1) seems to be lost. A second flute concerto attributed to Haydn (Hob. VIIf:D1) is the work of Leopold Hoffmann. An oboe concerto in C major (Hob. VIIg:C1), edited by A. Wunderer (Leipzig, 1926), is spurious. Likewise the second horn concerto (Hob. VIId:4) is probably the work of a follower of Haydn's. No proof of the authenticity of the concerto can be furnished. Yet it is a skillfully written, attractive composition, edited by H. H. Steves for Boosey and Hawkes (London, 1954). Steves was probably also the editor of the authentic horn concerto (Hob. VIId:3) published in the same year by Boosey and Hawkes.
[22] Cf. H. C. Robbins Landon, *The Symphonies of Joseph Haydn* (London, 1955), p. 230ff.

to enrich the rather impersonal character of his early symphonies by introducing elements of the concerto and of the suite. The most remarkable products of this experiment are the symphonies Nos. 6–8 known as "Le Matin," "Le Midi," and "Le Soir," dating from 1761.[23] In "Le Midi" the presence of two slow movements following each other in immediate succession appears to be most unusual. But a closer examination reveals the true meaning of this arrangement: the first slow movement is a sort of dramatic accompanied recitative, the second a beautiful aria of lyric character. In both pieces (as in Spohr's Violin Concerto No. 8, *in modo d'una scena cantante*) a solo violin is used for the recitative as well as for the aria. In a truly romantic way Haydn introduces the form of the vocal aria into his symphony, giving the part of the singer to a violinist. "Le Matin," "Le Midi," and "Le Soir" are based on a poetical program that Hermann Kretzschmar attempted to interpret. Such clearly defined pieces as the sunrise in the introductory adagio of "Le Matin," the amusing parody of a solmization class in the slow middle movement of the same work, and the effective thunderstorm, *la tempestà*, in "Le Soir" facilitated his task.

Solo instruments are widely distributed through these three symphonies. In its slow middle movement, "Le Matin" uses a solo violin; in the trio of the minuet, a solo bassoon and a solo violoncello; and in its finale, a solo flute, violin, and violoncello. In "Le Midi" and "Le Soir" the genuine concertino of two violins and violoncello used by Corelli and Handel alternates with the ripieno instruments.

In later symphonies of this period the influence of the concerto also is noticeable; a solo flute is used in the slow movements of Nos. 24 and 30, a solo violin and solo violoncello appear in the slow movement of No. 36. A good example of the graceful art of orchestration acquired by Haydn in the 1760s is provided by the adagio of No. 31, *Auf dem Anstand—mit dem Hornsignal* (On the lookout—with the horn signal), of 1765, with its delightful combination of the tones of the horns and the solo violin (Ex. 5). In this work Haydn used four rather than the traditional two horns. Two instruments are in the key of D, two in the key of G, so that their notes may supplement each other. (This expedient had to be used because valves for the brass instruments were unknown.) The

---

[23] Landon (*HCaW*, I, p. 8) suggests that Haydn in writing these symphonies was influenced by Vivaldi's *The Seasons*, a work performed in Eisenstadt (cf. János Harich, "Inventare der Esterházy-Hofmusikkapelle in Eisenstadt," *HYb*, IX (1975), p. 67ff.)

EXAMPLE 5    Symphony No. 31

Symphony No. 31, an interesting precursor of Haydn's famous "La Chasse," contains many attractive passages for the wind instruments and it seems hardly surprising that a theme with variations, the favorite form in the suite, is used as its finale. In other symphonies too, strongly idiomatic use of the wind instruments may be observed. In particular the trios of the minuets employ them to best advantage, conjuring up sounds of exquisite charm and folksonglike simplicity (see Nos. 22 and 40).

Haydn's tendency to unify certain movements of his works, so obvious in most types of his instrumental output, is developed with particular strength in his symphonies. Apart from the predilection for contrapuntal forms mentioned before, occasionally—as in the first movement of No. 28—a whole movement in sonata form grows out of a single motive. The tendency of the mature Haydn to develop the subsidiary theme out of the main idea is already noticeable; in the first movement of No. 39, for instance, the contrasting idea appears only in the epilogue. In the finale of No. 36, Haydn was so eager to give thematic material even to the accompanying parts that his exposition assumed certain aspects of a development; accordingly, the real development seems all but superfluous and is six bars in length. Johannes Brahms, who was a great admirer of Haydn and followed his example in many respects, used a similar device in the last movement of his first symphony. It brings so many elements of the development into the exposition as to make possible the omission of the sonata form's middle part.

The subject matter of the symphonies is at first merry and carefree, with a rather robust popular note in some of the minuets. The pleasure in little surprises, in sudden unexpected changes of a slightly humorous character is already evident. At the same time a quality of grave seriousness is by no means absent. It is indicated in the first movement of No. 22 ("The Philosopher"). Here the grave notes of the *canto fermo* intoned by horns and English horns (replacing the oboes) create an atmosphere foreshadowing the solemn passages of Mozart's *The Magic Flute*. The tragic Symphony No. 26 in D minor was probably written around 1768. From the stirring syncopation of the beginning to the passionate lament of the minuet (Ex. 6), this work strikes a note of suffering and despair. The title "Lamentatione," under which the work usually is known, seems

EXAMPLE 6   Symphony No. 26, *Menuett*

fully justified; this all the more as the *canti fermi* used show a definite resemblance to the Gregorian chants sung during Holy Week. The Symphony No. 39 in G minor was also written before 1770 and in its first movement anticipates the mood of suffering and grief in Mozart's string quintet in the same key. The climax of these efforts to give greater depth of feeling to the symphonies is reached in No. 49 of the year 1768, with the characteristic name of "La Passione." This work displays, particularly in its second movement in F minor, a feverish fierceness of expression that few musical or poetical works of the eighteenth century surpassed.

But intensity does not prevail only in the expression of dark moods. The lighter colors also assume greater brilliance, and thus the second movement of No. 34, composed before 1766, creates an atmosphere of turbulent gaiety.

These symphonies of the 1760s reveal Haydn's tenacity in keeping to territory previously occupied. Even where he makes progress, he tries not to completely relinquish the area in which he started. Thus, among the symphonies of this era of transition occur features reminiscent of Haydn's early attempts. Thus, for instance, No. 39, composed around 1768, offers an andante in two parts that cannot dispense with a filling continuo part. This stubborn clinging to acquired possessions, inherited from his peasant and artisan forebears, mingled as it was with a keen interest in novel experiments, constitutes one of the salient features of Haydn's personality.

• • •

Haydn wrote during his second period of composition five works for the stage of which, unfortunately, not a single one is preserved in its entirety. It does not seem impossible that the composer himself was responsible for this sad state of affairs. In later years he may well have given away parts of his scores in order to satisfy his admirers' ever increasing demand for new contributions.

Haydn's *festa teatrale, Acide* (Hob. XXVIII:1), was composed in 1762 and first performed in Eisenstadt on January 11, 1763 at the wedding of Count Anton Esterházy, the Prince's eldest son, to Countess Teresa Erdödy. The autograph score is incomplete. There also exists the fragment of a second version, started in 1773, but never performed, which contains an aria of Nettuno, as well as the overture to the opera.[24]

[24]Cf. Dénes Bartha and László Somfai, *Haydn als Opernkapellmeister* (Budapest, 1960), p. 381ff.

Since the libretto of the work survived in a copy made by the untiring C. F. Pohl, and we also possess substantial parts of Haydn's autograph, enough remains to give a good idea of the character of a work that is concerned with a subject treated by Handel some forty years earlier. Haydn's *festa teatrale* gives a rather long-winded account of the love story of Acis and Galatea and the murder of the handsome shepherd by the giant Polyphemus. The intervention of the traditional deus ex machina, in this case the sea-goddess Thetis, makes possible the happy ending that an eighteenth-century audience expected. The hero, Acis, after being murdered, returns to life as a fountain and—as a fountain—joins vigorously in the final quartet, the only ensemble in the whole opera. The music closely follows the style of the Italian *opera seria*, containing numerous secco recitatives and isolated recitatives with orchestral accompaniment. It keeps pedantically to the *da capo* aria trimmed with ornate coloratura, never attempting to reach more dramatic expression. The overture in three movements conforms to the shallow type of the symphony of the Italian opera. The melodies are merry and rather trivial. This overture is nothing but a glorified signal to indicate the beginning of the performance, a piece that might easily be replaced on the modern stage by the ringing of a bell. As this overture has no connection whatever with the opera, there is no objection to its being performed as a separate instrumental piece without any reference to the stage work. In fact, this has often been done; conversely, the eighteenth century did not hesitate to use as overtures to vocal compositions symphonies composed as separate instrumental pieces.

Haydn's *comedia*, *La marchesa nespola*, was probably written in the same year as *Acide*[25] and may also have had its premiere at the same occasion as the *festa teatrale*.[26] Unfortunately, only seven arias of the *comedia*, as well as an accompagnato recitative, are preserved. Moreover, two of the arias are incomplete, and the libretto is missing. No secco recitatives are contained in the score, which may well indicate that the connecting dialog was not sung but spoken.

[25] The date, 762, on the autograph is not clearly legible.
[26] The *Wiener Diarium* (January 20, 1763) reports from Eisenstadt that on the second day of the festivities in honor of Count Esterházy's marriage, Haydn's *Acide* and, on the third day, an opera buffa were performed. This second work may well have been *La marchesa nespola*. Ulrich Tank ("Die Dokumente der Esterházy-Archive," *H-St*, IV/3–4 [May 1980], p. 85) contends, however, on the basis of a copyist's bill, that the *comedia* had its premiere in July 1763, at the occasion of the Prince's return from Italy. This assumption ignores the fact that, like *Acide*, the *comedia* seems to have been revised by the composer (cf. *HCaW*, I, p. 453). If a performance took place in July 1763, it was, in all likelihood, no longer the premiere of the work.

The idea for *La marchesa nespola* might have been conceived by Haydn earlier in the year when a group of Italian comedians visited Eisenstadt during the months of May and June. The use of the term *nespola* (loquat) indicates the burlesque character of the text, as the work has the rather unusual title "The Marchioness of the Loquat." Likewise some characters of Haydn's work have names borrowed from the Italian commedia dell'arte. One is called Columbina, another Pantalone, and a third Scanarello, while the remaining characters are given Christian names. It seems that Haydn referred here to some members of the Esterházy ensemble. There is, for instance, a Signora Barbara (Fux) and a Leopoldo (Dichtler).[27] It seems tempting, but unfortunately pure conjecture, to speculate what the role of these various characters in the complete *comedia* would have been.

The longest and, for the singer, most demanding aria with its preceding accompagnato recitative exists also as a contrafactum with a sacred Latin text. The words of this hymn, which are in complete contrast to the original Italian text of the two numbers, are even inserted by the hand of a stranger into Haydn's autograph.

In both *Acide* and *Marchesa* the idiom of the Italian opera is mastered with consummate skill. It seems hardly believable that these works were written by a young composer with very little experience in the field. Although they reflect the style of Haydn's models, such as Hasse and Jomelli, they display no awkwardness or uncertainty. Right from the beginning the author presents himself as a skillful opera composer.[28]

Haydn's opera, *La canterina* (The Songstress), composed in 1766, continues the merry spirit of *La marchesa nespola*, though in a work of rather different character. The new composition is a lively farce taken from everyday life. It is an intermezzo, similar in character to Pergolesi's *La serva padrona*. It has no overture, and its two parts are meant to be performed in the intermissions of a three-act serious opera. *La canterina* is the first of Haydn's operas of which a nearly complete score has been preserved.[29] It is the earliest of Haydn's dramatic compositions that can be enjoyed without reserve in our day.

---

[27] Cf. Bartha and Somfai, *Haydn als Opernkapellmeister*, p. 378.
[28] A critical edition of the hitherto unpublished scores of *Acide* and *Marchesa* is being prepared by Karl Geiringer for *JHW*.
[29] In the finale of the second act a short solo and the beginning of the concluding tutti are missing. A piano score of the opera with Italian and English text, translated by C. Zytowski, (The Songstress) was edited by Karl Geiringer for Presser (Bryn Mawr, Pa., 1981). The full score, edited by Dénes Bartha, appeared in *JHW*, XXV/2.

No one could uphold the morality of the plot, for the young vocalist Gasparina sees no impropriety in encouraging two lovers at the same time. Her double-dealing is discovered, and this places her in a very embarrassing position, but she is clever enough to know the well-worn trick of threatening to commit suicide and pretending to faint, whereupon the fury of her lovers gives way to compassion. They repent of their anger and once more shower gifts upon her. The music is simple and graceful, following, like the libretto, the tradition of the Italian intermezzo. The composer replaces the schematic construction of the *opera seria* with a freer, more lively dramatic spirit. The undramatic *da capo* aria is avoided; instead, there is a preference for Logroscino's trick of introducing recitatives into the aria. The very first aria of the work is interrupted and concluded by a recitative. Accents of tragedy are used only for the purpose of burlesquing the pathos of the *opera seria*. Gasparina's aria in the second act, intended to move the heart of her infuriated lover, assumes—by the use of the somber English horns, the key of C minor, the tremolo of the strings, the "sighs," and augmented intervals of the melody—a mood of exaggerated grief, easily recognized as a parody. The fits of despair of the lovers, produced by Gasparina's fainting, are of a similar nature. Such agitated syncopations and wild runs were used in the *opera seria* in moments that decided life and death for its heroes. In the quartet that concludes the first act, Haydn attempted what Mozart was to accomplish in his great masterpieces: the expression of the personality of each of his characters, without violation of the musical beauty of the whole. The fury of the singing teacher, the cowardice of the second lover, the despair of Gasparina, and the impudence of the duenna all find expression in this charming piece of music. In spite, or perhaps because, of its great simplicity, *La canterina* is a really effective stage work. At its first performance, which took place at Pressburg during the carnival of 1767, the effect on the audience must have been particularly hilarious, as the part of the young male lover was sung by a female soprano, while the part of the duenna, originally intended for a soprano, was entrusted to a male tenor.[30]

*Lo speziale* (The Apothecary), written in 1768, carries on the tendencies of *La canterina*. In this opera in three acts, based on a libretto by Goldoni, as many as three suitors compete to win the love of pretty Grilletta. Sempronio, an old apothecary, who is thinking too much of distant countries and not enough of his business, wishes to marry his ward Grilletta; Mengone, a serious young man, is inspired by his love for the young girl to enter the apothecary's shop as a clerk; and the bold and frivolous Volpino tries to win Grilletta's love by pert little improvisations. Sempronio and Mengone are tenors; the part of Volpino, like that of Don Ettore in *La canterina* and Cherubino in Mozart's *Figaro*, is for a soprano, to be sung not by a man, but by a disguised woman. Among these four characters, two sopranos and two tenors, the comedy is enacted, and eventually the faithful Mengone wins Grilletta's hand.

Haydn succeeded in making *Lo speziale* a true musical comedy. The conceit of narrow-minded Sempronio, whose knowledge is based mainly on newspaper reports, is beautifully described in his very first aria. Mengone's aria in A major paints the sufferings of indigestion and the soothing effect of rhubarb with a daring realism that makes the piece hardly suitable for a prudish audience. Very different is the attitude of the young man in the trio at the end of the first act. Here Grilletta and Mengone whisper tender words of love while the old man meditates on war in the Far East (a conflict that seemed fantastic and improbable in Haydn's time), but as soon as the apothecary leaves the room, the flame of suppressed passion starts to blaze. The bold impudence of Volpino is well expressed in his second-act aria in E major. An interesting detail in this number deserves special attention. When Volpino mentions Grilletta's lovers, he sings a tune that reappears in the quartet finale of the act as soon as the names of the apothecary and the two young men are uttered. It is probably the first, though by no means the only, time that Haydn used the technique of the "leading motive." In this finale, Sempronio dictates to the two suitors, disguised as lawyers, his marriage contract with Grilletta. While pretending to repeat the words, they really burlesque them, changing every sentence to their own purposes. A tender melody of the oboe accompanies the main part of this scene. Repeated changes of tempo and the introduction of roguish, but also affectionate, mirth make this piece one of the most attractive numbers of ensemble music in the pre-Mozart *opera buffa*.

Unfortunately, a small part of this score has also been lost. The arrangement of the opera by Robert Hirschfeld that is ordinarily used in modern performances[31] condenses the three acts of the original into a single act and interpolates in lieu of missing numbers a

---

[31] The opera was first presented in Dresden in 1895 and published in Vienna in 1909. The score of the opera, edited by H. Wirth, appeared in *JHW*, XXV/3.

duet from Haydn's *Orlando paladino*. Unfortunately, the arranger did not know of the existence of the overture, missing in the autograph, but found since; moreover, he replaced the tenor Sempronio with a baritone.

*Le pescatrici*, composed in 1769 and performed in the following year, belongs stylistically to the great operas of the following decade and will therefore be discussed in our next chapter.

• • •

Haydn's early cantatas are closely related to his early operas. Three of these works were written in honor of his patron. *Destatevi o miei fidi* (Hob. XXXIVa:2) was composed in 1763 to celebrate the name day (December 6) of Prince Nicolaus; *Qual dubbio ormai* (Hob. XXIVa:4) was written in the following year for the same occasion. *Al tuo arrivo felice* (*Da qual gioja improviso*) (Hob. XXIVa: 3) welcomed the Prince in 1764 on his return from a trip abroad. A fourth cantata, *Applausus* (Hob. XXIVa:6) of 1768, celebrated the fiftieth anniversary of the abbot's profession in the monastery of Zwettl (Lower Austria).[32] These works, which follow Neapolitan models, consist of a succession of *da capo* arias introduced by recitatives and only rarely interrupted by ensemble numbers or choruses. In the *Applausus*, the text of which is written in Latin, the conversation conducted by the four Cardinal Virtues and Theology[33] about the merits of life in the seclusion of a monastery is of such a dry and abstract quality that the composer found it extremely difficult to get inspiration from the words. A happier choice of subjects was provided in the earlier works, which assume a heroic note in their glorification of Haydn's patron. Here the composer was more in sympathy with his theme. Consequently, the D minor aria, "Quanti il mar," in the cantata *Destatevi o miei fidi* of 1763, has the quality of inspired passion. The accompaniment in fast-moving sixteenth notes describes the roaring of the ocean and at the same time reflects a deep emotion; the wide intervals of the melody display unusual fervor (Ex. 7).

Arias of an equally impressive character are, however, not very frequent in these works. It is true that the instrumentation offers some variety; very attractive use is made, for instance, of the solo

[32] Hob. XXIVa:2 and 3 were not yet published in 1981; Hob. XXIVa:4 was edited by H. C. Robbins Landon for Doblinger (Vienna, 1971); and Hob. XXIVa:6 by Landon for Doblinger (Vienna, 1969) and by Wiens/Becker-Glauch in *JHW*, XXVII/2.

[33] *Theologia* is replaced in the libretto by *Sapientia*.

EXAMPLE 7   Cantata *Destateri*

harpsichord, and occasionally in the *Applausus* Haydn employs a solo violin, muted strings, and divided violas. Yet it must be admitted that the composer's approach to his subject was slightly mechanical. Here Haydn followed a certain tendency of Neapolitan art to manufacture rather than to create music.

The composer was unable to be present at the first performance of *Applausus* on April 17, 1768, at the monastery of Zwettl. He therefore accompanied the score with a memorandum in German enumerating his wishes about its production. The following are the main features of the ten points he stressed in this remarkable document:

1. The composer asks that his indications of tempo be carefully observed and that, in accord with the festive character of the text, the allegros be taken a little faster than usual.

2. As an overture, the allegro and andante of any symphony may be used; its finale is to be replaced by the first ritornello of the cantata.

3. In the recitatives, the instrumentalists should come in immediately after the vocalist has finished, but on no account is the vocalist to be interrupted, even if such a procedure were prescribed in the score.

4. The composer requires that the dynamic signs be strictly observed and points out that there is a great difference between piano and pianissimo, forte and fortissimo, crescendo and sforzando.

5. He professes to have been annoyed often by musicians who neglected slurs and warns the violinists to avoid such an "unpleasant and faulty" way of playing.

6. He wishes the viola part to be performed by two

musicians, "as the middle parts are sometimes more important than the melody," and adds the interesting remark: "It can be seen in all my compositions that the viola rarely doubles the bass."

7. He advises the copyist to write out the parts in such a way as not to have all the violinists turn the pages at the same time, as that reduces the volume of sound in a small ensemble.

8. He requests good slow diction of the soloists, so that every syllable may be understood.

9. He hopes that at least three or four rehearsals will be given to his composition.

10. He recommends the addition of a bassoon to the violoncello and double bass, as this makes the bass of the composition more distinct than in a work scored only for string basses. He asks the musicians to work hard on the production in their own interest and his, and concludes: "If I have failed to guess your taste, it must not be taken amiss, as I did not know the performers or the locality. My ignorance of these matters really has made the work hard for me."

This document is of unusual importance. Not only does it show what a good music director Haydn was—many of his wishes still are expressed by twentieth-century conductors—but it indicates his progressive attitude as a musician. His request for strict observance of the dynamic indications, the emphasis on the importance of the middle parts, the desire for a lively tempo: all these show that Haydn was eager to fight obsolete traditions of the past. On the other hand, the end of the letter emphasizes how important it was for a composer of the eighteenth century to be familiar with the abilities of the singers and the equipment of the stage for which his work was destined.

Some of Haydn's secular works written for a special occasion achieved wider circulation through their transformation into sacred compositions. Sometimes textual changes were sufficient to achieve this goal, in other cases substantial alterations in form and orchestration had to be made. Such "contrafacta" were quite frequently produced in the eighteenth century. A substantial number of J. S. Bach's compositions for the church are based on his own secular works. However, the Thomas cantor transcribed his own compositions, while the contrafacta of Haydn's secular works were usually made by others, though with the knowledge and consent of the composer. Thus an offertory "Plausus honores date" has survived which uses Latin texts to music from the Esterházy cantata *Al tuo arrivo felice*. Several numbers were transcribed from the *Applausus*, the result being the offertories "Dictamina mea," "Concertantes jugiter per calamitatem," and "Christus coeli atria" (with preceding recitative "Quae admiranda res"), the bass aria "Resonant tympana," and the motet "O Jesu te invocamus."[34] The method employed here may be explained through two examples. For the Latin offertory "Plausus honores date," two pieces with an Italian secular text were used. As instrumental prelude, a condensed version of the introduction to the recitative from *Da qual gioja improviso* is employed. The recitative itself is omitted and the music to the chorus "Sembra in questo giorno" follows straight away. Apart from minor deviations, the contrast between soli and tutti is newly introduced into the offertory; moreover, the melody played in the cantata by the cembalist's right hand is now entrusted to the solo violin, the harpsichord's sound apparently being considered unsuitable for church music. A different procedure was adopted for the offertory "Dictamina mea." As the original employed Latin words with an allegoric meaning, comparatively few changes had to be made in the text. On the other hand, the *da capo* form of the duet in the *Applausus* was not preserved in the offertory, which omitted the repeat of the first section. To round off the work a short Alleluja for four-part mixed chorus, strings, and organ (Hob. XXIIIc:3) was added. This graceful, brisk finale, not to be found in the original cantata, has been preserved in Haydn's hand[35] and is well suited to serve as the end piece of the offertory. The first part of the duet is in C major and the middle section ends in the dominant G. As there is no *da capo*, the Alleluja is in G major. Thus an offertory starting in C major ends in G major, a bold feature rarely found in eighteenth-century music.

The *Motetto di Sancta Thecla: Quis stellae radius* (Hob. XXIIIa:4) for soprano solo, mixed chorus, strings, and organ dates probably from the early sixties. It starts with a secco recitative for soprano, followed by an attractive *da capo* aria, whereupon a merry, simple

[34] See Karl Geiringer, "Joseph Haydn als Kirchenmusiker," *Kirchenmusikalisches Jahrbuch* (1960).

[35] The autograph is at present divided, with one part kept in Eisenstadt and one in Vienna.

hymn for mixed chorus brings the work to a close. The melodic material of this amiable little piece displays a certain affinity to Austrian folk songs.[36]

An independent composition is the first *Te Deum* in C major (Hob. XXIIIc:1), written before 1765. The relation of the first chorus "Te Deum laudamus" to the following tenor solo "Tu Rex Gloriae" by means of the same impetuously rising motive in thirty-second notes shows the hand of a master. The transition from a trio of solo voices to the full chorus at "Per singulos dies" anticipates the contrast between solo and tutti that Haydn was to use so effectively in his later church compositions. A very poetical thought is expressed at the end of the work, where the music to "Non confundar in aeternum" is immediately added to the motive of "In te Domine speravi" as a sort of counterpoint. Haydn's attitude in religious questions is shown by this little detail: to put one's hope in the Almighty is identical with the certainty of salvation.

The *Stabat Mater* of 1767 points in various ways to the idiom of the "romantic crisis" that was to sway Haydn decisively within a few years. Chromatic runs, "sighs," and syncopations combined with sudden dynamic changes create an atmosphere of restlessness and suffering superbly matching that of the text. Especially stirring is the solo quartet with chorus "Virgo virginum praeclara." Here the soloists have the leadership, while the chorus, in somber responses, merely enunciates brief passages and frequently only single words. Most impressive are the moments when to the soloists' fervent utterance "Passionis fac consortem—fac ut portem Christi mortem—fac me plagis vulnerari," the chorus again and again adds the word "fac," like an urgent prayer. Yet, in the manner of Haydn's youthful cantatas, the *Stabat Mater* employs Neapolitan formal principles, and it is not surprising that the work was given particular praise by Hasse.[37] The text is divided into individual numbers, those for soloists taking up twice as much room as those for chorus. It is interesting to observe the way in which the Neapolitan

[36] Parts of this *Motetto*, written by a copyist, were found in the Eisenstadt Pfarrkirche, their authenticity being proved by Haydn's signature in the bass part. Karl Geiringer, in "The Small Sacred Works by Haydn in the Esterházy Archives in Eisenstadt," *Musical Quarterly*, XLV/4 (Oct. 1959), p. 467, offers a facsimile of the signature: "Del giuseppe Haydn mpria." Irmgard Becker-Glauch, in "Neue Forschungen zu Haydns Kirchenmusik," *H-St*, II/3 (May 1970), p. 177ff., tries to prove that the *Motetto* is a contrafactum of a lost secular cantata in honor of Prince Esterházy. The composition is edited by Landon for Doblinger (Vienna, 1981).

[37] See Haydn's autobiographical sketch and his letter to Anton Scheffstoss dated March 20, 1768 (pp. 66, 69).

predilection for coloratura is combined here with Haydn's zest for intense expression (Ex. 8). Despite the text's lack of contrasts and the tendency toward large lyrical structures, Haydn succeeded in creating a work displaying dramatic vigor and stirring diversity.

EXAMPLE 8

Approximately contemporary with the *Stabat Mater* are the four *Responsoria de venerabili* "Lauda Sion Salvatorem" (Hob. XXIIIc:4)[38] for four voices, two violins, two horns, bass, and organ. These are unassuming pieces of simple beauty and charm, such as Haydn was apt to produce quickly for specific occasions. Another "Lauda Sion" (Hob. XXIIIc:6) for contralto solo, two flutes, strings, and organ might have likewise originated in the sixties. Here the flutes, which are rarely to be found in Haydn's early church music, create a mood of gentle exaltation. Deeply felt is also the German language *Cantilena pro Adventu* "Ein' Magd, ein' Dienerin" (Hob. XXIIId:1)[39] for solo soprano, two oboes, two horns, strings, and organ, built in the form of a *da capo* aria. This song in praise of the Virgin combines fervor of expression with vocal brilliance in a manner significant for Haydn's works of this period.

• • •

Around 1970 an autograph fragment from a Haydn mass was found in the Central State Library of Bucharest (Rumania). This torso was dated 1766 and consisted of a Kyrie and a Christe preceded by a title page inscribed: *Missa Cellensis in honorem Beatissimae Virginis Mariae*. It created a sensation among Haydn scholars.

There were three reasons for the strong effect of this unexpected discovery. The composition, which had been heretofore known as *Missa Sanctae Caeciliae* (Hob. XXII:5),[40] was not dedicated to the patroness of music, but to the Holy Virgin. It was

[38] Discovered and edited by Irmgard Becker-Glauch for Henle-Verlag (Munich, 1964).
[39] Edited by H. C. Robbins Landon for Haydn-Mozart Presse (Vienna, 1957).
[40] Edited by C. M. Brand for the Haydn Society Edition, Series XXIII/1 (Boston, 1951).

meant for Mariazell, the city of pilgrimage in Austrian Styria, beloved by Haydn and by the Esterházy family, and a place of worship for which he was to write a second Mass in C major sixteen years later. Most of all, the Mass was composed considerably earlier than had been previously assumed.[41]

This new date helps us better to understand the somewhat archaic character of the work, its dependence on earlier models, and also the exuberance of feeling that tempted the composer to write a Mass which, owing to its enormous dimensions, is unsuitable for liturgical use. The first *Missa Cellensis* is the longest work of its kind composed by Haydn, and also the one most nearly approaching the style of the Neapolitan cantata. The seven parts of the Gloria, for instance, consist of more than eight hundred measures, several choruses interrupted by solo episodes, a coloratura aria for soprano, and a trio for alto, tenor, and bass. Like J. S. Bach's B minor Mass, this work was not intended for regular liturgical use. The connection between text and music is fairly loose. The old printed edition of the Mass, published by Breitkopf and Härtel, omits whole movements of the composition, and the surplus text is used as well as possible for the remaining music. Thus, for example, in the shortened edition the words "Dominus Deus, rex coelestis, Deus pater omnipotens" are set to music originally composed to the words "et in terra pax hominibus bonae voluntatis," but the change of text does not seem bad, as in this section the music happens to be uncharacteristic. In other parts of his score, Haydn shows, however, real understanding of the dramatic possibilities of the text of the Mass, one instance being the striking contrast used for "iudicare vivos—et mortuos" (to judge the quick and the dead). Also the repetition of the word *credo* after each section of the profession of faith and the use of the orchestral recitative in "et incarnatus est," anticipating Beethoven, show that Haydn was not satisfied merely to copy the Neapolitan models. In the employment of the strings, in the emphasis on oboes and trumpets among the wind instruments, and, above all, in the work's expressive impact, there is a notable return to the baroque idiom, resulting in a composition imbued with vigor and grandeur.

The influence of the Neapolitan style is still noticeable in Haydn's next Mass, known as the *Grosse Orgel Messe* (Great Organ

[41] The Haydn biographer Carl Ferdinand Pohl dated the work 1782 (*Joseph Haydn* [Berlin, 1882], II, p. 191) and George Feder dated it 1774 ("Manuscript Sources of Haydn's Works," *HYb*, IV (1968), p. 108.

Mass, Hob. XXII:4),[42] and probably composed around 1768. This is again a brilliant work in a grand style, though avoiding the excesses of the *Missa Cellensis*. It calls for a four-part chorus, four solo singers, string instruments, an obbligato organ part, two English horns, bassoon, and two horns. The parts of the vocal soloists are enriched with coloratura like arias in a Neapolitan opera, and the organ part is also embellished with brilliant ornaments and runs (especially in the Kyrie and the Benedictus). Some numbers of the Mass, such as the beautiful "Qui tollis" (Ex. 9) exhibit a distinct

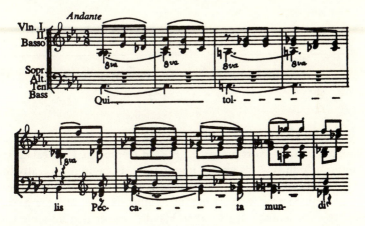

EXAMPLE 9

tendency to express the meaning of the words in sounds, but on the whole Haydn was more interested in the musical possibilities offered by a composition on so large a scale than in the interpretation of the mysteries of the Mass text. This is clearly shown in the "Dona nobis pacem," a presto in six-eight time introducing in the organ part a playful motive in triplets which seems better suited to an instrumental finale than to a Mass, a detail criticized even by one of Haydn's earliest biographers.[43]

---

[42] Edited by C. M. Brand for the Haydn Society Edition, Series XXIII/1 (Boston, 1951).
[43] Giuseppe Carpani, *Le Haydine* (Milan, 1812), p. 159.

CHAPTER FOURTEEN

A Romantic
Crisis

## THE THIRD PERIOD
## 1771 - 1780

The author of a short article on Haydn printed in 1766 called the
composer's music "charming, ingratiating, engaging, naturally humorous and enticing."[1] If the man who wrote these words had read
them again a few years later, he would have found them surprisingly inadequate, for by then Haydn's music had lost many of
the characteristics he had mentioned. The composer had grown
tired of the charm and gracefulness of rococo music, so dear to him
in his earlier days. To express personal feelings and strong emotion
now seemed one of the main aims of Haydn's art, and his creative
activity experienced what the great French Mozart scholar Theodor
de Wyzewa called "a romantic crisis."

As was noted earlier, the impulse for such a change came to
Haydn from the outside. The slogan "back to nature," which implied a return to sincerity of feeling, originated with Jean-Jacques
Rousseau, and German literature and music accepted it eagerly. In
the early seventies of the eighteenth century Goethe wrote his *Sorrows of Young Werther*, and all over the world its unrestrained emotionalism moved people to bitter tears, even to suicide. At about
the same time, Mozart wrote his first G minor symphony (K. 183,
not to be mistaken for the great symphony K. 550 of 1788), a surprisingly deep and moving work for a youth in his teens.

[1] *Wiener Diarium*, no. 84 (1766), supp., "*Gelehrte Nachrichten*," no. 36.

No musician felt the importance of the new movement more keenly than Joseph Haydn, for it opened his eyes to qualities that had been lacking in his own music. It is true that even during the sixties the composer's work exhibited several attempts to introduce a more emotional musical language, but this tendency broke forth with full power only after 1770. The composer found himself in complete accord with the artistic tendencies of his time and there was no longer any reason for him to suppress his passionate feelings.

As always in outbreaks of a revolutionary character, the reaction against the past went beyond the mark. Haydn's *Sturm und Drang* (storm and stress)— as the movement was frequently called in Germany—reached its climax in 1772, a year in which works of a strangely exaggerated character were created. Thereafter, Haydn's compositions gradually assumed a more restrained aspect, though the aftereffects of the "romantic crisis" were destined to be felt all through the seventies. Just as the French Revolution, despite its aberrations, made an essential contribution toward the formation of human society, so the crisis of the *Sturm und Drang* period through which Haydn passed played a vital part in his development and in the attainment of his full maturity. It was indispensable to him as an antidote against the excessive lightness of the rococo style.

The movement toward subjectivity and sentimentality brought Haydn closer and closer to the *Empfindsamkeit* that Philipp Emanuel Bach had revealed in his compositions more than twenty years previously. But Haydn really did not copy Bach. The relation between the two composers was not so much that of teacher and pupil as that of two artists who for a short time were pursuing the same artistic goal. The study of Bach's works helped Haydn overcome a deficiency in his own compositions, and as soon as he had succeeded in doing so, he freed himself from the overpowering influence of the older master.

•   •   •

The pianoforte sonata of 1771 (Hob. XVI:20) shows Haydn in the midst of his "romantic crisis." In this composition, the master's only piano sonata in C minor, all the formal restraints of the *style galant* are broken, and passion and subjective feeling triumph. The finale of the C minor Sonata is no longer a carefree affair destined solely to dismiss the listener in a happy mood; it becomes the climax of the whole work and is imbued with dramatic tension. In the first movement, the beginning of the development exhibits Haydn's art as constituting a link between the music of C. P. E. Bach and that of Beethoven. The contrapuntal style used in the elaboration of the main theme, the daring modulation to B-flat minor, the sudden change from tragic feeling to a completely lighthearted mood point both to the past and to the future. In all likelihood, this sonata is no longer meant for the harpsichord. The first movement contains a melodic line in which eighth notes marked *piano* regularly alternate with eighth notes marked *forte*. This dynamic effect could hardly be produced on a harpsichord, although it seems suitable for a clavichord or a pianoforte. Even on a clavichord the sudden emphasis on a note is apt to produce a tone slightly out of tune. Thus it seems most likely that the C minor Sonata of 1771 was intended for the new pianoforte.[2]

The next six sonatas (Hob. XVI:21–26), written in 1773 and dedicated to Prince Nicolaus Esterházy, were rather different from the work composed two years earlier. As a reaction against the previous subjectivism, and probably also to conform with the taste of his patron, Haydn's style was, at least temporarily, becoming less personal. No strong expression of feeling is noticeable here. These six sonatas contain only two real adagios, and in No. 26 the slow movement is replaced by a minuet. The insignificant finale of the same sonata certainly deviates from the remarkable last movement of No. 20. At the same time there is a tendency to make the form of the sonata increasingly compact. In No. 24 the adagio leads straight into the finale, and in No. 30, composed between 1774 and 1776, the dividing lines between the movements are omitted altogether. As the last two movements of this sonata are rhythmically related to each other, the connection is particularly strong. Within individual movements, too, the subjects are intimately linked and often grow out of the germ cells of a few basic motives. The first movement of No. 21, for instance, is based entirely on a dotted march rhythm and a motive in sextuplets; its subsidiary theme is derived from the main subject. A fairly frequent use is now being made of polyphonic devices. In No. 25 the finale is a canon. In No. 26 the minuet and trio are composed *al rovescio*, each being designed to be played forward, the way it is written, then backward, as a "crab canon."[3]

---

[2] Cf. also *HCaW*, II, p. 343. H. Walter, in "Haydns Klaviere," *H-St*, II/4 (Dec. 1970), p. 256ff., is, however, of the opinion that Haydn did not use the pianoforte before the late 1780s.

[3] The minuet *al rovescio* of No. 26 also occurs as the third movement of Symphony No. 47, composed in 1772.

The piano sonatas Nos. 27–39, written between 1773 and 1780, again display the "sensibility" of the *Sturm und Drang* period, though not with the intensity of the C minor Sonata. Three sonatas of this time were written in the minor key. The development section of the finale of No. 32 in B minor introduces a remarkable contrapuntal elaboration of the theme. Moreover, the unexpected rumbling unison of the coda furnishes a good example of Haydn's sense of humor. At the beginning of Sonata No. 34 in E minor, written before 1778, bass and melody answer each other in a rather original way. (Beethoven attempted a similar device in the first movement of his String Quartet Op. 18, No. 5.) The very first theme of the Sonata No. 36 in C sharp minor, written before 1780, displays an unconventional contrast of moods between the fragments of the main subject, while the development is characterized by rich modulations. The second movement of this sonata is a merry scherzando in two-four time, the finale a minuet in C-sharp minor with a trio in C-sharp major. Although the use of a minuet as the last movement of a sonata reminds one of the old suite form, the inversion of the traditional key relation (minuet in the minor, trio in the major) and the personal expression of this movement, with its now vigorous, now tender melodies, offer a striking contrast to the *style galant* of the previous period.

Particularly charming are the sets of variations that Haydn often introduced as finales to his sonatas. He was continually experimenting with fresh possibilities. In both No. 27 and No. 28, a passage in the minor key is suddenly inserted into a set of variations in the major; in No. 29 the minor passage is used to separate the theme from its variations; in No. 33 a theme in major and a theme in minor are varied in turn, a technique immortalized in the slow movement of his Symphony No. 103 ("Drum Roll"). The technique of the variation is also applied occasionally to the rondo form. Haydn now wrote rondos in which, as in the works of Philipp Emanuel Bach, each entrance of the main theme displays new figurations, and even episodes are variations of the main theme. It is interesting to note that the second movement of No. 36 and the first movement of No. 39 grow out of the same theme. In an *avertimento* preceding the publication of the sonatas through Artaria and Company in Vienna in 1780, the master himself stated: "Among these sonatas are two movements that begin with the same theme. . . . The composer explains in advance that he has done this on purpose, modifying the continuation of the movement in each case." Haydn obviously was interested in the problem of developing two different movements from a single theme. The movement in A major displays a light, frisking gaiety, whereas that in G major, in spite of its buoyancy, distinguishes itself by vigor and expressiveness.

The *Arietta con 12 Variazioni* (Hob. XVII:3) was probably written in the early seventies. As its theme the composer used the "celebrated Minuet" from his own String Quartet Op. 9, No. 2 (Hob. III:20). These are simple variations, probably intended for educational purposes. The melodic line is modified and ornamented in a somewhat mechanical manner resulting in an elegant, impersonal composition that won immediate success among the music lovers of the time. Hoboken's catalogue lists nine different editions of the work published in various countries.[4]

The most interesting of Haydn's trios for baryton, viola, and violoncello were composed during his third period. The erudite "Canone in Diapente" in the minuet of Hob. XI:94 (composed about 1771), the attractive variations in No. 95 and No. 111 (composed about 1771 and 1772, respectively), and the unusual intensity of expression of the largo of No. 96 (about 1771) are examples of the many beauties to be found among these charming pieces. Of the few surviving autographs, that of No. 109[5] (about 1772) deserves special mention. It was stained by water, and Haydn wrote at the beginning *fatto a posta—nihil sine causa* (done on purpose—nothing without reason). It must be left to the reader's imagination to conjecture what little drama provoked the composer to make this cryptic remark.[6] Number 97 (around 1771) is the longest of all baryton trios. It consists of seven movements which include two minuets and, as centerpiece, a polonaise. It was apparently intended for the birthday of Prince Nicolaus, as the inscription on the cover reads: *Fatto per la felicissima nascita di S.A.S. Prencipe Estorházy.*

•  •  •

Hadyn wrote twelve string quartets during his third period of composition. The six quartets Op. 17 (Hob. III:25–30) were finished in 1771; in the following year originated the six "Sun" quartets Op. 20 (Nos. 31–36), so called because of the lovely symbol of the rising sun in an old edition.[7]

[4]Hob., I, pp. 786–787.
[5]Preserved in the National Library, Budapest.
[6]Landon (*HCaW*, II, p. 353) quotes the baryton player Riki Gerardy, who assumed that Mrs. Haydn may have been responsible for the stain on the manuscript and consequently for Haydn's observation.
[7]Dated autographs of the two collections are preserved in the library of the Society

The quartets of Op. 17 show how closely Haydn approached the art of C. P. E. Bach during this period. Like the middle movement of the north German master's first Prussian sonata, the adagio of No. 5 includes a dramatic scene with recitatives and ariosos. The austere sternness in the beginning of the adagio of No. 1 and, still more, the bold harmonies in the slow movement of No. 3 also show the north German influence. In the first movement of No. 5, Haydn wrote a development longer than the exposition. He carried on with tendencies noticeable at an earlier period; at the same time these tendencies harmonized with Emanuel Bach's aim to give greater solidity and concentration to his works. The unexpected pianissimo ending of the finale of No. 2 is true Haydn, but it also reminds us of the pleasure Bach took in such sudden surprises.

These quartets are full of interesting effects of timbre. In the adagio of No. 2, Haydn introduced a theme first on the two highest strings, and then repeated it immediately on the G string. In the trio of the minuet of No. 3, the second violin was given the melody while the first accompanied. Haydn apparently took into consideration the fact that the player who usually performed a part of minor importance assumed in the long run a quality of tone different from that of the leader of the ensemble.

Rousseau's "back to nature" movement resulted in a general reawakening of interest in national folk music. Haydn showed himself in complete sympathy with this tendency. In the minuet of No. 1, for instance, lively skips of an octave and a tenth exhibit the character of Austrian popular music; the last subject of the finale of No. 6 shows clear traces of the Hungarian atmosphere in which Haydn had lived since he was twenty-eight years old.[8]

In the "Sun" quartets, Op. 20, all the features of the quartets of Op. 17 are intensified. The designation *affettuoso* found twice in the directions for the tempo of slow movements can be applied to the whole opus. Here an artist is aiming at intensification and deepening of expression, and it is not surprising that Beethoven felt induced to make a copy of the first work in this superb set. To

---

of Friends of Music in Vienna. Those of the "Sun" quartets were bequeathed by Johannes Brahms, who was a great admirer of Haydn's quartets and owned miniature scores of the complete "eighty-three." Brahms carefully compared the printed with the written text and marked in the miniature scores all deviations from the originals.

[8] A critical edition of the string quartets Op. 17 was supplied by Georg Feder in *JHW*, XII/2.

emphasize his rejection of rococo lightness, Haydn reverted to baroque features, adopting contrapuntal devices that also approach
the ideal of emotional concentration. Thus he introduced the architectural form of the fugue into the finales of three of the six quartets
in this series. In a naïve way he boasted of his scholarly achievements. The fugues were inscribed *a due*, *a tre*, and *a quattro soggetti*;
the canon cancrizans ("crab canon") was marked *al roverscio* [*sic*],
and the stretto, *in canone*. Such remarks seem to indicate that he
considered the contrapuntal idiom not quite a natural form for expressing his feelings. Yet it should be pointed out that Haydn's
string quartets with fugues were by no means isolated in this period. In 1773, Florian Leopold Gassmann, the composer of the opera *La contessina*, wrote six quartets, each of which contained two
fugues; in the same year Mozart (influenced by Haydn) finished six
quartets, twice using fugues as finales. The use of the fugue is not
the only instance of Haydn's return to baroque devices. The adagio
of No. 2, with the unusual name *Capriccio*, has an introduction of
four bars, and its weighty unison is reminiscent of the ritornello in
a concerto of the Bach-Handel period.

The Haydn's markings now were far more explicit than before. We
find such directions as *allegro di molto e scherzando* and *mancando*
(dying away).

The Haydn of the *Sturm und Drang* period was more daring in
the choice of keys than most composers of his time. The use of C-
sharp minor and C-sharp major in the piano sonata No. 36 certainly was a proof of boldness, and accordingly, it seems hardly
surprising that the "Sun" quartets should display a predilection for
the minor mode. Number 3 is in G minor, No. 5 in the then unusual key of F minor, and modulations into the minor are frequent
in the other works. Except for the first violin, the violoncello becomes the melody instrument in these quartets; in the beginning of
No. 2 and in the fourth variation of No. 4, a role of unexpected
importance is entrusted to it. The national element is again conspicuous, and Haydn openly confessed his predilection for the music of
the Hungarian gypsies in the *menuet alla zingarese* and the following
*presto e scherzando* of No. 4. This finale is certainly one of the most
fiery and, at the same time, one of the most amusing pieces that
Haydn ever wrote.

The composer liked to reveal his sense of humor in still another
way. At the end of the fugue that forms the finale to No. 2, he
wrote: *Laus omnip. Deo. Sic fugit amicus amicum* (Praise to the Almighty Lord. Thus one friend runs away from the other). This is

certainly an apt description of the fugue, in which the themes appear repeatedly in the different voices as if fleeing from each other.[9]

• • •

As the climax of his compositions for Prince Esterházy's favorite instrument, Haydn in 1775 wrote seven Divertissements (Hob. X:1–6 and 12), scored for baryton, string quartet, two horns, and contrabass, which turned out to also be his farewell to the genre. To make these valuable compositions available to a wider circle of music lovers, skillful arrangers replaced the baryton with a flute or oboe, transposing the part up an octave where necessary. In this arranged form six octets (Hob. X:12 and 1–5) were published by Artaria in 1781 as Op. 31.[10] Haydn's earlier divertimenti consisted of as many as five movements, but these pieces have no more than three. However, a diversity of forms is to be found in them. They contain sets of variations in which the theme is repeated after each variation and a little coda is attached at the end. The result is one of the many different mixtures of the rondo with variation forms that Haydn liked. Moreover, some minuets have two trios, a form not very frequent in Haydn's time. The subject matter of these pieces reveals their origin in the composer's *Sturm und Drang* period. They are imbued with severe dignity, passionate fervor, and dramatic intensity. Particularly expressive are the adagios of Nos. 1 and 12.[11] In the development section of the opening movement of No. 12 the thematic material is allotted impartially to all the instruments (Ex. 10), a feature heralding Haydn's period of maturity.[12]

• • •

Like most other types of Haydn's instrumental music, the symphonies show a decrease in number and an increase in quality during the seventies. Against some thirty symphonies written before 1771, we find only about twenty-five in the third period. A similar reduction in number is evident in later decades, too.

[9] A critical edition of the string quartets Op. 20, prepared by Georg Feder and S. Gerlach, is published in *JHW*, XII/3.

[10] Hob. X:1–6 are listed in the Haydn-Elssler catalog. Number 12 is missing in this list, but in view of its stylistic similarity to the other pieces of the set, we may assume that it likewise originated from an octet with baryton.

[11] The second and third movements of No. 12 were edited by Karl Geiringer (London, 1940), the complete No. 12 as well as No. 4 by Ernst Fritz Schmid (Kassel, 1952).

[12] A critical edition of the seven octets was edited by S. Gerlach in *JHW*, XIII. In certain cases the lost baryton part was reconstructed by Ms. Gerlach from the flute and oboe parts of the earliest prints.

EXAMPLE 10    Divertissement à huit parties concertantes, in G

In the 1770s, Haydn's symphonic style was determined by a striving for truth and strength of expression. The composer wrote works that almost remind us of Beethoven, so obvious is their emphatic diction. The powerful unison at the beginnings of Nos. 46 and 53 and the first and last movements of No. 44 express the unbending energy characteristic of this period. This symphony No. 44, known as "Trauer-Symphonie" (Symphony of Mourning), laments the death of a hero. Haydn wanted its beautiful adagio in E major, in which the dramatic impetus of the first and last movements is replaced by a gentle expression of grief, to be played at his own funeral service.

The changed feeling in this period made Haydn eager to find

new means of expression. Particularly daring is his choice of keys. One symphony is in C minor (No. 52), another in E minor (No. 44), a third in F-sharp minor (No. 45), and a fourth even in B major (No. 46). In the finale of No. 46, Haydn introduced a little reminiscence of the preceding movement (a minuet) just before the beginning of the coda. This seems to foreshadow the cyclical form so important in the nineteenth century.

The most unorthodox of these symphonies is in all likelihood also the most important. This is the famous "Farewell" Symphony No. 45 of November 1772.[13] In this work, "back to nature" results in a process of simplification. The orchestra of strings, two oboes, and two horns[14] is no larger than that of Haydn's first symphony. The initial movement has only about thirty measures of real development; the exposition is more than twice as long. This short development ends dramatically on a general pause, and a new melody of heavenly calm, not used in the exposition, is then presented. At the end of this lovely section, which equals the development in length, the recapitulation begins. In an earlier symphony (No. 42, composed in 1771) Haydn corrected a few measures of the original manuscript and remarked: "Dieses war vor gar zu gelehrte Ohren" (This was for too scholarly an ear). In the "Farewell" Symphony too, Haydn meant to avoid making too learned an impression. He wanted (like Beethoven) to write music "coming from the heart, to go to the heart." An adagio in A major and a minuet in the unusual key of F-sharp major are followed by a presto finale. As a coda, this presto has an adagio resuming the tempo and key of the slow second movement. According to the poetical program, one instrument after another falls silent in this long, drawn-out coda. By the end, only one first and one second violin are left, and they finish the movement pianissimo on a sixth chord. From an artistic point of view this adagio ending of a symphony in several movements was even bolder than Haydn's attempt to teach his inconsiderate prince a lesson.

It is interesting to note that in the symphonies of the early seventies also a certain display of contrapuntal techniques may be observed. Number 44 has a canon in its minuet; in No. 47 the minuet and trio are *al rovescio*. The second movement of No. 47 is constructed in double counterpoint at the octave. Here we have the

---

[13] A fine facsimile edition of the autograph owned by the National Library, Budapest, was edited by László Somfai (Budapest, 1959).
[14] Bassoons may have been used to reinforce the violoncellos and basses, but they have only a few independent bars in the last movement.

same combination of such contrasting elements as free expression of personal feeling and polyphonic severity that we found in the quartets of this period.

Haydn's innate pleasure in the use of unexpected ideas, noticeable in the "Farewell" Symphony, may also be observed in other orchestral works. In the first movements of Nos. 43 and 55, the main theme appears in the tonic soon after the beginning of the development. But this apparent recapitulation turns out to be merely a deception; presently the merry game of the development starts all over again with increased intensity. Even the famous "Surprise," to which Haydn owed so much of his popularity in England, had made an earlier appearance. After a diminuendo, the first movement of No. 60 brings a sudden loud tutti, in which the timpani greatly contribute to the intensity. The same work, a sort of suite based on Haydn's incidental music to the comedy *Il distratto* (performed in 1774 at Eszterháza), contains in its adagio a sudden fanfare, and its affinity to a program is obvious. The symphony embodies in its finale a joke that was certain to amuse any audience in the eighteenth century. After a grand pause of the whole orchestra, Haydn required the violinists to retune their instruments. The E, A, and D strings proved to be correct. But when they tried the G string, they found to their dismay that its pitch was no longer G, but had gone down to F. Disregarding the listening audience, the players raised the lowest string again to G; whereupon they continued as though nothing at all had happened. To play wrong notes purposely is one of the oldest and most effective comic devices. Haydn also did this in the second movement of "Le Matin," Mozart in "Ein musikalischer Spass" (K. 522).

The symphony "Il distratto" was probably written in 1774. By that time the climax of the *Sturm und Drang* movement had passed and Haydn gradually returned to his former path, though he had almost been lured away by the "romantic crisis." Problems of musical form and color regained much of their previous interest for him. In the first movement of No. 54 of 1774, for instance, he connected the slow introduction thematically with the following *allegro quasi presto*. He again showed a preference for the highly artistic form of the variation with frequent changes of major and minor within the same set. In No. 55, "Der Schulmeister" (The Schoolmaster), also of 1774, Haydn even used two sets of variations, one in the slow movement, the other in the finale. Particularly interesting is the "Loudon" Symphony, No. 69, probably composed in 1778–79 and named in honor of the great Austrian field marshal Gideon Ernst von Laudon. Its first theme is practically identical with the first theme of the Symphony "Maria Theresa," No. 48, written a few years earlier (Ex. 11).

EXAMPLE 11    Maria Theresa

At about the same time, Haydn did something similar in his compositions for the pianoforte (cf. p. 255). He wanted to show that the main problem in a composition was how to deal with a theme, not how to invent one; it is an idea that Beethoven brought to full development.

Haydn now also showed greater interest in the wind instruments. In No. 54 the main theme of the allegro was given to bassoons and horns. The effects that Haydn produced by entrusting the violins with the melody and accompanying them in the lower octave by bassoons are interesting (cf. the third movements in Nos. 54 and 66). A particularly wide field of activity was offered to the woodwind and the brass sections in the numerous movements in variation form.

Many features in the symphonies written between 1774 and 1780 prove that even in later years the *Sturm und Drang* movement did not completely lose its significance for Haydn. Thus, the first movement of No. 67, composed around 1778–79, introduces, like the "Farewell," a new idea in the development section; moreover, its finale is so crammed with musical themes as to replace sonata form by three-part form, the middle part introducing a new idea, new tempo, and new rhythm. The second movement of this remarkable symphony contains, near the end in the string parts, the surprising direction *col legno del arco*. Instead of the hair, the wooden part of the bow is to be used to give an insubstantial and ghostlike quality to the tone.

•   •   •

During the seventies the majority of Haydn's works for the stage had their premieres at Eszterháza, and it may be more than a mere coincidence that the largest number of dramatic works were written in a period characterized by loosening of emotional expression. Similarly, during the nineteenth century, when the era of romantic art reached a climax, two of the greatest masters of dramatic music were active: Wagner and Verdi.

Haydn wrote no fewer than six seriocomic operas during this period. They are more ambitious and longer than similar works the composer had previously written and decided prominence is given to the music. It is not surprising that in the long run the farcical character of *La canterina* (The Songstress), which offered no scope for deeper musical expression, was no longer able to satisfy the artistic leanings of a Haydn than was the shallow pathos of the *opera seria*. The composer now tried to combine comic and serious elements; the beginning of such tendencies could be noticed in *Lo speziale* (The Apothecary). In the seventies, Haydn's comic operas were increasingly permeated with warmth and tenderness, his lighthearted characters more and more contrasted with serious and dignified figures, and thereby a type of serio-comic or mixed opera was created, a type that Mozart was to develop to perfection. It was no mere accident that Goldoni, the Venetian playwright mainly responsible for the division into *parti serie* and *parti buffe* (serious and comic characters), should have supplied the libretto for three of Haydn's operas.

A similar distinction is clear in the music. The language of the serious characters is practically that of the great *opera seria* of Naples. Preference is given to big arias in three-part form, with rich coloratura and frequent repetitions of the text. The recitative accompanied by the orchestra is used in moments of dramatic tension. The *parti buffe*, however, employ two-part song or strophic form, simple melodies with folk-song tendencies and free from flourishes and coloratura.

Haydn's tendency to attach increased importance to the music may be seen in his growing use of ensembles. At Eszterháza he had no chorus at his disposal; therefore he usually combined his soloists into quartets, quintets, and occasionally even septets and octets. Of special importance are the finales, which show the composer at the height of his dramatic mastery. The tempo, the rhythm, the key, and the number of singers are constantly varied, but the musical unity is always maintained. In each finale a great climax is reached after several interruptions. In some of these operas Haydn included purely instrumental numbers of an illustrative or "programmatic" character, and also some ballets.

It is interesting to analyze Haydn's arias of the seventies. At first they show, like the arias of Hasse, a great similarity to the forms of instrumental music. In two-part arias in the major, the first part modulates to the dominant; in two-part arias in the minor, to the relative major. The second part begins like a *da capo* and keeps the tonic up to the end. In arias in three-part form, the first part assumes the function of an exposition, the third part that of a recapitulation; the middle part rarely brings in any contrasting new idea, but consists as a rule of a sort of development of the text and music of the outside parts.

Toward the end of this period, Haydn occasionally discarded this principle. Arias in three, four, and five different parts, sometimes interspersed with recitatives, were used. The form of these arias was dictated by the exigencies of the libretto rather than by musical considerations. Haydn began to realize the deep truth of Gluck's axiom, that in the opera, music always has to serve the drama and never dominate it.

*Le pescatrici* (The Fishermaids), *dramma giocoso per musica* (Hob. XXVIII:4) was composed in 1769 and performed in 1770. It is based on a libretto by Goldoni which was, however, altered before Haydn set it to music. Unfortunately, the autograph of the score, preserved in the National Library, Budapest, is incomplete. There are substantial gaps in both the first and second acts, so that more than one-fourth of the music is missing.[15] This first of Haydn's mixed operas introduces one serious couple, Prince Lindoro and his bride, Eurilda, and two lively pairs: the fishermen Burlotto and Frisellino and their sweethearts, Nerina and Lesbina. The contrast between the couples is also shown in the choice of voices. The prince is a bass, Eurilda a contralto, whereas the merry couples consist of sopranos and tenors. The second act of the work provides an excellent example of the pleasure Haydn took in ridiculing the stiffness of the *opera seria*. In a solemn manner, Lesbina praises her own beauty, and this part of her aria in B-flat major would be quite in place in any of the great Neapolitan operas. But suddenly her roguish temperament gets the better of her, and in conformity with the best traditions of the *opera buffa*, she calls her rivals all sorts of names. It is interesting to note that in Pergolesi's lovely intermezzo *La serva padrona*, an aria of Serpina's displaying a similar character is

---

[15] A critical edition of the score was presented by D. Bartha, J. Vecsey, and M. Eckhardt in *JHW*, XXV/4. A practical edition in which the missing numbers are supplemented by H. C. Robbins Landon was published by Haydn-Mozart Presse (Vienna, 1965).

in the same key, B-flat major. Haydn apparently knew the work of the great Neapolitan composer. Also full of humor is Frisellino's F major aria, in which a bassoon conjures up the sounds of a bagpipe. On the other hand, scenes of a more contemplative character are not missing, and the orchestral sound assumes a more lyrical quality through the occasional use of English horns.

Besides effective arias, a considerable amount of ensemble music is used in this work. The first act has two quartets, a sextet, and a septet. *La canterina* and *Lo speziale* employed four vocalists, but now even seven were not enough for Haydn; in the introduction to the third act he used several choristers, probably imported from Eisenstadt, besides the regular cast.

*L'infedeltà delusa* (Unfaithfulness Deluded), *burletta per musica* (Hob. XXVIII:5) was composed in 1773 and performed in September of that year during the visit of Empress Maria Theresa to Eszterháza. The libretto is based on a book by M. Coltellini, who had also provided the texts for operas of Hasse, Salieri, Gluck, and Mozart. The autograph score of *L'infedeltà delusa* is, for once, preserved in its entirety. The work won international acclaim at its revival in modern times thanks to the untiring efforts of Robbins Landon.[16]

The opera's libretto deals with the triumph of true love over all obstacles; the number of ensembles is small and most pieces are arias, though of a rich variety of expression. True dramatic passion as in the arias of the serious heroine, Sandrina, and of her lover, Nanni, is replaced by insolent mirth in those of the gay and energetic Vespina. Altogether, the portrayal of human characters in music is particularly successful in this work. An interesting feature in the bass aria of Nanni is the introduction of a violoncello obbligato. (The association of a solo instrument and a voice of the same range is often seen in compositions of J. S. Bach.) The aria "Come piglia si bene la mira" deals with a favorite subject of the rococo period, describing how Cupid, in spite of the bandage over his eyes, does not fail to pierce the heart of his victims. Although the piece abounds in coloratura, the expression is warm and deeply felt.

*L'incontro improvviso* (The Chance Encounter), *dramma giocoso per musica* (Hob. XXVIII:6), composed in 1775, is based on a text arranged after the French book of Dancourt by Karl Friberth. It is interesting to note that Haydn uses here, as in *Philemon und Baucis*

[16] Critical editions of the score were presented by D. Bartha and J. Vecsey in *JHW*, XXVIII/5, and by H. C. Robbins Landon for Haydn-Mozart Presse (Vienna, 1961). Landon edited also a miniature score for Philharmonia (Vienna).

and later in *Armida* and *L'anima del filosofo* (*Orfeo ed Euridice*), topics earlier employed by Gluck (*Orfeo ed Euridice*, 1762; *La rencontre imprévue*, 1764; *Bauci e Filemone*, 1769; *Armide*, 1777).

In *L'incontro improvviso* Haydn treats, moreover, a Turkish subject as Mozart was to do in 1781 (*Die Entführung aus dem Serail*), although it is unlikely that the younger master knew his friend's work. In Haydn's opera,[17] Calandro, a real *basso buffo*, and his servant Osmin are comic parts; the noble Rezia and the Sultan of Egypt are completely serious characters. It is interesting that, according to the fashion of the time, the clergy is ridiculed in the person of the roguish monk Calandro. The score is full of charming details. Ali, for instance, sought by the Egyptian soldiers, disguises himself as a painter. He shows the officers a number of pictures and describes their subjects to them, the orchestra offering exquisite portrayals. His aria in D major illustrates a magnificent Italian banquet, a sweetly murmuring little brook, and an appalling battle scene with the discharge of muskets and guns. Delightful effects of tone color are attained in the trio "Mi sembra un sogno" for three sopranos, accompanied by muted strings, English horns, and French horns. Another remarkable number is an orchestral interlude in the third act, in which such conventional Turkish instruments as the triangle and tambourine are used to evoke the atmosphere of an oriental fairy tale. The opera has three important finales, the most interesting being that of the second act which consists of three sections contrasting in tempo and rhythm. It is preceded by a duet in E major, which together with this finale forms a sort of larger unit.

*Il mondo della luna* (The World of the Moon; Hob. XXVIII:7) *dramma giocoso*, composed in 1777,[18] is based on a libretto by Goldoni and is related in its content to *Lo speziale*, the first Goldoni opera composed by Haydn. The apothecary Sempronio in the earlier work is crazy about geography, and Buonafede in *Il mondo della luna* is all too fond of astronomy. His excessive interest in it is destined to become his undoing. Thinking that he lives on that distant satellite, he permits his daughters to marry suitors whom he would never have approved on earth. This rather amusing farce was very popular in the eighteenth century, and composers such as Galuppi and Paisiello successfully set it to music. *Il mondo della luna*

[17] A piano-vocal score with German text was edited by H. Schultz for Musikwissenschaftlicher Verlag (Leipzig, 1939) and a critical edition of the full score by H. Wirth for *JHW*, XXV/6.

[18] Critical edition edited by H. C. Robbins Landon for Bärenreiter (Kassel). A new edition presenting various revisions of the work is being prepared by G. Thomas for *JHW*, XXV/7. As of 1981 two of its three volumes are available.

includes an unusually large number of instrumental movements. In the first act a short orchestra piece leads us into the world of the moon, and three times the trusting Buonafede looks through a telescope prepared by a fraudulent astronomer, Ecclitico. On each occasion the same instrumental piece is played, only to be interrupted by a *recitativo secco* and an arietta in which Buonafede explains what he sees. The orchestration changes after each observation; for its original appearance Haydn used strings in the instrumental piece and oboes, horns, and strings in the arietta. At the first repetition in both pieces flutes are added. Buonafede's last observation is particularly unpleasant, which induced Haydn to add bassoons to his orchestra and to change the key of the piece from D to E flat. The introduction to Act II, Scene 5, with its dotted rhythms and the use of timpani, describes the pompous entry of the sovereign of the moon. Similarly, at the beginning of the first finale the sensations of flying are painted with realism by the orchestra. Haydn was obviously following the tradition of Gluck's reform operas composed for Vienna, in which descriptive orchestral preludes and ballets were of great importance. In this opera Haydn uses a male alto. From 1776 to 1778 the castrato Pietro Gherardi was in Prince Esterházy's service. The composer at first entrusted the important part of the astrologer Ecclitico to him, but later changed his mind and had him sing the relatively insignificant role of the cavaliere Ernesto instead. Instances of Haydn's composing for a castrato are rare. The one-movement overture to the opera has no direct connection with the work. According to the custom of the time, Haydn also used it for other purposes. Without the opera's extensive coda, and with a somewhat smaller orchestra, it appears as the first movement of the Symphony No. 63, "La Roxolane."

*La vera costanza* (True Constancy; Hob. XXVIII:8) *dramma giocoso per musica*, composed in 1778 or 1779, makes use of a libretto by Fr. Puttini. According to Haydn's earliest biographers, the composer was commissioned to write this opera for performances in Vienna. He did so, but when he went to the capital to rehearse with the singers, such a flood of intrigues was let loose against him that he withdrew his work in disgust. The opera then had its premiere in Eszterháza. Recent Haydn research found it impossible to confirm this story. It is only certain that an opera *La vera costanza* by Pasquale Anfossi was performed in Vienna during April 1777. Haydn certainly knew this work. He even included a recitative and aria (No. 28) from Anfossi's opera in his own score, which had its premiere in Eszterháza during April 1779.

The original score of Haydn's *La vera costanza* seems to have been destroyed during the big fire which devastated Eszterháza in November 1779. For a new performance in 1785, the composer recreated the work with the assistance of trusted helpers and some parts of the earlier manuscript that had been previously copied. Thus a new, partly autograph score was created which is today preserved in the Bibliothèque Nationale of Paris. It is our main source for the critical edition of the opera,[19] but it is impossible to determine how much of the composition in its definite form goes back to the original version performed in 1779.

*La vera costanza* shows an interesting relationship to a work by Mozart. By an odd coincidence, the heroine, who rises from humble beginnings to the position of countess, bears the name Rosina, and like the Countess Rosina in Mozart's *Le nozze di Figaro*, she is devoted in deep love and faithfulness to her husband, though the count, despite his own gallant adventures, torments her with his unfounded jealousy. The tender, sensitive Rosina has as a counterpart the merry Villotto, who tries to win her love. *La vera costanza* is perhaps the most mature of Haydn's comic operas. Typical is the count's aria in the first act. It is introduced by an accompanied recitative in preparation for the tempestuous atmosphere of the first part of the aria; the second section, with an abrupt change of mood, is a tender adagio inspired by the thought of his beloved. Irritated by a motion of his clumsy rival, the count suddenly starts; another recitative accompanied by the orchestra leads to the third part of the aria, bringing in new thematic material. The free form of this passionate piece perfectly expresses the count's overwrought state of mind; his agitation is again portrayed in his solo in the second act. An accompanied recitative built on the thematic material of the first part of the aria is followed by an intricate vocal number consisting of as many as five sections. These contrast in tempo, rhythm, and character and are interspersed with occasional recitatives. This second aria (No. 28) is, as mentioned before, borrowed from Anfossi's opera *La vera costanza*. Haydn had it included in his own score as he felt that it was ideally suited to picture the weak, unstable character of the count. The finales, too, reveal the artist's maturity: the first consists of seven contrasting parts in different keys related to each other; the number of singers gradually increases from three to seven; and in the second finale nine sections can be distinguished. At the begin-

---

[19]Critical editions were prepared by Landon for Universal-Edition (Vienna, 1975) and by H. Walter in *JHW*, XXV/8. A piano score with German text was prepared by G. Schwalbe and W. Zimmer for Henschel Verlag (Berlin, 1959).

ning one singer and one sleeping person are on the stage, but at the
end all the seven characters take part. The composer gives a great
amount of variety to these finales without ever endangering the
continuity of the plot and the musical unity.

Despite the "inanities" of the libretto, rightly criticized by
Landon,[20] the opera enjoyed great success in Haydn's lifetime. It
was performed twenty-one times in Eszterháza, as well as in Bratislava, Brno, Budapest, Vienna, and even in Paris.

*L'isola disabitata* (The Deserted Island; Hob. XXVIII:9) *azione
teatrale*, composed in 1779, is based on a text by P. Metastasio.[21] *La
vera costanza* showed Haydn's growing interest in the serious opera,
but he took a more important step in the same direction in *L'isola
disabitata*. This is a real *opera seria*, based on a simple, short drama
by Metastasio, previously set to music by composers like Bonno,
Holzbauer, Jommelli, and Traetta. Costanza, separated by pirates
from her husband Ernesto, lives with her sister Silvia on a deserted
island until, after many years, she finds her beloved spouse. The
work shows that the composer knew Gluck's operas and allowed
himself to be influenced by them. It is hardly mere chance that
Haydn called *L'isola disabitata* an "azione teatrale," the designation
Gluck had used for his *Orfeo ed Euridice*. The *recitativo secco* accompanied by harpsichord only is banished from Haydn's opera, as it
was from Gluck's work. It is replaced by a carefully designed recitative accompanied by the orchestra and fills the greatest part of the
score. Unity among the scenes is achieved through the use of simple, constantly recurring motives. The recitative is sometimes transformed into a real arioso; the arias themselves are unaffected and
powerful, without excessive development of the musical element.
To some extent, however, Haydn deviated from this role in the
arias of Silvia, which he wrote for Luigia Polzelli. In these lovely
pieces he attained a tenderness of expression reminiscent of Mozart.
It is a pity that he included only a single ensemble number, the final
quartet, in the score; the fire that had ravaged the theater at Eszterháza shortly before may have been responsible for such economy.
As Haydn did not have a real stage at his disposal, he had to be
satisfied with four singers and to abstain from ballets and changes
of scenery. There is only one instrumental number in this opera, the
overture in G minor (Hob. Ia:13), the slow introduction of which
uses the same main idea as the following allegro. The fast move-

---

[20] *HCaW*, II, p. 527.
[21] A critical edition of the opera was presented by H. C. Robbins Landon for Bärenreiter Verlag (Kassel, 1976).

ment gains unity from the prevailing accompaniment in eighth notes. After a short contrasting allegretto in G major, the first allegro returns as a kind of coda. In the restless allegros Haydn meant to describe the terrible existence on the desolate island; the allegretto voiced the hope of the eventual union of the loving couple.

The static, oratoriolike character of this opera did not win it many friends. Thus Haydn's next work for the stage returned to the successful genre of the mixed, serio-comical opera. *La fedeltà premiata* (Faithfulness Rewarded; Hob. XXVIII:10) *dramma pastorale giocoso*[22] was composed in 1780 and first performed on February 25, 1781, to celebrate the reopening of the Eszterháza theatre, rebuilt after the great fire of 1779. The libretto of Haydn's opera is based on G. B. Lorenzi's *L'infedeltà fedele*, previously set to music by D. Cimarosa.

The composer's efforts were in this case particularly successful. It is characteristic for his unconventional approach that he reversed the traditional distribution of serious and comical characters. Instead of highborn persons, a pair of shepherds are treated as *parti serie*, whereas the antics of a foolish count are meant to amuse the audience. Undoubtedly this is a remarkable score. The free organization of the arias, the colorful use of the chorus (for which Haydn probably borrowed singers from Eisenstadt), the inspired finales with their effective changes in tempo, key, combination of voices, and, last but not least, the brilliant overture to the opera (which Haydn later used as finale for his Symphony No. 73, "La Chasse"), all contribute to create a work that surpasses all Haydn's previous efforts in the field of dramatic composition. Particularly successful were an aria and preceding *accompagnato* recitative from the second act: "Ah, come il core mi palpita nel seno." In a slightly altered version they were published in 1782 by Artaria in Vienna as a separate cantata. The recitative introduces in flute and horn a moving melody that expresses longing for a beloved person who has died, and this tune is used again in the slow part of the succeeding aria, thus giving greater unity to the composition. In 1783 C. F. Cramer, editor of the noted *Magazin der Musik*, wrote an enthusiastic article, "About the Beauty and the Expression of Passion in a Cantata by J. Haydn," in which he declared that he could sing the melody of the aria to himself for days without getting tired of it.

Different in character from the Italian operas are two German stage works. *Philemon und Baucis* (Hob. XXIXa:1) was originally

[22] Critical edition by G. Thomas in *JHW*, XXV/10.

conceived as a German puppet opera[23] and, like *L'infedeltà delusa*, performed to celebrate Empress Maria Theresa's visit to Eszterháza in September 1773. It was preceded by a prologue *Der Götterrat* (The Deliberation of the Gods; Hob. XXIXa:1a). Apart from the libretto and a few fragments of the music, this version is lost, but a later arrangement of the work as a German Singspiel with spoken dialogue has survived. It probably originated around the middle of the seventies. In this Singspiel not only is the dialogue spoken, but also the gods Jupiter and Mercury are entrusted with purely spoken parts so as to stress their difference from mortal beings. The overture consists of only two movements because by the custom of the period the introduction to the first vocal number was used instead of a finale. Both movements have passages full of tenderness, illustrating the moving idyl enacted by the loving couple. To deepen the picture of conjugal affection the work introduces the couple's son Aret and his bride Narcissa, who were felled on their wedding day by lightning. Philemon's canzonet "Ein Tag der allen Freude bringt" voices his grief over these events. All shades of emotion are expressed here, and sad resignation is ultimately called forth in this simple piece, which dies away pianissimo. Revived upon Jupiter's command, the young people express their affection for each other in moving terms. A gem of the score is Aret's aria, which with its poignant oboe solo stirringly conveys the feeling of bewildered happiness experienced by a man returned to earth from another world. It is supplemented by Narcissa's aria portraying with the help of a delicate orchestral accompaniment the young girl's tender sweetness and charm. Significantly enough, Haydn again used this exquisite piece—offering a highly rewarding task for the singer—with different words, in his opera *Il mondo della luna*. As the reference to the empress' visit at the end of the original marionette opera (see p. 64) had to be omitted from the Singspiel, it concluded with a ballet taken from Gluck's opera *Paride ed Elena* (1769). This insertion seemed altogether fitting, as Haydn's score reveals in many aspects affinities with Gluck's idiom.[24]

---

[23] "Haydn's Marionette Operas" were thoroughly discussed in a basic study by H. C. Robbins Landon in *HYb*, I (1962), pp. 111–199.

[24] A reconstructed version of the lost marionette opera *Philemon und Baucis* was edited by J. Braun in *JHW*, XXIV/1. The Singspiel version, found by Jens Peter Larsen in the Bibliothèque du Conservatoire, Paris, was edited by H. C. Robbins Landon for Bärenreiter Verlag (Kassel). In his article "Haydn's Marionette Operas" (p. 150), Landon points out that the poignant little minuet accompanying the revival of the young couple through Jupiter appears also in Ordonez's marionette opera *Alceste*; apparently this is one of the by no means rare instances of one eighteenth-century composer borrowing from another.

Probably likewise intended for marionettes was the comic opera *Die Feuersbrunst oder Das abgebrannte Haus* (The Conflagration—
The Burned House; Hob XXIXb:A) written after 1775. The musical numbers of this work, as well as the cues preceding each piece,
are preserved, while neither the connecting spoken dialogue nor
a libretto is any longer to be found. The torso indicates, however, that the composer reverts to the low comedy and commedia
dell'arte atmosphere of earlier works, such as *Der krumme Teufel* and
*La marchesa nespola.*[25] This is a typically Austrian work, introducing
*Hanswurst*, the clown of the Viennese stage, a mischievous hostler,
a fierce dragon, and a pathetic ghost. Very coarse language and at
times a thick Viennese dialect are sported by some of the characters,
and the traditional disguises (*Hanswurst* appears in both male and
female attire) add to the fun. The music is light, merry, and uncomplicated. Coloratura is avoided in the vocal pieces, as the composer
aims at maximum clarity of the text while matching the popular
nature of the libretto. Yet the individual characters are subtly portrayed with the help of melodic and orchestral devices.

Also preserved are the librettos of three additional marionette
operas from the years between 1776 and 1779, for which Haydn's
music has not yet been found. They are *Dido* (Hob. XXIXa:3),
*Genovevens vierter Theil* (Hob. XXIXa:5) and *Die bestrafte Rach-
begierde* (Hob. XXIXb:3).

•  •  •

Haydn produced no cantatas during his third period of composition, but in 1774–75 he wrote an even larger work. It was his
first oratorio, *Il ritorno di Tobia* (The Return of Tobias; Hob.
XXI:1), based on a book by G. G. Boccherini, a brother of the
composer.[26] This composition still adheres to some extent to the
Neapolitan vocal style. Even a cursory glance at the many arias
with abundant coloratura discloses the influence of Italian art. At
the same time the intricacy of the musical craftsmanship and the
close connection between words and music give this oratorio a
character all its own. The libretto differs favorably from the typical
Neapolitan oratorio text; instead of the traditional feeble allegories,
a definite plot is established, a plot by no means lacking dramatic

[25] The score of *Die Feuersbrunst* was found by H. C. Robbins Landon at the Music
Library of Yale University, New Haven, Connecticut. He attempted to reconstruct
the missing dialogue and edited the work in this version for Schott (London, 1961).
[26] A critical edition of the score was prepared by Ernst Fritz Schmidt for *JHW*,
XXVIII/1. As he died before the score went into production, the editorial work was
concluded by Georg Feder.

episodes, such as his parents' meeting with Tobias, whom they thought dead; the miraculous healing of old Tobit's blindness; the revelation of the archangel's identity, and his return to heaven. This oratorio, written for Vienna, follows the best musical traditions of the Austrian capital. The Habsburgs always preferred a more severe musical style, and, accordingly, oratorios in Vienna were kept free from the aberrations of Neapolitan music. In his *Sturm und Drang* period, Haydn himself was striving for an expressive musical language; now he was emotionally qualified to write a work in accord with the exacting tradition of Viennese art. The remarkable overture to the work consists of a largo in C minor, the lofty character of which reminds us of Gluck, and an *allegro di molto* in C major in sonata form. The slow introduction is thematically related to the first chorus, "Pietà d'un infelice," and a spiritual affinity exists between the allegro of the overture and the final chorus of the work. In this overture, Haydn deals with the main idea of the oratorio: out of sorrow and darkness a way leads to happiness and light. The basic idea of Beethoven's C minor and D minor symphonies is not very different.

The arias frequently renounce the stereotyped *da capo* form. They show the same strong influences of sonata form that can be noticed in the opera arias. There are two contrasting ideas in the first part of the aria. The middle section brings development of feeling and action, and the last part once more recapitulates it. Dramatic and musical points of view are in complete accord here. Haydn by no means dispenses with the antitheses so important for the dramatic impact of an aria, but introduces such contrasts between the first and second ideas of the main section. In her first aria, for instance, the mother of Tobias deplores the weakness of her husband. In the initial section, the achievements of the warrior and peasant are glorified and then, after a modulation to the dominant, the passivity of the husband is lamented. In the second (development) section in the minor, the passionate reproaches increase. Anna cannot help remembering once more (recapitulation) the gallant warrior and the diligent peasant, both of them so sadly contrasting with her husband.

The recitatives too are most carefully treated. The delicate portrait of Tobias's young wife in No. 8 of the first part and the healing of blind Tobit in No. 7 (16) of the second part are strikingly depicted, surpassing by far the average recitatives of the period.

The most important numbers of the score, however, are the choruses. At first the work contained only three choruses, one each at the beginning and end of the first part and one as the finale of the second part. For a performance in 1784, Haydn added two more choruses, one in each part.[27] Most effective in the very first chorus are the combination of solo voices and chorus and the use of the instruments to which the melody is frequently entrusted while the chorus provides a harmonic basis. The last number of the first part is in a sort of rondo form. Again and again the chorus repeats its moving supplication, "Rendi a Tobit la luce, o della luce autor" (Return the light to Tobit, Creator of the light), interrupted only by the five soloists, who send their individual prayers to the heavenly Father. Particularly dramatic is the moment when the humble wailing of "mira le calde lacrime" (notice our scalding tears) suddenly changes into the passionate outcry "odi le nostre voci" (listen to our voices). Perhaps the most important of the ensemble numbers is the chorus No. 13c, "Svanisce in un momento," which Haydn added in 1784 to the second part.[28] The effective contrast between pictures of darkest horror and of heavenly peace makes this piece equal to the best creations of the mature Haydn. In this oratorio, Haydn bestowed particular care on the instrumentation. He did not content himself with clothing almost every number in its own coloristic garb; he also achieved superb clarity and transparency of texture. A passage for wind instruments like the following (Ex. 12) anticipates the orchestral technique of the London symphonies.

EXAMPLE 12    *Ritorno di Tobia*, second part, Aria No. 2 (Sara)

Three years before Haydn's death his pupil Sigismund Neukomm arranged *Il ritorno di Tobia* on behalf of the composer. Some of the unnecessary repetitions of the text and excessive coloratura were eliminated, which is all to the good. Neukomm's changes and

---

[27] They are I/6c, "Ah gran Dio," and II/13c, "Svanisce in un momento." Haydn also shortened some of the arias, while, at the same time, enlarging the orchestra through the addition of two horns and two trombones. The alto part of Anna was entrusted to the well-known soprano, Nancy Storace (Mozart's first Susanna in *Le nozze di Figaro*), and probably accordingly altered.

[28] This chorus, 13c, was also printed separately as a motet with Latin and German text (*Insanae et vanae curae—Des Staubes eitle Sorgen*). It is known as the "Storm Chorus."

enlargements of the orchestration, however, might well have been avoided, for they coarsened some charming details of Haydn's original instrumentation. Even if the pupil acted in conformity with Haydn's own wishes, it is doubtful that the composer himself, after the passing of more than thirty years, was able to conjure up the atmosphere of the original work in order to judge the merits of this "improvement."

• • •

Haydn's church compositions of this period start with a *Salve Regina* in G minor (Hob. XXIIIb:2) written for four voices, solo organ and strings.[29] At the beginning of the work, the keyboard instrument is entrusted with an extensive, solo; subsequently its cantilena attractively alternates with the singers' utterances. In accord with the organization of the text, Haydn wrote a composition in three movements in an effective tempo sequence. The fastest section is in the middle, whereas an adagio forms the beginning and an allegretto with an introductory largo concludes it. It is an attractive composition, clearly showing the characteristic Viennese version of the Italian style that Haydn used in this period for sacred compositions and oratorios.

The end of the autograph of the *Salve Regina* contains two prayers to the Holy Virgin imploring her to help the composer. Each of them has the form of a chronogram—written perhaps by the composer himself—whose capitals express the year of composition (1771):

oro te o pIa et DVLCIs VIrgo Vt assIstas CoMposItorI
pIa DVLCIsqVe VIrgo assIste CoMposItorI

The offertory "Animae Deo gratae" is also known with the text *Agite properate* (Hob. XXIIIa:2). This is a spirited, festive piece in C major, concluding with a jubilant Alleluja. It employs a solo trio of two sopranos and tenor, whose brilliant coloratura alternates with the tutti of the four choral parts. Violins, oboes, trumpets, basses, timpani, and organ create an effective instrumental background. Parts, formerly in the monastery of Göttweig and dated 1776, prove that the work originated in that year at the latest.[30] This

---

[29] A critical edition was edited by H. C. Robbins Landon for Doblinger (Vienna, 1961).

[30] Irmgard Becker-Glauch ("Neue Forschungen zu Haydns Kirchenmusik," *H-St*, II/3 (May 1970), p. 212) is of the opinion that the work fits stylistically better into the sixties than into the seventies.

is certainly one of Haydn's sacred works that fully expresses his positive and unquestioning faith.[31]

The monumental chorus in *da capo* form "Ens aeternum" (Hob. XXIIIa:3), using for accompaniment strings, oboes, bassoon, trumpets, timpani, and organ, was written before 1772.[32] This solemn, powerful offertory, which combines elegance of structure with textural solidity, seems to have enjoyed great favor, since it was published by both Breitkopf and Härtel and Simrock with the German text "Walte gnädig, o ew'ge Liebe" added to the Latin original.[33]

After the large-scale masses of the sixties, the masses of the seventies appear surprisingly condensed. The *Missa Sti. Nicolai* (Hob. XXII:6) is a *missa brevis*, written in 1772, probably soon after the "Farewell" Symphony, to celebrate the name day of Prince Nicolaus.[34] The composition, which was obviously produced in great haste, is scored for four solo voices, mixed chorus, two oboes, two horns, bassoon, strings, and organ. This Mass is one of the most lyrical and tender of Haydn's church compositions. The Kyrie, which is quoted in the "Dona nobis pacem," has the character of a pastorale in six-quarter time, the Gratias is a soprano solo, the Benedictus a solo quartet of winning gracefulness. The modern critic finds it somewhat disconcerting that in the Credo different sections of the text are sung simultaneously; however, similar devices to save time were used not only by Haydn, but also by other composers of the period. The sensibility of the *Sturm und Drang* period perhaps is not so strongly expressed in this Mass as in other compositions of 1772. But the frequent sforzandi in the Kyrie, the mournful repetition of the words "et homo factus est" mingled with the menacing Crucifixus, and the moving accents of the Agnus Dei show that Haydn was well aware of the supreme drama unfolding in the text of the Mass.

Landon has noted that the peaceful, pastoral character prevalent in this Mass stands in "breathtaking" contrast to the tragic and pessimistic mood of the "Farewell" Symphony which immediately precedes it.[35] We must consider, however, that radical changes

[31] Cf. Karl Geiringer, "The Small Sacred Works by Haydn in the Esterházy Archives at Eisenstadt," *Musical Quarterly*, XLV/4 (Oct. 1959), p. 467.
[32] Becker-Glauch ("Neue Forschungen zu Haydns Kirchenmusik," p. 210) believes that this work too is a product of the sixties.
[33] A critical edition of the work was edited by H. C. Robbins Landon for Doblinger (Vienna).
[34] Critical score edited by C. M. Brand for the Haydn Society Edition, Series XXIII/1 (Boston, 1951).
[35] *HCaW*, II, p. 252.

in mood are characteristic features of human nature. Deeply felt, sad adagios are quite often followed by ebullient scherzos; Italian eighteenth-century *opera seria* was frequently interspersed with burlesque intermezzi; and even Wagner's *Tristan und Isolde*, the most tragic of his music dramas, was immediately followed by *Die Meistersinger*, his merriest work.

It was probably around 1777 or 1778 that Haydn created the little organ solo Mass in B-flat, to which he gave the title *Missa brevis Sti. Joannis de Deo.*[36] Saint John of God was the founder of the Brothers of the Order of Mercy, for whose Eisenstadt church the Mass was apparently destined. As the organ loft of this sanctuary was very small, the number of performers had to be restricted. Only in the more broadly treated Benedictus does a solo soprano compete with the concertizing organ. All the other movements are entrusted to the chorus and the small instrumental apparatus of two violins and bass. In accordance with the limited number of performers, the structure of the score is kept on quite a small scale. In the Gloria and at the beginning of the Credo, different sections of the text are simultaneously presented. Thus, for instance, in the Credo the soprano sings "Credo in unum Deum," and almost simultaneously the alto "Genitum non factum," the tenor "Qui propter nos," and the bass "Et ex patre natum." The trend toward deepened expression characteristic of the works of the seventies is also noticeable in this short Mass. Deeply felt is the Crucifixus. At the dramatic climax of the text, the beginning of "et resurrexit" after the end of the crucifixion, Haydn quotes the music of the Gloria. Better than a date on the manuscript, the expression-mark *perdendosi* used at the end of the "Dona nobis pacem" indicates the period in which this work was written. The pianissimo at the end of the prayer for peace certainly conforms to the idea of the text, though it deviates from the traditional musical construction.[37]

[36] Critical edition by H. C. Robbins Landon, in collaboration with K. H. Füssl and Christa Landon, in *JHW*, XXIII/2.

[37] In Haydn's original manuscript of the Mass, the notes for the bass and the organ parts were written about twice as large as those of the rest. Apparently the organist—probably Haydn himself—intended to play from the full score.

# CHAPTER FIFTEEN

# *Maturity*

# THE FOURTH PERIOD
# 1781–1790

With the year 1781 Haydn entered upon his classical period of composition. Both the frills of the rococo period and the exaggerated emotionalism of the *Sturm und Drang* period were overcome, though they left their imprint on the master's work. Out of the combination of features in the second and third periods of composition there grew the classical style of his full maturity, in which the principle of "thematic elaboration" (see p. 284) found its widest use.

The term "classical" can hardly be better explained than by the words "well balanced." In classical music one finds a perfect blend of the work of the mind and the work of the heart; inspiration is as important as the action of the intellect. Cheerfulness and seriousness, the tragic and the comic spirit are all called upon to make their contributions. Classical works seem to be born out of the fundamental qualities of the instruments or voices for which they were written. All technical problems are completely solved, and the compositions are neither too long nor too short. The musical ideas fit the musical form to perfection. Those works that deserve the term "classical" exhibit a beauty and composure comparable to those of the best architecture and sculpture of ancient Greece.

Although Haydn had undergone an artistic development that seemed to lead him inevitably toward classicism, his work would hardly have reached the full height of perfection had he not associ-

279

ated artistically with Mozart, who moved to Vienna in 1781. It has been shown in the first section of this book that the friendship between the two masters resulted in an amazing musical relationship. Not only did Haydn influence Mozart (this is not particularly surprising, as he was twenty-four years older and by far the more successful of the two), but he also allowed himself to be influenced by the young genius. It was a perfect example of mutual give-and-take, equally beneficial to Mozart and Haydn, for in helping one another, each of the two composers reached in the eighties the consummation of his classical style and with it his full artistic maturity.

•  •  •

It is evident that even before the first meeting of the two composers, Haydn had studied Mozart's work, for some of his pianoforte sonatas published before the date of that meeting show clear signs of Mozart's influence. For instance, the melodic invention in the second movement of sonata Hob. XVI:35 and the striking separation of the subsidiary subject from the main subject in the first movement of sonata No. 37 (both sonatas were published in 1780) show a certain similarity to Mozart's works, as does the connection of the end of the exposition with the beginning of the development in the first movements of Nos. 41 and 49, two sonatas composed after the musicians first met. In the adagio of No. 49, too, the melodic character appears to be inspired by Mozart to some extent.

However, pianoforte sonatas are not among Haydn's most inspired works of this period. In 1784, three sonatas (Nos. 40–42) were published and dedicated to Princess Marie Esterházy. Each sonata has only two movements, and the influence of the divertimento seems to be particularly strong (especially so in No. 40). A comparison of the scintillating *prestissimo* finale of No. 39 with the tame *allegretto e innocente* at the beginning of No. 40 reveals a striking difference of character. Obviously the Princess was not in favor of bold innovations, and the finales of Nos. 41 and 42 seem to show that a display of strict counterpoint was more to her taste. These sonatas denote a decided lack of deeper interest in the form, and in the following years Haydn completely neglected the piano sonata.[1] Chamber and orchestral music in which "thematic elaboration" could be displayed to best advantage occupied his mind to such an extent that other forms receded into the background. Only at the end of the eighties did he revert to the piano sonata. Early in 1789

[1] Numbers 44–47, published in 1788–89, are earlier works, probably composed between 1765 and 1768.

he wrote a work that had been commissioned by the renowned Leipzig publisher Ch. G. Breitkopf. The resulting sonata (Hob. XVI:48) belongs to the most remarkable compositions Haydn has written for the clavier. It consists of two movements only. The first, an *andante con espressione*, is a kind of fantasy in which three interrelated sections in C major alternate with episodes in the minor mode. A wealth of dynamic changes from pianissimo to fortissimo, including numerous crescendi and sforzandi help to impart a passionate, dramatic quality to the movement. An effective contrast is achieved by the brisk and amusing finale, a forceful piece in masterly structured rondo form. Despite its great artistic significance, this work was surpassed in the following year by the large Sonata No. 49 in E-flat major, intended for Marianne von Genzinger. In this composition too Haydn completely forgot the educational purpose of his piano music and followed only his inspiration. In the exposition of the first movement, the subsidiary and concluding subjects, though derived from the main idea, show an independent character of their own; the retransition to the recapitulation is full of dramatic tension, and the important coda seems to be a sort of second development. The solemn adagio, with its dramatic episode in B-flat minor, is reminiscent of Mozart. Haydn himself considered this movement the climax of the whole work, as his letter to Marianne von Genzinger shows (see p. 94). The finale is very different from this middle movement. In its amusing, energetic character it supplies a cheerful solution of the conflict. Thus Haydn's interest in the piano sonata got a fresh impetus from his devotion to Marianne von Genzinger, for everything connected with her had to be perfect. It is significant that the composer could not even bear the thought of his friend playing the sonata on her old, inferior piano. He was not satisfied until he had persuaded Prince Esterházy to present Frau von Genzinger with a new instrument, he himself giving elaborate advice as to the final choice.[2]

[2] Although Haydn wrote to Marianne von Genzinger: "This Sonata . . . is quite new and eternally intended for Your Honor," the autograph of the work bears in Haydn's hand the dedication "Composta per la stimatissima Signora Anna de Jerlischek." This lady, a friend of Marianne and housekeeper at the Esterházy court, later married Johann Tost, to whom Haydn dedicated twelve string quartets (see p. 288). As we learn from Haydn's letters to Marianne, while he was composing this sonata for her, Fräulein de Jerlischek commissioned him to write a piano sonata meant as a gift for Frau von Genzinger. Haydn complied and dedicated the work to the housekeeper, who paid for it, but as he was obliged to "be very careful not to lose her favor," he concealed the fact that he had meant to write a sonata for Marianne in any case. It seems likely that when the manuscript finally reached the Viennese lady, it was inscribed to her. Hoboken (Hob., I, p. 773) remarks that the dedication to Fräulein Jerlischek in the autograph apparently had been pasted over.

Two smaller piano compositions by Haydn, a Fantasia (Hob. XVII:4) and an Andante with Six Variations (Hob. XVII:5), were composed in the same years (1789 and 1790) as the two sonatas discussed above. Haydn had a high opinion of the Fantasia, which he offered to Artaria with the following words: "In a humorous mood I have composed an entirely new capriccio for the piano; its good taste, singularity, and careful execution are sure to please both experts and amateurs. It is in a single movement, rather long, but not particularly difficult." The Fantasia, which might have been influenced by similar works of C. P. E. Bach, shows, even better than the sonatas, the colorful character of Haydn's piano-playing. We seem to hear in this piece the tone of violins and double basses, of horns and flutes; moreover the rapid crossing of the hands, the arpeggios, and the distribution of passages between the hands exhibit the composer's concern for purely pianistic devices. The effect that Haydn achieved by holding notes in the bass until they die away (*tenuto intanto finchè no si sente più il sono*) is rather notable. This Fantasia was written by a master who exploited the possibilities of piano technique in transcribing ideas of an essentially orchestral nature. The Andante with Six Variations was characterized by Artaria, the firm which published the little work in 1791, as *facile et agréable*. This is indeed an apt description. The work is unassuming and pleasant, presenting no particular difficulties for amateur performers.

• • •

During his period of maturity Haydn composed thirteen piano trios: Hob. XV:5–10 in 1784–85, 11–13 in 1788–89 and 14–17 in 1789 and 1790.[3] The trios 5–14 were written for clavier "accompanied" by violin and cello; 15 and 16 replaced the violin by a flute, and in 17, a violin *or* a flute could be used. All these works were immediately printed, partly by English publishers and partly by Artaria in Vienna. In addition, Haydn sent a trio (Hob. XV:2), which was arranged from an earlier quartet for baryton, two violins, and clavier (Hob. XIV:2) to the publisher Forster in London. Moreover, he mailed to Forster by mistake two trios of his former pupil I. Pleyel, indicating on the title page of the manuscript in his own hand: *Di me Giuseppe Haydn* (By me J. H.). The publisher saw no reason to doubt the authenticity of the compositions and printed

[3] There are two critical editions of Haydn's collected piano trios. One was revised by H. C. Robbins Landon for Doblinger (Vienna), the other, comprising the trios written before 1791, by W. Stockmeier for *JHW*, XVII/1 and 2.

them together with a genuine Haydn trio (Hob. XV:5) in 1785. Later, the pupil got even with his teacher. In 1797 the two trios by Pleyel and the one by Haydn were printed in Paris, indicating Pleyel as the author of all three compositions.[4]

Haydn's error might be interpreted as a sign that the composer did not feel particular interest in the form and hardly examined works he had written to satisfy the public's demand. This is by no means the case, however. On the contrary, the trios seem to have allowed the composer to experiment with unusual devices. The individual works are sometimes in two and sometimes in three movements, but each of them shows a different sequence of tempi, with such unusual combinations as andante—andante—allegro assai (No. 7) or adagio non tanto—allegro—allegro (No. 5). In many trios the violin part shows a remarkable independence from that of the clavier. Its melodic line repeatedly reaches g³ in the fifth position, while in No. 7 the composer prescribes *sopra una corda*, a coloristic effect indicating that the phrase ought to be played on the G string only. There are dazzling harmonic progressions and enharmonic changes. Thus No. 14 starts in A-flat major, modulating to F major. After a grand pause without any transition, G-flat major is intoned, which presently leads, with the help of enharmonic changes, to B major and finally back to A-flat. The following adagio is in E major with a middle section in E minor. It ends in D-sharp (E-flat) major and from there it moves *attacca* to the finale in A-flat. Haydn displays here a spirit of enterprise that appears rather unusual considering that the date of this publication is 1790. Most of the old prints of the trios refer to the keyboard instruments as "clavecin ou pianoforte." However, *fz* is frequently prescribed, a dynamic effect easily achieved on a pianoforte, although impossible on a harpsichord. Thus is appears that the composer had the new instrument in mind, while the publishers, for practical reasons, referred also to the traditional cembalo, still to be found at that time in the homes of most music-lovers.

In 1784, Haydn sent to England his six divertimenti for first violin or flute, second violin, and violoncello (Hob. IV:6–11), which were published by William Forster as Op. 38. According to Haydn's receipt for the honorarium, which accompanied the manuscripts, these trios may also be performed by two flutes and violoncello. They are pleasant pieces of no great consequence, largely ar-

---

[4]Cf. Alan Tyson, "Haydn and Two Stolen Trios," *Music Review*, XXII/1 (Feb. 1961), p. 21ff., and Hob., I, p. 684. The two Pleyel trios are published in an appendix to *JHW*, XVII/2.

ranged from baryton trios and the opera *Il mondo della luna*. It is regrettable that these attractive works are (in 1982) not yet available in a modern edition.

•  •  •

The string quartet, a kind of counterpart to the vocal quartet, is a perfectly balanced, harmonious form of chamber music. It is therefore not surprising that it was particularly cultivated by Haydn during the decade in which the classical style reached a climax in his work. No less than twenty-five quartets—more than one-third of his whole output in this field—were completed between 1781 and 1790.

The quartets Op. 33 of 1781 (Hob. III:37–42), were dedicated to the Grand Duke Paul of Russia, and therefore are known as the "Russian" quartets. The six pieces are also called both *Gli scherzi*, as in this series the composer gave the name of scherzo to most minuet movements, and the *Jungfernquartette*, from the title page of an old edition.[5] Since the composition of the preceding series of string quartets, Op. 20, of 1772, no less than nine years had elapsed, during which Haydn had composed several operas, the oratorio *Il ritorno di Tobia*, and many symphonies. The string quartet had been abandoned temporarily, probably because Haydn felt that further progress along the lines established in his Op. 20 was impossible. In the fugue movements of the "Sun" quartets, a strong concentration of both form and content had been attained, but in time this sort of solution seemed too radical to him and not in conformity with the spirit of the string quartet. The progressive Haydn was not satisfied to use an antiquated contrapuntal form of the baroque period in the young string quartet. He wanted unification and concentration, but not knowing how to achieve them adequately, he renounced the composition of string quartets for the time being and it was not until nine years later that he found a solution to his problem.

The "Russian" quartets, which, according to Haydn himself, were written "in an entirely new and particular manner," raised the principle of "thematic elaboration" to the status of a main stylistic feature. Haydn had used thematic elaboration—a method of dissecting the subjects of the exposition and then developing and reassembling the resulting fragments in an unexpected manner—in his

[5] Critical editions by Reginald Barrett-Ayres and H. C. Robbins Landon for these and the following quartets for Doblinger (Vienna, 1968–   ).

earlier works, but never with such logic and determination. Henceforth this device, combined with modulations, ruled the development sections of the sonata form. Each of the six "Russian" quartets
provides examples of this technique. Thus, for instance, in the first
movement of No. 5, part of the main subject (Ex. 13a) grows into
the succeeding intricate texture (Ex. 13b). Thematic elaboration is

EXAMPLE 13    (a) String Quartet, Op. 33, No. 5
              (b) String Quartet, Op. 33, No. 5

by no means confined to the development sections. Even the transition from the first to the second subject in the exposition might
make use of an elaboration of the main theme, and occasionally
new developing episodes can be found in the recapitulation. The

quartets Op. 20, with their fugues, already had done away with the predominance of the first violin. In the "Russian" quartets, all instruments as a matter of course were given equal shares in the melodic work. Even the accompanying and purely filling parts were based on motives taken from the main subjects.

Haydn exercised wise economy in using the sonata form only in the first movements of the "Russian" quartets. The slow movements are mainly in three-part (romanza) form, with a contrasting middle part instead of a development, whereas in the finales there is a return to the rondo form. Only in his last period was Haydn to give to the rondo the characteristic features of sonata form, thus creating at the end of the cycle a counterpart to its beginning. The most apparent innovation of the "Russian" quartets, the use of a scherzo or scherzando instead of the traditional minuet, should not be taken too seriously. An analysis of these pieces shows that the change is limited to the name of the movement and does not affect its character. Only the scherzo of No. 5 foreshadows the piquant flavor and fire of Beethoven's movements of the same title.

The synthesis of the homophonic rococo style with the contrapuntal idiom noticeable in the form of these quartets also may be discerned in their contents. Without avoiding the earlier grace and liveliness, they reveal greater depth of feeling. The last traces of *galant* superficiality have disappeared, and the music breathes quiet serenity and classical nobility. Still, an experience of the importance of the "romantic crisis" necessarily left its imprint on the composer's work. The augmented octaves in the introduction of No. 1, and the last movement of No. 2, with its adagio episode, its grand pauses of increasing length, and the unusual pianissimo ending bear witness to it. However, these paraphernalia of tragedy are employed to achieve a purely comical effect. This finale rightly bears the nickname "The Joke." It seems to be a pleasant, though not particularly amusing, rondo with two episodes. The real fun comes in the coda, for after a solemn adagio episode, the eight measures of the main subject are repeated in an odd manner. Each phrase of two measures is followed by a rest of two. When the whole subject is played, Haydn doubles his rests and starts all over with the first measures of the melody, and before anybody in the audience has a chance of voicing a protest, the end has come, leaving the listener puzzled and amused. Perhaps the best known work of the set is No. 3, "The Bird." Both the grace notes in the main subject of the first movement, and the trio of the scherzando, an unusually

charming duet between first and second violin, are responsible for
the nickname of the work.

The next quartet, Op. 42 (Hob. III:43), is a sort of foreign
body within the quartets of the eighties. The very terse construction of its four movements induced Pohl and Sandberger to classify
this composition as one of Haydn's earlier works. Some details,
however, such as the dramatic development of the first movement,
the pianissimo endings of the first and last movements, and the use
of contrapuntal devices in the finale, prove Op. 42 to be the product of a later period. Additional evidence is provided by the autograph, which bears the date 1785. The work must certainly be considered a composition of Haydn's maturity which—for unknown
reasons—was conceived in a particularly unassuming manner.[6]

In 1787, six new quartets (Hob. III:44–49) were published
by Artaria in Vienna as Op. 50 and dedicated to King Friedrich
Wilhelm II of Prussia. In these "Prussian" quartets the thematic
elaboration employed in Op. 33 is continued. The four stringed
instruments are again treated individually, but cooperate on a single
task: to discuss each subject thoroughly so as to cast full light upon
all its potentialities. It is most significant that Haydn, who increasingly exploited the possibilities of the transformation of
themes, often rejected the use of a contrasting subsidiary subject.
He was eager to concentrate his compositions not only by using
thematic elaboration, but also by letting a whole movement unfold
from a single germ. The complete expression of his straightforward and undivided personality is to be found in movements that
seem hewn from a single block. Thus, the finale of No. 1 shows a
monothematic construction. The main subject stated in the first
two measures is treated either as a whole or in halves all through the
movement. In No. 2, the second section of the minuet (the name
scherzo vanishes again in this set of quartets, though the character
of Beethoven's scherzo is occasionally intimated) is a development of the first section, not a new idea, thus again emphasizing the
idea of unity. Similar tendencies prevail in the first movement of
No. 4, in F-sharp minor, possibly the most interesting of the six
"Prussian" quartets. Although the main subject is in the minor

---

[6]Landon (*HCaW*, II, pp. 490 and 621) conjectures that Op. 42 was written for
Spain. He bases this hypothesis on a remark in a Haydn letter to Artaria (dated April
5, 1784). Here the composer mentions that he is working on three very small quartets intended for Spain. It seems possible—though not very likely—that Op. 42 is
the only composition of this group that was really written or that survived.

mode and the subsidiary subject in the major, this subsidiary subject is obviously derived from the first idea. The impassioned, subjective character of the movement, together with the fugue of the finale, seems to indicate that No. 4 originated during the early seventies, but a very important detail shows that the quartet belongs to a later period: both the transition to the subsidiary subject and the subject itself display the spirit of Mozart. In the andante of this quartet, the main theme in the major mode is followed by a contrasting melody in the minor, and there is one variation each in the major and minor sections, followed by a second variation of the main theme which brings the movement to an end. Similar combinations of the variation form with that of the rondo were of the greatest importance in Haydn's later compositions. In No. 5, the slow movement, which has some elaborate solo passages for the violin, is known as "A Dream." In the third movement, both the minuet and its trio are governed by the same grace note motive, showing that the idea of unity seemed to Haydn more important than the traditional contrast between minuet and trio. In this rather serious and thoughtful series, there is one quartet imbued with Haydn's particular sense of humor. It is No. 6, "The Frog," and its finale is filled with gay croaking sounds produced with the help of the so-called *bariolage* (French, derived from Latin *variare*; to change or switch): playing the same notes in quick alternation on adjoining strings. Haydn, and later Brahms, made repeated use of this amusing coloristic effect.

Between the quartets Op. 50 and those of Op. 54, the arrangement of Haydn's *The Seven Last Words* for string quartet is inserted in some editions as Op. 51 (Hob. III:50–56). This work is discussed on page 302ff.

The quartets Op. 54, Nos. 1–3, and Op. 55, Nos. 1–3 (Hob. III:57–62), were composed around the year 1788. In 1790 Haydn wrote six additional quartets, known as Op. 64, Nos. 1–6 (Hob. III:63–68). The quartets Op. 64 were dedicated to Johann Tost, and the same is probably true of the six earlier quartets. Commonly, Op. 54 and 55 are therefore referred to as "the first series of Tost quartets," and Op. 64 as "the second series of Tost quartets."[7]

[7]The man whom Haydn thus honored had been a violinist in the orchestra of Prince Esterházy from 1783 to 1788. In 1789 he traveled to Paris where he sold, with Haydn's consent, the quartets Op. 54 and 55, as well as two of the composer's symphonies, to the publisher Sieber. (Less satisfactory was the fact that he included in the deal a symphony of Gyrowetz, designated as a work of Haydn, cf. p. 200). On his return to Austria, Tost married the wealthy Anna de Jerlischek (or Gerlischek), the

The boldness and variety of invention in these works, and their well-balanced musical form, show Haydn at the summit of his quartet production. A characteristic feature of the compositions is again structuring a whole movement upon a single subject. The adagio in Op. 55, No. 1, grows out of one idea only; so do the finale of Op. 64, No. 2, and the first movement of Op. 64, No. 1, both in sonata form. In each of these two compositions the subsidiary subject is developed out of the first subject and the composer revealed his desire for unity by using in the recapitulation the main subject itself rather than its transformation. Occasionally Haydn employed contrasting ideas but postponed their entrance as long as possible so that they became epilogues rather than subsidiary subjects (see the first movements of Op. 54, No. 1, and Op. 64, No. 1). Mozart's type of construction, in which the subsidiary idea is a countermelody of sweet and tender character, is not often found in these works (the finale of Op. 64, No. 4, provides one of the infrequent examples), and it is significant of the difference in character between the two masters that the older composer stressed unity, the younger contrast.

The "Tost" quartets are full of attractive surprises. Haydn liked to introduce into his rondos and the developments of his sonata forms interesting fugato sections, as in the finales of Op. 55, No. 1, Op. 64, No. 2, Op. 64, No. 5, and the second movement of Op. 55, No. 2. Harmony and modulation sometimes seem to foreshadow the romantic period. The delicately veiled episode of the second subject in the allegretto of Op. 54, No. 1, introduces tender modulations of a hazy, elusive character. With the help of hardly noticeable chromatic progressions and enharmonic changes Haydn modulates from G major over C, B-flat, and E-flat to D-flat, and back to the initial key. We seem to be lifted by some magic in a fantastic flight through the air, eventually to be deposited at the spot from which we started. Similarly the harsh dissonances in the trio of the minuet of Op. 54, No. 2, contradict all sentimental conceptions of good old "Papa" Haydn. The same quartet has a rather striking adagio finale that in all likelihood was originally meant

---

lady who had served as intermediary in the matter of the piano sonata for Frau von Genzinger. Tost seems to have been not only a musician, but also a good businessman, as he owned a cloth factory and was described as *Grosshandlungs-Gremialist*. Unfortunately nothing is known about his personal relationship to Haydn. (See Jens Peter Larsen, *Die Haydn-Überlieferung*, (Copenhagen, 1939), pp. 154–155, Hob., I, p. 415, and *HCaW*, II, p. 81.)

merely as the slow introduction to a presto. It assumed such proportions, however, that it developed into the main section of the
movement while the short presto was reduced to a mere episode
losing its significance through the reentry of the adagio, which
brings the movement to an end. The arrangement of the voices in
this movement is also most unusual; the first violin carries the melody while the violoncello keeps crossing the middle parts, passing
again and again into the treble register. The Quartet in F minor,
Op. 55, No. 2, is known as the "Razor" Quartet. In this work the
first two movements change places. It begins with a set of variations in slow time, alternately in minor and major, but the second
movement is an allegro in sonata form of peculiar charm, with
sudden half-tone progressions. A forte cadence in F minor is followed, after a grand pause, by a delicate piano passage beginning
in G-flat major; later a cadence in A-flat is succeeded in the same
way by a passage beginning in A major. Similar devices were used
by Philipp Emanuel Bach, for instance, in the big "Heilig" published by Breitkopf and Härtel in 1779. Op. 64, No. 1, exhibits
in the development section of its finale an excellent example of
Haydn's strong sense of humor. The drumming main subject is
used here for a little fugato, the constant note repetitions of which
make an irresistibly droll impression. Op. 64, No. 2, in B minor, is
filled with passionate energy. Although the exposition of the first
movement has a subsidiary subject in the relative major, the recapitulation reintroduces it, surprisingly enough, in the tonic minor, and
only the following simple, sweet *adagio ma non troppo* in B major
brings a harmonious solution. The trio of the minuet, taking the
first violin up to the highest positions, shows what great demands
Haydn made at that time on the technical abilities of his players. It
should not be assumed, however, that the master's reason for inserting this trio was to give the player of the first violin a chance to
show off his technical ability. Haydn's motives were purely artistic,
for after the ponderous heaviness of the minuet the silvery lightness
of the high registers was needed to achieve a perfect balance. The
finale brings yet another example of Haydn's sense of humor in
the entertaining interplay between piano passages as the seeming
bearers of timid and faltering questions and replies to them in the
form of brusque, loudly declaimed unisons. Here again the technique of the comic opera is employed in a work of chamber music.
The slow movement of Op. 64, No. 4, has in its parts for the second violin and viola an accompaniment that is surprisingly pianistic in its whole conception. Haydn, like other eighteenth-century

composers, sometimes wrote pianoforte parts that showed the influence of stringed instruments, but he occasionally inverted this relationship. The lovely first movement of Op. 64, No. 5, is responsible for the name, "The Lark," given to the quartet. From the earthbound accompaniment of the lower parts, the first violin soars up to heavenly heights. The finale of this quartet, with its unrelenting motion in sixteenths, forms a sort of *perpetuum mobile*. The trio of the minuet in Op. 64, No. 6, a counterpart of the same movement in Op. 55, No. 1, again presents technical difficulties that almost equal those of a violin concerto. The second violin carries the subject while the first violin accompanies like a tenuous chime, with notes ascending to more than three octaves above middle C (see Ex. 14):

EXAMPLE 14    String Quartet, Op. 64, No. 6, Trio

• • •

In the years between 1782 and 1784, Breitkopf and Härtel's catalogues listed "VI Divertimenti da Giuseppe Haydn," three of which were scored for two oboes, two clarinets, two horns, and two bassoons, the other three for two oboes, two horns, three bassoons, and a serpent, an obsolete bass cornet in the form of a snake. These divertimenti (Hob. II:41–46) are no longer considered authentic Haydn compositions.[8] We mention them only because one movement from the set has achieved lasting fame. In 1870 the Haydn biographer C. F. Pohl showed a copy of the divertimenti to his friend Johannes Brahms, who immediately copied the second movement of No. 6, in B-flat major, in his notebook. Fascinated by the "Chorale St. Antoni," apparently an old Austrian pilgrims' song upon which this movement was based, Brahms used it as the theme for his *Variations on a Theme by Joseph Haydn*, Op. 56a and b, which he wrote during the summer of 1873. This divertimento is in four movements, all of which exhibit a close melodic relationship;[9] in fact, it may be said that the first movement, the minuet, and the finale are in a way variations of the "Chorale St. Antoni," introduced in the second movement. The old German variation suite of the seventeenth century, in which the different dances of a suite are made up of variations of a main dance, seems here to be revived, and the cyclical form so dear to the composers of the nineteenth century foreshadowed. Brahms, who liked to use for his variations themes which had been previously employed for this purpose, acted true to form here also.

The "Toy" symphony or "Sinfonia Berchtolsgadensis" (Hob. II:47), for seven toy instruments and strings, is traditionally considered to be a work of Joseph Haydn, though in recent years it has been assigned to various other composers, among them Michael Haydn and Leopold Mozart.[10] It is a charming piece in three brief movements displaying an amiable sense of fun and a true understanding of the world of children.

• • •

Closely related to Haydn's divertimenti are the five concertos for two lire organizzate (Hob. VIIh:1–5), composed in 1786.[11] This instrument was a sort of hurdy-gurdy and looked like a big guitar.[12] A wooden wheel, turned by a crank, pressed on the strings from

---

[8] *Grove's Dictionary of Music and Musicians*, 5th ed. (London: Macmillan; New York: St. Martin's Press, 1954), IV, 177, ascribes them to Haydn's pupil Pleyel. There is, however, no proof for this assertion either. R. Benton in *Ignace Pleyel: A Thematic Catalogue of his Compositions* (New York, 1977) does not even mention the divertimenti.

[9] It was first edited by Karl Geiringer for Edition Schuberth (Leipzig, 1932).

[10] Cf. Ernst Fritz Schmid, "Leopold Mozart und die Kindersinfonie," *Mozart-Jahrbuch*, 1951, p. 69ff. and the same author's "Nochmals zur Kindersinfonie," *Mozart-Jahrbuch*, 1952, p. 117.

[11] Number 3 was edited by Karl Geiringer for Edition Adler (Berlin, 1932). Critical editions of all five concertos were edited by H. C. Robbins Landon for Doblinger (Vienna, 1959) and Makoto Ohmiya in *JHW*, VI.

[12] Cf. Harry R. Edwall, "Ferdinand IV and Haydn's Concertos for the 'Lira Orga-

below and set them vibrating. Four of these strings, tuned in G c g c¹ (or d¹), were mere drones that could be connected or disconnected at will; two were meant for the performance of the melody and both were tuned in g¹. These melody strings were shortened with the aid of wooden bridges or tangents, which in turn were operated by a system of keys. A little pipe organ attachment was built into the instrument, and the keys, besides shortening the strings, admitted air to the tiny pipes. Smaller instruments were equipped with one set of pipes, tuned in unison with the notes produced on the strings. Larger lire organizzate also contained a second series of pipes tuned an octave higher. The wheel had the double function of serving as a bow and working the bellows. However, the player did not have to use pipes and strings together; it was possible to disconnect either of them.

As mentioned before (cf. p. 86), these concertos were composed at the order of the King of Naples, who delighted in playing duets for lire organizzate with his teacher, the Austrian minister, Norbert Hadrava. To stimulate the august pupil's interest, Hadrava commissioned original compositions for the lira from Haydn, Gyrowetz, Pleyel, and Sterkel. A close examination of Haydn's works will show that they are not so much concertos as divertimenti in which the various partners, in the manner of chamber music, compete with each other. The technical possibilities of the clumsy lira were less than modest: as a rule the keys of C, F, and G had to be used, and its range scarcely reached two octaves. Haydn wrote these pieces as a sort of ensemble music for nine or ten instruments: two violins, two violas, violoncello (possibly reinforced by double bass), two horns, and two lire. A very modest amount of prominence is accorded to the solo instruments. As their parts resemble those of woodwinds, it is possible to replace them in modern performances by oboe, flute, or even recorder. The high-spirited compositions, including several dances and even a hunting scene (finale of No. 2), display classic balance in the distribution of the thematic material. Accordingly the composer was in a position to use two movements of the fifth lira concerto for his Symphony No. 89, written in 1787. In the same concerto's first movement, Haydn employed as a kind of motto a well-known motive consisting of four notes, which had previously played an important part in the last movement of his Symphony No. 13. Mozart was captivated by the

nizzata,'" *Musical Quarterly*, XLVIII/2 (Apr. 1962) and M. Bröcker, *Die Drehleier* (Düsseldorf, 1973).

same idea. He used it in the Credo of his Missa Brevis in F major (K. 192), and finally glorified it by introducing it as the main theme of the finale of his "Jupiter" Symphony. The third concerto is a particularly remarkable member of the set. Out of its middle movement grew later one of Haydn's best-loved movements, the allegretto of the Symphony No. 100 ("Military").

The lira concertos pleased the King of Naples so much that he also commissioned eight notturni for two lire organizzate, two clarinets, two horns, two violas, and bass (Hob. II:25–32).[13] In order to make wider use of these charming works the composer himself later changed their instrumentation by replacing the lire with flute and oboe or two flutes, the clarinets with violins. It is interesting that in making these alterations Haydn did not substantially change his scores. He merely added an occasional double bass part and placed at the head of No. 3 (Hob II:27) a newly composed, dramatic largo introduction. In this form, some of the notturni were also played in Haydn's London concerts.

The notturni are delightful pieces, but in them Haydn's fantasy is somewhat restrained by the technical limitations of the two principal instruments. The works are again in C, F, or G major and display for the most part the traditional three movements. Pieces like the spirited fugue in the last movement of No. 5 (Hob. II:29) or the almost symphonic allegro moderato in No. 4 (Hob. II:28) are exceptions. More characteristic is the gentle character of the middle movement in No. 3 (Hob. II:27), whose poetical mood Robbins Landon describes in the following manner:[14]

A profound sadness overcomes Haydn, which wells out of this marvellous Adagio in its measured quavers, the interweaving parts slowly moving in a modulation that seems to foretell Brahms. It is a magic moment which we are all privileged to share with this lonely man who filled this music of 1790 with a special mood which he never quite recaptured after his life became so very different.

• • •

The few well-known solo concertos by Haydn were written during the eighties. The authenticity of the Violoncello Concerto in D major (Hob. VIIb:2) has been doubted; it has been suggested that Anton Kraft, a cellist of the Esterházy orchestra and pupil of

---

[13] A critical edition was presented by Makoto Ohmiya in *JHW*, VII.
[14] *HCaW*, II, p. 655.

Haydn, was its author, though the first edition, published by André (Offenbach) in Haydn's lifetime, bore the inscription "Édition d'après le manuscrit original de l'auteur," and Köchel, the great Mozart scholar, testified to having seen this autograph. Fortunately it was rediscovered in Vienna by the middle of this century, and all doubts of Haydn's authorship were thus removed. In this work, composed in 1783, the part for the solo instrument not only is brilliant, but also has been made the center of the composition: all the other instruments look to it for leadership. The concerto is often performed with an enlarged orchestral accompaniment that was provided by François-Auguste Gevaert in 1890. The original version, using only two oboes and two horns is also available and is certainly preferable in every respect.[15]

In 1784 another D major concerto, this time *pour le clavecin ou pianoforte*, was published. This work (Hob. XVIII:11) not only has an attractive solo part, but also a very effective accompaniment by the orchestra. The middle movement grows out of the thematic material of the first eight measures of the tutti; and a simple motive, in which the same note is repeated six times, expands into an important dialogue between solo instrument and orchestra. This six-note motive comes to life only if the strength of the individual notes is modulated, which can be done on a pianoforte, but is impossible on a harpsichord. This seems to indicate that the choice of solo instrument, mentioned in the concerto's title, in reality does not exist. Apparently the composer had in mind here the modern pianoforte and not the old-fashioned harpsichord. The most interesting movement of the concerto is the final *rondo all'ungarese*. It contains two episodes in the minor, the impassioned strength of the second reminding us of nineteenth-century romantic music (see Ex. 15):

EXAMPLE 15   Piano Concerto in D major

[15] Edited by K. Soldau for Peters (Leipzig, 1934).

• • •

Haydn's symphonies of the eighties use the same guiding principles of construction as his string quartets and also show the increasing influence of Mozart's compositions. Haydn renounced the contrapuntal constructions so important during the seventies and replaced them with the free, unconventional polyphony evolved from the principle of thematic elaboration, using motives taken from the main melodies to weave a rich thematic texture of accompanying voices.

The finale of the Symphony No. 73, "La Chasse"—the famous hunting movement making extensive use not only of horns and oboes, but also of trumpets and timpani—was written in 1780 as a prelude to Haydn's opera *La fedeltà premiata*. To make this piece available to a larger audience, in the following year the composer added three movements, one of which, an andante in G major, is also connected with a vocal work, as it appears in condensed form in the song "Gegenliebe," likewise written in 1781.[16] The other two movements are independent pieces, and the opening allegro in particular displays in its harmonic language and structure a brilliance and technical mastery heralding the beginning of Haydn's maturity.

Number 74, composed at about the same time, is one of the earliest symphonic works to show the influence of Mozart. The opening movement (which is also distinguished by an exceptional development section) has a subsidiary subject in clear contrast to the first theme, and likewise the main idea of the second movement has all the ingratiating qualities of Mozart's melodies.

Number 75, written in 1779, affords a delightful contrast between a set of melancholy variations on a songlike theme and an extremely cheerful minuet and finale. The work was performed by Haydn in England, and the composer noted in his diary that an English clergyman thought that he heard the prediction of his imminent death in the slow movement, and actually died shortly afterward.

The symphonies Nos. 76–78 were composed in 1782. Haydn sent them to Forster in London, who published them in 1784. No. 76 has a more conventional first movement, but it also contains a fine slow movement whose dark sections in the minor mode foreshadow trends in romantic music. The middle section in the first movement of No. 77 has a kind of *stretto maestrale*, a short-

16 Edited by P. Mies in *JHW*, XXIX/1, p. 20.

EXAMPLE 16    Symphony No. 77

range imitation of the first bar of the main subject in which all the string and woodwind instruments join (Ex. 16):

Number 78 starts in C minor, seemingly reviving the passionate spirit of the seventies. However, a lighter, more playful mood gradually takes root, and even the last movement in C minor contains a merry C major section.

The symphonies Nos. 79–81 were written in the years 1783 and 1784. The first work of this group does not seem quite equal in importance to the other two. From a purely formal point of view, however, the first movement deserves special attention, as it resumes the work of development even in the recapitulation. In No. 80 in D minor the stylistic elements are not yet fully blended, but rather presented in close juxtaposition.[17] The dark and dramatic beginning of the initial *allegro spiritoso* might have been remembered by Mozart, when he started to write his tempestuous Piano Concerto in D minor (K. 466) in February 1785. In Haydn's movement it does not take long, however, before a complete change of atmosphere can be observed. At the end of the exposition an amusing waltzlike theme is introduced, a carefree idea which also dominates the following development section. The following adagio is among the most exquisite slow movements Haydn wrote in these years. In particular the second subject with its broad cantilena, supported by fast-moving strings, is deeply stirring. The concluding presto in D major is full of exuberant gaiety. Among the humorous pieces the composer liked to offer in his finales, this piece deserves a place of honor.

The ambivalent character of No. 80 is missing in No. 81 in G major. The initial vivace is a cheerful and energetic composition which displays some of the features of an overture to a comic opera. When Haydn wrote the gaily skipping third subject, he may have recalled a comical duet from his own opera *Orlando paladino* of 1782, a number that was to thrill London audiences in later years. Similarly, in the minuet a group of peasant musicians seems to present the Austrian country dance, the *Ländler*. They are by no means dismayed when a wrong note slips in and cheerfully repeat the same mistake.

The symphonies Nos. 82–92 were composed between 1785 and 1788, largely for performances and publishers in Paris.[18] In 1784 the board of directors of the Concerts de la Loge Olympique asked Haydn to compose six symphonies for them, which he did during the two following years. These works (Nos. 82–87) are usually referred to as the Paris symphonies.

Number 82, the so-called "First Paris" symphony, was, according to the testimonial of the autograph, written in 1786, one year after the Paris symphonies No. 2 and No. 6. It is affectionately known as "L'Ours" (The Bear) on account of the peculiar character of its finale. Here a growling bear seems to be portrayed by repeated low-pitched notes, each preceded by a brief grace note. The

[17] In our discussions of Symphonies Nos. 80–91 we refer to our own jacket notes to the recordings of these symphonies played by the Vienna Chamber Orchestra under the direction of Ernst Maerzendorfer and published by The Musical Heritage Society, Inc. (New York).

[18] These eleven symphonies were edited by H. C. Robbins Landon in volumes I/9 and I/10 of the Haydn Society Edition before he edited all the symphonies for Doblinger and Universal Edition (cf. p. 196).

beast is in a good mood and not averse to showing off its dancing skill. In no time merriment proves to be contagious, and the bystanders join in the fun. The grunting of cellos and double basses turns into the squealing of oboes and violins. A general dance evolves whose driving force seems to foreshadow the finale of Beethoven's Seventh Symphony. The first movement too is an energetic, zestful piece with a joyful emphasis on harsh dissonances. The thematic development is here so abundant that even the transition from the first to the second subject is imbued with it. The following allegretto is a typical representative of the *style galant*. Haydn presents three times a captivating tune that shows features of the old French *gavotte*. A Gallic flavor is also apparent in the minuet. We do not witness the merrymaking of Austrian peasants, but rather an entertainment at the court of Louis XVI. The predilection for the use of wind instruments, apparent throughout the French set, is particularly noticeable in this movement. There are delightful oboe solos in the minuet, and the trio offers an episode in which the wind instruments are on their own while the strings drop out.

Number 83, the second of the Paris symphonies, got its name "La Poule" (The Hen) from the subsidiary subject of the first movement, in which the oboe peevishly repeats the same note while the first violin offers a piquant melody adorned with many grace notes. On the whole, however, this movement in G minor shows a surprisingly serious character; the dramatic quality of the following andante is equally unusual. A stubborn minuet and a charming finale in the style of a siciliano contribute a peculiar charm to this work.

Number 84, the third of the Paris symphonies, has a first movement that almost completely grows out of the main idea. Haydn postpones the entrance of the contrasting subject so long that it assumes the role of an epilogue rather than a subsidiary subject. The second movement, an andante with variations, separates the theme in the major from its first variation by a rather dramatic passage in the minor. The finale is merry and carefree; its sudden changes from the pianissimo of a few instruments to the forte of the whole orchestra anticipate the famous "surprise" of Symphony No. 94.

Symphony No. 85, the fourth of the Paris symphonies, is known as "La Reine" (The Queen), as Marie Antoinette is said to have voiced her predilection for this work. The composition starts with a stately adagio using the dotted rhythm characteristic of the early French operatic overture. Here Haydn anticipates the rocketlike ascending runs that play an important part in the movement's main section. The turbulent second subject surprisingly appears in the minor mode. It sounds like a quotation from the beginning of Haydn's "Farewell" Symphony written more than a dozen years earlier. Possibly the composer meant to refer to this very unusual work which had been printed in Paris one year before the performance of "La Reine." The second movement is entitled *Romanze*. This is a set of four variations on the popular French song "La gentille et jeune Lisette," presenting a dainty and charming rococo canvas in the style of Watteau and Lancret.

The autograph of Symphony No. 86, the fifth of the Paris symphonies, bears the date 1786 in the composer's own hand. Various sketches for this work have been preserved, showing that the symphony's apparent lightness and brilliance were the result of protracted work. The formal construction becomes more and more artistic, but Haydn does not fail to counterbalance it occasionally with movements of a looser structure. The symphony's slow movement shows an affinity with both the sonata and the rondo forms, but without adopting either. Haydn called this surprisingly serious movement *Capriccio*. The final *Allegro con spirito* once more furnishes evidence that Italian *opera buffa* made its contribution to the classical symphony. A musical comedy with its flirtatious girl, its miserly old bachelor, and hilarious disguises seems to come to life in this amusing piece.

Number 87, known as the sixth of the Paris symphonies, was actually composed in 1785, thus before the first, third, and fifth works of the set. Here again the middle movements are particularly attractive. The tender and moving adagio appears like a concerto for wind instruments accompanied by the string players. Flute, oboes, and bassoon are entrusted with delightful solos, and even opportunities for unaccompanied cadenzas are provided. The final vivace achieves effects of dramatic vigor through the use of contrapuntal devices. The composer is so engrossed in his exacting task that he even extends the development at the expense of a complete recapitulation of the first section.

The symphonies Nos. 88 and 89, which were probably both written in 1787, were likewise intended for Paris. Haydn gave them to Johann Tost, together with the quartets Op. 54 and 55 (cf. p. 288), before the violinist left for France. They were eventually sold to the publisher Sieber, who printed the parts in 1789.

The G major Symphony No. 88 is one of the most important orchestral compositions Haydn had written up to that time. The composer's superb artistry is evident in the structure of the initial allegro. The main subject is joined by a counterpoint in its first forte entrance, and this counterpoint also appears in the transition to the second subject. Moreover, the subsidiary subject is so completely embedded in material taken from the main theme that the listener hardly notices the break in the homogeneous structure of the movement. In the following movement, a solemn largo with variations, a climax is achieved by the unexpected fortissimo entrance of trumpets and drums (here prescribed for the very first time in the whole symphony!). On the other hand, characteristic of Haydn's newly acquired unconventional treatment of instruments, is the use of horns and timpani in the minuet. In the composer's early works, such instruments were employed as the typical reinforcements of the tutti; now, however, he presents them also in mysterious piano as an accompaniment of the main subject. Then, in the trio, Haydn prescribes forte assai for the bassoons while the other voices have to play piano.

Contrary to the magnificent No. 88, the following F major Symphony No. 89 is a work of lesser significance. Haydn used for the second and fourth movements material from the fifth concerto for lire organizzate (cf. p. 292), while the newly composed first and third movements are treated in a somewhat perfunctory manner. Nevertheless, here too attractive details are not lacking. Thus, for instance, the orchestration of the trio in the minuet is particularly attractive. The traditional Austrian *Ländler* is first played by woodwind and violins in octaves. The flute and first oboe gain the upper hand until the first violin forces its way back into the game. Supported by bassoon and flute in the lower and upper octave, respectively, it celebrates a triumphant return. The final *Vivace assai* displays a rather uncomplicated rondo form. An unusual instruction for the performers is here to be found. At the return of the main theme, Haydn prescribes *trascinando* (dragging) to assure that the musicians achieve the proper suspense before the entrance of the victorious protagonist.

In 1788–89 Haydn wrote three symphonies (Nos. 90–92) that were probably commissioned by the Comte d'Ogny, a young French nobleman who had also been instrumental in producing the Paris symphonies. Orchestral parts of the same works were sold by the composer in the following years to the Bavarian Prince Krafft Ernst of Öttingen-Wallerstein.

Number 90 again proclaims the achievements of Haydn's maturity. Its andante uses variations on a theme in the major and one in the parallel minor, a form that became increasingly interesting to

Haydn at that time. In the last movement, an episode near the end is remarkable. A blustering fortissimo of the full orchestra in C major is followed after a pause of four full measures by a timid pianissimo of the strings and a single bassoon in D-flat major (a similar device is also used in the slow movement of the "Razor" Quartet). Frightened voices are raised from all sides, until laughter and loud shouts of the full company announce the happy ending of the hilarious game.

In No. 91 the main theme of the first movement's *allegro assai* rises rather laboriously with the help of chromatic progressions. This idea is conceived in double counterpoint. As soon as its eight measures have been sounded, Haydn lets the theme, so to speak, stand on its head by entrusting the former melody to the basses, while the original bass accompaniment is used as the new melody. Likewise the construction of the finale deserves special attention. It assumes regular sonata form with a main and a contrasting subsidiary theme. However, the second theme is not used in the development section, and even the impudent grace notes of the first theme quickly recede into the background. The principle of unification is here applied in modified form. Haydn seems to have thought very highly of this symphony, for in his letters from London to Frau von Genzinger he again and again asked his friend to send him the score from Vienna.

The Oxford Symphony, No. 92, will be discussed in the next chapter, together with the London symphonies, for it is related to them in both style and content.

•   •   •

Hardly any other of Haydn's works has so interesting a history as *The Seven Last Words of Our Saviour on the Cross* (Hob. XX:1), composed in 1786.[19] In the preceding year the composer had received the invitation to write an instrumental composition based on *The Seven Last Words*, to be performed in Cádiz during Lent. He accordingly wrote, as he explained in a letter dated April 8, 1787, to the English publisher William Forster, a "work consisting merely of instrumental music, divided into seven sonatas, each lasting from seven to eight minutes, as well as an introduction and ultimately a *terremoto* or earthquake. These sonatas," he added, "are so conceived as to fit the words Christ Our Saviour uttered on the cross. . . . The whole work requires a little over an hour, but after each

[19]Critical edition presented by Hubert Unverricht in *JHW*, IV.

sonata there is a pause to ponder the ensuing text in advance."
Haydn's orchestra consisted of two flutes, two oboes, two bassoons, four horns, two trumpets, two timpani, and strings. The
parts for this version were published in 1787 by Artaria, Vienna. In
the same year an arrangement of the work appeared for string
quartet. This was made by the composer, who also revised a transcription of *The Seven Last Words* for piano.

As we stated earlier (cf. p. 83), Haydn himself said of this
work:[20] "It was no easy matter to compose seven adagios lasting
nearly ten minutes each and following one after the other without
fatiguing the listener." The warm reception given everywhere to
*The Seven Last Words* proved that he had succeeded completely in
this task. This is all the more admirable as throughout the work
Haydn employs a homophonic idiom and makes hardly any use of
the thematic elaboration. He wished to keep his composition read-
ily understandable in order to be sure of the effect "from the heart
to the heart" that he was most eager to achieve. Just this economy
of style enabled Haydn to rouse the listener's emotions. A *maestoso
ed adagio* in a single movement serves as an introduction. With its
baroque dotted rhythms, frequent changes between forte and piano,
and repeated sforzandi, this brief piece in D minor unfolds a dramatic, deeply moving picture of the crucifixion. Haydn is not satisfied, however, merely to describe suffering and torment. In the
middle section and in the coda, ending pianissimo, Jesus' divine
mercy and love are expressed. The second "sonata," based on the
words "Verily I say unto thee, today shalt thou be with me in paradise," is developed entirely out of a single idea.[21] It appears timidly
at first in the key of C minor, as if the poor malefactor did not dare
to believe in his own good fortune. Gradually, however, the knowledge of God's mercy enters the heart of the tormented man; the
main idea is now transposed to E-flat major as a noble cantilena full
of sweet happiness. In the development section the shadows of
death seem to obscure the mind of the dying man, but the return of
the cantilena, this time in C major, again conjures up all the wonders of paradise. The art of developing, as it were, out of a single
germ cell ideas of wholly different emotional substance shows that

[20] In the preface to the oratorio version published by Breitkopf and Härtel (Leipzig,
1801).
[21] The main themes of each sonata fit the Latin translation of the respective "word" of
Christ. According to Haydn's wish, expressed in a letter to Artaria, these Latin
"words" were also printed in some of the instrumental parts at the beginning of the
sonatas.

this work is a product of Haydn's maturity. The third "sonata" is based on the words "Woman, behold thy son!" and "Behold thy mother!" Jesus brings his beloved disciple and his mother together. Accordingly, the beginning of the piece is imbued with beauty and love, but at the same time the drama of Golgotha is not forgotten, and the subsidiary theme that grows out of the main idea leads us to its anguish and suffering. The original motive, played here by the basses, now seems like a nightmare. It is of interest that No. 5, "I thirst," is based on the same motive as No. 3. Here Haydn resumed the idea originally used to describe the love of a mother for her son. In his agony the Saviour becomes a child again, asking his mother for help. This can also explain the idyllic character of No. 5. Later, however, when vinegar mingled with gall is given to Jesus, the distress of extreme misery breaks through with elemental force.

In his *The Seven Last Words*, Haydn successfully avoids the danger of monotony presented by the text. From the stirring introduction to the forceful earthquake, new musical pictures are presented again and again, illustrating not only the drama of the Passion but also the miracle of salvation that grows out of the sacrifice on the cross.

The vocal version of *The Seven Last Words* made by Haydn in the 1790s will be discussed in the next chapter.

•  •  •

For composers in the classical time the song did not have the importance that was attributed to it in the romantic period. To Haydn, Mozart, and even Beethoven it was a form of relatively little consequence, too unimportant to be given much attention. It is well known that in spite of this attitude a few real masterworks were created; but the courage of Schubert, who had a single song ("The Erlking") printed as his Op. 1, was inconceivable in the eighteenth century. Only in his maturity did Haydn become interested in the song. His first collection of twelve Lieder was published in 1781, a second set in 1784, both through Artaria and Company in Vienna.[22] These Lieder clearly show their derivation from the rhythmically and harmonically simple songs of the German Singspiel (a type of opera using simple melodies of folk-song character and spoken dialogue). Italian influences may be found in the graceful melodic lines; the mastery of instrumental composition is revealed in important preludes, interludes, and postludes. In the

[22] Haydn's collected songs were edited by P. Mies for *JHW*, XXIX/1.

selection of texts, Haydn was helped by his friend Hofrat Franz S. Greiner. Nevertheless, or perhaps because of such help, their poetical value is often doubtful.

In a letter to Artaria dated July 20, 1781, Haydn pointed out that three of his songs had previously been set to music by the Viennese kapellmeister, Leopold Hoffmann, and added: "Just because this braggart thinks he has swallowed Mount Parnassus and at every opportunity tries to belittle me in the eyes of certain circles of society, I have composed these same three songs to show these circles the difference—*sed hoc inter nos.*" In the same letter he says: "I particularly request you not to allow anyone to copy or sing these songs at present or spoil them in any way whatever, for when they are finished I intend to sing them myself to critical audiences. A composer must maintain his rights by his presence and by the proper execution of his works. They are indeed merely songs but not 'street songs' like those of Hoffmann, devoid of ideas, of expression, and, above all, of melody."

The twenty-four songs are printed on two staves only. A separate line for the voice is not necessary, as its melody is identical with that of the top line of the piano part. Haydn frequently used the form of the strophic song (stanza form). The influence of music for the stage is shown in the employment of chromatic progressions, little coloratura phrases, and melodies of a more cantabile character. In the serious or sentimental songs Haydn approaches the character of the aria. "Die Verlassene" (The Deserted Woman, Hob. XXVIa:5), for instance, is filled with the pathos of dramatic grief. If the *opera seria* is godmother here, the charmingly humorous "Lob der Faulheit" (Praise of Laziness, Hob. XXVIa:22) certainly owes much to the *opera buffa.*

•  •  •

During the late seventies and especially during the eighties Haydn wrote a sizable number of arias to be inserted, according to the custom of the period, into the operas of other composers. Haydn arranged the works he performed at Eszterháza according to the prevailing conditions, the abilities of the singers, the taste of the audience and the technical possibilities of the theatre.[23] As his interest in the composition of complete operas gradually subsided, these short pieces composed during Haydn's maturity are of great interest

[23] Cf. p. 77f. and Dénes Bartha and László Somfai, *Haydn als Opernkapellmeister* (Budapest, 1960).

to the Haydn student.[24] Gay and light is the bass aria "Dice benissimo" (Hob. XXIVb:5), written in 1780 for Salieri's *Scuola de' gelosi*, in which men are warned against the fetters of matrimony. Its counterpart is formed by the graceful soprano aria of 1785(?), "Dica pure" (Hob. XXIVb:8), destined for Anfossi's *Il geloso in cimento*, in which women's qualities are extolled and men's evil nature condemned. Somewhat similar are the soprano aria of Giannina, "La moglie quando e buona," composed in 1790 for Cimarosa's *Giannina e Bernardone*, in which the perils of jealousy are pointed out, and the soprano aria of Donna Stella, "D'una sposa meschinella," composed in 1777 for Paisiello's *La frascatana*. This latter starts with a tender, fervent adagio featuring an oboe solo and a pizzicato accompaniment by the basses and rises to a brilliantly virtuoso presto section. A delightfully graceful and whimsical soprano aria, "Son pietosa, son bonina," was provided by Haydn for the pasticcio *La Circe, ossia l'isola incantata*, which he performed in 1789, also using material from two other operas (*Ipocondriaco* by Naumann and *La Circe*, whose composer has not yet been ascertained). The same pasticcio contains a dramatic scene for Pedrillo (tenor), an extended *accompagnato* recitative in which Haydn displays a number of amusing tone-paintings.

A serious tenor aria, "Ah tu non senti amico" (Hob. XXIVb: 10) was contributed by Haydn in 1786 to Traetta's *Ifigenia in Tauride*. With its dramatic *accompagnato* recitative, which leads to an F minor aria full of pathos, it fits admirably into the grand, tragic opera of the time. Deeply stirring in its outbursts of passionate grief is the soprano aria of Beatrice, "Infelice sventurata," written in 1789 for Cimarosa's *I due supposti conti*.

Several arias are intended for the composer's mistress, the mezzo-soprano Luigia Polzelli. These pieces ("Signor, voi sapete," for Anfossi's *Il matrimonio per inganno*, 1785; "Chi vive amante," for Bianchi's *Alessandro nell'Indie*, 1787; "Il meglio mio carattere," for Cimarosa's *L'impresario in angustie*, 1790; etc.) have a certain affinity in character. Andante seems to be the favorite tempo indication. The arias use simple, tender melodies; they display a gentle, graceful, and somewhat impish nature and avoid excessive technical difficulties. Haydn, while deeply in love with the attractive singer, certainly had no illusions about her technical abilities.

•   •   •

[24]The aria for soprano and orchestra "Chi vive amante" was edited by A. Orel (Leipzig, 1937); fourteen additional arias for soprano and orchestra and the cantata

Similar to the insertion arias, though conceived on a larger scale, are the independent scenes Haydn composed for the concert hall. Only the voice part is left of the solo cantata *Deutschlands Klage auf den Tod Friedrich des Grossen* (Hob. XXVIb:1) for voice and baryton, which Haydn wrote around 1786 for the baryton player Karl Franz, a former member of the Esterházy orchestra. Another solo cantata *Miseri noi, misera patria* (Hob. XXIVa:7), for soprano and orchestra, which may have originated around 1790, apparently was taken by Haydn to England. This is a heroic work with a brilliant and rather difficult solo part consisting of an extensive orchestral recitative and an aria abounding in virtuoso coloratura.

Haydn was particularly successful with the Italian cantata *Arianna a Naxos* (Hob. XXVIb:2), for mezzo-soprano with piano accompaniment, which he composed in 1789. The aria, in which Haydn challenges comparison with no less a composer than Claudio Monteverdi, was a favorite of the master. He called it his "dear Arianna" and accompanied it personally at a most successful London performance (one of the two recitals in which he appeared as pianist in the English capital). Although the work has only a piano accompaniment, this part seems like the reduction of an orchestral score, and the various instrumentations that have been made of the cantata certainly are defensible. The relation to the opera genre is also quite obvious here. As in a dramatic scene by Gluck, not the aria but the recitative forms the main part of the piece, and this recitative not only precedes, but also interrupts, the aria. The music is completely dependent on the dramatic spirit of the text. *Arianna a Naxos* is enriched by many striking passages, such as the interlude before the denouement, with its chromatic progressions describing Ariadne's climbing up the rock and at the same time her utter despair.

•  •  •

Only two complete works for the stage were written by Haydn during his fourth period of composition. His "drama eroicomico" *Orlando paladino* (Hob. XXVIII:11) was performed in 1782.[25] The

*Miseri noi* were edited by H. C. Robbins Landon for Haydn-Mozart Presse (Vienna, 1959–1961); the scena of Pedrillo for tenor and orchestra by D. Bartha and L. Somfai as a supplement to their work *Haydn als Opernkapellmeister*.

[25] A critically revised score of the opera presented by Karl Geiringer is published in *JHW*, XXV/11, vols. 1 and 2, a piano score of the work, likewise revised by Karl Geiringer is published by Bärenreiter Verlag (Kassel, 1982).

libretto was written by Nunziato Porta, who stood as librettist and stage director in the service of Prince Esterházy.

The subject of *Orlando paladino* has been repeatedly treated before. Bojardo wrote his *Orlando inamorato* in 1495; Ariosto his *Orlando furioso* from 1516 to 1532. Handel, who composed an *Orlando* in 1733, considered the subject as completely serious. However, Lope de Vega had already written various comedies on this topic, and Guglielmi's *Le pazzie d'Orlando* of 1771 is partly humorous. Haydn too conceived his work as an opera in the mixed genre, and this last of his partly serious and partly comical operas was also extremely successful. At Eszterháza it was performed thirty times during the seasons from 1782 to 1784. During the composer's lifetime, thirty-three opera houses in Germany and Austria—among them those at Prague, Budapest, Frankfurt, Cologne, Nuremberg, Berlin, Bremen, Leipzig, Munich, Königsberg, Hamburg, Breslau, and Dresden—performed it; no other stage work by Haydn was so frequently produced. The composition's music combines Italian operatic elements with the spirit of Austrian folk music. It abounds in melodious and brilliant arias, highly dramatic orchestral recitatives, effectively constructed finales which reach a climax in the *coro* of the third act, a charming dance piece, of which Haydn himself was so fond that he used it again in his last opera. Above all, the treatment of the individual characters and the emphasis on comical elements were responsible for the opera's very friendly reception. The exaggerated outbursts of savagery from Rodomonte, King of the Barbarians, whom H. Wirth rightly describes as a "saber-rattling bumpkin squire,"[26] the crazy passion of Orlando, who attempts to impose his love on a completely unresponsive Angelica, the pitiful weakness of the flute-playing swain Medoro, and the magic tricks of the sorceress Alcina—all these portrayals are made with unfailing dramatic skill. Particularly funny is Orlando's servant, Pasquale, a boastful swaggerer rivaling his seventeenth-century brother, Cervantes's Sancho Panza. The charming aria demonstrating the performance practice and musical ornaments of the period, and the cavatina in which Pasquale, on horseback and heralded by trumpets and horns, boasts of his feats of valor, rank among the best numbers that the comic opera of the eighteenth century produced.

It seems unlikely that Mozart or his librettist knew Haydn's

[26] Cf. *Orlando paladino*, analytical notes to the Haydn Society recording of *Orfeo ed Euridice* (Boston, 1951), p. 38.

*Orlando paladino.* Nevertheless there appears a certain affinity in the musical characterization of Haydn's Medoro and Mozart's Don Ottavio. Similarly, Angelica impresses us almost as a sister to Donna Anna, and Pasquale's personality seems to herald the character of Leporello. In particular an aria in which Orlando's squire boasts of his travels all over the world appears to anticipate Leporello's bragging about the amorous conquests of his patron. It is also remarkable that both in *Orlando paladino* and in *Don Giovanni* three serious characters (two female and one male) are balanced by three comic ones (two males and one female). In the middle stand the main heroes of the two works, Orlando and Don Giovanni, who appear as equally tragic and funny. Evidently these masterworks by Haydn and Mozart grew out of the same artistic soil.[27]

In 1784 Haydn's "dramma eroico" *Armida* (Hob. XXVIII:12), based on Tasso's *Gerusalemme liberata* was performed at Eszterháza.[28] The composer used in this work one of the most popular opera subjects of his time. Salieri, Anfossi, Sacchini, Jomelli, Handel, and Gluck, to mention only a few composers, had written operas on this or a closely related topic. Haydn's own libretto seems to have been compiled from various sources, possibly by the skillful N. Porta, who had made so important a contribution to *Orlando paladino. Armida* represents a new phase in Haydn's output for the stage. Between 1769 and 1782, he had written no less than seven mixed operas, the last being in many respects the most significant. He felt that he had exhausted the potentialities of this genre, and he turned accordingly to *opera seria*, a genre he had cultivated only in an early work and in one more recent composition where he had labored under specific restrictions. *Armida* displays a completely homogeneous character renouncing all contrasting elements, and thus conforms to the attitude of the mature Haydn, who was increasingly eager to unify his instrumental music. In its dignity and unrelieved seriousness it appears like a secular counterpart to *The Seven Last Words*, written in the following year. *Armida* is an imposing work full of dramatic power, and Prince Nicolaus was greatly impressed by it. *Armida* was performed no less than fifty-four times in Eszterháza, thus more often than any other of Haydn's operas. However, outside the princely domain the reception was consider-

---

[27] Cf. also Karl Geiringer's jacket notes to the beautiful recording of *Orlando paladino* directed by Antal Dorati for the Philips company.
[28] A critically revised edition of the score was presented by W. Pfannkuch in *JHW*, XXV/12.

ably cooler. Only a handful of performances of the complete work took place, since music lovers apparently felt that the score was lacking in some of the greatest assets of Haydn's art: charm, naturalness, simplicity and humor.

Haydn's *Armida* is to some extent influenced by the tenets of Gluck. The older composer said of his overture to Alceste: "My idea was that the overture ought to indicate the subject and prepare the spectators for the character of the piece they are about to see." The same might have been said of the prelude to Haydn's *Armida*. Whereas in the older Italian operas the overture was independent of the work to follow, in this case Haydn has produced a sort of tone poem covering the whole plot of Rinaldo's sinful passion for the lovely sorceress Armida, and his eventual return to duty. In its first four measures, the opening theme of the overture depicts Rinaldo's carefree life of knighthood and in its second half his youthful longing for love.[29] The energetic second subject portrays the hero's attachment to his military duties, but the development of the movement introduces a serious conflict. Abruptly a yearning allegretto is heard, and this corresponds to that part of the opera in which the hero arrives at Armida's paradise. At last Rinaldo breaks away from the arms of the sorceress. The return of the first part of the prelude then reveals the victory of duty over love, and the overture closes with the Rinaldo theme, but without the love motive of its second half. This interesting prelude resembles in its form Mozart's overture to *Die Entführung aus dem Serail*, performed two years before Haydn's *Armida*.

In the opera itself, Haydn unfortunately does not follow Gluck's method to the same extent. The old *recitativo secco* of the Italian opera takes up whole scenes, but the number of ensemble pieces is very small (one duet in the first act, one trio in the second, and a sextet at the end of the opera). The lovely finales of the earlier operas are completely absent. The best numbers of the score are the big solo scenes, such as the aria describing Rinaldo's attempts to escape from the bondage of Armida. The accompanied recitative, in which the orchestra follows each fluctuation of Rinaldo's expression, the aria growing organically out of this recitative, and the final presto bringing the tragic episode to its climax—all these display such strong dramatic vigor that they counterbalance the formal coloratura arias in other parts of the score. Of almost equal importance is the long monologue of despair by the deserted Ar-

[29] The overture was edited for Augener's by H. Gál (London, 1939).

mida; and particularly attractive, in spite of the use of conventional means of expression, is a scene in the third act in which Armida displays her witchcraft.

With *Armida*, Haydn's operatic output reached a crisis. Apparently he felt unable to give of his best in a purely serious work; yet the mixed genre no longer interested him. Thus he may not have regretted too much that his arduous duties made it impossible for him to write more works for the stage at Eszterháza.

• • •

During his fourth period of composition, Haydn wrote only a single Mass, a *Missa Cellensis* (Mass of Mariazell) in C major, composed in 1782.[30] The inscription on the autograph, "Fatta per il Signor Liebe de Kreutzner," gives the name of the person who commissioned the work. C. F. Pohl assumes that Herr Liebe meant the Mass to be played in the famous pilgrims' church of Mariazell in thanksgiving for his elevation to nobility.[31]

In comparison with the first *Missa Cellensis*, written in 1766, this second one shows a completely different character. The earlier work, with its gargantuan proportions, was strongly dependent on older Neapolitan models and as good as unusable for liturgical purposes. The later composition, on the other hand, is reduced to customary size; it mixes in its style traditional and progressive elements, and has developed into one of Haydn's most beloved compositions for the church.

The *Missa Cellensis* shows a decrease in the number of solo arias; on the other hand, Haydn begins to employ the quartet of solo voices that was to become extremely important in the Masses of his last period. The quartet offers the same possibilities for drama and color as do the voices in separate solos, but without their excessive display of virtuosity.

In this work, both elements of a purely musical style and a style inspired by the content of the text are to be found. The Kyrie is given the shape of an instrumental movement in sonata-allegro form, and the Gratias, an aria for soprano, includes some real coloratura. The Resurrexit uses the superficial technique of the earlier *missae breves*, bringing simultaneously in each of its voices a different section of the text, so that while the soprano sings "et resurrexit," the alto has the words "et in spiritum sanctum," the tenor

---

[30] The work was edited by H. C. Robbins Landon, K. H. Füssl, and Christa Landon in *JHW*, XXIII/2.
[31] Carl Ferdinand Pohl, *Joseph Haydn*, (Leipzig, 1875) II, p. 197.

"et iterum venturus," and the bass "qui cum patre." This return to the technique of the *missa brevis* is all the more surprising, as it is applied only to an episode of thirteen measures which, in the prevailing tempo vivace, takes less than half a minute to perform. Haydn's reasons for inserting this strange interlude are even harder to understand, as the telescoped section is immediately preceded by the Crucifixus, one of the most expressive and moving sections of the score. The Benedictus uses an aria originally written for the comic opera *Il mondo della luna*; yet the poignant piece, with its powerful baroque beginning and the effective changes between chorus and solo quartet, by no means disgraces the score. We must not forget that likewise many of the most beautiful numbers in Bach's church music grew out of the transformation of his own secular compositions.

Numerous passages in this Mass show a deep understanding of the true meaning of the text. An excellent example is provided by the aria for tenor, "Et incarnatus est." Beginning in A minor, it modulates to C major at the words "homo factus est" and reaches the melancholy C minor when the catastrophe of the Crucifixus approaches. The climax of the work is fittingly reached in the concluding "Dona nobis pacem," based on a very unusual syncopated theme. It begins quietly in the bass, gradually involving more and more voices, until heaven and earth seem to be filled with the passionate prayer for peace.

The style of this second *Missa Cellensis* is not exactly homogeneous. We gain the impression that Haydn has reached a kind of crisis in this field. Thus he may have even welcomed it when, in 1783, the Emperor Joseph II passed a decree that practically banned the more complicated forms of instrumental music from the church. Haydn accordingly stopped composing Masses, and when he resumed fourteen years later, after most of the confining regulations had been revoked by the Emperor's successors, his style had changed greatly. It seems almost providential that in all fields of Haydn's vocal music a long pause ensued before the composer felt ready to create his last and greatest masterpieces in each genre.

# CHAPTER SIXTEEN

# Consummate Mastery

## THE FIFTH PERIOD
## 1791 – 1803

Haydn reached the summit of his artistic achievements in his fifth period of composition. As kapellmeister for Prince Esterházy he had done outstanding work and attracted the attention of the whole musical world, but after thirty years of life in a remote castle, toiling mostly with the same artists and for the same narrowly restricted audience, he found that Eszterháza was becoming less and less a challenge to his genius. Some of his very best works of the eighties, such as the Paris symphonies and *The Seven Last Words*, were not written for Haydn's Prince. It is therefore not surprising that the composer accepted without a moment's hesitation the invitation to go to London.

The trip provided a complete change of atmosphere: a new landscape, new people with a new culture, a strange language, and the experience of living in the largest city in the world. Of still greater importance was the change in social standing, combined with a change in working conditions. The esteem accorded to Haydn at Eszterháza never allowed him to forget that he was living there as a servant, dependent on every whim of his employer. In England he was free to do what he liked, free to go where he pleased, and responsible to no one but himself. He felt like a man who had escaped from a golden cage. Furthermore Haydn was now in a position to conduct an excellently trained large orchestra and

313

his compositions were to be played to a most exacting and fastidious audience of a size he had seldom encountered.

The effect of these favorable conditions on Haydn's creative output was amazing. Even though he was nearly sixty years old, he started to write compositions surpassing in both accomplishment and daring enterprise anything he had previously attempted. The beautiful balance of the classical style was noticeable in these works, their quality surpassing even that of his best achievements in the eighties. Practically every work of this latest period was a masterpiece, belonging among those compositions for which Haydn is still admired.

Even after Haydn had returned from London to settle down in Vienna, the influence of his English journeys remained alive. He composed more slowly than in any of the earlier periods, often relying on preliminary sketches, and the quality of his creative products was permanently on the highest possible level.

The most remarkable feature of these compositions written in the nineties is that they occasionally present a somewhat problematical and experimental character. They show a definite tendency toward trying out new devices, even at the sacrifice of the poise of former years. Fundamentally, Haydn remained a classical composer, but again and again episodes are to be found in his music in which expressiveness and passionate feeling break through classical composure. Under the influence of the new experience of freedom, Haydn's musical style lost some of its former restraint. He seemed to revive characteristic features of his *Sturm und Drang* period. But we shall be nearer the truth if we consider the little irregularities in his later music to be the first indications of a movement that was shortly to exercise a profound influence over the whole artistic world: romanticism.

It is significant that at the age of sixty-three Haydn, in his love for experiments, abandoned the symphony, which had brought him such overwhelming success, in order to devote his powers to vocal composition. And it is of symbolic importance that his first great achievement of this sort, *The Creation*, begins with a piece that in its whole conception unmistakably heralds the great romantic revolution of the future.

• • •

Only three sonatas for the pianoforte (Hob. XVI:50–52) were written during Haydn's fifth period of composition. All three were probably composed in 1794–95 for the English pianist Theresa Jan-sen, who married Gaetano Bartolozzi, son of the famous engraver Francesco Bartolozzi, in May 1795. (Haydn was one of the witnesses at the wedding.) According to Strunk, the Sonata in E flat major (No. 52) is the first of the set, No. 51 in D major the second, and No. 50 in C major the third, the last composition written by Haydn for the piano alone.[1] While No. 49, the sonata composed for Marianne von Genzinger, displays the full maturity of the classical style, these last works aim to employ a more personal and expressive musical language. No. 52 uses in its first movement all the devices of Philipp Emanuel Bach's style. At the same time the second movement, an adagio in the unexpected key of E major, introduces ornaments that may almost be compared to those of Chopin. The loose construction in the first movement of No. 51 and its charming second subject presage Schubert; the powerful energy and mysterious character disclosed in the first movement of No. 50 occasionally foreshadow Beethoven (Ex. 17):

EXAMPLE 17    Piano Sonata No. 50

This is no longer music intended for the weak little square pianos popular in Vienna at that time. Apparently Haydn had a powerful grand instrument in mind, with a range up to $a^3$ (a note used in the finale of No. 50, but not in any other of his keyboard compositions). The last traces of music written for technically inept amateurs have disappeared from this music. The three sonatas are intended for an accomplished performer, which Mrs. Bartolozzi apparently was. They make a valuable contribution to the development of piano composition around the turn of the century.

Among the smaller compositions for piano, the Variations in F minor (Hob. XVII:6), composed in 1793 and published in 1799, are of special importance. They belong to the type of variations with two themes in which Haydn proved particularly successful. The main theme is in the style of a funeral march and is followed by a trio in the major mode. Both are varied twice, and a most imaginative

[1] William Oliver Strunk, "Notes on a Haydn Autograph," *Musical Quarterly*, XX/2 (Apr. 1934), p. 192–205.

coda ends the composition. The harmonic and coloristic idiom of this magnificent work anticipates certain aspects of the romantic style. Landon may be justified in assuming that the tragic composition originated under the impact of Marianne von Genzinger's sudden death.[2]

• • •

Haydn's compositions for musical clocks are related to his smaller works for the piano. Pater Primitivus Niemecz, Prince Esterházy's librarian, was an expert in constructing tiny organs equipped with flute pipes and played mechanically. So great was his reputation that the clocks provided with his organs were exported even to England. We know he constructed a clock for Prince Liechtenstein in 1792 and another the following year for Prince Esterházy; he probably made a third clock, which originated around 1789.[3] All three instruments have a light, gay, very clear tone; their repertoire consists mainly of music by Niemecz's friend and teacher, Joseph Haydn. E. F. Schmid, who edited these pieces for the first time,[4] has compiled thirty-two compositions, partly from autographs of Haydn and old manuscripts, partly from notes written down while the tunes were played by the instruments. He adapted them for the piano by making slight alterations and thus presented some short and unpretentious though very attractive pieces.

The sixteen numbers played by the clock made in 1789 (Hob. XIX: 1–16) contain an aria from Haydn's *Il mondo della luna* (No. 1), one piece with a charming middle part in F minor, *all'ungarese* (No. 2), a Russian dance (No. 4), and a fuga (No. 16), whose pseudo-erudition sounds particularly amusing on the toylike instrument. The Russian dance is based on a composition by the violinist Giornovichi; this same piece was later used by Beethoven as a theme for his twelve variations in A major. Owing to the character of its accompaniment, the composition was nicknamed "The Bagpipe" by the clock's original owners. Similarly, No. 8 was named "The Call of the Quail," No. 6 "Gossip at the Coffee Table."

The 1792 clock, with its sweet, weak tone, plays twelve pieces, one each hour. Twelve numbers also form the repertoire of the 1793 clock, which Haydn gave to Prince Esterházy before leaving on his

---

[2]H. C. Robbins Landon, *The Symphonies of Joseph Haydn* (London, 1955), p. 559.
[3]Cf. Renate Federhofer-Königs, "Der Haydn-Kongress in Bratislava," *Die Musikforschung*, XIII (1960), p. 63.
[4]Nagel's *Musikarchiv* (Hanover [now Kassel], 1931 and 1954). Cf. also Ernst Fritz Schmid, "Joseph Haydn und die Flötenuhr," *Zeitschrift für Musikwissenschaft*, XIV/4 (Jan. 1932).

second trip to England. Of the twenty-four numbers performed by the two instruments, ten (Hob. XIX:7–16) also appear on the 1789 clock. The remaining fourteen numbers belong partly to the eighties, partly to the nineties. No. 20 shows a certain relationship to the trio of the minuet from Symphony No. 85, "La Reine." Number 25, a March in D major, is also in the repertoire of a musical clock constructed in the beginning of the nineteenth century. This instrument plays it after a grenadier march by Beethoven, a fact responsible for the erroneous attribution of the D major March to the younger composer. No. 28 is a simplified version of the finale of the String Quartet Op. 71, No. 2 (composed in 1793). Number 29 is a minuet that was used the following year in Symphony No. 101 ("The Clock"), and No. 30 is a sort of piano arrangement of the *perpetuum mobile* from the Quartet Op. 64, No. 5 (composed in 1790). Two pieces (Nos. 31 and 32) are preserved in Haydn's original manuscript, but none of the clocks known so far plays them. Number 32 is a sketch for the finale of Symphony No. 99 of 1793. All together, these tiny pieces, in spite of their unassuming garb, are not entirely lacking in importance. They point to Beethoven's bagatelles, Schubert's *moments musicaux*, and all those short pianoforte pieces that were instrumental in building up nineteenth-century keyboard music.

●   ●   ●

Although a fair number of violin sonatas by Haydn have appeared in print, not many music lovers avail themselves of this opportunity, since the part of the violinist is of too little interest for the performer. The bowed instrument moves in unison or in thirds with the upper part of the piano score; it accompanies or performs little imitations, but even when short melodic fragments are entrusted to it, they may be omitted without really endangering the effect of the composition. No true cooperation between the two instruments is attempted, as the violin part is always considered *ad libitum*, and it seems quite likely that not one of the so-called violin sonatas was originally conceived for this combination.[5] Haydn may not even have taken part in the transcription. In the well-known collection of eight violin sonatas published by Peters, Nos. 2–4 are ordinary piano sonatas (Hob. XVI:24–26), to which Burney added a violin part.[6] Likewise, No. 5 is a transcription of the Piano Sonata

[5] See Hoboken, I, p. 727.
[6] This scholar manufactured violin parts to no less than eighteen of Haydn's piano sonatas (Hob., XVI:20–32, 35–39).

No. 43, No. 6 an arrangement of the Piano Sonata No. 15, which in turn is based on the Divertimento in C major for strings, flute, and oboe (Hob. II:11). The original was more extensive than the arrangement, and in an apparent reflection of the ideas Haydn eventually developed of matrimony, the latter version eliminates the andante *Mann und Weib*, which was supposed to describe the harmonious cooperation of husband and wife (cf. p. 215). The Violin Sonatas Nos. 7 and 8 are arrangements of the String Quartets Op. 77, Nos. 1 and 2, eliminating in each case the minuet and trio of the original composition. The only violin sonata independent of piano sonatas and string quartets therefore seems to be No. 1 of the Peters edition, an unpretentious piece in two movements. And even with this work it seems quite likely that it was originally conceived as a trio for piano, violin, and cello (Hob. XV:32). In spite of attractive episodes to be found in almost any of the eight compositions, this type of violin sonata, in which the bowed instrument always serves and accompanies the keyboard instrument, is of only historical interest today. As long as merely weak and fragile pianos were built, with tonal volumes hardly equaling those of the violins, such an arrangement was well designed, but with the arrival of heavier and stronger pianofortes, violin sonatas were developed that gave full equality to the two instruments. It is noteworthy that Mozart's later sonatas for violin and piano already displayed such a progressive attitude.

•  •  •

The closest Haydn came to writing violin sonatas was in his clavier trios, or, as they were called at that time, the "sonatas for pianoforte with the accompaniment of a violin and violoncello." Since the cello part served mainly as a reinforcement of the keyboard's bass, the leading piano part and the subservient violin part offered in reality a sort of duet.

Between 1792 and 1796 Haydn wrote, mostly for English publishers, fifteen trios (Hob. XV:18–32). Following the style prevalent in Britain at that time, the composer kept the violin part of these pieces rather simple, while the keyboard part was apparently meant for amateurs of greater technical abilities. The trios of the nineties are often larger compositions than the earlier ones, and their contents are of greater importance. The wealth of modulations in these last trios is remarkable. In the first movement of No. 26, in F-sharp minor, the development, with the help of enharmonic changes, reaches the key of E-flat minor; gently sliding passages of the kind used by Mozart lead back to the tonic. In a similar way, the first movement of No. 28, in E major, introduces in the development a section in A-flat major. Such well-planned modulations are symptomatic of the importance that the piano trio now assumed for Haydn. Characteristic pieces, such as the lovely theme and variations in the first movement of No. 25, in G major, the simple and fervent prayer in E major of its second movement, and the high-spirited *rondo all'ungarese* of the finale would hardly have been written by the earlier Haydn in the form of a piano trio. Remarkable also is the middle movement of No. 28. Its unrelenting ground bass in eighth notes, on which the whole piece is based, makes it appear as a sort of passacaglia, reminding us of Johann Sebastian Bach, whose works Haydn heard in Baron van Swieten's home. The finale of Haydn's Trio No. 30 of 1795, a presto with some traits of Beethoven's scherzos, abandons completely the old idea of the piano sonata accompanied by violin and violoncello. Here the parts of the two bowed instruments are organically linked together while the accompanying clavier supports their melody (Ex. 18). A new type of piano trio in which all three members share

EXAMPLE 18   Piano Trio No. 30, Finale

responsibility is breaking through, a type that was to gain increasing importance in the future.

The so-called London trios (Hob. IV : 1–4) were written in 1794 for two aristocratic flute lovers among Haydn's English friends (cf. p. 142). They are scored for an unusual combination of two flutes and violoncello, and consist of nine movements altogether, partly in C and partly in G major, whose definite arrangement is not quite certain.[7] Haydn may not have spent much time on the composition of these attractive miniatures; nevertheless, one andante exists in two versions, a sign of the greater care the composer bestowed in this period even on compositions of lesser consequence.

* * *

Haydn produced fifteen string quartets during his last period of composition; among them are some of the greatest works he has given to this form. According to the autographs, Haydn composed six string quartets in 1793. They were printed as Op. 71, Nos. 1–3, and Op. 74, Nos. 1–3 (Hob. III:69–74), and were dedicated to Count Apponyi. Haydn wrote them at a time when he was strongly interested in orchestral composition, and they accordingly display a certain symphonic character. An innovation in these quartets is the use of introductions to the first movements, a feature so important in Haydn's symphonies. In Op. 71, Nos. 1 and 3, and Op. 74, No. 1, this introduction consists only of chords of the full ensemble; in Op. 71, No. 2, however, it is a real adagio of four bars. In Op. 74, Nos. 2 and 3, the preliminary sections are unison passages of eight measures, of great significance in the following movement. Particularly in Op. 74, No. 3, the connection between introduction and exposition is so intimate that the listener is surprised when he finds the main idea, and not the unison of the introduction, which he had been led to expect, at the beginning of the recapitulation. In the first movement of Op. 71, No. 2, the defiant downward octave leaps given to all four instruments are completely alien to the intimacy of chamber music and approach the realm of symphonic composition. The first violin introduces whirling passages in sixteenths, and the other instruments come in gradually to carry the melody to a climax. When, at the end, the violoncello joins the general uproar, one feels that a contrabass should accompany in the lower octave in order to give the necessary foundation to this im-

---

[7] The trios were first edited by L. Balet for Nagel (Hanover, 1931).

posing structure. In the first movement of Op. 71, No. 3, the viola part goes below the violoncello part (measures 21–23 of the development), thus causing undesired six-four chords. While writing this passage, Haydn may have been under the illusion that contra-basses doubling the violoncello part in the lower octave would take care of the situation.

The dawn of romanticism is noticeable in the string quartets of Op. 74. Haydn resumes his experiments with the sonata form, and the first and last movements of No. 1 contain development work in the recapitulation. The A major trio of its minuet in C major introduces a softly rocking melody with roots in Austrian folk songs and contains passages that make us think of Schubert. The lovely Quartet No. 2 goes even further in the key relations between its minuet and trio. Here the former is in F major and the latter stands a major third lower, in D-flat major. This daring combination certainly would not have been attempted by the younger Haydn. In the first movement of the "Rider" Quartet, No. 3, the main subject following the powerful introduction is of less significance than the subsidiary idea accompanied by the triplets of the transitional section. Innumerable romantic compositions of the nineteenth century show this phenomenon, assigning more importance to the second subject than to the first (cf. Schubert's "Unfinished" Symphony). This quartet in G minor uses as a slow movement a *largo assai* in E major. A climax is reached in the brilliant finale, with its first and second themes in the Hungarian and Austrian folk vein, introducing some charmingly merry passages in the development.

In 1797, six string quartets (Hob. III:75–80) were written and published as Op. 76, with a dedication to Count Erdödy. If an appropriate motto were sought for this series, the word "Excelsior" should have the first choice. Everything here is condensed and intensified, the expression more personal and more direct. It is characteristic of Haydn that he now repeatedly increases the tempo in the course of a movement, as in Nos. 5 and 6, in which the initial allegretto is transformed into allegro; likewise the concluding *allegro ma non troppo* of No. 4 twice increases its speed. In these quartets, the minuet has lost completely the character of a graceful allegretto. In Nos. 1 and 6, Haydn's tempo marks are presto, and an approach to Beethoven's scherzo is also evident in the spirit of the compositions. The same quartet No. 1, in G major, has a finale beginning in G minor. It would seem that Haydn wanted to change the mood of the composition, but the opposite is true: he desired merely to introduce a retardation before the definite solution; the finale, in its second half, passes quite regularly from minor to major so that the beginning and end of the quartet conform. A similar situation may be found in No. 3.[8] As the quartets of Op. 76 are contemporary with Haydn's *The Creation*, it is not surprising that the last movements of two of them should be based on the idea expressed in the great passage from minor to major at the words "Let there be light."

Number 2 of this set is known as the "Quintenquartett" because of the use of fifths in its main subject. A strange piece is its *Hexen-Menuett* (Witches Minuet), a canon in which the two violins play the melody in octaves while viola and violoncello (also in octaves) perform the imitation. Number 3, in C major, is a comparatively uninspired quartet that hardly would deserve its place among Haydn's last works of this type were it not for its *poco adagio cantabile*. Like Schubert in his quartet "Death and the Maiden" and in his "Trout" Quintet, in this slow movement Haydn presents variations on one of his own songs, the Austrian national anthem, "Gott erhalte Franz den Kaiser." There are only four variations, and in each a different member of the quartet is entrusted with the melody. It is a composition of great simplicity and dignity, fully deserving the great popularity that it enjoys. Number 4 is known as the "Sunrise"; the main subject of the first movement beautifully expresses the feeling of growth and expansion that we experience on an early summer morning. Number 5, based on a single melody, presents in its first movement a greatly simplified sonata form. As Haydn liked to use two movements of the same form within a single work, the succeeding famous *largo cantabile e mesto* in F-sharp major (the first movement being in D major!) is similarly constructed. It is a piece full of luxuriant beauty, just as romantic in its whole conception as the variations on the Austrian hymn in the preceding quartet were classical. The first movement of No. 6 introduces a set of variations on an allegretto theme. The last of these variations reveals traces of serious polyphonic construction. Like many nineteenth-century composers, Haydn concludes his set of variations with a display of counterpoint. The following fantasia moves from B major throught the keys of E, G, B-flat, B, A-flat, and finally back to the tonic. This unconventional piece, rich in enharmonic changes, at first has no key signature at all. As in works by Philipp Emanuel Bach, and by some twentieth-century com-

[8] Sir Donald Tovey points out that Brahms's Third Symphony shows quite similar tendencies. This is by no means the only point the two composers have in common, and as Brahms was a most diligent student of Haydn's scores, the resemblance does not seem to be accidental.

posers, the accidentals are written separately for each note. The trio (*alternativo*) of the minuet of this quartet uses as a theme the scale of E-flat. It runs through all parts, sometimes ascending and sometimes descending, while Haydn constantly invents new counterpoints to it. Beethoven may have remembered this humorous piece when composing his canon on the words "I beg you, write down the E-flat scale for me."

In 1799 the composer wrote two string quartets (Hob. III: 81–82) that were printed as Op. 77, with a dedication to Prince Lobkowitz. More than ever, Haydn delighted at this time in little experiments in form. For instance, in the recapitulation of the first movement of No. 1, the subsidiary subject has been omitted because he thought that it had been sufficiently used in the development section. In the second quartet, the minuet is in F major, the trio in D-flat major. The coda also starts in D-flat major, but as it is thematically related to the minuet, it unites the two contrasting sections of the movement. Both this piece and the minuet of the preceding quartet exhibit features characteristic of Beethoven's scherzos. Striking is the beginning of the andante of No. 2. It is limited to two parts only, thus recalling the distinctive "thinness" of Philipp Emanuel Bach's piano compositions. In this period, when true expression seemed more important to Haydn than a perfect balance between form and content, he was getting closer to the style of Johann Sebastian Bach's second son, and at the same time to that of his own *Sturm und Drang* period.

In 1803, Haydn began his last string quartet, Op. 103 (Hob. III:83), in B-flat major. He wrote only two movements, an *andante grazioso* and a minuet. These movements show complete technical mastery, but at the same time a certain lack of inventive power. Haydn was unable to add the initial movement and finale to these two middle pieces. The quartet remained unfinished and was eventually published in 1806 as the master's swan song. As a humorous explanation and apology, it has at the end of the minuet a reproduction of the visiting card that Haydn used during the last years of his life. On it was printed a quotation from his favorite four-part song "Der Greis" (The Old Man): "Hin ist alle meine Kraft, alt und schwach bin ich" (Gone forever is my strength, old and weak am I).

• • •

The Concertante Op. 84 (Hob. I:105), for violin, oboe, violoncello, and bassoon, accompanied by a small orchestra, was composed in London in 1792. Landon is probably right in assuming that the artistic competition in which Haydn was involved with Pleyel was responsible for the creation of the work.[9] As a matter of fact, Haydn's composition was performed on March 9, 1792, closely following and preceding similar works by Pleyel. Traditions of the preclassic *concerto grosso* are revived in Haydn's score. The composer was mainly interested in the problem of contrasting a group of concertante instruments consisting of high- and deep-pitched strings and woodwind with the ripieno instruments used to accompany it. During most of the time the four soloists, who vary so greatly in technical possibilities, are used together, or at least in the same way, rendering impracticable the development of a style that takes into consideration the technical accomplishments of each individual instrument, and limiting the players' possibilities of displaying technical virtuosity. The finale, however, includes some remarkable little recitative episodes for the violin (intended, of course, for Salomon), which revive similar features in Haydn's earliest symphonies and also anticipate similar ideas in nineteenth-century romantic compositions. It is to be regretted that this attractive work, like other concertantes of the late eighteenth and nineteenth centuries (J. C. Bach's, C. Stamitz's, Mozart's *Sinfonies concertantes*; Beethoven's Triple Concerto; Brahms's Double Concerto), is performed so seldom.

In 1796, Haydn wrote a concerto for the keyed trumpet (Hob. VIIe:1). This is a trumpet with holes in the wall of the tube that are closed by keys. As a rule there are five such keys, which raise the pitch by successive semitones. They are so arranged that the performer can play them with his left hand while holding the trumpet in his right. The invention of the keyed trumpet has been ascribed to the Viennese Anton Weidinger, who is said to have constructed it in 1801, but the instrument is older than that, as Haydn's concerto was written five years earlier. The composition reveals the characteristics of the new invention; one looks in vain for the usual triad melodies. The concerto is predominantly diatonic, though there are chromatic passages even in the deeper register of the instrument. Great demands are made on the nimbleness of the trumpet, and in the allegro, runs of sixteenth notes are not unusual. With youthful enthusiasm, the aged composer threw himself into the novel task, creating the finest solo concerto of his whole career and proving once more his flexibility and ability to absorb new ideas.

Despite Haydn's efforts, the keyed trumpet had no real success. The explanation may be that the holes detracted greatly from the

[9] *HCaW*, III, p. 536.

brilliant tone of the instrument. Accordingly it never succeeded in obtaining admittance to the symphonic orchestra. However, Haydn's work was edited in various arrangements for valve trumpet and piano[10] and is today in the repertoire of most trumpeters.

A review of Haydn's whole output in the field of the concerto forces one to admit that he showed no particular interest in this form of composition. The few masterworks among the concertos hardly make up for the number of routine compositions written for a single performance and never meant for wider circulation. This will not surprise anyone familiar with Haydn's personality. Unlike Mozart, he was no virtuoso. Neither on the piano nor on the violin was his technique particularly brilliant. Above all, his natural disposition was alien to that of a virtuoso. The rather dramatic gifts of the professional performer, which great virtuosos like Liszt, Paganini, and even Mozart possessed in abundance, were completely lacking in Haydn. His reserve made it impossible for him to become a success as a soloist, and while he progressed as a composer, his interest in the concerto form gradually faded. Most of Haydn's concertos were written during the 1750s and 1760s, the smallest number of them (though these include the finest works) during the eighties and nineties.

•  •  •

At different periods of his lifetime, Haydn composed a number of marches and dances, but he does not seem to have attributed great importance to them. The catalogue of 1805 mentions only two marches and omits the dances altogether.

Seven marches,[11] mostly written during the composer's last creative period and preserved in autograph, are known today. One of them was written in London for the Prince of Wales (Hob. VIII:3), two were for the Derbyshire Cavalry Regiment (Hob. VIII:1, 2); the last march, the "Hungarischer Nationalmarsch" (Hob. VIII:4) is dated 1802. These are very concise pieces, the longest of which consists of only forty-six measures. As the marching bands of the eighteenth century usually performed without music, it seemed advisable to keep down the length of the pieces they had to memorize. The marches are mostly in the key of E-flat major and are scored for two clarinets (and/or oboes), two bassoons, and two horns, to which at times a trumpet and a serpent (a wooden horn in snake form, equipped with finger holes) were

[10] First edited by A. Goeyens for Walpot (Brussels, 1929).
[11] Edited by H. C. Robbins Landon for Doblinger (Vienna, 1960–1961).

added. The "March for the Royal Society of Musicians" (Hob. VIII:3 *bis*), written in 1792 for a banquet of the society, adds two flutes and strings. However, this piece is an arrangement of the "March for the Prince of Wales," scored for wind instruments only. The little marches, strongly rhythmical pieces of vigorous and virile character, enjoyed popularity in Haydn's lifetime, as is proved by the fact that one of them (Hob. VIII:6), in slightly changed form, is played by the musical clock of 1793 (Hob. XIX:25).

Many minuets and German dances were written by Haydn for balls and dances. A contemporary author even goes so far as to mention four hundred such pieces contributed by the composer.[12] The earliest of them go back to Haydn's first two periods of composition, while the last and best were written in the nineties. Graceful utility music is provided in the six allemandes (Hob. IX:9) of the middle eighties. A climax was reached with the twelve minuets and twelve German dances (Hob. IX:11, 12)[13] for large orchestra which Haydn offered in the fall of 1792 to the Pensionsgesellschaft bildender Künstler Wiens (Pension Fund of Vienna's Artists) for their masked ball. It took place on November 25, the name day of St. Catherine, and the compositions were therefore called "Catherine Dances." These twenty-four pieces are jewels of musical inspiration pervaded by amiable humor and chiseled with exquisite understanding of the individual instruments' potentialities. Haydn, who, after the triumphs won in England, may have felt the reception given to him in Vienna to be somewhat cool, was probably eager to bring his art to the attention of the Viennese, and these dances seemed particularly suitable for such a purpose. That the composer attached significance to the dainty and unassuming pieces is proved by the various sketches he made for them.

• • •

The twelve London or Salomon symphonies (Hob. I:93–104), composed between 1791 and 1795, plus an additional one, the Thirteenth or Oxford Symphony (No. 92 of 1789), represent the climax of Haydn's symphonic output. Never before had he written orchestral works of equal significance, and no other musician composed in quick succession so large a number of great symphonic

[12]Carl Bertuch, *Bemerkungen auf einer Reise aus Thüringen nach Wien im Winter 1805–1806* (Weimar, 1808–1810), 12th letter.
[13]Hob. IX:9 was edited by H. C. Robbins Landon for Doblinger (Vienna, 1960); Hob. IX:11 by Ernst Fritz Schmid for Kistner and Siegel (Leipzig, 1940); Hob. IX:12 by Otto Erich Deutsch for Kistner and Siegel (Leipzig, 1931).

masterpieces. Although each of these thirteen works has its own outstanding merits, a gradual improvement in quality may be noticed. The symphonies Nos. 99–104, written for the second sojourn in London, surpass, if that be possible, the Nos. 93–98, composed for the first visit. No others of Haydn's scores show such virtuosity of instrumentation or such delightful unorthodox treatment of musical forms and contrapuntal devices in the development sections. Remarkable is the imagination displayed by Haydn at such a comparatively unimportant place as the recapitulation in sonata form. Occasionally composers introduce an almost mechanical repetition of the exposition as soon as the development is finished. Haydn, on the other hand, presents the material of the first section in a new way, writing a recapitulation as rich in inspiration as the exposition itself. A last climax is often reached in the coda. This coda, far from being a mere "tail," develops into a final dramatic concentration of the thematic material. The whole nineteenth century, beginning with Beethoven and ending with Brahms, was able to draw rich inspiration from Haydn's last thirteen symphonies.

The mosaic style of the thematic development has become a matter of course; filling and accompanying voices enjoy the same privileges as the parts carrying the melody, for the same motives are used by all. The baroque division into leading instruments, whose parts are florid and ornamental, and subordinate instruments, whose function is that of giving a foundation to the evolutions of the others, reflects the social cleavage of the period into a ruling and a subservient class, a division that here has been abandoned entirely.

Hermann Kretzschmar called the Oxford Symphony (No. 92 in G major) Haydn's "Eroica," as it is the first work to display the full perfection of Haydn's fifth period of composition. In its whole architecture it belongs to the works of the nineties rather than to the Paris symphonies, though it was actually composed in 1789. Tovey is mistaken when he points out that the Oxford Symphony "was written for the occasion of Haydn's receiving the Doctorate of Music at Oxford."[14] The fact is that this Symphony No. 92, written in 1789 for the Count d'Ogny but not known in England, was presented as a new work at the Oxford celebration.

The Oxford Symphony displays thematic development in every measure, and all the devices of counterpoint are introduced to reveal new sides of the subjects again and again. The work is gay and carefree, but at the same time filled with dramatic excitement.

[14]Donald Francis Tovey, *Essays in Musical Analysis* (London, 1935–1944), I, p. 143.

The climax is reached in the brilliant finale, which shows so many different forms of its main theme that it seems hard to determine which is the original and which a variation. The score, laid out at first for an orchestra of only medium size, was later enlarged by the addition of trumpets and timpani.

Symphony No. 93, in D major, composed in 1791, starts with a slow introduction of lofty grandeur, its dramatic impact enhanced by frequent pauses. The *largo cantabile* of the second movement may have been in Beethoven's mind when he worked on the hymnic finale of the Pastoral symphony. However, near the end, Haydn intentionally destroys the deeply moving atmosphere by allowing the bassoon to break in with a rather vulgar statement. The finale shows the combination of rondo and sonata form that Haydn liked so much in his last period. Such a combination is also used in the symphonies Nos. 94, 95, 100, 101, and 102, and it is characteristic of the consummate mastery of the composer that no two of these movements solve the problem in the same way.

Symphony No. 94, in G major, known as the "Surprise"[15] and composed in 1791, owes its name to an episode in the andante of its second movement, which has a folk-song character. Haydn introduced eight measures of his theme at first piano, played by strings only, and then a second time pianissimo. At the end of this repetition, when the tone may be expected to fade out, quite suddenly a fortissimo of the full orchestra, including the drums, sets in. This sort of surprise had been used by Haydn before, and the movement owes its popularity more to the graceful, simple melodic invention than to the little joke. The andante displays a mixture of variation and three-part-song form, as the freely constructed second variation in C minor takes the place of the middle part. Haydn had the good taste not to repeat in the individual variations the little prank he introduced in the theme. In the coda, the childlike, naïve melody of the main subject suddenly assumes an enigmatic character because of the romantic harmonies of the stringed instruments used as an accompaniment (measures 145–152). Here we reach once more the threshold of Beethoven's art.

The other movements match the andante in artistic perfection. In the slow introduction to the first movement, Haydn boldly employs chromatic progressions of an almost romantic fervor. The

---

[15] An incomplete autograph is preserved in the Staatsbibliothek Preussischer Kulturbesitz, Berlin. Some of the pages missing there are included in the copy in the Library of Congress, Washington, D.C. These sheets contain the first version of the andante in which the "surprise" effect has not yet been achieved.

ensuing *vivace assai* built on three subjects is worked out with the zest and ingenuity we have learned to expect in these symphonies. Much more amusing than the "surprise" of the andante is a detail in the minuet. At the end of the second part (measures 39–40), a ridiculous snort and groan in the violoncellos and bassoons lead us back to the beginning of the main melody. This movement bears no relation to the graceful French minuet of the rococo period. It is a typical Austrian *Ländler*, foreshadowing the waltz of the nineteenth century.

In the final rondo, too, the retransitions to the main theme show unusual humor and fantasy and a brilliant coda concludes this great movement.

The dramatic beginning in unison of Symphony No. 95, in C minor, composed in 1791, reminds us of the *Sturm und Drang* period. The lack of a slow introduction to the first movement, the frequent doubling by the strings of the parts of the woodwind instruments, and the baroque use of polyphonic devices in the finale are equally characteristic of an earlier phase in Haydn's creative output. The variations of the andante, however, displaying in their whole construction a great resemblance to the "surprise" movement of the preceding symphony, and the rather difficult violoncello solo in the trio of the minuet show that in Haydn's latest period old and new elements are blended together with perfect success.

The Symphony No. 96, in D major, written in 1791, may well be the first number of the set Haydn composed in London. It is known as the "Miracle," a nickname not owing to aesthetic qualities (well deserved though it would be), but rather to a story told about the first performance. At the end of the concert, the applauding crowd rushed toward the platform to have a better view of the composer. At this moment a chandelier in the rear crashed down. Thanks to the enthusiasm the audience had shown, nobody was hurt, and exclamations were heard that a miracle had happened.[16]

In the vigorous first movement a bold effect may be observed which Haydn used with great skill in various compositions of the time. In the middle section the composer concludes a passage in F-sharp major and, after a pause, unexpectedly starts a half-tone higher, with a chord in G. The slow movement seems to recapture the best spirit of rococo art, and its dainty charm and exquisitely

---

[16] According to Landon, *Symphonies*, p. 535, the event happened in February 1795 at the premiere of Symphony No. 103. Yet the nickname has been indissolubly linked with Symphony No. 96.

soft pastel coloring bring Watteau's masterpieces to mind. Robust jocularity reigns in the minuet, while the trio presents a dance tune of poignant sweetness, deeply rooted in Austrian folklore. The finale offers a brilliant *perpetuum mobile*, allowing Haydn to display his uncanny resourcefulness in achieving a variety of humorous effects while obstinately clinging to the same rhythm.

In the Symphony No. 97, in C major, composed in 1792, the introduction to the first movement is intimately connected with the main part. The characteristic motive of its second measure returns all through the movement, the last time in the coda. Near the beginning of the development section, the strings toss backward and forward a little motive derived from the main subject. The "Jacob's ladder" effect in the finale of Beethoven's Eighth Symphony (measures 458–469) is foreshadowed in this little episode. In the following variation movement, the unexpected forte entrance of trumpets and timpani in the second variation is particularly stirring. A gem, outstanding even in this set of masterpieces, is the minuet, in which Haydn displays his magical touch as orchestrator. Here the traditional repetitions are written out completely, introducing attractive little variations instead of mechanical reiteration. The same is true of the trio, incidentally one of the most typically Austrian pieces Haydn ever wrote. The finale of this symphony displays an obvious mirthfulness; near the end, however, in a dramatic move, the composer introduces a passage imbued with the spirit of tragedy, taking the listener completely by surprise. Immediately afterward, cheerfulness is restored; the dark shades were used only to give a more effective background to the prevailing bright colors.

In the Symphony No. 98, in B-flat major, composed in 1792, the slow introduction in B-flat minor anticipates the main subject of the following allegro (B-flat major) in a way that was to become customary in romantic music. The *adagio cantabile* of the second movement, according to Tovey, might almost be called Haydn's "requiem for Mozart, the news of whose death had so deeply shocked him during his London visit." It certainly is an unusually serious piece, anticipating in its hymnlike character the prayer "Be now gracious" (No. 6) in *The Seasons*. However, the last two movements once more sparkle with the composer's typical love of fun. The finale, which conjures up a hilarious operatic scene, achieves a particularly amusing effect by suddenly slowing up its brisk motion near the end. It is noteworthy that a manuscript score of the work, written by one of Haydn's copyists in London, contains arpeggios for the harpsichord (pianoforte?) in bars 365–375 of the finale.

Haydn, who liked to conduct from a keyboard instrument, apparently had them inserted for his own use.[17]

The last six symphonies were performed during Haydn's second stay in England. They were written between 1793 and 1795 in a little over two years, and represent a culmination of eighteenth-century art, opening up, at the same time, magnificent vistas into the development of nineteenth-century music.

The Symphony No. 99, in E-flat major, composed in 1793 between the two trips to England, is the first symphony in which Haydn uses clarinets, though these instruments had been prescribed by him in such earlier compositions as the notturni with lire organizzate. How well he understood the potentialities of this wind instrument is shown in the very first measures of the score. The sonorous chalumeau register of the clarinet provides an effective bass for the stringed instruments. Daring modulations give this introduction a decidedly progressive character. In the main section of the movement, the second subject is of greater significance than the first, and a similar romantic preponderance of the subsidiary idea may be noted in the following adagio, one of the deepest and most stirring pieces written by Haydn. As in the preceding symphony, the mood changes completely with the beginning of the minuet. This scherzolike movement and, to an even greater extent, the finale employ all the devices of instrumentation and counterpoint to create pictures of uncontrollable gaiety. Thus Haydn could count on pleasing the exacting Londoners with the first symphony he planned to present to them after his return.

In the first movement of the Symphony No. 100, in G major, composed in 1794 and known as the "Military" Symphony, a trio consisting of a flute and two oboes introduces the main subject; no other instruments are added for support. So revolutionary a treatment of the high woodwinds, which in the earlier symphonies are almost never used independently, shows that the aged Haydn did not cease experimenting and trying out new effects. The subsidiary subject bears a certain resemblance to both the main idea of the first movement of Mozart's great G minor Symphony and to one of the most popular Austrian tunes of the nineteenth century, the "Radetzky March" by the elder Johann Strauss. Even the use of the first three notes of both Mozart's and Haydn's subjects in the respective development sections displays a striking similarity. The work owes

---

[17] Cf. Landon, *Symphonies*, p. 589. The score in question is the property of the Royal Philharmonic Society. It is on loan to the British Library, London.

its name to the allegretto of the second movement. In this piece Haydn's ordinary symphonic orchestra is enlarged by the introduction of military instruments: triangle, cymbals, bass drum, and the penetrating C clarinet. The composer uses here the allegretto from his third lira concerto, changing only the orchestration and the end of the movement. Even the division of the violas used in the original composition is preserved in the adaptation for the "Military" Symphony. Haydn frequently prescribes the percussion instruments in piano and pianissimo, thus producing charming effects of color. Rather strange is the unaccompanied trumpet signal near the end of the movement, followed by a roll of the kettledrum, increasing from pianissimo to fortissimo. It can hardly be doubted that Haydn, in a purely romantic way, meant to express with this dramatic episode a certain poetical program. From here the way leads directly to the trumpet signals in Beethoven's *Leonore* overtures. The brisk final presto uses the same percussion instruments as the andante. It is distinguished by interesting modulations and contains several little replicas of the famous "surprise" from the Symphony No. 94 which are hardly less effective than the original itself. Particularly amusing are measures 118–123. Two chords are played by violins and viola, first piano, then after a general pause, diminuendo, and finally after a second general pause, pianissimo. Before this charming effect can be fully grasped, the kettledrum crashes in with six powerful fortissimo beats. By omitting the third general pause, which the listener anticipates, Haydn set a sort of trap for his audience, the humorous effect of which nobody can miss.

The Symphony No. 101, in D major, commonly known as "The Clock," was written in 1794. The presto of the first movement and its six-eight time are what one would expect in the finale of a symphony rather than in its initial movement. The andante introduces an accompaniment of bassoons and plucked strings that sounds like the ticktock of a big clock and is responsible for the symphony's nickname. This movement displays Haydn's favorite mixture of variation and rondo form, which so strongly impressed Beethoven that one finds traces of it even in the slow movement of his "Choral" Symphony. In Haydn's andante, continual changes of the orchestration occur. Particularly attractive is the entrance of the charming main theme after the dramatic episode in G minor. Here the ticktock is taken over by a flute, so that a tiny clock seems to replace the big timepiece heard at the beginning. The trio of the succeeding minuet belongs to the type now frequently used by Haydn, which does not contrast with the preceding dance, but

rather supplements it. Both sections are in the same key, a fact that
has induced some conductors to omit the repetition of the minuet
after the trio. It is hardly necessary to point out that such a procedure completely destroys the architecture of the movement. The
finale, imbued with mellow joyfulness, shows a construction greatly
resembling that of the andante. In spite of its prevailing light, gay
character, the entrance of the main theme after the episode in the
minor mode assumes the form of a double fugue in miniature. How
solidly this finale is constructed may be gathered from the fact that
the first three notes of the main subject are used throughout the
movement, giving the greatest unity to the composition. One is
reminded of the thematic "germ cell" that plays so important a part
in the symphonies of Johannes Brahms.

In the Symphony No. 102, in B-flat major (composed in 1794),
the slowly gliding chords of the introductory largo intoned by the
wind instruments transport us to a world of mystery. A brisk vivace follows, its second subject once more revealing the aged composer's joy in experimentation. Haydn has the theme start on a fortissimo outcry. A general pause ensues, and then the rest of the
melody is uttered piano. Equally striking are the violent dissonances in the canonic episode of the development. The soul-stirring
adagio displays an orchestration of unusual subtlety, introducing
muted trumpets and muffled kettledrums. It is a simple piece imbued with serenity, and it is not surprising that it was arranged as an
anthem at a later date. Haydn himself used this adagio in F major a
second time: in the Piano Trio in F-sharp minor (Hob. XV : 26) it
serves as the middle movement. The hearty, robust minuet of the
symphony has a romantic trio in which chromatic progressions express ardor and yearning that one would expect in a composition by
Mozart rather than a piece by Haydn. The brilliant finale employs
an old Croatian folk tune as its main subject. Near the end, the
great musical humorist produces another of his delightful jokes.
The first violin suddenly begins to stutter: it tries to present the
main theme, but succeeds in uttering no more than its first few
notes. These grow more and more confused, whereupon the chorus of attending instruments rudely breaks in, and with loud laughter carries the movement to an exuberant conclusion.

Among the many romantic and highly dramatic introductions
that head the first movements of Haydn's London symphonies, the
one written in 1795 for the Symphony No. 103, in E-flat major,
"with the Drum Roll," is particularly remarkable. It starts with a
completely unaccompanied long roll of the kettledrum. This mys-

terious first measure is followed by an impressive unison of bassoons, violoncellos, and double basses. Here Haydn wrote the basses an octave higher than the cellos, so that the two groups of instruments sound at the same pitch. Only in this way can the lonely majesty of the passage be expressed fully. This is another example of the special care that Haydn then bestowed on the problems of orchestration. In the succeeding *allegro con spirito* the composer uses a real waltz tune as a subsidiary subject, and a happy and warm spirit pervades the movement. Twice, however, reminiscences of the solemn adagio introduction are heard, and thus a new dimension seems to be added to the sparkling gaiety of the piece. The following andante is in variation form, using two themes of folk-songlike character which show a certain relationship to each other. The first theme is in C minor, the second in C major, and Haydn wrote variations on them alternately. Particularly delightful is the second C major variation, which has the oboes sound the theme while the bassoons offer a ponderous accompaniment and the flutes chime in like little bells. This *andante più tosto allegretto*, with its superb treatment of the variation form, is followed by a minuet that introduces in its second section an effective stretto of the main subject, showing that the use of polyphonic devices need not be restricted to the first and last movements of a symphony. The beginning of the finale is just as daring as that of the first movement. Two horns play an unaccompanied signal of the type later used by Schubert and Schumann. This horn theme is nothing but a counterpoint to the main idea, which is presently introduced by the first violin. (Incidentally, these two ideas have a striking resemblance to the beginning of the finale in Mozart's "Jupiter" Symphony.) The whole movement is based entirely on the one main melody. Its first five notes—a variation of the old "sigh motive"—lend themselves particularly well to the contrapuntal work that Haydn uses extensively all through this masterly piece.

Haydn's last symphony, No. 104 in D major, composed in 1795, is sometimes known as his "London" or "Salomon" Symphony, though these names may be applied to any of the last twelve symphonies. The autograph preserved in the Staatsbibliothek, Berlin, bears the inscription (in English) "the 12th which I have composed in England." In writing this, Haydn may have felt that he was not only finishing the last symphony he had promised to compose for the English public, but that he also was completing his output in the field of orchestral composition. The first movement starts with a solemn adagio in D minor, after which the D major

allegro section presents a warm, tender subject of Mozartean nature. It is typical of Haydn's art that a slightly modified repetition of
the main idea is used instead of the subsidiary subject. There is also
a contrasting melody near the end of the exposition, which at first
seems to be quite insignificant. However, like Beethoven in later
years, Haydn chooses as a foundation for his developing work the
very theme that appeared least likely to attract his attention. The
andante of the second movement is in three-part form, and here
Haydn achieves greater coherence by using material from the first
section for the contrasting *minore* of the middle part. The movement's sweetly poignant theme and its deeply moving coda once
more bring Mozart to mind. The mood changes completely when
we reach the zestful minuet in D major (with trio in B-flat major).
Here the accents on the last beats of measures and the general pause
near the end, followed by a trill of the woodwind and strings, anticipate the scherzos of Beethoven. In the finale the composer employs
two subjects, one based on the old English street song "Hot Cross
Buns," the contrasting one imbued with tender longing. The main
subject is accompanied by the deep drone of horns and violoncellos
holding the tonic note D as a pedal point for long stretches, creating
the illusion of a rustic dance tune played on a bagpipe.

Admiring the facets of Haydn's art displayed in these last symphonies, we feel that they fittingly serve as a final and most important feature in the gigantic structure erected by the composer's orchestral work.

• • •

The vocal compositions of Haydn's fifth period are on the same
high level as his creations in the field of instrumental music. The
artistic imprint of English music is on quite a few of these works,
even on some of them written in Austria after he left England.

Haydn devoted a surprisingly large amount of his time to the
writing of songs. Nevertheless, the creation of songs never became
for him a matter of great importance.

The first set of Haydn's *Six Original Canzonettas*, written
in England to English words, was printed by Corri, Dussek and
Company in London in 1794, a second set of six English canzonettas
the following year (Hob. XXVIa:25–36). In these songs, the inclusion of the vocal part in the right-hand part of the piano accompaniment, as exemplified by Haydn's first twenty-four German songs, is
abandoned. The composer now uses a separate line for the voice part;
his instrumental introductions become larger and more important,

and the piano accompaniment is of greater significance. Occasionally it is obvious that Haydn was thinking in terms of the orchestra even when composing for the piano only. The influence of the aria in these songs is just as conspicuous as it is in Beethoven's *Adelaide*, for soprano with piano, written at about the same time. Haydn's use of coloratura and chromatic progressions, the wide range of the voice part, and the occasional influx of the dramatic spirit show the opera composer at work. However, it is not always the Italian opera, but occasionally, as in the "Sailor's Song," the simpler German Singspiel that influenced him. At the same time, Haydn still preferred the strophic arrangement, which he had also used in the first twenty-four German songs. "A Pastoral Song" and "She Never Told Her Love" belong among the more attractive pieces of the two English sets; for the latter, Haydn used a text from Shakespeare's *Twelfth Night*.

Two songs not included in the twelve canzonettas are settings of English words. "O Tuneful Voice" (Hob. XXVIa:42) is based on a poem given to Haydn by Mrs. Hunter before his departure from England (see p. 151). It is to be wondered whether this almost tragic composition in the style of *opera seria* does not take the simple text a little too seriously. To Haydn's best pieces for voice and piano belongs "The Spirit's Song" (Hob. XXVIa:41), again on a text by Anne Hunter. Apparently the author's romantic manner of conveying the idea of life after death struck a responsive note in the aging composer's mind. For once, this expressive composition is void of operatic influence; in its mysterious atmosphere and deep feeling it anticipates Schubert's Lied.

Yet Haydn's most successful song is his "Gott erhalte Franz den Kaiser" (Hob. XXVIa:43), composed in 1797 as the Austrian national anthem. For more than a century this melody was used with at least a dozen different texts as the anthem of the Austro-Hungarian monarchy. In Germany, Haydn's tune has been employed for the patriotic song "Deutschland, Deutschland, über alles," and in the English-speaking countries as a church hymn.

In this work, folk song and art music came to a classical union. Hardly ever did a composer create with such simple means a work imbued with such fervor and solemnity. Like every tune of simple folk-song character, "Gott erhalte" resembles other melodies in certain details. Dr. Kuhač found analogies between Haydn's hymn and the Croatian folk song "Vjutro runo," and came to the conclusion that the master's melody must be of Croatian origin. Even if the

Croatian folk song were older than Haydn's anthem, the melodic relationship would not prove anything, as similar slight resemblances may be discovered in a great number of other pieces that Haydn most certainly never saw. Tappert,[18] Friedländer,[19] and Botstiber[20] made lists of such "relations" and proved that some of the melodic successions of Haydn's song are also to be found in: Hasse's *Pilgrime von Golgatha*; a rondeau for piano by Georg Philipp Telemann; a hymnbook from 1786; Mozart's *Exsultate jubilate* of 1773; and Haydn's own setting of *The Seven Last Words*. (Even long after Haydn's death, Brahms used in his Piano Sonata in F minor a tune with a certain similarity.) This does not mean that Haydn studied all these works; it only shows that he succeeded in creating one of those basic melodies of which elements are to be found in works by the most different composers. This fundamental quality, which was reached only after long and arduous work (Haydn made many sketches to this short, uncomplicated song and they are preserved in the Vienna National Library), also accounts for its unparalleled success.

Inspired by Nelson's victory at Aboukir Bay in 1798, Haydn wrote his aria for soprano or tenor and piano, "Lines from the Battle of the Nile" (Hob. XXVIb:4) in 1800. As in *Arianna a Naxos*, the piano part bears the character of an orchestral arrangement; thus Ludwig Landshoff's instrumentation[21] of this piece is to a certain extent justified. The cheerful principal subject of the aria, characterizing the victorious hero, makes its appearance in the introductory recitative. Like an operatic scene by Gluck, "Lines from the Battle of the Nile" subordinates the music to the text. Consequently, the recitative, which also interrupts the continuous flow of the aria, is almost more important than the aria itself.

In London in 1795 Haydn wrote for Brigida Giorgi-Banti "Berenice che fai" (Hob. XXIVa:10)[22] for soprano accompanied by strings and woodwind, a grand concert aria full of impressive modulations and harmonic changes. Three years later he composed the soprano aria "Solo e pensoso" (Hob. XXIVb:20)[23] on a sonnet by

[18] Wilhelm Tappert, *Musikalische Studien* (Berlin: Guttentag, 1868).
[19] Max Friedländer's introduction to the volume of songs in the first collected edition (Leipzig: Breitkopf & Härtel, 1932).
[20] Carl Ferdinand Pohl and Hugo Botstiber, *Joseph Haydn* (Leipzig, 1927), III, p. 320ff.
[21] Edition Adler (Berlin, 1932).
[22] Edited by A. Orel for the Musikwissenschaftlicher Verlag (Leipzig, 1937).
[23] Edited by H. C. Robbins Landon for the Haydn-Mozart Presse (Salzburg, 1961).

Petrarch. It starts with an *adagio cantabile,* dispensing almost completely with wind instruments, and leads to an allegretto in which the soloist and instruments (now including two clarinets) are offered ever greater opportunities for displaying their art.[24]

• • •

Haydn's arrangements of Scottish and Welsh folk songs belong to a special group. Starting on this work in London in 1791, he continued it in Vienna with the help of Sigismund Neukomm and possibly other pupils, carrying it on even after his failing health made really creative work impossible. The incentive to undertake these arrangements came first from England and later from Scotland. While in London he established contacts with William Napier, whereas later George Thomson and William Whyte approached him through middlemen (cf. p. 169f.). No less a poet than Robert Burns provided new texts for some of the songs ordered by Thomson. Among the composers who worked at that time or afterwards along similar lines were Pleyel, Koželuch, and even Beethoven.

Between 1791 and 1805, Haydn delivered close to three hundred fifty such arrangements of Scottish, Welsh, and Irish folk songs, an easy task for which he was well paid by Thomson and Whyte.

The Napier arrangements [25] were printed in three lines only, the top one destined for the violin, the second (under which the text is placed) for the melody, the third for the figured bass. The two lower lines are apparently intended for singer and clavierist, the use of a cello to reinforce the bass being optional. The setting is rather thin here, requiring the addition of filling notes by the clavierist, but the Thomson and Whyte editions offer a different picture. In them, as a rule, a separate line is allotted to the singer's part; the two lines underneath contain the completely elaborated clavier part. In separate volumes, the violin and cello parts are also presented, and though they could be omitted in performance, and in all likelihood were used but rarely, they contribute considerably to the coloristic enrichment and the poetic interpretation of the songs. A novelty in

---

[24] Cf. also the cantata *What Art Expresses,* known under the title *Dr. Harington's Compliment,* mentioned on p. 146.
[25] Cf. Karl Geiringer, "Haydn and the Folk Song of the British Isles," *Musical Quarterly,* XXXV/2 (Apr. 1949); Cecil Hopkinson and C. B. Oldman, "Haydn's Settings of Scottish Songs in the Collections of Napier and Whyte," *Edinburgh Bibliographical Society Transactions,* III/2 (1949–1951). One hundred Scottish songs arranged for Napier were edited by Karl Geiringer in *JHW,* XXXII/1.

these arrangements for both Thomson and Whyte are instrumental preludes and postludes, on which the arrangers bestowed particular care.

There can be no doubt that the one hundred fifty settings of folk songs made for Napier were all done by Haydn himself. The same is probably true of the first arrangements the composer did in Vienna. Later, however, the enfeebled old man depended increasingly on some help. We know today that at least forty-three, but possibly over seventy, of the "Haydn arrangements" were in fact done by S. Neukomm in 1804 and 1805.[26]

Unfortunately, the arrangers, including Haydn himself, were in no way familiar with the true character of Scottish and Welsh folk music. They did not necessarily receive an authentic version of the airs, and, worst of all, they always got them without texts. In addition, Haydn was urged by Thomson to keep the accompaniments quite simple, so that even amateurs of limited technical abilities could perform them. Under these circumstances the results of the arranger's labors were disappointing, and neither in Haydn's own time nor afterwards did these adaptations meet with much success.

• • •

In 1796, Haydn wrote two Italian chamber duets of Nina and Tirsi, "Saper vorrei" and "Guarda qui" (Hob. XXVa:1, 2),[27] using texts by C. F. Badini, the librettist of his London opera *L'anima del filosofo*. The compositions, which are set for soprano, tenor, and clavier, have the character of simple operatic duets. They make no particular demands on the singers' technical abilities and were apparently meant for music-making in the home. Quite different is the great tercet for two sopranos, tenor, and orchestra, "Pietà di me, benigni Dei" (Hob. XXVb:5), probably written for Mrs. Billington: in it there is no lack of fast runs and wide leaps in the vocal parts. As a counterpart to the trio of singers, Haydn here introduces

[26] Cf. Cecil Hopkinson and C. B. Oldman, "Thomson's Collections of National Song with Special Reference to the Contributions of Haydn and Beethoven," *Edinburgh Bibliographical Society Transactions*, II/1 (1938–1939), and Rudolph Angermüller, "Sigismund Ritter von Neukomm (1778–1858) und seine Lehrer Michael und Joseph Haydn," *H-St*, III/1, (Jan. 1973), p. 39. Selected folk songs were edited by B. Engelke for Steingräber (Leipzig, 1927). The Scottish folk-song arrangements are listed in the Hoboken catalogue as XXXIa:1–273, the Welsh arrangements as XXXIb:1–60, and the Irish arrangement as XXXIb:61.
[27] Edited by H. C. Robbins Landon for Doblinger (Vienna, 1960).

a concertant trio of English horn, French horn, and bassoon; its parts match those of the vocalists in virtuosity.[28]

Haydn's thirteen songs for three or four voices with continuo or clavier accompaniment were begun in 1796, according to the testimony of the autograph.[29] Griesinger contends that in 1801 Haydn told him that he wanted to write twenty-five of these pieces, but old age apparently made this impossible. He probably received the impulse to create these works in England, where part singing had always been popular. As a true instrumental composer, Haydn added piano accompaniments to his compositions. The simple, naturally flowing melodies—avoiding all virtuosity and closely following the intentions of the poet—and the complete lack of theatrical pathos give these pieces a unique position among Haydn's vocal output. Full of humor are the trio "An den Vetter" (To the Cousin) with its quaint coloratura, and the quartet "Harmonie in der Ehe" (Harmony in Marriage), in which Haydn delights in mocking a meaningless marriage. A special joke can be found at the end of the delightful quartet "Die Beredsamkeit" (Eloquence). Here the last word, *stumm* (still), must not be sung, but should only be mouthed soundlessly by the singers, as Haydn prescribes in the autograph. The other extreme is marked by the powerful religious songs "Aus dem Danklied zu Gott" (From the Song of Thanks to God) and "Abendlied zu Gott" (Evensong to God), pieces that, despite their having more the character of chamber music, can well stand comparison with the great choruses of *The Creation* and *The Seasons*. Haydn himself suggested that Friedrich Zelter should make an arrangement of the "Abendlied" for chorus, solo quartet, and pianoforte.

● ● ●

All of Haydn's fifty-seven canons (Hob. XXVIIa and b) are products of his last period of composition.[30] The famous *Ten Commandments*, ten individual canons each setting one of the command-

---

[28] The tercet was edited by H. C. Robbins Landon for Doblinger (Vienna, 1971).
[29] Three of the tercets and six of the quartets are accompanied by continuo only; one tercet and three quartets have simple clavier accompaniments. The thirteen songs (Hob. XXVb:1–4 and XXVc:1–9) were edited by P. Mies in *JHW*, XXX. Karl Geiringer edited (with English translations by H. S. Drinker) the following: "Harmony in Marriage" and "From the Song of Thanks to God" (New York: Music Press), "Evensong to God" (New York: Boosey and Hawkes), "The Old Man" and "Eloquence" (New York: Carl Fischer), "To the Women" (New York: Schirmer).
[30] They were edited by Otto Erich Deutsch in *JHW*, XXXI. Fifty-six *Rounds and Canons by Haydn* were edited by W. G. Whittacker with English texts for Oxford University Press (London, 1932).

ments to music, were probably written in England to German words and completed by June 1792.[31] Haydn sent the first of these canons to Oxford University in 1792 as a sign of appreciation of the doctorate of music conferred upon him. He changed, however, at this occasion the original text "Du sollst an einen Gott glauben" (Thou shalt have no other gods before me) to the more appropriate words "Thy voice, O Harmony." The *Ten Commandments* were printed frequently, the German and the English versions appearing at approximately the same time (1810).

After Haydn's return to Vienna, the new interest he took in vocal music prompted him to write a substantial number of secular canons, of which forty-six have survived. He was very fond of these pieces and used fair copies, glazed and framed, as wall decorations in his study. After his death, these copies were bought by Prince Esterházy. They were kept for a time in the castle of Eszterháza, but can no longer be traced. Breitkopf and Härtel, Leipzig, published forty-two of them in the year 1810, during which the *Ten Commandments* appeared in print.

These canons and rounds are usually for three or four parts, but pieces for two, five, six, seven, and eight voices occur. Particularly subtle is the three-part canon "Thy Voice, O Harmony," which may also be sung backward as a canon cancrizans. A further possibility is that of turning the score of this canon upside down; held in this way the canon may again be sung forward and backward. The canon "Das gröszte Gut" (entitled "The Best" in Whittaker's edition) introduces an imitation at the third and fifth below; and there are several canons for two voices at the fifth below. They all show that Haydn's contrapuntal skill was considerable. In the seventh of the *Ten Commandments*, according to an unproved old story, he used a melody that he himself had taken from another composer, as if to poke fun at the seventh commandment, "Thou shalt not steal." The tale is based on an unconfirmed rumor, but it would be very much in keeping with Haydn's delightful sense of humor.

The texts of the rounds and canons are, following the classical tradition, often facetious and not always sensible; some of them are unintelligible, as Haydn liked to set to music brief verses he had found in extensive poems; taken out of their context, the verses are likely to make no sense. As early as 1810 the German edition changed many of Haydn's original texts and this procedure was unfortunately continued, though in many cases the expurgated ver-

[31] Cf. *HCaW*, III, p. 178.

sions definitely are inferior to the originals. In particular the Latin words of Horace, the Italian of Federico (used also in the first aria of Pergolesi's *La serva padrona*), and the funny verses of Lessing belong among the best texts used for this kind of composition.[32]

• • •

Haydn's last opera (Hob. XXVIII:13) *L'anima del filosofo ossia Orfeo ed Euridice*, "dramma per musica," written in 1791 to a libretto by C. F. Badini, offers problems which defy a definite solution. The work was not performed in the composer's lifetime (cf. p. 112), and no libretto was printed. Moreover, the autograph score does not indicate the order of the individual numbers. The best source seems to be an early nineteenth-century copy of the score probably based on material owned by Gallini and preserved today in the Bibliothèque Nationale, Paris. None of the scores contains scenic remarks (which are usually to be found in librettos only), and it is not even certain whether the music is complete. According to letters Haydn wrote in 1791, he worked on an opera in five acts while the manuscript scores contain only four.

Nevertheless, thanks to the efforts of various scholars, such as H. Wirth, H. C. R. Landon, and, recently, G. Feder, reconstructions of the score have been undertaken, and we may hope that the results approach the composer's original intentions fairly closely. Since its "premiere" in 1951, the opera has been variously performed with such stars as Maria Callas, Boris Christoff, Joan Sutherland, and Nicolai Gedda in leading parts. In 1951 the complete work was recorded by the Haydn Society.[33]

*L'anima del filosofo* was the only opera in which Haydn did not have to take into account the small group of singers of Prince Esterházy's company. He was thus in a position to make ample use of the chorus, which, as in Gluck's operas, plays an important part in the dramatic events. For instance, the fourth act (this is Haydn's only opera in four acts) contains, besides recitatives and a short instrumental piece, six choral numbers but only a single aria. In the

---

[32] The Horace text *Ille potens sui laetusque deget* is used in Hob. XXVIIb:10; the Federico text *Aspettare e non venire* in Hob. XXVIIb:17; the Lessing text *Ein einzig böses Weib* in Hob. XXVIIb:23. Cf. also Otto Erich Deutsch, "Haydns Kanons," *Zeitschrift für Musikwissenschaft*, XV/31 (Dec. 1932), p. 112f.

[33] In 1806–1807 Breitkopf and Härtel, Leipzig, issued first in piano score and later in full score eleven numbers (recitatives, arias, a duet and choruses) from *Orfeo ed Euridice*. H. C. Robbins Landon edited all the extant music in 1951 for the Haydn Society (Boston) as did H. Wirth in 1974 for *JHW*, XXV/13. Georg Feder offered a reconstructed libretto in 1980.

third act too there are more choral numbers than arias. Mixed choruses alternate with women's and men's choruses. Also the tragic final scene of the work, in which the bacchantes administer poison to Orpheus, and the boat carrying the body of the singer founders in a storm, is treated as a women's chorus interrupted by a short accompanied recitative. All through the work Haydn alternates choral and solo numbers. Thus, the second act starts with a cheerful songlike women's chorus (Ex. 19) based on a charming chorus in

Fin- chè   cir—co- la  il   vi-   go-   re, fin- chè  sei  nell  e- · tà

bion- da  be- vi'l  Net-  ta-  re  d'a- mo- re nel-.la  taz- za  di pia-  cer

EXAMPLE 19   *L'anima del filosofo*, Act II

*Orlando paladino* (No. 26). It is followed by a dialogue in secco recitative between Orfeo and Euridice, whereupon the women's chorus repeats its initial song. The lovers again take over and ultimately the two soloists cooperate with the chorus. The important part assigned to the choruses, the tragic ending of the opera, the more concise form in which most of the numbers are cast, and the stirring effect of some scenes (especially of the simple, deeply moving death-song of Euridice) show that Haydn was aiming at improving the Neapolitan *opera seria* along the lines of Gluck's operatic reform. Yet he must have encountered a serious obstacle in the verbosity and tediousness of Badini's libretto. Besides, he was not able to dispense completely with the *recitativo secco*, and some of the pieces, such as the conventional coloratura aria of the Spirit in the third act, definitely point back into the past. In spite of its many beauties, *L'anima del filosofo* is hardly on a level with the composer's other great vocal and instrumental works of the same period. The opera shows again that Haydn did not feel sufficiently at home in the composition of serious operas to free himself completely from the bondage of prevailing taste and to create real musical drama.

   Haydn's last work for the stage was incidental music to an English tragedy, *The Patriot King, or Alfred and Elvida*, by Alexander Bicknell (1788), which was performed in 1796 in Vienna in a translation by J. W. Cowmeadow, as *Alfred oder der patriotische König* but had little success and before long disappeared from the repertoire.

Haydn composed for this drama a three-part "Chorus of Danes" for sopranos, tenors, and basses;[34] a recitative and aria for the Guardian Spirit, and a duet for Alfred and Odun, Earl of Devon (Hob. XXX:5). The chorus was published after Haydn's death with changed words and piano accompaniment as "Kriegerischer Chor" (Martial Chorus). It is a showy, somewhat shallow piece employing trumpets and timpani. The soprano aria of the Guardian Spirit "Ausgesandt vom Strahlenthrone" (Sent forth from the radiant throne) is in fact a dialogue between a heavenly and a terrestrial being. The Spirit sings accompanied by a sextet of clarinets, horns, and bassoons, and the woman who receives the celestial message answers with spoken words to instrumental accompaniment. Evidently it was Haydn's aim to establish a clear distinction between supernatural and human beings. The duet "Der Morgen graut, es ruft der Hahn" (Dawn breaks, the cock is crowing) presents a solemn melody accompanied by pizzicato strings. In the orchestral ritornelli, the cantilena likewise played pizzicato by the first violins is accompanied by a *violino principale* in the upper octave, achieving a remarkable coloristic effect. Haydn originally planned to have a harp cooperate, but he left the respective staff in the score empty, deciding that the plucked strings sufficed to produce the desired effect.

As this music concludes Haydn's production for the stage, it seems appropriate to review his operatic output as a whole here. The memorandum with which Haydn in the 1760s accompanied his cantata *Applausus* contained the significant words: "If I have failed to guess the taste of the musicians, it must not be taken amiss, as I did not know the performers or the locality. My ignorance of these matters really has made the work hard for me." In the famous letter of 1787 to Roth in Prague, he gave the following reason for his refusal to have one of his earlier operas performed there: "All my operas are too closely connected with our personal circle (Eszterháza in Hungary); they could never produce the proper effect, which I have calculated in accordance with the locality." These utterances, made at different periods, reflect the basic attitude natural to a composer of the eighteenth century writing in the style of the Italian opera. The personality of the performers and the place of performance always had to be taken into consideration. The virtuosity of the singers, the technical equipment of the stage, the beauty of the costumes and decorations, and the skill of the stage architect were

[34] The elimination of the alto voice is equally characteristic of the choice of soloists in Haydn's two great oratorios written soon afterward.

factors the composer took into serious account. It is significant that after the failure to have *L'anima del filosofo* performed in London, Haydn did not attempt to have it staged elsewhere. With the enormous prestige he enjoyed, he certainly could have obtained a production in Austria or Germany, and it would not have been too difficult to get a release from the London owner.[35]

Dependence on outside conditions was no rarity among eighteenth-century opera composers. Haydn, however, exaggerated his own subservience to this trend. His operas were not only performed in Eszterháza during his lifetime, but also with greatest success in other places and by ensembles with whom he had no contact whatever. It is true that during the climax of the romantic era, Haydn's work for the st~ge was badly neglected, as it appeared too naïve and unsophisticated to an audience used to Wagner and Verdi. In our time, however, the delicate beauty of these works appeals more and more to the music lover. It is largely due to the untiring efforts of Robbins Landon that the music of some fine Haydn operas is again available. Thus the attraction and charm—of the semicomical operas, in particular—can be enjoyed by performers and audiences alike.

• • •

Around 1800, Haydn composed a *Te Deum* in C major (Hob. XXIIIc:2) for the Empress Maria Theresa (second wife of Francis II).[36] Although nearly forty years separate this work from the first *Te Deum*, written in the early 1760s, the two compositions resemble each other not only in the use of the same key, but also in many details, such as the traditional combination of a melody to the words "In te Domine speravi" with a counterpoint to the words "Non confundar in aeternum" in the concluding double fugue. But the second *Te Deum* calls for a choir only and no solo voices. The orchestra is larger, including even three trombones in the definitive version; the setting is simpler and clearer than in the earlier composition. Its expressive power is heightened by the introduction of the Eighth Psalm-Tone at the beginning of the *Te Deum*. In its concise structure and forceful language, this magnificent work counts among the aged Haydn's most significant contributions.

[35] In this respect the edition printed by Breitkopf and Härtel is significant: it does not reveal the sequence of numbers in the opera. Evidently Haydn wanted merely to present individual pieces, not a complete opera suitable for performance.
[36] J. Atkins edited the work with organ accompaniment for Oxford University Press (London); H. C. Robbins Landon edited the full score for Doblinger (Vienna, 1959).

A place of its own is occupied by the "Offertorio in Stilo a Capella" (as the draft catalogue lists it), "Non nobis Domine," set merely for four vocalists and a figured bass. This brief motet (Hob. XXIIIa:1), based on Psalm 115, verse 1 ("Not unto us, O Lord"), was probably written after Haydn's return from his second trip to England, and later changed slightly by the composer himself.[37] The work starts with an impressive fugato, which leads to a homophonic section. This imposing composition, adopting the Palestrina style, testifies again to the great significance strict polyphony held for Haydn, particularly in his later works.

In the six Masses (Hob. XXII:9–14), written between 1796 and 1802 for the name day of Princess Marie Hermenegild Esterházy, Haydn again displayed supreme mastery.[38]

The Mass in C major (Hob. XXII:9) was composed in 1796. Haydn wrote at the head of the score *Missa in tempore belli* (Mass in Wartime), as Napoleon, coming from Italy, was threatening Vienna at that time. In German-speaking countries the work is known as *Paukenmesse* (Kettledrum Mass). In the Agnus Dei the use of trumpets and kettledrums emphasizes the war atmosphere; in particular, the fanfare of the wind instruments at the beginning of the "Dona nobis pacem" creates an intimidating, ominous atmosphere.

A Mass in B-flat major (Hob. XXII:10), entitled *Missa Sancti Bernardi de Offida*, was likewise written in 1796.[39] St. Bernard (1604–1694) was a Capuchin monk who was beatified by Pope Pius VI in 1795. Haydn, who had lived in Vienna close to the Capuchin monastery, was so impressed by the personality of this monk whose life was spent in helping others that he dedicated the Mass to his memory. In German-speaking countries the work is known as *Heiligmesse* because of the use of the hymn "Heilig, heilig, heilig" (Holy, holy, holy) in the alto and tenor parts of the Sanctus.

The Mass in D minor (Hob. XXII:11) was Haydn's only Mass in a minor key. According to the autograph in the National Library, Vienna, it was composed in 1798 at Eisenstadt within the surprisingly short time of fifty-three days (July 10 to August 31).

---

[37] The first version was edited by Karl Geiringer with Latin and English text for Concordia (St. Louis, Mo., 1960). Both versions were edited by H. C. Robbins Landon for Doblinger (Vienna).

[38] H. C. Robbins Landon, H. H. Füssl and Christa Landon edited Hob. XXII:9 and 10 for *JHW*, XXIII/2; G. Thomas edited Hob. XXII:11 and 12 for *JHW*, XXIII/3; Irmgard Becker-Glauch edited Hob. XXII:13 for *JHW*, XXIII/4; F. Lippmann edited Hob. XXII:14 for *JHW*, XXIII/5.

[39] It is not known which of the two Masses belonging to the year 1796 was written first.

While Haydn was engaged in this composition, the news of the battle of the Nile arrived. The striking use of the trumpets in the Benedictus is usually thought to be associated with the report of Nelson's decisive victory over Napoleon, which made a tremendous impression all over Europe.[40] As the work was written in a period of devastating wars, Haydn gave it the title *Missa in angustiis* (Mass in Distress) in his draft catalog, but it is usually known as the *Nelson Mass*. In England it is—possibly as a reference to its outstanding beauty—often called the *Coronation* or *Imperial Mass*. This is the most exciting and dramatic work of its kind Haydn wrote, and probably also the best known and most popular among his Masses.

A Mass in B-flat major (Hob. XXII:12) was composed in 1799. Although it was again written for the name day of Princess Esterházy, the work is known as *Theresienmesse*, as Haydn may have dedicated it later to the Empress Maria Theresa, who was a great admirer of his art.

A Mass in B-flat major (Hob. XXII:13) was composed in 1801 within forty-five days (July 28 to September 11), thus even faster than the *Nelson Mass*. As it introduces in the "Qui tollis" of the Gloria a quotation from Haydn's oratorio *Die Schöpfung*, this Mass is known as the *Schöpfungsmesse* (Creation Mass). Griesinger reports that when the work was performed in Vienna, the Empress objected to the introduction of a well-known secular tune into the sacred composition and demanded its removal. As a matter of fact, in the imperial castle of Vienna parts for the performance of the Mass are preserved that show the demanded alteration.

A Mass in B-flat major (Hob. XXII:14) was composed in 1802. It is scored for an orchestra of strings, flute, and two each of oboes, clarinets, bassoons, horns, trumpets, and timpani as well as an organ. On account of its emphatic use of wind instruments, it is known as *Harmoniemesse* (Wind Band Mass). This is Haydn's last great composition, and it represents a kind of farewell not only to the Mass form but to music itself. Motives and moods from earlier Masses reoccur, and Haydn displays once more his magical ability to use all elements of the contrapuntal style.

In his valuable book on Haydn's symphonies, Robbins Landon expounds on the idea that Haydn's last six Masses represent a direct continuation of his activity as a composer of symphonies. He states that "in their fundamental construction the late Haydn Masses are

---

[40] After Haydn's death a chart of the Battle of the Nile was found among his papers.

symphonies for voices and orchestra."[41] Martin Chusid continues this trend of thought by stating that each of the Masses represents a cycle of three vocal symphonies.[42] He explains that through the interpolation of segments from the Proper of the Mass, the Ordinary is subdivided into three main sections: (1) Kyrie and Gloria; (2) Credo; (3) Sanctus, Benedictus, and Agnus. Within each of these sections, Haydn uses a fast movement (occasionally with slow introduction) at the beginning and likewise a fast movement at the end, while a slow movement in a contrasting key, and also mostly a more cheerful movement, stands in the middle. Thus the formal structure of a vocal symphony is achieved. Moreover, many of the individual sections clearly adopt the forms of symphonic movements such as sonatas or rondos.

On the whole, however, the features of the older Masses are still preserved in these later works, but the distribution of the individual elements has changed, and their connection has become tighter and more organic. The use of vocal solos is greatly reduced and their melodic line simplified in a classical manner. Instead of single voices, Haydn largely employs the solo quartet, the four voices of which are treated in a loose contrapuntal style, thus effectively contrasting with the plain tutti of the chorus, which predominantly are conceived on purely harmonic lines. The importance of polyphony is increased in these last Masses, and fugues are frequently introduced. The Credo of the *Nelsonmesse* includes a canon at the fifth, and the Incarnatus of the *Heiligmesse* a three-part canon. Particularly impressive are the magnificent Credo fugue of the *Missa in tempore belli* and the "In gloria Dei" fugue of the *Heiligmesse*. Sketches for the latter prove the care that Haydn bestowed on it. In the earlier Masses, the instruments of the orchestra were used mainly to reinforce the vocal parts; in the works written after 1796, they frequently are employed independently, carrying melodies of their own. The choice of instruments used in the different Masses reflects the changing size of Prince Esterházy's orchestra; at the same time it reveals Haydn's joy in diversity—no two of the Masses have the same orchestral garb. The original version of the *Nelsonmesse* prescribes three trumpets and timpani besides strings and concertizing organ, thus achieving a sparse tonal

---

[41] Landon, *Symphonies*, p. 596.
[42] Martin Chusid, "Some Observations on Liturgy, Text and Structure in Haydn's Late Masses" in *Studies in Eighteenth Century Music. A Tribute to Karl Geiringer on His Seventieth Birthday*, edited by H. C. Robbins Landon and Roger E. Chapman (London, 1970), p. 125ff.

language full of vigor and intensity. The use of brass instruments gives the Benedictus of this Mass a particularly brilliant and power-ful character. The *Theresienmesse* calls for only two clarinets and two trumpets among the wind instruments. The most extensive orchestral body is required in the *Harmoniemesse*, the last large work that Haydn completed. Truly romantic sound effects are achieved here by the wind instruments; for example, the mysterious, soft employment of brass and timpani in the "Et incarnatus est" is ex-quisitely poetic. Of equal significance is the lovely Incarnatus in the *Creation Mass*, in which Haydn again introduces an organ solo. The delicate warbling and twittering provided here with the help of the flautino stop is intended to describe the advent of the Holy Ghost symbolized by a dove. Beethoven uses a somewhat related idea in his *Missa Solemnis*. One of Haydn's main aims during this period was to furnish an adequate musical interpretation of his text; the composition tries to follow the Ordinary of the Mass in every detail and to deepen its expression. The occasions are becoming less and less frequent when Haydn's musicianship makes him oblivious to the dramatic possibilities of his subject. As an example of such neg-lect, the Incarnatus of the *Theresienmesse* should be mentioned. Its first part in B-flat minor is followed by a second in D-flat major. The mild, tender character of the second section is musically justi-fied, but it hardly fits the words of the Crucifixus with which it is used. It is also noteworthy that in the same work Haydn neglects setting to music the words "Et in unum Dominum Jesum Christum filium Dei unigenitum" despite their liturgical importance. But in-stances of excellent interpretation of the text in terms of music are far more frequent. The *Heiligmesse* contains a Crucifixus, the tragic expression of which could hardly be surpassed. In the Incarnatus of the *Missa in tempore belli*, Haydn, like Beethoven after him, uses the word *et* (and) in order to increase the dramatic suspense. The whole chorus sings it in a long, drawn-out forte based on a diminished seventh chord before the words "incarnatus est" sung in piano de-scribe the miracle of the union of divinity with humanity in Christ. An anticipation of Beethoven may also be discerned in the menac-ing use of trumpets and timpani in the Agnus Dei of the same Mass. Beethoven's "prayer for inner and outer peace" is somewhat forecast in this deeply moving section. In this connection it may be pointed out that the inclusion of trumpet fanfares in the Mass is based on an old Austrian tradition. Christoph Strauss, a choirmas-ter of St. Stephen's Cathedral in Vienna, used it as early as 1631 in his *Missa veni sponsa Christi*. As in Haydn's late instrumental works, so in his late Masses, the influence of Mozart may be detected. A good example is provided by the Gratias of the *Theresienmesse,* which displays much of Mozart's grace and fervor.

Summarizing the results of the analysis of Haydn's church music, we notice that at first he used elements of style that had originated in various parts of Italy. Subsequently he succeeded in synthesizing these trends and creating, out of baroque and classical elements, with the help of simple, often folkloristic melodies, a language of his own, definitely of Austrian character. The type of sacred composition that was thus created from different building stones helped to establish the foundation for the imposing edifice of nineteenth-century Austrian Mass composition.

•  •  •

In 1792 Haydn's "madrigal" for chorus and orchestra, *The Storm* (Hob. XXIVa:8),[43] based on a text by John Wolcot (better known under his pen name of Peter Pindar), was performed with great success in London. This work shows an effective contrast between an imposing musical description of a storm (in D minor) and a melodious, gently flowing andante (in D major) expressing hope for the return of "blessed calm." The contrast also is expressed in the instrumental coloring, as the trumpets, timpani, and trombones, included in the first part of the work's definitive version, are dismissed in the second section and the chorus is replaced by a quartet of soloists. This piece seems like a precursor of the thunderstorm in *The Seasons,* but the repetition of both sections, though certainly justified from a musical point of view, somewhat weakens its dramatic power.

The British Library possesses the autograph of an oratorio fragment by Haydn, written in 1794. This work (Hob. XXIVa:9)[44] consists of two numbers only, an aria for bass and a five-part chorus accompanied by full orchestra. The words are taken from M. Nedham's poem "Neptune to the Commonwealth of England," which he used as an introduction to his English translation of John Selden's Latin treatise *Mare clausum.* The composition was undertaken at the request of Lord Abingdon. But when Haydn found out that three other men before him, among them his former pupil Pleyel, had composed on the same subject, he lost interest in the

[43] Edited by F. Burkhart with English and German text for Doblinger (Vienna, 1958).
[44] Edited by H. C. Robbins Landon for Doblinger (Vienna, 1971).

work.[45] Only the second and third of the six stanzas of Nedham's poem were set. The aria "Nor can I think my suit is vain" brilliantly employs the woodwinds (including clarinets); the chorus "Thy great endeavours to increase the Marine power" is a vivid, radiant piece easily captivating the audience. It is most regrettable that this lively and inspired composition, one of the few works Haydn wrote to an English text, never was completed.

•   •   •

The singularly expressive character of Haydn's music to *The Seven Last Words* has always been noticed. In 1788 the *Musikalische Realzeitung* wrote about the work: "We are able to guess in practically every note what the composer meant to convey by it." It was therefore an obvious idea to convert this instrumental composition into a vocal Passion piece by the introduction of voices. The first attempt in this direction was made by Joseph Friebert, a musician in the little city of Passau in south Germany. Haydn heard this arrangement in 1794, on his second trip to England. He did not approve of the new version, but was so interested in it that he decided to use it as a basis for a similar work of his own. The adaptation of the words was made by Gottfried van Swieten, who collaborated with Haydn for the first time in this work. The new text, dealing with the sufferings of Our Lord and the redemption of mankind, is lacking in action and is in complete conformity with the sentimental German oratorios of the second half of the eighteenth century, which were based on the story of the Messiah. Its content is altogether lyrical, and dramatic elements are eschewed as far as possible; apparently Ramler's *Tod Jesu* served van Swieten as a model. The librettist even appropriated episodes from that work, such as the gloomy and portentous text on the earthquake that concludes Haydn's work. Fortunately the stilted pomposity characteristic of so many German oratorio texts of the eighteenth century hardly is noticeable in *The Seven Last Words*.

The autograph of the oratorio,[46] preserved in the National Library, Budapest, plainly reveals the technique adopted by Haydn for his arrangement. He first had the original instrumental version copied onto music paper ruled with a great many staves, only some of which were used. Then he himself started to insert the vocal

[45] Cf. Pohl and Botstiber, *Joseph Haydn*, III, p. 84.
[46] The composition (Hob. XX:2) has been edited in a revised edition by Hubert Unverricht for *JHW*, XXVIII/2.

parts and the new instruments, two clarinets and two trombones, into the score. At the same time, several minor changes were made in the original instrumentation. For instance, in order to increase the harsh grandeur of the introduction, Haydn omitted the flutes of the older version. An important addition to the arrangement consists of a new number inserted between the fourth and fifth sonatas. It is a largo performed by wind instruments only. As a counterpart to the introduction, it once more expresses the prevailing tragic spirit by instrumental means. At the same time, the oratorio adopts a significant feature, each of its movements being preceded by the relevant utterance of the Saviour. The full chorus is employed to pronounce the "word" in simple recitation. Apart from these details, the original construction of the composition has not been changed. A chorus and a quartet of solo voices were added to the instrumental composition without any considerable alteration of the original music. Nevertheless, the text is mostly so well adjusted that the listener who is not informed about the genesis of *The Seven Last Words* is inclined to accept the work as an oratorio conceived in the normal way. Only occasionally are text and music incompatible. In the choral section of No. 6, for instance, the words "Woe ye wicked, woe ye blind" are accompanied by music imbued with an almost serene spirit. While the composer, inspired by the words "It is finished," expresses the confidence of mankind in the salvation through Jesus' sacrifice, the poet still is concerned with the drama of Golgotha. Either point of view is justified, but their combination certainly is unsatisfactory. Such shortcomings are, however, infrequent, and on the whole it is remarkable how admirably the poet follows the musician, though the peculiarities of the instrumental forms, such as the development and recapitulation sections, do not make his task an easy one.

The vocal version impresses the listener as a work fully realizing the composer's innermost intentions. Sandberger feels that a large part of its success is owing to Friebert's work, as Haydn's arrangement, particularly in its first part, is strongly dependent on the model.[47] However, we cannot help admiring Haydn's sure instinct and singular lack of prejudice in allowing himself to be guided by an artist of mediocre abilities at a time when he himself had reached the pinnacle of his creative output.

•   •   •

[47] Adolf Sandberger, "Zur Entstehungsgeschichte von Haydns 'Die Sieben Worte des Erlösers am Kreuze,'" *Jahrbuch Peters*, X (1903).

It is of interest that the exponents of the later romanticism, around the year 1900, looked with a very superior air, almost with contempt, at the early evidence of romantic feeling as displayed in Haydn's *Die Schöpfung* (The Creation) and *Die Jahreszeiten* (The Seasons). I. F. Runciman sums up his discussion of *The Creation* with the words:[48] "After considering the songs, the recitatives, and the choruses in detail it really seems to contain very little. Perhaps it may be described as a third-rate oratorio, whose interest is largely historic and literary."

It no longer is necessary to apologize for Haydn's last two oratorios. Nevertheless, they do not enjoy the position they deserve in the English-speaking countries. Performances of *The Creation* are still relatively infrequent, and *The Seasons* is almost unknown even to many choral conductors. The great popularity that these oratorios enjoy in Austria and Germany is not paralleled in England and America, though in several respects the two works are more English than German.

Haydn had been among the audience of the great Handel Festival of 1791. He found a whole nation aroused by compositions offered in monumental performances. Compared with these concerts on a large scale, his own efforts of earlier years to entertain a small group of music lovers at Eszterháza must have seemed almost insignificant to him. He desired intensely to write, as Handel had written, works meant for a whole nation. Different types of oratorios were used at that time in Austria and Germany, but none of them really satisfied the master. There was the Italian oratorio, which he had employed in his *Il ritorno di Tobia*. But Haydn was now reluctant to use a language foreign to the people for whom the composition was written, reluctant to commit himself to the formalism of this genre, with its weak arias and neglect of powerful choruses. There was, on the other hand, the contemplative, sentimental German oratorio; but he had just finished the arrangement of *The Seven Last Words* and had no wish to lose himself again in tearful mellowness. Neither did he care for the dramatic type of German oratorio as cultivated by J. H. Rolle, which produced a sort of disguised sacred opera. After having written more than a dozen operas, Haydn felt too clearly that he would never give his very best in a work of predominantly dramatic character. There remained only one type of oratorio to which he really felt attracted, and that was again the oratorio of Handel, of the type exemplified

[48] I. F. Runciman, *Old Scores and New Reading* (London, 1899), p. 92.

by his *Israel in Egypt* and *L'allegro, il pensieroso, ed il moderato*. The unorthodox construction of these works, the hymnic impetus of their choruses, and their strong feeling for nature deeply impressed Haydn, and he decided to follow the example of these great English oratorios rather than use a German model.

Also, a wholly suitable subject for his work was offered to Haydn in England. This was an oratorio text that an unknown author had compiled from the contents of the first chapter of Genesis and the seventh and eighth books of Milton's *Paradise Lost*. According to tradition, this text, entitled "The Creation," had originally been destined for Handel himself. Haydn took the English libretto to Vienna, entrusting Baron van Swieten with the translation and proper adaptation. Van Swieten was certainly the right person for the task, as he had proved his skill with his work on *The Seven Last Words*, and moreover he was a great admirer of Handel. Therefore it is not surprising that the German text of "The Creation," based in its recitatives on the Vulgate, was in many respects akin to the texts of Handel's oratorios. Wherever it was possible, the powerful words of the Bible replaced the sentimental paraphrases used in German oratorios at that time. The old narrator was revived in the persons of three singers: the archangels Gabriel (soprano), Uriel (tenor), and Raphael (bass), who take turns telling the story of the Creation. Most of all, the important share awarded to the chorus reminds us of the oratorios of Handel.

Van Swieten did not restrict himself to the arrangement of the text; the imperious baron also gave Haydn directions on how to set the words to music.[49] Far from resenting such tutoring, Haydn followed van Swieten's advice in most cases, and it cannot be denied that this was beneficial for the composition. What insight is revealed, for instance, by the baron's advice: " 'Let there be light' must be sung only once"!

Not only van Swieten's text, but also Haydn's music breathes the spirit of Handel. Haydn certainly did not copy the older master, but he found in the works of his great model an excuse for his tendency to abandon formulas generally employed in Austria. In Haydn's oratorio,[50] chorus and soloists are sometimes used to-

[49] The autograph of van Swieten's libretto is preserved by the National Library, Budapest. Cf. also Horst Walter, "Gottfried van Swieten's handschriftliche Textbücher zu 'Schöpfung' und 'Jahreszeiten,'" *H-St*, I/4 (Apr. 1967), p. 241.

[50] Haydn was engaged in work on *Die Schöpfung* (Hob. XXI:2) in the years from 1796 to 1798. His autograph of the score seems to be lost. The work was originally printed in 1800 with Haydn himself serving as the publisher. A critical edition of the oratorio was presented by E. Mandyczewski in *Haydns Werke* (Leipzig: Breitkopf &

gether, at other times alternate quickly; the form of the arias changes from number to number, but is always dependent on the text; the recitatives often assume the form of charmingly accompanied ariosos, displaying in their tone-paintings the composer's deep love of nature. All this is typical of Haydn's last period of composition, but it is doubtful that he would have dared to follow his instinct so completely, had it not been for the encouragement provided by Handel's oratorios. In his early cantatas, Haydn often subordinated the text to the music; in *Il ritorno di Tobia* they were treated as equals; finally, in *The Creation* and *The Seasons* the musical construction was determined by the substance of the text in the same way as it has been in all truly great oratorios before and after those of Haydn.

The apparently spontaneous freedom of expression in *The Creation* is really the product of an extraordinary intensity of work. Haydn now worked very slowly and carefully, first making sketches as Beethoven did after him. Of that easy reliance on sure instinct that his youthful works had revealed there is not a trace in *The Creation*.

The master used drafts for many works of this period, such as the last Masses and various marches, songs, and canons. None of these sketches is so extensive and so important as those of *The Creation*, twenty-three pages of which are preserved in the National Library, Vienna.[51] As they afford a valuable insight into the gradual shaping of Haydn's ideas, it seems appropriate to mention two characteristic instances.[52]

Particularly interesting are the sketches for the chorus "By thee with bliss" (No. 30),[53] which in its final form presents only a shadowy foundation on which the swelling hymn of the two soloists is raised. Haydn did not arrive at this justly admired color effect at first inspiration. As originally conceived, this chorus was a lively movement opening with imitations and set in C minor, not C major. But Haydn did not let matters rest there, and the passage appears on another page of the sketches in C major. The soprano solo

Härtel, 1924), XVI no. 5. The Eulenburg pocket score is based on Mandyczewski's revision.

[51] MSS. 16835 and 18987. Individual sheets with sketches to *The Creation* are also preserved in the Public Library, New York; the British Library, London; and the Bibliothèque Nationale, Paris.

[52] Cf. Karl Geiringer, "Haydn's Sketches for 'The Creation,'" *Musical Quarterly*, XVIII/2 (Apr. 1932), p. 299ff. Reprint by Da Capo Press (New York, 1982).

[53] In the following analysis the numbering of individual pieces follows the Eulenburg score of *The Creation*.

now occurs in its present form and the chorus is handled far more simply. In the margin Haydn appended the words, so indicative of his irrepressible sense of humor: "It is not good to be interesting," the obvious reasoning behind this comment being: This example proves that it is not good to write too complicated music. In fact, the final form of the chorus is far simpler than either of the sketches.

For the instrumental introduction to the oratorio, entitled "Representation of Chaos," no less than seven different sketches exist. The passage for the first violin in the third and fourth measures, describing the boundless loneliness of lifeless chaos, is missing in an early sketch, and the ascending triplet figure is not given the completely subdued coloring expressing infinite desolation. Haydn entrusts it to the first violin, horn, and clarinet, whereas he subsequently has it played by bassoon, viola, cello, and, occasionally, the second violin (which probably sounds less brilliant than the first). The D-flat major section is merely outlined in this early draft. A later sketch presents the first part of the introduction in practically the same form in which we know it today, but the contrasting section in D-flat major still lacks the significant accompaniment in sixteenth notes in the bassoon, which contributes so substantially to mellowing the austerity of the beginning. It also is characteristic that in measure forty-nine of the final version, Haydn has written a single ascending figure for the bassoon, whereas in the sketch he had put an ornate flourish, twice as long, for the clarinet. The composer worked steadily toward the simplification of expression, banning all rococo affectation from his work.

One of the greatest numbers in the score of *The Creation* is this very first one, describing Chaos. Zelter, the friend of Goethe, called it "the crown on a God's head." The romantic touch in these dark harmonies full of chromatic passing notes and suspensions is unmistakable, and Tovey even goes so far as to compare them to the music of Wagner's *Tristan und Isolde*. He suggests moreover, that Haydn, who had met the astronomer Herschel, may have heard about the evolution of the cosmos out of chaos, and that these ideas inspired him to write his overture. The economy of the composer's thematic work deserves greatest admiration. The first twenty measures of this prelude in C minor describing the sadness of Chaos are based on the stepwise descending "sigh motive." As soon as the idea of cosmic life is introduced, the gentle key of D-flat major sets in, and with it an ascending instead of the former descending motive in the woodwind. Such monumental simplicity is largely responsible for the piece's overwhelming effect. The following recitative and chorus contain the famous passage "And there was light," with its change from C minor to C major, and from piano to forte. A hundred years later, Richard Strauss, in his *Also sprach Zarathustra*, described the mighty appearance of the sun with similar means of expression. The ensuing "Now vanish" (No. 2), is one of the many numbers of this score in which Haydn connects a soloist with the chorus, displaying in these mixed pieces an unrivaled imagination and variety of form. Here the chorus repeatedly sings the words "A new created world springs up at God's command." Whenever the words "a new created world" recur, Haydn changes the harmony. No. 3, Raphael's recitative "And God made the firmament," contains some of the innumerable descriptions of nature in which *The Creation* excels. Storm, lightning, thunder, rain, hail, snow, and, later on, a whole menagerie of mammals, birds, fishes, and insects— all this Haydn's orchestra describes with a great sense of humor. He, who clung to nature and all earthly things more fervently than most other composers, fully succeeded in reflecting the youthful purity of the newly created universe. So sure was Haydn of the expressive power of his music that his descriptions always precede the explaining text. A powerful solo by Gabriel with a choral accompaniment concludes the second day of the Creation. No. 6, Raphael's aria "Rolling in foaming billows," is partly modeled on Italian examples. It is not free from ornamental coloratura, and its key sequences are reminiscent of those used in instrumental music. Nevertheless, the text predominates over the form here too, and an equal number of musical sections corresponds to the four pictures of the poem (ocean, mountains, river, and brook, the latter characteristically treated with special love). The beautiful, purely lyrical aria of Gabriel, "With verdure clad" (No. 8), contrasts very effectively with the majestic chorus "Awake the harp" (No. 10). The simple, terse first ten measures of the recitative "In splendor bright" (No. 12), describing the sunrise, belong among Haydn's greatest inspirations. The melody is lifted slowly stepwise through the interval of a tenth. In almost every measure a fresh instrument is added to the orchestra until the delicate pianissimo has been changed into an overwhelming fortissimo. The chorus with a trio of the soloists, "The heavens are telling" (No. 13), ends the first part of *The Creation*. It is one of the best-known pieces of the score, but its popularity ought not to induce the conductors of small choruses to perform it as a separate piece with the omission of the solo voices, as this procedure deprives the composition of much of its charm.

The second part of the oratorio begins with the fifth day of the

Creation, when the animals come to life. In the coloratura aria of Gabriel "On mighty pens" (No. 15), the cooing sounds of the pigeons are particularly well imitated by the bassoons and violins. A stroke of genius is found in No. 16, which begins as a recitative, but presently assumes the character of an arioso. At the words "Be fruitful and multiply," divided violas, violoncellos, and double basses are employed to express mysterious saturation and abundance. Here is it imperative that the double basses should play the lowest notes $F_1$, $E_1$, $D_1$, and $C_1$, as prescribed by Haydn, for the frequent transposition of this passage an octave upward is likely to nullify the majestic effect he intended. In No. 19, "The Lord is great and great His might," the three soloists join in praise of the Almighty, the chorus supporting them in an exuberant paean. The recitative "Straight opening her fertile womb" (No. 21) takes us to the sixth day of the Creation and with it to a further extension of the zoological cast of characters. Here, Haydn's resourcefulness in the invention of effects of color is matched only by his economy in their employment. The aria of Uriel, "In native worth" (No. 24), deals with the achievement of the seventh day, the creation of the first human couple. Its proud bearing expresses the optimistic attitude toward mankind which Haydn shared with many great spirits of the eighteenth century, the age of humanism and enlightenment. The end of the second part of the oratorio consists of two great choruses in the same key (Nos. 26 and 28), partly based on identical words ("Achieved is the glorious work") and music, but separated by a trio for the soloists, the result being a sort of three-part form. The second of these choruses contains a double fugue of Handelian dignity and simplicity.

The third part of *The Creation* is dedicated to the praise of the Creation through the first human beings, Adam (bass) and Eve (soprano), who now replace the archangels Gabriel and Raphael. In the E major introduction to this part, Haydn uses three flutes accompanied by the pizzicato of the strings. This intensely romantic description of the early morning seems to anticipate the beginning of the prelude to Wagner's *Lohengrin*. The duet and chorus "By thee with bliss" (No. 30) has already been mentioned in connection with the sketches for the oratorio. With its approximately four hundred measures, it is one of the longest, and at the same time one of the most inspired and powerful, numbers of the entire work. In a way it marks the end of the oratorio, as the succeeding love duet between Adam and Eve displays a slightly incongruous and commonplace character. Its ostentatious show in the *style galant* seems better suited to a rococo Singspiel than an oratorio based on the Bible and Milton's great epic. The very last number, a prayer of thanks for solo quartet (the only number of the score in which a contralto solo is prescribed) and chorus, culminates in a mighty double fugue that brings the work to an imposing conclusion. Better than any personal document, *The Creation* testifies to the breadth of Haydn's inner world. In this work, childlike naïveté, joy in the world of the senses, and gentle humor are combined with profound faith, nobility of expression, and hymnlike fervor. The diversity inherent in this spiritual landscape may account for the strong echo that the work, since its first performance, has evoked in the hearts of listeners.

Soon after the completion of *The Creation* (1798), Haydn started on another big vocal composition, on which he worked up to the year 1801. Again, van Swieten adapted the text from an English poem, James Thomson's *The Seasons*, printed in four sections in 1726, 1727, 1728, and 1730. This work, filled with cheerful optimism, describes with an abundance of detail the beauties of nature; any kind of dramatic action is completely absent from it. The poem offers a continuous series of images full of picturesque variety, and these provide an excellent foundation for a musical libretto. Van Swieten showed a certain attitude of independence toward the original work. He eliminated philosophical and historical details, while emphasizing Thomson's tender lyrical observations of nature. The English poet's fundamental attitude, however, that of depicting the seasons with love and deep understanding but without any attempt to establish a relationship with human emotions, has been preserved by van Swieten. Thomson's work and the baron's adaptation do not present subjective feelings, but only objective descriptions. The exaggerated praises of the "merry shepherd," the "gay herd," and the wonderful "daughters of nature" all breathe the shallow playfulness of rococo art.

The English poem did not furnish van Swieten with any suggestions for the arrangement of the text into recitatives, arias, choruses; in this regard he again displayed a thorough understanding of the possibilities of musical setting, and particularly an appreciation of Haydn's specific talents. Far less successful was the arranger in transforming the unhappy ending of Thomson's "Winter," in which the wanderer perishes in the cold. But the baron had just as little appreciation of the beauties of nature in wintertime as Thomson himself, and accordingly he moved the scene from the open air to a peasant's house, where the soloists and chorus perform two pieces. For this episode, van Swieten used texts written by other poets: "The Spinning Song" by Gottfried August Bürger and a little poem by Christian Felix Weisse (based on a French text by Madame Favart) that Johann Adam Hiller had employed thirty years earlier in his Singspiel *Liebe auf dem Land*. But as the playful tune of the Singspiel seemed to the baron unsuitable for the conclusion of an oratorio, he made a sudden about-face and boldy ventured into the realm of symbolism. Comparing the seasons in nature to the seasons of human life, he came to the conclusion that virtue alone can lead to eternal happiness. The vision of Paradise assures a dignified ending for the work. However, it cannot be denied that the heterogeneous elements of van Swieten's "Winter" do not blend too well.

Again, the Baron was not satisfied with merely writing the libretto. Just as he had done when working on *The Creation*, he advised Haydn on how to set the words to music. Max Friedländer, the German musicologist, owned the copy of van Swieten's libretto that Haydn had made the basis of his composition.[54] The pages of the manuscript were folded, and in the margin the Baron had noted hints for the benefit of the composer. For instance, he remarked near the end of "Spring": "I believe that at the words 'God of Light! Hail Gracious Lord' [No. 8][55] a key strikingly different from the one used in the preceding 'Song of Joy' would make a good effect and contribute to the solemn and devout character of the utterance." The highly effective change from D major to B-flat major in the majestic invocation of the Lord near the end of "Spring" is thus intimated. It is well known that Haydn disliked certain sections of the text of *The Seasons*, and he particularly resented van Swieten's suggestions of inserting little tone-paintings and genre scenes into the music. As stated earlier in this book, the composer remarked: "This Frenchified trash was forced upon me." But the librettist should not be blamed too severely for having done the "forcing." Although van Swieten was no great poet, his text furnished Haydn

---

[54] See Max Friedländer, "Van Swieten und das Textbuch zu Haydn's 'Jahreszeiten,'" *Jahrbuch Peters* XVI (1909), p. 47ff. The autograph of the libretto was partly photographed and partly copied in 1931–32 by Ernst Fritz Schmid. This reproduction is preserved in the J. Haydn Institute in Cologne and served as a basis for Horst Walter's "Gottfried van Swietens handschriftliche Textbücher zu 'Schöptfung' und 'Jahreszeiten,'" p. 241ff. The autograph of the libretto itself has unfortunately been lost.
[55] The numbering of the individual pieces in this anlysis is based on the Philharmonia miniature score, which reproduces the critical revision of the work by E. Mandyczewski published in *Joseph Haydn Werke*, Series 16, Vols. VI–VII (Leipzig: Breitkopf & Härtel, 1922). The Eulenburg and Peters scores use the Philharmonia edition as their model.

with an abundance of musical possibilities, and even the notorious episode of the croaking frogs in "Summer" by no means disgraces the composition. The composer's complaint about the unpoetical chorus "Joyful, joyful the liquor flows," is equally unjustified. This piece gave him a chance to introduce a typically Austrian note into the work, and even if the words are neither dignified nor poetic, the finished number ranks among the jewels of the score. This is a case of the great and naïve musician Haydn versus the reflective aesthete Haydn, and we must be grateful to van Swieten for having encouraged the former rather than the latter.

Haydn used sketches for *The Seasons* as he had in the case of *The Creation*.[56] He emphasized again and again how strenuous the work was, and he must be admired all the more in that the finished product displays no signs of the toil and labor involved in its making. The apparently easy flow of the musical language was really the result of a strain on the composer's every nerve.

It cannot surprise us that *The Creation* and *The Seasons* (Hob. XXI:3), having been conceived in quick succession, display frequent similarities. Haydn again uses a solo trio consisting of Simon, a farmer (bass); Lucas, a countryman (tenor); and Hanne (Jane), Simon's daughter (soprano), instead of the traditional solo quartet. The free, unorthodox construction of the sections is particularly marked in the later work. It seems to be, in effect, a succession of four loosely connected cantatas, and many editions (among them the first one) do not carry the designation "oratorio" at all.

As in *The Creation*, the introductions to the different parts of the work express a poetical program. The art of description is so highly developed that some of the instrumental pieces tell a story of their own, after which the ensuing vocal number carries on the account from where the instrumental introduction left off. These instrumental numbers rank among the very best sections of the score.

The first part of *The Seasons*,[57] called "Spring," opens with an overture "expressing the passage from winter to spring." Here the master orchestrator asserts himself. The icy terror of winter is described by a menacing unison of the strings at the start and subsequently by syncopations and sforzandi, as well as by the threaten-

[56] See G. Schünemann, "Ein Skizzenblatt Joseph Haydns," *Die Musik*, (1908–09), p. 16. Only a single sheet with sketches (to Nos. 33 and 36) is known to have survived. It is the property of the Staatsbibliothek Preussischer Kulturbesitz, Berlin.
[57] The autograph of the work seems to be lost. The score was first printed in 1802 by Breitkopf and Härtel (Leipzig), with German and English text. An edition with French and German text followed soon after.

ing voices of trombones and timpani. Later, the instruments toss to each other a high-spirited new subject (measure 56); clearly, spring is on its way and a more transparent instrumentation suggests the melting of the ice.

The overture to *The Seasons* is followed by one of those recitatives with highly expressive orchestral accompaniments in which this composition so excels. The lovely chorus of peasants, "Come gentle spring" (No. 2), uses in its middle section alternate groups of women and men, providing an effective contrast to the full chorus employed at the beginning and end of the number. In other sections of the oratorio, too, Haydn at times divided his mixed chorus in order to obtain greater variety of color. The succeeding aria of Simon (No. 4) displays the same attractive simplicity as the chorus. The bass describes the plowman tilling his field and whistling a folk tune, which the piccolo intones in a few instrumental measures after the first stanza. It is none other than the theme of the andante in Haydn's "Surprise" Symphony; even farmers were presumed to know it at that time. Two mighty ensemble numbers constitute the second half of "Spring." The prayer for a blessing of the fields (No. 8) reveals Haydn's art in having soloists and chorus alternate or cooperate, thus building up a musical texture of greatest diversity. It starts with a rapturous solo of the soprano, later joined by tenor and chorus, extolling the beauties of the fields in bloom. After a jubilant ending in D major, the chorus boldly intones a hymn to the Creator in the solemn key of B-flat major. A short section for the solo trio leads to an imposing choral fugue imbued with the ingenious majesty of the choruses in *The Messiah*. In this piece, Haydn gives special prominence to the first three notes of his subject, and they are used in the second half of the fugue in a very effective augmentation. The analogy with some of his own symphonic movements is obvious.

"Summer" starts with an introduction "representing the idea of morning twilight." The anxieties and fears of the night are described at first in order to create a dark background for the light, cheerful atmosphere of the following scenes. It is interesting to note that Haydn intended this passage in its original form to sound even more mournful. An old manuscript score,[58] which belonged to the Tonkünstlersocietät in Vienna and shows a version of the instrumentation earlier than the one in the first printed edition, used no violins at all in this number. The melody of the strings was con-

[58] Preserved in the City Library of Vienna.

fined to the violas and basses, an idea that Brahms later used in his *Ein deutsches Requiem*. As soon as the "crested harbinger of the day with lively note the shepherd wakes," the amusing oboe solo effectively dispels the gloomy mood of the beginning. The vision of sunrise (No. 11) is equal, if not superior, in significance to the parallel description in *The Creation*. Haydn depicts the ascent of the sun with the help of instruments, solo voices, and chorus, and the device of chromatic modulation is most impressively employed. It takes the composer, who begins the movement piano, only six measures to reach the climax, and in these few measures, urging, growing, driving, and expansion are expressed, which we would expect in the work of a youth rather than in that of a man of almost seventy. After a hymn in which soloists and chorus jointly glorify the sun, a striking contrast is achieved by the recitative and cavatina (Nos. 12 and 13) of Lucas, painting a most realistic picture of languid prostration with the help of muted strings, flute, and oboe. Jane's ensuing recitative and aria (Nos. 14 and 15) are inserted as a retarding element before the cataclysm of the thunderstorm, announced by scary pizzicatos in the strings and two ominous timpani rolls. Of the storm choruses that Haydn composed, the one in "Summer" (No. 17) is not only the last but also certainly the greatest. Its first part describes with striking realism the uproar of nature; its second section, a fugue with a lamenting subject, the distress of frightened mankind. A disaster and its reflection in the human heart are depicted in colors of sublime grandeur. For the second time in the course of "Summer" the composer introduces a dark, almost tragic element in order to produce a change in the predominantly optimistic gaiety of the composition. The last trio and chorus of this section (No. 18) is an idyll very different from the majestic endings of "Spring" and "Winter." The dramatic episode of the thunderstorm is over, and beast and man enjoy the return of peace. Here Haydn presents some of his most charming nature studies: the lowing of cows, the chirping of crickets, the croaking of frogs, and the ringing of evening bells. How delightful is all this "Frenchified trash," and how beautifully it fits into the score. Evening has come, the stars shine, and the country people go to sleep. In delicate pianissimo the rustic scene reaches its tranquil end.

If this conclusion of "Summer" is reminiscent of the slow movement of a symphony, the following "Autumn" contains many numbers recalling a scherzo. The instrumental introduction (No. 19) "indicating the husbandman's satisfaction at the abundant harvest" presents a graceful tune reflecting a happiness that Haydn, who spent most of his life in the country, must often have experienced at harvest time. This introduction was originally much longer. The score of the Tonkünstlersocietät contained, after measure thirty of this piece, twenty-four measures that Haydn later cut. The composer always avoided drawing out a composition unnecessarily if he could achieve the same effect with fewer notes. The ensuing trio with chorus (No. 20), praising industry, was, as Haydn himself admitted, composed very reluctantly because of its pedantic text; yet the vivid fugue placed in its center imbued the philistine phrases with life and spirit. The succeeding duet (No. 22) expresses the tender affection between the young peasant, Lucas, and the farmer's daughter, Jane. The words of both are sung to the same melody, thus making the close connection of the couple obvious. This piece, with its coloratura passages and two changes of time, recalls to some extent the form of the grand Italian arias. The *style galant* of the rococo period is in evidence in this pastoral scene, and it would not be surprising if in spite of, or rather because of, its ostentatious show of artless simplicity, Lucas and Jane were replaced by Damon and Phyllis.

There follow various scenes devoted to hunting (Nos. 24–26). We witness dogs flushing birds, then a battue aimed at killing hares, and finally a stag hunt. Haydn, who loved hunting, here creates a composition full of verve and color. Four French horns, the traditional interpreters of hunting scenes, are used to excellent effect. The fact that this piece begins in D and ends in E-flat is characteristic of the composer's daring inspiration. The best is, however, yet to come: the final chorus of "Autumn," depicting the merrymaking after the gathering of the grapes (No. 28). The orchestra, reinforced by triangle and tambourine, greatly contributes to the exhilarating scene, and one is reminded of old Dutch paintings, showing lusty peasants dancing, drinking, and shouting. Haydn's musical portraits are, however, typically Austrian in character, and in their earthy vigor they are far removed from the coy lovers described earlier. He does not hesitate to depict the effect of wine on the merry tipplers, relying on his own observations in wine-growing country.

The instrumental introduction to "Winter" (No. 29), depicting the thick fogs at the approach of that season, resembles the "Representation of Chaos" in *The Creation*, written in the same key, C minor. It is interesting that this stirring piece was originally longer. In the manuscript score of the Tonkünstlersocietät, a sequence of nineteen measures is found which in the printed version is replaced by measures eleven and twelve only; obviously the introduction, as originally planned, had forty-nine instead of thirty-one measures. This again is proof of Haydn's tendency to concentrate his composition as much as possible. The eighteenth century did not feel any appreciation for the beauties of outdoor life in winter, and thus Haydn, after describing the desolation and danger threatening the wanderer in icy expanses guides him into a hospitable farmhouse with obvious relief. A delightful genre picture unfolds, with the girls spinning and singing under Jane's leadership (No. 34). The combination of the whirring and humming noise of the wheels in the instrumental accompaniment with the simple, ingratiating melody of the voices has left its traces in the spinning song of Wagner's *The Flying Dutchman* written forty years later. The next number, which is separated from the spinning song only by a recitative of eight measures, is again for solo soprano and chorus (No. 36). The droll story of the conceited lord who is taken in by the "honest country lass" is treated like a number in a German Singspiel, and is so completely different from the preceding piece that an entire change in the means of expression could not have provided a greater variety of effects.

Once more the mood of the oratorio becomes serious. The author draws a parallel between winter and old age (No. 38), and the thought of the imminence of death leads him to hope for God's mercy. As this final number (No. 39) marks the climax of the whole work, the chorus is subdivided into two groups, and the marked use of brass instruments (three horns, three trumpets, three trombones) enhances the grandeur of the conclusion. The antiphonal questions and answers exchanged between the trio of soloists and the two choruses remind us of the ideas expressed in *The Magic Flute*: "But who shall dare those gates to pass?" "The man whose life was incorrupt." "And who the holy hill ascend?" "The man whose tongue was void of guile." A magnificent fugue, "Direct us on thy ways, O God," leads to a short though very impressive "Amen," which brings the work to a majestic conclusion.

Looking at *The Seasons* as a whole, we find that van Swieten's rather dry libretto furnished just the right basis for Haydn. The objective description of nature was transformed through music into powerful expression, and it may well be that a more emotional text would have hampered rather than inspired the composer. The glaringly optimistic attitude of the text is put into correct balance by the music, which creates countless shadings in the bright colors and brings them into relief by stressing darkness wherever possible. Thus, "Summer" not only offers the catastrophic thunderstorm, but also starts with an introduction conjuring up the mood of an anguished, sleepless night. Against this somber background, the ensuing scenes radiate greater sparkle. In "Winter," the labored text becomes fully convincing in the composition, leading us through gloom to gaiety, and finally to feelings of gratitude to the Almighty. Through the magic of his genius Haydn transformed a somewhat pedestrian text into a work of sublime art.

# Conclusion

Unbroken homogeneity and steadiness of purpose were basic features of Haydn's nature. Throughout his artistic career, he entered no dead-end streets, and no real rebounds are noticeable. Though the direction of his progress may have changed at times, Haydn constantly moved forward, and every inch of territory captured by him was preserved and cultivated. Thus, through more than half a century his art steadily gained in significance.

The composer by no means started as a pioneer; his point of departure was the very place occupied by his predecessors. When he turned from the rococo idiom toward that of sensibility, the change of style was heralded years in advance and achieved step by step. By the time he attained full maturity, the rococo lightness, purified in the fiery tide of the *Sturm und Drang* movement and deepened by the impact of earlier masterworks, had changed into noble popularity. Out of *galant*, expressive, and baroque elements, Haydn evolved a classical synthesis, but he still moved forward, and the last phase in his artistic growth again revealed a stronger emphasis on subjective and expressive features.

A powerful nature averse to dualism is expressed in Haydn's music. Even in an early symphony (No. 31 of 1765) he achieved a thematic connection between the beginning and the end. He often avoided the use of a contrasting second subject in the sonata form and replaced it by one growing out of the main idea. At the same time, the development section became more concise, eschewing the employment of new thematic material. In his vocal arias, Haydn similarly confined the middle section to subject matter introduced in the first part.

The composer's manuscripts clearly reveal his steadfastness. Unlike Mozart, who at times broke off in the midst of a composition, he completed almost every work he started. His composing progressed slowly and steadily. "I never was a fast worker," he remarked to Griesinger, "and always composed carefully and diligently." As a rule he worked out his compositions in his mind before committing them to paper and produced very clear manuscripts. This does not quite apply to the works of the opera and oratorio composer. Following his experiences during rehearsals and early performances, or accommodating ensembles for which his composition had not originally been intended, he occasionally altered his scores. By and large, however, Haydn's autographs exhibit but few changes. In his last creative period the composer seems to have relied on sketches. He was aware that his work was listened to by the entire musical world, and he aimed to give it the definitive shape that would remain valid through changing times. Again and again the aged composer stirringly expressed his hope "not wholly to die," but to live on in his music.

The admiration given Haydn in his lifetime was largely the result of his peculiar development. As the young composer's work revealed no pioneering or unusual features, it did not offend anyone; on the other hand, the greater significance of his idiom and the obvious talent it displayed were bound to attract attention. Thus Haydn laid the foundation of his fame in the 1760s. Thenceforth the growth and expansion of his spiritual world occurred at so slow a pace that even the enemies of progress found it possible to follow him. The mature master then captured all hearts by the humor and the noble popularity of his idiom. Thanks to these irresistible qualities, such provoking features as concentrated thematic elaboration, daring modulations, and instrumental devices pointing toward the future were accepted, without protest. On the other hand, the very gaiety and naturalness of his idiom, combined with unbroken homogeneity, earned Haydn the disdain of the romantic era. The scarcity of discordant and ambiguous moods in his music made people look down on "good old Papa Haydn." Only in the twentieth century, when romantic ideals began to lose their hold on artistic thinking, did a true appreciation of Haydn's greatness become possible.

Haydn was endowed with a truly mundane spirit. Healthy sensuality pervaded his nature. He was a shrewd observer who watched everything around him with clear, sharp eyes and never-failing interest. His feeling for nature was deep, far deeper than Mozart's, perhaps even than Beethoven's. He loved to hunt and fish; he was conversant with the habits of many creatures, and it is significant that as a crowning achievement in his life's work he praised the creation in its smallest as well as largest manifestations. The *Laus Deo* at the foot of almost every Haydn autograph is enhanced to outsized proportions in *The Creation*.

Out of Haydn's love for the beauties of our world grew the gaiety and affirmative spirit apparent throughout all his creative periods. At first constrained by modish *galant* precepts, they assumed their rightful place as soon as Haydn embraced the expressive style. To counterbalance the dark passion of the *Sturm und Drang*, he often was, as he himself stated, "seized by uncontrollable humor." Even in his advanced age, this gaiety did not entirely desert him. Nurtured by his noble humanity and a victorious optimism maintained through all the vicissitudes of a long and arduous life, this radiant joyfulness again and again manifested itself, and Haydn considered it his mission to let his fellow beings share in this unique gift. This was touchingly expressed in the letter he wrote a few years before his death to admirers in the German town of Bergen:[1] "Often when contending with obstacles of every sort that interfered with my work, often when my powers both of body and mind were failing and I felt it a hard matter to persevere on the course I had entered on, a secret feeling within me whispered: 'There are but few contented and happy men here below; grief and care prevail everywhere; perhaps your labors may one day be the source from which the weary and worn, or the man burdened with affairs, may derive a few moments' rest and refreshment.' What a powerful motive for pressing onward!"

[1] Cf. p. 178f.

# *Bibliography*

ABBREVIATIONS USED IN BIBLIOGRAPHY

*DjH*  *Der junge Haydn*. Edited by V. Schwarz.

*GFs*  *Studies in Eighteenth-Century Music. A Tribute to Karl Geiringer on His Seventieth Birthday*. Edited by H. C. R. Landon and R. Chapman.

*HCW*  *Haydn Studies: Proceedings of the International Haydn Conference, Washington, D.C., 1975*. Edited by J. P. Larsen, H. Serwer, and J. Webster.

*HFs*  *Anthony van Hoboken. Festschrift zum 75. Geburtstag*. Edited by J. Schmidt-Görg.

*H-St*  *Haydn-Studien*

*HYb*  *Haydn Yearbook*

*JbP*  *Jahrbuch Peters*

*Mf*  *Die Musikforschung*

*ML*  *Music and Letters*

*MQ*  *Musical Quarterly*

*MR*  *The Music Review*

*MT*  *The Musical Times*

*OeMz*  *Oesterreichische Musikzeitschrift*

*PRMA*  *Proceedings of the [Royal] Musical Association*

*StzMw*  *Studien zur Musikwissenschaft*

*ZfMw*  *Zeitschrift für Musikwissenschaft*

Abert, Hermann. "Joseph Haydns Klaviersonaten." *ZfMw*, III/9–10 (June–July 1921), 535–552.

——. "Joseph Haydns Klavierwerke." *ZfMw*, II/10 (July 1920), 553–573.

Adler, Guido. "Haydn and the Viennese Classical School." *MQ*, XVIII/2 (Apr. 1932), 191–207.

Angermüller, Rudolph. "Neukomms schottische Liedbearbeitungen für Joseph Haydn." *H-St*, III/2 (Apr. 1974), 151–153.

——. "Sigismund Ritter von Neukomm (1778–1858) und seine Lehrer Michael und Joseph Haydn. Eine Dokumentation." *H-St*, III/1 (Jan. 1973), 29–42.

Artaria, Franz, and Botstiber, Hugo. *Joseph Haydn und das Verlagshaus Artaria. Nach den Briefen des Meisters an das Haus Artaria & Compagnie dargestellt.* Vienna: Artaria, 1909.

Badura-Skoda, Eva. "The Influence of the Viennese Popular Comedy on Haydn and Mozart." *PRMA*, C (1974), 185–199.

——. "Personal Contacts and Mutual Influences in the Field of Opera." In *HCW*, pp. 419–421.

——. "'Teutsche Comoedie-Arien' und Joseph Haydn." In *DjH*, pp. 59–73.

Barrett-Ayres, Reginald. *Joseph Haydn and the String Quartet.* London, 1974.

Bartha, Dénes, ed. *Joseph Haydn: Gesammelte Briefe und Aufzeichnungen. Unter Benützung der Quellensammlung von H. C. R. Landon.* Kassel: Bärenreiter, 1965.

——. "Remarks on Haydn as an Opera Conductor." In *HCW*, pp. 51–53.

Bartha, Dénes, and Somfai, László. *Haydn als Opernkapellmeister. Die Haydn-Dokumente der Esterházy-Opernsammlung.* Budapest: Ungarische Akademie der Wissenschaften, 1960.

Becker-Glauch, Irmgard. "Die Kirchenmusik des jungen Haydn." In *DjH*, pp. 74–85.

——. "Neue Forschungen zu Haydns Kirchenmusik." *H-St*, II/3 (May 1970), 167–241.

——. "Remarks on [Haydn's] Late Church Music." In *HCW*, pp. 206–207.

Benton, Rita. "A Resumé of the Haydn-Pleyel 'Trio Controversy' with Some Added Contributions." *H-St*, IV/2 (May 1978), 114–116.

Bernhardt, Reinhold. "Aus der Umwelt der Wiener Klassiker. Freiherr Gottfried van Swieten (1734–1803)." *Der Bär. Jahrbuch von Breitkopf & Härtel.* VI/9 (1929–1930), 74–164.

Bertuch, Carl. *Bermerkungen auf einer Reise aus Thüringen nach Wien im Winter 1805 bis 1806.* Weimar: Landes-Industrie-Comptoir, 1808–1810.

*Beschreibung des Hochfürstlichen Schlosses Esterháss im Königreiche Ungern* [sic]. Pressburg: Anton Löwe, 1784.

Beyle, Marie Henri. *Lives of Haydn, Mozart and Metastasio.* Translated and introduced by Richard N. Coe. London: Calder & Boyars, 1972.

Biba, Otto. "Nachrichten zur Musikpflege in der gräflichen Familie Harrach." *HYb*, X (1978), 36–44.

Blume, Friedrich. "Josef Haydns künstlerische Persönlichkeit in seinen Streichquartetten." *JbP*, XXXVIII (1931), 24–48.

Botstiber, Hugo. "Haydn and Luigia Polzelli." *MQ*, XVIII/2 (Apr. 1932), 208–217.

Brand, Carl Maria. *Die Messen von Joseph Haydn.* Würzburg: Triltsch, 1941.

Brenet, Michel. *Haydn.* Paris: Alcan, 1909.

Brook, Barry S., ed. *The Breitkopf Thematic Catalogues. The Six Parts and Sixteen Supplements, 1762–1787.* New York: Dover, 1966.

Brown, A. Peter. "The Earliest English Biography of Haydn." *MQ*, LIX/3 (July 1973), 339–354.

———. "The Structure of the Exposition in Haydn's Keyboard Sonatas." *MR*, XXXVI/2 (May 1975), 102–129.

Brown, Peter J. "New Light on Haydn's 'London' Symphonies." *MT*, May 1959, 260–261.

Burney, Charles. *A General History of Music from the Earliest Ages to the Present Period, to Which is Prefixed a Dissertation on the Music of the Ancients.* 4 vols. London, 1776–1789. Reprint by F. Mercer, New York: Dover, 1957.

———. *The Present State of Music in Germany, the Netherlands and United Provinces.* 2 vols. London: Becket, Robson & Robinson, 1773–1775. Facsimile edition by R. Schaal, Kassel: Bärenreiter, 1959.

Carpani, Giuseppe. *Le Haydine.* Milan: C. Buccinelli, 1812. Reprint, Bologna: Forni, 1969.

Chailley, Jacques. "Joseph Haydn and the Freemasons." In *GFs*, pp. 117–124.

Chapman, Roger E. "Modulation in Haydn's Piano Trios in the Light of Schoenberg's Theories." In *HCW*, pp. 471–475.

Chusid, Martin. "Some Observations on Liturgy, Text and Structure in Haydn's Late Masses." In *GFs*, pp. 125–135.

Conrat, Hugo. "Joseph Haydn und das kroatische Volkslied." *Die Musik*, IV/7 (Jan.–Mar. 1905), 14–20.

Csatkai, André. "Beiträge zur Geschichte der Musikkultur in Eisenstadt." *Mitteilungen des Burgenländischen Heimat- und Naturschutzvereines*, V/2 (1931), 21–27.

———. "Die fürstlich Esterházyschen Druckereien in Eisenstadt." *Burgenländische Heimatblätter* (Eisenstadt), V/1 (Mar. 1936), 4–10.

Daffner, Hugo. *Die Entwicklung des Klavierkonzerts bis Mozart.* Leipzig: Breitkopf & Härtel, 1906.

Deutsch, Otto Erich. "Haydn als Sammler." *OeMz*, XIV/5–6 (May–June 1959), 188–193.

———. "Haydn und Nelson." *Die Musik*, XXIV/6 (Mar. 1932), 436–440.

———. "Haydn's Hymn and Burney's Translation." *MR*, IV/3 (Aug. 1943), 157–162.

———. "Haydns Kanons." *ZfMw*, XV/3 (Dec. 1932), 112–124; XV/4 (Jan. 1933), 172.

Dies, Albert Christoph. *Biographische Nachrichten von Joseph Haydn.* Vienna: Camesinaische Buchhandlung, 1810. English translation by V. Gotwals, Madison, Wisc.: University of Wisconsin Press, 1968.

Dworschak, Fritz. "Joseph Haydn und Karl Joseph Weber von Fürnberg." *Unsere Heimat* (Vienna), V/6–7 (June–July 1932), 187–204.

Edwall, Harry R. "Ferdinand IV and Haydn's Concertos for the 'Lira Organizzata.'" *MQ*, XLVIII/2 (Apr. 1962), 190–203.

Engl, Johann Evangelist. *Joseph Haydns handschriftliches Tagebuch aus der Zeit seines zweiten Aufenthaltes in London, 1794 und 1795.* Leipzig: Breitkopf & Härtel, 1909.

Feder, Georg. "Apokryphe 'Haydn'-Streichquartette." *H-St*, III/2 (Apr. 1974), 125–150.

--------. "Bemerkungen über die Ausbildung der klassischen Tonsprache in der Instrumentalmusik Haydns." In *International Musicological Society. Report of the Eighth Congress*, edited by J. LaRue. Kassel: Bärenreiter, 1961, pp. 305–313.

--------. "Bemerkungen zu Haydns Skizzen." *Beethoven-Jahrbuch 1973/1977*. Bonn, 1977, pp. 69–86.

--------. "The Collected Works of Joseph Haydn." In *HCW*, pp. 26–34.

--------. "Haydn-Entdeckungen." *Musica*, XIX/4 (July–Aug. 1965), 189–192.

--------. "Haydns frühe Klaviertrios. Eine Untersuchung zur Echtheit und Chronologie." *H-St*, II/4 (Dec. 1970), 289–316.

--------. "Haydns Opern und ihre Ausgaben." In *Musik-Edition, Interpretation. Gedenkschrift Günter Henle*. Munich, 1980, pp. 165–179.

--------. "Joseph Haydns Skizzen und Entwürfe. Übersicht der Manuskripte, Werkregister, Literatur- und Ausgabenverzeichnis." *Fontes Artis Musicae*, XXVI (1979), 172–188.

--------. "Probleme einer Neuordnung der Klaviersonaten Haydns." In *Festschrift Friedrich Blume zum 70. Geburtstag*, edited by A. A. Abert and W. Pfannkuch. Kassel: Bärenreiter, 1963, pp. 92–103.

--------. "Similarities in the Works of Haydn." In *GFs*, pp. 65–70.

--------. "Stilelemente Haydns in Beethovens Werken." In *Gesellschaft für Musikforschung. Bericht über den Internationalen Musikwissenschaftlichen Kongress, Bonn 1970*. Kassel [1973], pp. 65–70.

--------. "Wieviel Orgelkonzerte hat Haydn geschrieben?" *Mf*, XXIII/4 (Oct.–Dec. 1970), 440–444.

--------. "Zur Datierung Haydnscher Werke." In *HFs*, pp. 50–54.

Feder, Georg, and Gerlach, Sonja. "Haydn-Dokumente aus dem Esterházy-Archiv in Forchtenstein." *H-St*, III/2 (Apr. 1974), 92–105.

Fellerer, Karl Gustav. "Zum Joseph-Haydn-Bild im frühen 19. Jahrhundert." In *HFs*, pp. 73–86.

Finscher, Ludwig. *Studien zur Geschichte des Streichquartetts*. Vol. I: *Die Entstehung des klassischen Streichquartetts*. Kassel: Bärenreiter, 1974.

Fischer, Wilhelm. "Instrumentalmusik." In *Handbuch der Musikgeschichte*, edited by G. Adler. Berlin, 1929.

——. "Stilkritischer Anhang" to A. Schnerich's *Joseph Haydn und seine Sendung*. Zürich: Amalthea, 1926.

——. "Zur Entwicklungsgeschichte des Wiener klassischen Stils." *StzMw*, III (1915), 24–84.

Framery, Nicolas E. *Notice de Joseph Haydn*. Paris: Barba, 1810.

Freeman, Robert N. "The Function of Haydn's Instrumental Compositions in the Abbeys." In *HCW*, pp. 199–202.

Friedlaender, Max. "Van Swieten und das Textbuch zu Haydns 'Jahreszeiten.'" *JbP*, XVI (1909), 47–56.

Gardiner, William. *Music and Friends: Or, Pleasant Recollections of a Dilettante*. 3 vols. London, 1838–1853.

Geiringer, Karl. "The 'Comedia La Marchesa Nespola': Some Documentary Problems." In *HCW*, pp. 53–55.

——. "Eigenhändige Bemerkungen Haydns in seinen Musikhandschriften." In *HFs*, pp. 87–92.

——. "From Guglielmi to Haydn: The Transformation of an Opera." In *International Musicological Society. Report of the Eleventh Congress, Copenhagen 1972*, vol. I. Copenhagen: Edition Wilhelm Hansen, 1974. Pp. 391–395.

——. *Franz Joseph Haydn. Symphonie No. 103 in E-flat major ("Drum Roll"): Historical Background, Analysis, Views and Comments*. Norton Critical Scores. New York: Norton, 1974.

——. "Haydn and His Viennese Background." In *HCW*, pp. 3–13.

——. "Haydn and the Folk Song of the British Isles." *MQ*, XXXV/2 (Apr. 1949), 179–208.

——. "Das Haydn-Bild im Wandel der Zeiten." *Die Musik*, XXIV/6 (Mar. 1932), 430–436.

——. "Haydn's Sketches for 'The Creation.'" *MQ*, XVIII/2 (Apr. 1932), 299–308.

——. *Joseph Haydn. Die grossen Meister der Musik*. Potsdam: Athenaion, 1932.

——. *Joseph Haydn. Der schöpferische Werdegang eines Meisters der Klassik*. Mainz: Schott, 1959.

——. "Joseph Haydn, Protagonist of the Enlightenment." *Studies on Voltaire and the Eighteenth Century* (Institut et Musée Voltaire, Geneva), XXV (1963), 683–690.

——. "The Small Sacred Works by Haydn in the Esterházy Archives at Eisenstadt." *MQ*, XLV/4 (Oct. 1959), 460–472.

——. "Stylistic Changes in Haydn's Oratorios: 'Il Ritorno di Tobia' and 'The Creation.'" In *HCW*, pp. 392–394.

——. *A Thematic Catalogue of Haydn's Settings of Folksongs from the British Isles*. Studies in Musicology, Series A, no. 2. Superior, Wisc.: Research Microfilm Publishers, 1953.

Georgiades, Thrasybulos. "Zur Musiksprache der Wiener Klassiker." *Mozart-Jahrbuch*, II (1951), 50–60.

Gotwals, Vernon. "The Earliest Biographies of Haydn." *MQ*, XLV/4 (Oct. 1959), 439–459.

——, ed. *Joseph Haydn: Eighteenth-Century Gentleman and Genius*. Madison, Wisc.: University of Wisconsin Press, 1963.

——. "Joseph Haydn's Last Will and Testament." *MQ*, XLVII/3 (July 1961), 331–353.

Griesinger, Georg August. *Biographische Notizen über Joseph Haydn*. Leipzig: Breitkopf & Härtel, 1810; Reprint with an epilogue, corrections and supplements by P. Krause, Leipzig, 1979. English translation by V. Gotwals, Madison, Wisc.: University of Wisconsin Press, 1968.

Gyrowetz, Adalbert. *Biographie des Adalbert Gyrowetz*. Vienna, 1848. New edition by Alfred Einstein, Leipzig: Kistner und Siegel, 1915.

Haas, Robert. "Abt Stadlers vergessene Selbstbiographie." *Mozart-Jahrbuch*, VIII (1957), 78–84.

——. "Die Musik in der Wiener deutschen Stegreifkomödie." *StzMw*, XII (1925), 3–64.

——. "Teutsche Comedie Arien." *ZfMw*, III/7 (Apr. 1921), 405–415.

Hadden, James Cuthbert. "George Thomson and Haydn." *The Monthly Musical Record*, XL/472 (Apr. 1, 1910), 76–78.

——. *Haydn*. The Master Musicians. 1902. Revised edition, London: J. M. Dent & Co., 1934.

Hadow, Sir William Henry. *A Croatian Composer*. London: Seeley & Co., 1897.

Harich, János. *Esterházy-Musikgeschichte im Spiegel der zeitgenössischen Textbücher.* Eisenstadt, 1959.

——. "Haydn Documenta." *HYb,* II (1964), 2–44; III (1966), 122–152; IV (1968), 39–101; VII (1970), 47–168; VIII (1971), 70–163.

——. "Das Haydn-Orchester im Jahr 1780." *HYb,* VIII (1971), 5–69.

——. "Das Opernensemble zu Eszterháza im Jahr 1780." *HYb,* VII (1970), 5–46.

——. "Das Repertoire des Opernkapellmeisters Joseph Haydn in Eszterháza (1780–1790)." *HYb,* I (1962), 9–110.

Hase, Hermann von. *Joseph Haydn und Breitkopf & Härtel.* Leipzig: Breitkopf & Härtel, 1909.

*Haydn-Studien.* Edited by the Joseph Haydn Institute, Cologne. (1965–   ). (Also see articles cited by individual authors.)

*Haydn Yearbook.* Edited by H. C. R. Landon and colleagues, Vienna. (1962–   ). (Also see articles cited by individual authors.)

Heuss, Alfred. "Haydns Kaiserhymne." *ZfMw,* I/1 (Oct. 1918), 5–26.

Hoboken, Anthony van. *Joseph Haydn: Thematisch-bibliographisches Werkverzeichnis.* Vol. I: *Instrumentalwerke.* Vol. II: *Vokalwerke.* Vol. III: *Register. Addenda und Corrigenda.* Mainz: Schott, 1957–1978.

——. "Nunziato Porta und der Text von Joseph Haydns Oper 'Orlando Paladino.'" In *Symbolae Historiae Musicae.* Mainz: Schott, 1971, pp. 170–179.

——. "A Rare Contemporary Edition of Haydn's 'Hymn for the Emperor.'" In *GFs,* pp. 292–296.

Hodgson, Anthony. *The Music of Joseph Haydn—The Symphonies.* London, 1976.

Hopkinson, Cecil, and Oldman, C. B. "Haydn's Settings of Scottish Songs in the Collections of Napier and Whyte." *Edinburgh Bibliographical Society Transactions,* III/2 (1949–1951), 85–120.

——. "Thomson's Collections of National Song, with Special Reference to the Contributions of Haydn and Beethoven." *Edinburgh Bibliographical Society Transactions,* II/1 (1938–1939), 1–64.

Horányi, Mátyás. *Das Esterházysche Feenreich.* Budapest: Ungarische Akademie der Wissenschaften, 1959.

Hughes, Rosemary S. M. "Dr. Burney's Championship of Haydn." *MQ*, XXVII/1 (Jan. 1941), 90–96.

———. *Haydn.* The Master Musicians, New Series. London: Dent, 1950.

———. "Haydn at Oxford: 1773–1791." *ML*, XX/3 (July 1939), 242–249.

Jancik, Hans. "Joseph Haydn als Kirchenmusiker." *Singende Kirche*, VI/3 (Mar.–May 1959), 98–99.

———. *Michael Haydn. Ein vergessener Meister.* Vienna: Amalthea-Verlag, 1952.

*Joseph Haydn Werke.* Edited by the Joseph Haydn Institute, Cologne. (1958–    ). (Also see articles cited by individual authors.)

Kelly, Michael. *Reminiscences.* London: H. Colburn, 1826. See also Ellis, Stewart Marsh. *The Life of Michael Kelly.* London, 1930.

Kinsky, Georg. "Haydn und das Hammerklavier." *ZfMw*, XIII/9–10 (June–July 1931), 500–501.

Kirkendale, Warren. *Fuge und Fugato in der Kammermusik des Rokoko und der Klassik.* Tutzing: Schneider, 1966.

Kobald, Karl. *Joseph Haydn. Bild seines Lebens und seiner Zeit.* Vienna: Epstein, 1932.

Kretzschmar, Hermann. "Die Jugendsinfonien Joseph Haydns." *JbP*, XV (1908), 69–90.

Lachmann, Robert. "Die Haydn-Autographen der Staatsbibliothek zu Berlin." *ZfMw*, XIV/6 (Mar. 1932), 289–298.

Landon, H. C. Robbins, ed. *The Collected Correspondence and London Notebooks of Joseph Haydn.* London: Barrie and Rockliff; Fair Lawn, N.J.: Essential Books, 1959.

———. *Haydn: Chronicle and Works.* Vol. I: *The Early Years, 1732–1765.* Vol. II: *Haydn at Eszterháza, 1766–1790.* Vol. III: *Haydn in England, 1791–1795.* Vol. IV: *Haydn: The Years of 'The Creation', 1796–1800.* Vol. V: *Haydn: The Late Years, 1801–1809.* Bloomington, Ind.: University of Indiana Press, 1976–1980.

———. *Haydn: A Documentary Study.* New York: Rizzoli, 1981.

———. "Haydn's Marionette Operas and the Repertoire of the Marionette Theatre at Esterház Castle." *HYb*, I (1962), 111–199.

————. "Das Marionettentheater auf Schloss Esterház." *OeMz*, XXVI/5–6 (May–June 1971), 272–280.

————. *The Symphonies of Joseph Haydn*. London: Rockliff, 1955.

————. "The Symphonies of Joseph Haydn: Addenda and Corrigenda." *MR*, XIX/4 (Nov. 1958), 311–319; XX/1 (Feb. 1959), 56–70.

————. "Die Verwendung gregorianischer Melodien in Haydns Frühsymphonien." *OeMz*, IX/4 (Apr. 1954), 119–126.

Landon, H. C. Robbins, and Chapman, Roger E., eds. *Studies in Eighteenth-Century Music. A Tribute to Karl Geiringer on His Seventieth Birthday*. London: Allen and Unwin, 1970. (Also see articles cited by individual authors.)

Larsen, Jens Peter, ed. *Drei Haydn Kataloge in Faksimile mit Einleitung und ergänzenden Themenverzeichnissen*. Copenhagen: Munksgaard, 1941. Second facsimile edition with a survey of Haydn's oeuvre, New York: Pendragon, 1979.

————. *Die Haydn-Überlieferung*. Copenhagen: Munksgaard, 1939.

————. "Probleme der chronologischen Ordnung von Haydns Sinfonien." In *Festschrift Otto Erich Deutsch zum 80. Geburtstag*, edited by W. Gerstenberg. Kassel: Bärenreiter, 1963, pp. 90–104.

————. "A Survey of the Development of Haydn Research: Solved and Unsolved Problems." In *HCW*, pp. 14–25.

————. "Zur Entstehung der österreichischen Symphonietradition (ca. 1750–1775)." *HYb*, X (1978), 72–80.

Larsen, Jens Peter, and Feder, Georg. "Haydn, (Franz) Joseph." In *The New Grove Dictionary of Music and Musicians*, vol. VIII. London: Macmillan, 1980, pp. 328–407.

Larsen, Jens Peter, Serwer, H., and Webster, J., eds. *Haydn Studies: Proceedings of the International Haydn Conference, Washington, D.C., 1975*. New York: Norton, 1981. (Also see articles cited by individual authors.)

Lesure, François. "Haydn en France." In *Bericht über die Internationale Konferenz zum Andenken Joseph Haydns*, edited by Bence Szabolcsi and Dénes Bartha. Budapest: Akadémiai Kiadó, 1961, pp. 79–84.

Lowens, Irving. *Haydn in America*. With "Haydn Autographs in the United States" by O. E. Albrecht. Bibliographies in American Music, no. 5. Detroit, Mich., 1979.

Luithlen, Victor. "Haydn-Erinnerungen in der Sammlung alter Musikinstrumente des Kunsthistorischen Museums zu Wien." In *HFs*, pp. 110–114.

Mann, Alfred. "Beethoven's Contrapuntal Studies with Haydn." *MQ* , LVI/4 (Oct. 1970), 7111–7126.

————. "Haydn as Student and Critic of Fux." In *GFs*, pp. 323–332.

Mayeda, Akio. "Nicola Antonio Porpora und der junge Haydn." In *DjH*, pp. 41–58.

Menčik, Ferdinand. "Haydn-Testamente." *Die Kultur*, IX (1908), 82–90.

Mies, Paul. "Joseph Haydn und seine Singkanons." *Musica sacra*, LXXX (1960), 45–49.

————. "Joseph Haydns geistliche Lieder für eine und mehrere Singstimmen mit Klavierbegleitung." *Musica sacra*, LXXVII/4 (Apr. 1957), 113–117.

Moe, Orin, Jr. "The Significance of Haydn's Op. 33." In *HCW*, pp. 445–450.

————. "Structure in Haydn's 'The Seasons.'" *HYb*, IX (1975), 340–348.

————. "Texture in Haydn's Early Quartets." *MR*, XXXV/1 (Feb.–May 1974), 4–22.

Mörner, C.-G. Stellan. "Haydniana aus Schweden um 1800." *H-St*, II/1 (Mar. 1969), 1–33.

Mount-Edgcumbe, Richard. *Musical Reminiscences*. Anonymously published, 1825.

Müller, Robert Franz. "Joseph Haydns letztes Testament. Nach der Urschrift veröffentlicht." *Die Musik*, XXIV/6 (Mar. 1932), 440–445.

————. "Heiratsbrief, Testament und Hinterlassenschaft der Gattin Joseph Haydns." *Die Musik*, XXII/2 (Nov. 1929), 93–99.

Müller-Blattau, Joseph. "Zu Haydns 'Philemon und Baucis.'" *H-St*, II/1 (Mar. 1969), 66–68.

Nef, Karl. "Haydn-Reminiszenzen bei Beethoven." In *Sammelbände der Internationalen Musikgesellschaft*, XIII (1911–1912), 336–348.

Neukomm, Sigismund. "Canon Énigmatique inscrit sur le Tombeau de J. Haydn." *Revue et Gazette musicale de Paris*, X/32 (Aug. 6, 1843), 274.

———. "Dix-huit mois de la vie de Haydn." *Revue et Gazette musicale de Paris*, XLI/10–11 (Mar. 8–15, 1874), 75–77, 82–84.

Neurath, Herbert. "Das Violinkonzert in der Wiener klassischen Schule." *StzMw*, XIV (1927), 123–142.

Newman, William S. *The Sonata in the Classic Era*. Chapel Hill, N.C.: University of North Carolina Press, 1963.

Nohl, Ludwig. *Letters of Distinguished Musicians: Gluck, Haydn, P. E. Bach, Weber, Mendelssohn*. Translated by Lady Wallace. London: Longmans, Green & Co., 1867.

Norton, M. D. Herter. "Haydn in America (before 1820)." *MQ*, XVIII/2 (Apr. 1932), 309–337.

Nowak, Leopold. *Joseph Haydn. Leben, Bedeutung und Werk*. Zürich: Amalthea, 1951. Second edition, Zürich: Amalthea, 1959.

———. "Die Skizzen zum Finale der Es-dur-Symphonie GA 99 von Joseph Haydn." *H-St*, II/3 (May 1970), 137–166.

Ohmiya, Makoto. *Joseph Haydn's Compositions for Lira*. Musicology Ochanomizu University, no. 1. Tokyo, 1973.

Olleson, D. Edward. "Georg August Griesinger's Correspondence with Breitkopf & Härtel." *HYb*, III (1966), 5–53.

———. "Gottfried van Swieten, Patron of Haydn and Mozart." *PRMA*, LXXXIX (1962–1963), 63–74.

———. "Haydn in the Diaries of Count Karl von Zinzendorf." *HYb*, II (1964), 45–63.

Parke, W. T. *Musical Memoirs, comprising an account of the general state of music in England, 1784–1830*. London, 1830.

Papendiek, Charlotte Louise Henrietta. *Court and Private Life in the Time of Queen Charlotte: Being the Journals of Mrs. Papendiek, Assistant Keeper of the Wardrobe and Reader to Her Majesty*. 2 vols. Edited by Mrs. Vernon Delves Broughton. London: R. Bentley and Son, 1887.

Pauly, Reinhard G. "The Reforms of Church Music under Joseph II." *MQ*, XVIII/3 (July 1957), 372–382.

Pohl, Carl Ferdinand. *Joseph Haydn*. 3 vols. Berlin, 1875 and 1882. 3d vol. completed by H. Botstiber. Leipzig, 1927.

———. *Mozart und Haydn in London*. Vienna: Gerold, 1867.

Porter, Andrew. "L'incontro improvviso." *MT*, CVII /1477 (Mar. 1966), 202–206.

————. "Practical Considerations in Modern Production." In *HCW*, pp. 259–266.

Radant, Else, ed. "Die Tagebücher von Joseph Carl Rosenbaum 1770–1829." *HYb*, V (1968), 7–159.

Reich, Willi. *Joseph Haydn. Chronik seines Lebens in Selbstzeugnissen.* Zurich: Manesse Verlag, 1962.

————. *Joseph Haydn: Leben, Briefe, Schaffen.* Lucerne: Josef Stocker, 1946.

Riedel-Martiny, Anke. "Das Verhältnis von Text und Musik in Haydns Oratorien." *H-St*, I/4 (Apr. 1967), 205 –240.

Rosen, Charles. *The Classical Style: Haydn, Mozart, Beethoven.* New York: Viking, 1971. Revised paperback edition, New York: Norton, 1972.

Roy, Klaus G. "The So-Called Violin Sonatas of Haydn." *Bulletin of the American Musicological Society*, Sept. 1948, 38–40.

Saint-Foix, Georges de. "Haydn and Clementi." *MQ*, XVIII/2 (Apr. 1932), 252–259.

————. "Les Sonates pour violon et alto de Haydn." *La Revue Musicale*, XIII/128 (July–Aug. 1932), 81–84.

Sandberger, Adolf. "Haydn und das kleine Quartbuch." *Acta Musicologica*, VIII/1–2 (Jan.–June 1936), 18–22.

————. "Neue Haydniana." *JbP*, XL (1933), 28–37.

————. "Zur Entstehungsgeschichte von Haydns 'Die Sieben Worten des Erlösers am Kreuze.'" *JbP*, X (1903), 47–59.

————. "Zur Geschichte des Haydnschen Streichquartetts." *Altbayerische Monatshefte*, 1900, 1–24.

Saslav, Isidor. "Tempos in the String Quartets of Joseph Haydn." D.M. document, Indiana University, 1969.

Schaal, Richard. "Die Autographen der Wiener Musiksammlung von Aloys Fuchs, unter Benützung der Originalkataloge." *HYb*, VI (1969), 5–191.

Schenk, Erich. "Ist die Göttweiger Rorate-Messe ein Werk Joseph Haydns?" *StzMw*, XXIV (1960), 87–105.

Schering, Arnold. "Bemerkungen zu J. Haydns Programmsinfonien." *JbP*, XLVI (1939), 9–27.

Schmid, Ernst Fritz. "Gottfried van Swieten als Komponist." *Mozart-Jahrbuch*, 1953, 15– 31.

————. *Joseph Haydn. Ein Buch von Vorfahren und Heimat des Meisters.* Kassel: Bärenreiter, 1934.

————. "Joseph Haydn und Carl Philipp Emanuel Bach." *ZfMw,* XIV/6 (Mar. 1932), 299–312.

————. "Joseph Haydn und die Flötenuhr." *ZfMw,* XIV/4 (Jan. 1932), 193–221.

————. "Neue Funde zu Haydns Flötenuhrstücken." *H-St,* II/4 (Dec. 1970), 249–255.

Schmidt-Görg, Joseph, ed. *Anthony van Hoboken. Festschrift zum 75. Geburtstag.* Mainz: Schott, 1962. (Also see articles cited by individual authors.)

Schnerich, Alfred. "Haydn-Gedenkstätte in Eisenstadt." *Burgenland* (Eisenstadt), I (1929), 15–21.

————. *Joseph Haydn und seine Sendung.* 2d ed. Zürich: Amalthea, 1926.

————. *Messe und Requiem seit Haydn und Mozart.* Vienna and Leipzig: C. W. Stern, 1909.

————. "Die textlichen Versehen in den Messen Haydns und deren Korrektur." In *Haydn-Zentenarfeier, III. Kongress der Internationalen Musikgesellschaft.* Vienna, 1909.

Scholes, Percy A. "Burney and Haydn." *The Monthly Musical Record,* LXXI (Sept.–Oct. 1941), 155–157, 172–178.

Schrade, Leo. "Das Haydn-Bild in den ältesten Biographien." *Die Musikerziehung* (Königsberg), IX/6–9 (June–Sept. 1932), 163–169, 200–213, 244–249.

Schwarz, Vera, ed. *Der junge Haydn.* Graz: Akademische Druck- und Verlagsanstalt, 1972. (Also see articles cited by individual authors.)

Scott, Marion M. "Dr. Haydn and Dr. Geiringer." *MT,* LXXXIX/1259 (Jan. 1948), 9–11.

————. "Haydn: Fresh Facts and Old Fancies." *PRMA,* LXVIII (1941–1942), 87–105.

————. "Haydn in England." *MQ,* XVIII/2 (Apr. 1932), 260–273.

————. "Haydn: Relics and Reminiscences in England." *ML,* XIII/2 (Apr. 1932), 126–136.

————. "Mi-Jo Haydn." *The Monthly Musical Record,* LXIX/805 (Mar.–Apr. 1939), 67–73.

Seeger, Horst. "Zur musikhistorischen Bedeutung der Haydn-

Biographie von Albert Christoph Dies (1810)." *Beiträge zur Musikwissenschaft*, I/3 (1959), 24–31.

Smith, Carleton Sprague. "Haydn's Chamber Music and the Flute." *MQ*, XIX/3–4 (July–Oct. 1933), 341–350, 434–455.

Somfai, László. "A Bold Enharmonic Modulatory Model in Joseph Haydn's String Quartets." In *GFs*, 370–381.

————. "Haydns Tribut an seinen Vorgänger Werner." *HYb*, II (1964), 75–80.

————. *Joseph Haydn: Sein Leben in zeitgenössischen Bildern*. Budapest: Corvina; Kassel: Bärenreiter, 1966.

————. "The London Revision of Haydn's Instrumental Style." *PRMA*, C (1974), 159–174.

Sondheimer, Robert. *Haydn: A Historical and Psychological Study Based on His Quartets*. London: Bernoulli, 1951.

Stadtlaender, Christina. *Joseph Haydn of Eisenstadt*. Translated by Percy M. Young. London: Dobson, 1968.

Stein, Fritz. "Der musikalische Instrumentalkalender. Zu Leben und Wirken von Gregorius Josephus Werner." *Musica*, XI/7–8 (July–Aug. 1957), 390– 396.

Strunk, William Oliver. "Haydn's Divertimenti for Baryton, Viola, and Bass." *MQ*, XVIII/2 (Apr. 1932), 216–251.

————. "Notes on a Haydn Autograph." *MQ*, XX/2 (Apr. 1934), 192–205.

Szabolcsi, Bence. "Joseph Haydn und die ungarische Musik." *Beiträge zur Musikwissenschaft*, I/2 (1959), 62–73.

————. "Der Zukunftsmusiker Haydn." In *Festschrift 1817–1967. Akademie für Musik und darstellende Kunst in Wien*. Vienna: Lafite, 1967, pp. 65–72.

Tandler, Julius. "Über den Schädel Haydns." *Mitteilungen der Anthropologischen Gesellschaft* (Vienna), XXXIX (1909), 260–279.

Tank, Ulrich. "Die Dokumente der Esterházy-Archive zur fürstlichen Hofkapelle in der Zeit von 1761 bis 1770." *H-St*, IV/3–4 (May 1980), 129–333.

Tenschert, Roland. *Frauen um Haydn*. Vienna: Donau-Verlag, 1946.

Tiersot, Julien. "Le Lied 'Ein Mädchen, das auf Ehre hielt' et ses prototypes français." *Zeitschrift der Internationalen Musikgesellschaft*, XII/8–9 (May–June 1911), 222–226.

Tovey, Sir Donald Francis. *Essays in Musical Analysis*. 7 vols. London: Oxford University Press, 1935–1944.

————. "Franz Joseph Haydn." In *Cyclopedic Survey of Chamber Music*, compiled and edited by Walter Willson Cobbett, vol. I. London: Oxford University Press, 1929, pp. 514–548.

Tyson, Alan, and Landon, H. C. Robbins. "Who Composed Haydn's Op. 3?" *MT*, CV/1457 (July 1964), 506–507.

Unger, Max. "Haydn-Studien, I." *Musikalisches Wochenblatt*, XL/24–25 (Sept. 9–16, 1909), 317–320, 333–334; XLI/28 (Oct. 13, 1910), 297–300.

————. "Haydn-Studien, II." *Musikalisches Wochenblatt*, XLI/37–39 (Dec. 15–22, 1910), 413–415, 440–441.

Unverricht, Hubert. *Geschichte des Streichtrios*. Tutzing: Schneider, 1969.

————. "Zur Chronologie der Barytontrios von Joseph Haydn." In *Symbolae Historiae Musicae*. Mainz: Schott, 1971, pp. 180–189.

Valkó, Arisztid. "Haydn magyarországi müködése a levéltári akták tükrében." In *Zenetudományi Tanulmányok*, VI (1957), pp. 627ff, and VII (1960), pp. 527ff.

Wackernagel, Bettina. "Joseph Haydns frühe Klaviersonaten. Ihre Beziehung zur Klaviermusik um die Mitte des 18. Jahrhunderts." Dissertation, University of Würzburg. Tutzing, 1976.

Wagner, Hans. *Wien von Maria Theresia bis zur Franzosenzeit. Aus den Tagebüchern des Grafen Karl von Zinzendorf*. Vienna, 1972.

Walter, Horst. "Die biographischen Beziehungen zwischen Haydn und Beethoven." *Gesellschaft für Musikforschung. Bericht über den Internationalen Musikwissenschaftlichen Kongress, Bonn 1970*. Kassel [1973], pp. 79–83.

————. "Gottfried van Swietens handschriftliche Textbücher zu 'Schöpfung' und 'Jahreszeiten.'" *H-St*, I/4 (Apr. 1967), 241–277.

————. "Haydn's Keyboard Instruments." In *HCW*, pp. 213–218.

————. "Das Tasteninstrument beim jungen Haydn." In *DjH*, pp. 237–248.

Wendschuh, Ludwig. "Über Joseph Haydn's Opern." Dissertation, Universität Rostock, 1896.

Wirth, Helmut. "Haydns letzte Oper 'Orfeo ed Euridice.'" *OeMz*, XXII/5 (May 1967), 249–252.

———. *Joseph Haydn als Dramatiker.* Wolfenbüttel, 1941.

Wyzewa, Théodore de. "A propos du centenaire de la mort de Joseph Haydn." *Revue des deux mondes*, LXXIX/51 (June 15, 1909), 935–946.

Zeman, Herbert. "Das Theaterlied zur Zeit Joseph Haydns, seine theatralische Gestaltung und seine gattungsgeschichtliche Entwicklung." *Jahrbuch für österreichische Kulturgeschichte*, VI (1976), 35–39.

Zinzendorf, Karl von. See Wagner, Hans.

# ℐndex of ℙersons

389

# Index of Compositions